From the Great Recession to Labour Market Recovery

The International Labour Organization

The International Labour Organization was founded in 1919 to promote social justice and, thereby, to contribute to universal and lasting peace. Its tripartite structure is unique among agencies affiliated to the United Nations; the ILO's Governing Body includes representatives of government, and of employers' and workers' organizations. These three constituencies are active participants in regional and other meetings sponsored by the ILO, as well as in the International Labour Conference – a world forum which meets annually to discuss social and labour questions.

Over the years the ILO has issued for adoption by member States a widely respected code of international labour Conventions and Recommendations on freedom of association, employment, social policy, conditions of work, social security, industrial relations and labour administration, among others.

The ILO provides expert advice and technical assistance to member States through a network of offices and multidisciplinary teams in over 40 countries. This assistance takes the form of labour rights and industrial relations counselling, employment promotion, training in small business development, project management, advice on social security, workplace safety and working conditions, the compiling and dissemination of labour statistics, and workers' education.

Other recent publications by ILO and Palgrave Macmillan:

OFFSHORING AND WORKING CONDITIONS IN REMOTE WORK (edited by Jon C. Messenger and Naj Ghosheh)

BLUNTING NEOLIBERALISM: TRIPARTISM AND ECONOMIC REFORMS IN THE DEVELOPING WORLD (edited by Lydia Fraile)

BUILDING DECENT SOCIETIES: RETHINKING THE ROLE OF SOCIAL SECURITY IN DEVELOPMENT (edited by Peter Townsend)

INTERNATIONAL AND COMPARATIVE LABOUR LAW (by Arturo Bronstein)

IN DEFENCE OF LABOUR MARKET INSTITUTIONS: CULTIVATING JUSTICE IN THE DEVELOPING WORLD (edited by Janine Berg and David Kucera)

MICROFINANCE AND PUBLIC POLICY: OUTREACH, PERFORMANCE AND EFFICIENCY (edited by Bernd Balkenhol)

GLOBALIZATION, EMPLOYMENT AND INCOME DISTRIBUTION IN DEVELOPING COUNTRIES (edited by Eddy Lee and Marco Vivarelli)

UNDERSTANDING GLOBALIZATION, EMPLOYMENT AND POVERTY REDUCTION (edited by Eddy Lee and Marco Vivarelli)

From the Great Recession to Labour Market Recovery

Issues, Evidence and Policy Options

Edited by

Iyanatul Islam

and

Sher Verick

palgrave
macmillan

First published 2011 by
PALGRAVE MACMILLAN

Palgrave Macmillan in the UK is an imprint of Macmillan Publishers Limited, registered in England, company number 785998, of Houndmills, Basingstoke, Hampshire RG21 6XS.

Palgrave Macmillan in the US is a division of St Martin's Press LLC, 175 Fifth Avenue, New York, NY 10010.

Palgrave Macmillan is the global academic imprint of the above companies and has companies and representatives throughout the world.

Palgrave® and Macmillan® are registered trademarks in the United States, the United Kingdom, Europe and other countries.

ISBN 978–0–230–28358–9 hardback
ILO ISBN 978–92–2–124031–0

This book is printed on paper suitable for recycling and made from fully managed and sustained forest sources. Logging, pulping and manufacturing processes are expected to conform to the environmental regulations of the country of origin.

A catalogue record for this book is available from the British Library.

Library of Congress Cataloging-in-Publication Data

From the great recession to labour market recovery: issues, evidence and policy options/edited by Iyanatul Islam and Sher Verick.
p. cm.
ISBN 978–0–230–28358–9
ILO ISBN 978–92–2–124031–0
1. Global Financial Crisis, 2008–2009. 2. Recessions. 3. Labor market.
4. Manpower policy. I. Islam, Iyanatul, 1953– II. Verick, Sher.
HB37172008.F76 2010
330.9'0511—dc22

2010027521

10 9 8 7 6 5 4 3 2 1
20 19 18 17 16 15 14 13 12 11

Printed and bound in Great Britain by
CPI Antony Rowe, Chippenham and Eastbourne

Contents

List of Tables, Figures and Boxes

Tables

Figures

Boxes

Foreword

This book showcases research undertaken by current and former ILO staff on the macroeconomic and labour market dimensions of the Great Recession of 2008–09. It offers a global overview, interpreting the causes, consequences and policy responses to the Great Recession from the perspective of both developing and developed countries.

With so many books on the Great Recession in the market place, it is important to clarify the value added of this one. The crisis has provided an opportunity for rethinking growth, macroeconomic and development policies and paradigms. This book makes a contribution to this endeavour in three respects: its focus on drawing lessons from efforts to ease the pain and mitigate the impact of the Great Recession in both developed and developing countries; the call for a rethinking of macroeconomic frameworks to make them more employment-friendly; and the delineation of the necessary elements for more balanced policies in a post-crisis world.

The contributors to this volume identify several other key messages. Firstly, contrary to widely-held perceptions during the boom years before the crisis, the global economy was by no means as stable as suggested, while at the same time the majority of the world's poor had benefited insufficiently from stronger economic growth. Secondly, there were complex and interlinked factors behind the emergence of the crisis in 2007, namely loose monetary policy, global imbalances, misperceptions of risk and lax financial regulation. Thirdly, beyond the aggregate picture of economic collapse and rising unemployment, the impact of the crisis is rather diverse, reflecting differences in initial conditions, transmission channels and vulnerabilities of economies, along with the role of government policy in mitigating the downturn. Fourthly, while the recovery phase has commenced, a number of risks remain that could derail improvements in economies and hinder efforts to ensure that the recovery is accompanied by job creation. These risks pertain in particular to persistent fragility in the financial system and the challenges of dealing with global imbalances.

The authors explore a range of policy options for a post-crisis future that are closely aligned with the ILO's Decent Work Agenda and Global Jobs Pact. The book argues that initiatives at the national level to secure inclusive, job-rich economic recovery need to be complemented by global and regional cooperation that would support an agenda of 'fair globalization'.

Jose Manuel Salazar-Xirinachs
Executive Director, Employment Sector
International Labour Office

Notes on the Contributors

Editors

Iyanatul ('Yan') Islam is currently Senior Employment Policy Specialist, in the Employment Policy Department of the International Labour Office in Geneva. He also holds the position of Professor of International Business, School of International Business and Asian Studies, Griffith University, Australia, and is currently on leave from his professorial duties. He is an economist educated at Manchester (Bachelor of Arts in Economics, First Class Honours), Western Ontario (Master of Arts in Economics) and Cambridge (Ph.D., Economic Development). He is the author of more than 10 books and co-edited volumes published by leading publishers, including Oxford University Press, Routledge and Edward Elgar. He co-authored two books on the Indonesian labour market published in 2009 and has published extensively in peer-reviewed international journals such as *Cambridge Journal of Economics, World Development*, and the *Journal of Development Studies*. He has worked as an external expert for United Nations agencies since the mid-1980s and has produced more than 20 policy reports on developing economies. He is one of the founding editors of the *Journal of Asia-Pacific Economy* and a member of the editorial board of the University of Michigan-based *Journal of Asian Business*.

Sher Verick is currently Senior Research Economist in the Employment Analysis and Research Unit of the International Labour Office in Geneva. Prior to joining the ILO, he worked for various research institutions in Europe and Australia, and the United Nations Economic Commission for Africa in Addis Ababa. He holds a masters degree in development economics from the Australian National University and Ph.D. in economics from the University of Bonn. Since December 2004, he has been a Research Fellow of the Institute for the Study of Labor (IZA). He has published in a range of journals, including the *Oxford Bulletin of Economics and Statistics, Economic Record* and *Development Policy Review*.

Contributors

Sandrine Cazes joined the ILO as an economist in 1997. Since December 2008, she has been the head of the Employment Analysis and

Research Unit of the International Labour Office. Prior to that she was a senior researcher at the International Institute for Labour Studies of the ILO, and the Employment Specialist of the ILO Subregional Office for Central and Eastern Europe in Budapest during the EU enlargement process. Her main topics of interest are labour market policy and social reforms, the role of labour market regulations and flexicurity. Her regional areas of interest are the OECD countries and Central and South Eastern Europe. She is author and co-author of numerous publications – books, research papers, policy advisory reports and articles in referenced economic journals.

Caroline Heuer is currently working at the Federal Ministry of Labour and Social Affairs in Germany. She has a master's degree from the University of Heidelberg, Germany.

Rizwanul Islam is former Special Adviser, Employment Sector, International Labour Office, Geneva. His previous positions include Director, Economic and Labour Market Analysis, and other directorial positions at the ILO. He did his Ph.D. in Economics at the London School of Economics and Political Science under the supervision of Professor (and Nobel Laureate) Amartya Sen. He received a Commonwealth Scholarship for doing his Ph.D. at the LSE. He specializes in development economics with a particular focus on employment, poverty and income distribution, and has published a number of journal articles and books in this field, including publications on development, poverty and employment. The topics of his current research include: (i) the challenge of jobless growth, employment intensity of economic growth and poverty reduction; and (ii) the impact of shocks like food price inflation and economic downturns on employment and poverty.

Nomaan Majid is a Senior Economist at the International Labour Office in Geneva. He works on employment and poverty-related policy issues in developing economies. He was educated in Pakistan and England and holds a D.Phil. in Economics from the University of Oxford. He has published in international journals such as the *Journal of Development Studies*, the *International Labour Review*, the *Journal of Peasant Studies* and *Pakistan Development Review*. He is also a co-author of a book entitled *The Global Employment Challenge*, published by the ILO and Academic Foundation in 2008.

Muhammed Muqtada is a Senior Economist with the ILO and is currently the Director of Policy Planning of the ILO's Employment Sector. He has carried out extensive research on issues related to employment and development, and has published several articles and books on labour markets, employment, macroeconomic policies, poverty and structural adjustment. His books include: *The Elusive Target: An Evaluation of Target Group Approaches to Employment Generation* (editor); *Employment Expansion and Macroeconomic Stability Under Increasing Globalization* (co-edited with Azizur Rahman Khan); and *Bangladesh: Economic and Social Challenges of Globalization* (co-edited with Andrea M. Singh and Mohammed Ali Rashid). Mr Muqtada holds a Ph.D. in Economics from the University of Cambridge.

Ludek Rychly is the Senior Labour Administration and Labour Inspection Specialist at the International Labour Office in Geneva. His previous professional experience includes serving as the Deputy Minister for the Ministry of Labour and Social Affairs, Prague. His other employment includes the Social and Wage Policy Department at the Czech and Moravian Trade Union Confederation in Prague as well as jobs in the private sector. He has extensive practical experience in the fields of labour administration, labour law and industrial relations and is the author of numerous publications and policy papers in these fields. He also has an extensive experience in cooperation with international institutions, such as the United Nations, the Council of Europe, the OECD and the European Commission. He has lectured at several universities and has carried out regular work for the ILO Training Centre in Turin. He is the honorary senior research fellow at the Birmingham University (Business School).

Acknowledgements

This book is the outcome of in-depth research conducted by current and former ILO officials in 2009 and 2010. This edited volume would not have been possible without the dedication and commitment of all contributors.

We are grateful to the former director, Duncan Campbell, and current director, Moazam Mahmood, of the Economic and Labour Market Analysis Department (EMP/ELM) of the International Labour Office (ILO) for the financing of the book. We also thank Azita Berar Awad, director of the Employment Policy Department (EMP/POLICY), for her support throughout the process.

The book has benefited enormously from comments provided by an external peer reviewer and two ILO peer reviewers, along with colleagues who have provided feedback on various versions of the manuscript, including Uma Rani Amara, Hielke Buddelmeyer, Sameer Khatiwada, Sangheon Lee and Markus Pilgrim. We would also like to thank Sarah Anwar, Tara Scharf and Leyla Shamchiyeva for their excellent research assistance.

Finally, we would like to thank Charlotte Beauchamp, Chris Edgar and Alison Irvine of ILO Publications for their untiring support in getting the manuscript into shape and working with the co-publisher, Palgrave Macmillan, to finalize the production of the book.

Iyanatul Islam

Sher Verick

List of Abbreviations

ADB	Asian Development Bank
ALMPs	Active labour market policies
ARRA	American Recovery and Reinvestment Act
ASEAN	Association of Southeast Asian Nations
BWIs	Bretton Woods institutions
CBO	Congressional Budget Office
CC.OO	Confederación Sindical de Comisiones Obreras (Spain)
CDOs	Collateralized debt obligations
CDS	Credit default swaps
CEA	Council of Economic Advisors
CEE	Central and Eastern Europe
CIS	Commonwealth of Independent States
CPI	Consumer price index
CRER	Constant real exchange rate rule
EIIP	Employment Intensive Investment Programme (ILO)
EIU	Economist Intelligence Unit
EPL	Employment protection legislation
EPWP	Extended Public Works Programme (South Africa)
EU	European Union
FCNA	Financial Crisis Alert Series
FDI	Foreign direct investment
GDP	Gross domestic product
GNI	Gross national income
HICP	Harmonized index of consumer prices (Eurostat)
I/GDP	Investment to GDP ratio
IFIs	International financial institutions
IILS	International Institute of Labour Studies
ILO	International Labour Organization

IMF	International Monetary Fund
INDEC	National Institute of Statistics and Census of Argentina
IPIM	Internal wholesale price index
IT	Information technology
ITUC	International Trade Union Confederation
JSA	Jobs search assistance
KILM	Key Indicators of the Labour Market (ILO)
LCU	Local currency unit
LDC	Least developed countries
LMPs	Labour market policies
MBS	Mortgage-backed securities
MDB	Multilateral development banks
MDGs	Millennium Development Goals
NEDLAC	National Economic Development and Labour Council (South Africa)
NERA	National Employment Rights Authority (Ireland)
NREG	National Rural Employment Guarantee (India)
ODA	Official development assistance
ODI	Overseas Development Institute
OECD	Organisation of Economic Co-operation and Development
PES	Public employment services
PLMPs	Passive labour market policies
PPP	Purchasing power parity
PRGF	Poverty Reduction and Growth Facility
PRSC	Poverty Reduction Support Credit
PRSPs	Poverty Reduction Strategy Papers
Rp	Rupiah (Indonesian currency)
Rs	Rupees (Mauritian currency)
SAPs	Structural adjustment programmes
SFA	Small Firms Association (Ireland)
SIVs	Structured investment vehicles

SMEs	Small and medium-sized enterprises
SPV	Special purpose vehicle
TIFT	Tax on international financial transactions
UB	Unemployment Benefits
UGT	Unión General de Trabajadores (Spain)
UNCTAD	United Nations Conference on Trade and Development
UNDP	United Nations Development Programme
VA	Value added
VAT	Value added tax
WDI	World Development Indicators (World Bank)
WTO	World Trade Organization

1
Introduction

I. Islam and S. Verick

Introduction

The global financial crisis of 2007 has cast its long shadow on the economic fortunes of many countries, resulting in what has often been called the 'Great Recession'.[1] By the end of 2007 what had started as seemingly isolated turbulence in the subprime segment of the US housing market had mutated into a full-blown recession. The old proverbial truth that the rest of the world catches a cold when the United States sneezes appeared to be vindicated as systemically important economies in the European Union and Japan went collectively into recession by mid-2008. Overall, 2009 was the first year since the Second World War that the world was in recession, a calamitous turn around on the boom years of 2002–07.

The crisis came largely as a surprise to policymakers, multilateral agencies, academics and investors. On the eve of the outbreak of the financial crisis, Jean-Philippe Cotis of the OECD (2007) had declared: '... for the OECD area as a whole growth is set to exceed its potential rate for the remainder of 2007 and 2008, supported by buoyancy in emerging market economies and favourable financial conditions'. In the wake of the global recession of 2008–2009, the economics profession has come under a great deal of criticism from leading scholars. Krugman (2009a) chides fellow economists for their '... blindness to the very possibility of catastrophic failures in a market economy'. Galbraith (2009) offers a robust critique of the economics profession and argues that both explicit and implicit intellectual collusion made it difficult for the leading members of the profession (invariably associated with elite American universities) to encourage a genuine discourse based on alternative views. The result was that a rather limited intellectual conversation took place between essentially like-minded scholars.

Therefore, it is unsurprising that for much of 2008, the severity of this global downturn was underestimated. Subsequently, leading forecasters, including the IMF and the World Bank, made a number of revisions to their growth forecasts during 2008 and into 2009 as the magnitude of the crisis grew.[2] Of course, there were some voices that issued dire warnings of a brewing storm, but they were not enough to catch the attention of many who were lulled into a collective sense of complacency in the years leading up to the crisis. Some policymakers, after being caught by surprise at the seemingly sudden appearance of a global downturn, noted confidently that nobody could have predicted the crisis. Thus, Glenn Stevens (2008), the Governor of the Reserve Bank of Australia, observed: 'I do not know anyone who predicted the course of events'. Yet there were economists and other professional analysts, albeit few in number, who were prescient enough to issue a warning about a gathering storm. One paper (Bezemer 2009a: table 1, p. 9) claims that between 2005 and 2007 12 economists and professional analysts predicted a likely recession based on models in which private sector debt accumulation played a major role,[3] while another cites an even smaller number (Foreign Policy 2009).

In retrospect, however, the warning signs were all present: large current deficits in the United States, the United Kingdom and other advanced economies that were being financed by the excess savings of emerging economies and oil exporters (the global current account imbalance); loose monetary policy (most notably in the United States in the wake of the mild recession of 2001); the search for yield and underestimation of risk; and lax financial regulation.

Following events in 2008, particularly the collapse of Lehman Brothers in September, previously risk-loving banks and investors around the world were hit by the fallout from the bank failures, and, subsequently, rapidly reversed their perceptions of risk. Due to the complexity of the mortgage-backed securities, they were, however, unaware of the true extent of the liabilities linked ultimately to a rapidly deteriorating US housing sector. Consequently, liquidity quickly dried up, almost bringing the global financial system to its knees. Some commentators even questioned whether American-style capitalism itself had been dealt a death blow.

Determined to avoid mistakes made by policymakers during previous crises, governments in both advanced and developing countries reacted aggressively by injecting massive amounts of credit into financial markets and nationalizing banks, slashing interest rates, and increasing discretionary spending through fiscal stimulus packages. This response helped avoid a catastrophic depression in many countries although the effectiveness of policies has varied depending on the magnitude of the response and vulnerabilities of the domestic economy. However, despite these interventions, the global financial crisis quickly evolved into a global jobs crisis, as the crisis-induced credit crunch strangled the real economy and trade flows collapsed. Unemployment in OECD countries has surged, while in countries without social security schemes, the downturn has threatened to push millions into poverty.

By the end of 2008 many – but by no means all – developing and emerging economies were feeling the deleterious effects of the US recession. The typical outcome was a deceleration ion growth (ranging from mild to major) in many parts of the developing world, but there were also cases of outright recessions. Among the hardest-hit countries were Armenia, Mexico, South Africa, Turkey, the Baltic States, and Ukraine. At the same time, the two most successful globalizers of recent times have avoided a major downturn, which has been crucial for kick-starting the recovery in 2009. China has, in particular, managed to keep its economy growing in 2009 at a rate of 8.7 per cent, which was supported by the massive stimulus package put together by the Chinese authorities (amounting to US$585 billion). With a smaller stimulus, the Indian economy has also proven to be resilient thanks to strong domestic demand, with growth only falling to 6.7 per cent in 2009.

Nonetheless, the world economy entered 2010 in an environment fraught with a considerable degree of uncertainty. While the worst seems to be over, and while one hears proclamations of a robust recovery, the jury is still out on the lessons and legacies of the tumultuous economic events of 2008 and 2009. How apposite is the epithet of the 'Great Recession'? What were the historical and global circumstances that led to its seemingly sudden emergence? To what extent were policy errors by past US administrations responsible for the crisis? How have policy-makers across the world responded to such economic volatility? How effective have these responses been? What is the way forward in a post-crisis world? These are the questions that are probed in this volume. In raising these questions and seeking to respond to them, the study does not intend to offer a blueprint for a post-crisis world, nor does it aim to offer policy prescriptions that seek to uphold the institutional agenda of any particular international organization or national government.

This chapter provides both an historical perspective on the period leading up to the crisis and insights into the events surrounding the crisis of 2007. This task is undertaken by discussing the notions of the 'Lost Decades' and the 'Great Moderation', and the prevalence of crises throughout history, before turning to the boom years of 2002–07, which was also accompanied by a food and oil crisis in developing countries. Next, the chapter provides a summary of the causes, consequences and policy responses of governments to the global financial crisis that took hold in 2007. The succinct account of these issues highlights both the severity of the crisis and the diversity in its impact on both advanced and developing economies. The chapter considers the recovery phase that tentatively began in mid-2009 and the potential risks that remain. It then proceeds to offer some concluding remarks.

Interpreting the pre-crisis period: alternative views

Over the years leading up to the global financial crisis of 2007 and the ensuing recession, commentators, including leading academics, postulated that the economy had entered a new era of low volatility (known as the 'Great Moderation'). Apart from this OECD-centric view, there are other interpretations of the economic trends of the past few decades, namely the insufficient rates of growth in developing countries in the 1980s and 1990s to tackle poverty (the 'Lost Decades'), and then, more recently, the devastating impact of the surge in oil and food prices on the poor (the so-called 'crisis-before-the-crisis'). Moreover, the financial crisis that hit the global economy in 2007 and 2008 was by no means the first. A review of previous crises reveals that these episodes have occurred frequently – a fact that was so easily overlooked during the boom years of the 2000s.

The 'Lost Decades' and the 'Great Moderation': different views on recent global economic trends

Traumatic external events have the potential to engender turning points in the evolution of the global economy. In this respect, the second oil price shock (1979) was followed by a prolonged global growth slowdown that lasted throughout the 1980s and well into the 1990s. The per capita median real per capita growth rate of the developing world between 1980 and 1998 was effectively zero. This situation was most pronounced in sub-Saharan Africa. This slowdown of growth happened despite the implementation of policy reforms under the rubric of the structural adjustment programmes (SAPs) led by the Bretton Woods institutions. Between 1980 and 1998, 958 SAPs were negotiated and implemented. Not surprisingly, the 1980s and 1990s have been dubbed by some as the 'Lost Decades'. The 'Lost Decades' seem to have emerged as a result of external factors, most notably the impact of the 'slowdown in growth in the industrial world'.[4]

Focusing on the situation in advanced economies, other commentators have referred to the decades leading up to the crisis as the 'Great Moderation', a term attributed to the current Federal Reserve Governor, Ben Bernanke, and other writers on the subject.[5] This claim refers to the decline in macroeconomic (output and inflation) volatility over the last 25 years, following the crises of the 1970s and 1980s. Bernanke (2004) states that the fall in macroeconomic volatility can be attributed to structural changes (meaning 'changes in economic institutions, technology, business practices, or other structural features of the economy have improved the ability of the economy to absorb shocks') and improved macroeconomic policies. In 2004, the Governor of the Federal Reserve stressed that 'improved monetary policy has likely made an important contribution not only to the reduced volatility of inflation... but to the reduced volatility of output as well.' At that time, this interpretation of recent economic history seemed to rest on 'solid' empirical evidence. However, this view contributed to the dangerous underestimation of risk (i.e. that low levels of macroeconomic volatility would continue), which was a major factor in the run-up to the crisis.

Thus, the global and historical circumstances surrounding the emergence of the crisis of 2008 and 2009 are subject to alternative interpretations. They are either marked by an excessive amount of optimism or afflicted by a bleak view of the past. This dichotomy in turn reflects dualism in the global economy: countries that were benefiting from globalization (OECD and emerging economies such as China and India) versus the losers (or the 'not so strong gainers') such as poorly integrated low-income countries.

The global financial crisis has called some of these views into question, particularly the notion that monetary policy was doing a good job of maintaining stability. The problem as discussed further in this chapter was that the instability was manifesting itself elsewhere, namely in asset markets (housing and stock markets).

A history of crises

Given the historical evidence, insufficient attention was paid to the costs associated with low-frequency, high-impact events, particularly among the proponents of the 'Great Moderation'. This inadequate perception of risk stands in contrast to the fact that between 1970 and 2008, there were: 124 systemic banking crises; 208 currency crises; 63 sovereign debt crises; 42 twin crises; 10 triple crises; a global economic downturn about every 10 years; and several price shocks (two oil shocks in the 1970s, the food and energy price shock in 2007–08 discussed below).[6]

Contemporary studies of the historical evidence – for example, IMF (2009i) and Reinhart and Rogoff (2009a) – have shown that such financial crises typically induce a sharp recession, which lasts for approximately two years. Consumption, private investment and credit flows are also slow to improve, which is driven by the deleveraging of debts and risk perceptions. As a consequence, recovery is slow with unemployment levels continuing to rise for a number of years after the economy has started to grow again.

Economic crises are not just a peculiarity of advanced economies. Indeed, in recent decades developing countries have been highly vulnerable to a plethora of banking, external debt, currency, and inflation crises. The debt crisis of the 1980s, the Asian financial crisis of the late 1990s and the more recent debt crisis in Latin America in the 1990s and 2000s have all resulted in deep recessions. Many developing countries have suffered repeated crises as the result of poor macroeconomic management and policymaking. For example, Argentina has experienced four banking crises since 1945 (Reinhart and Rogoff 2009a).

In developing countries, how households cope with economic downturns and external shocks impose social costs that are not always easy to reverse. For example, in the case of the Asian financial crisis, there was an increase in poverty incidence, ranging between 3.1 per cent (Thailand) and 7.6 per cent (Indonesia) and a decline in real wages ranging between −8.9 per cent (Korea) to about −40 per cent (Indonesia).[7]

Overall, it is clear that, despite the 'Great Moderation', there are high costs associated with low-frequency, high-impact events. This means that risk management strategies aimed at containing these costs should be a core part of economic policymaking.

The synchronized global boom of 2002–07

Amid the doom and gloom of 2008 and 2009, it was easy to forget that the pre-crisis period between 2002 and 2007 was one of historically high rates of growth, especially for the developing countries. There was a relatively mild global downturn in 2001 after the bursting of the dot.com bubble. This was followed by a synchronized boom that lasted until 2007. Many countries, particularly in such regions as Africa, grew at rates not seen since the 1960s and early 1970s, signalling a departure (at least statistically) from the 'Lost Decades'. This led some economists to hail the onset of a global 'platinum age'.[8] These advocates of the platinum age are pitted against those who still maintain that the golden age of global growth was the 1950–73 period. Indeed, a former Chief

Economist of the World Bank once noted that the 1960s represent the golden age of economic development.[9]

However, in hindsight, the 2002–07 period stands out as an example of an unsustainable boom. There was a surge in various forms of external finance (export revenues, remittances, private capital flows) that fed a consumption boom in advanced economies and a surge in investment and exports in the developing world led by China and other emerging economies.[10] Overall, the increase in credit flows pushed down the cost of capital (World Bank 2010). Such a growth experience bred a sense of robust optimism about the future, especially among investors in developed economies leading to an underestimation of risk. This state of mind perhaps contributed to the collective complacency of policymakers, development practitioners and multilateral agencies that were evident even at a time when the seeds of a rather severe global economic recession were being sown in the US heartland.

The crisis before the crisis – jobless growth, sluggish real wages and the food and energy crisis

One legacy of the global boom of 2002 and 2007 was that insufficient attention was being paid to the stresses and strains that afflicted labour markets across the world even during the high-growth era. Quantitative expansions in employment in many parts of the world, particularly in developing countries, were juxtaposed with sluggish real wage growth, the persistence of the informal economy, the 'casualization' of the workforce, declining wage shares in national output and rising levels of inequality. This is a familiar theme in recent ILO reports,[11] but other organizations, such as the OECD and the World Bank, have also highlighted the problems of growing economic insecurity and inequality in regional and global labour markets.[12] Decent work remains an elusive goal in many low- and middle-income countries.

One key shortcoming of the boom period was the failure of increases in economic growth to translate into improvements in household incomes. For example, in three major developing and emerging economies – Indonesia, South Africa and Turkey – real wages in the 2000s showed hardly any sustained improvement.[13] Even in consumption-led economies like the US, incomes remained relatively stagnant over this period (Figure 1.1). However, in contrast to developing countries where this situation translates into stubborn levels of poverty, American households were able to increase consumption by tapping into their wealth, namely the increase in household equity that accompanied rising prices (Baily et al. 2008).

In addition, during 2007 and the early part of 2008, many developing countries were buffeted by food and energy price shocks that impaired the fiscal and current balances of the affected economies, led to food riots and protests in many countries and pushed millions into poverty.[14] This phenomenon was also an outcome of the global boom and the surging demand for goods in China, India and other fast-growing emerging economies.

This situation was more pronounced for non-oil or mineral exporters, but even within countries benefiting from the commodity bonanza, the poor were suffering from skyrocketing inflation without seeing much of the returns from exports. The 2007–08 food and energy price shocks appears to have pushed more than 100 million people in the developing world into transient episodes of poverty.[15] In comparison, the World Bank estimates that the Great Recession of 2008–09 has resulted in an increase in poverty of 64 million people (by 2010) (World Bank 2010). The food and oil crisis was (and is), therefore, arguably a much greater concern for low- and middle-income countries than the global financial crisis that affected rich, highly globalized economies more severely.

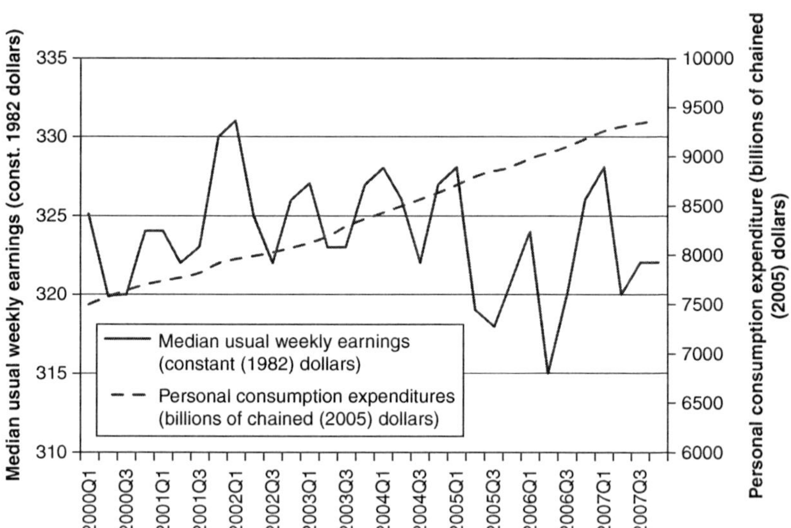

Figure 1.1 Growing consumption in the United States during the boom years despite stagnant real wages, 2000–07

Source: Bureau of Labor Statistics, www.bls.gov, and Bureau of Economic Administration, www.bea.gov.

The global financial and economic crisis of 2007–09

This historical perspective on the decades leading up to the global financial crisis provides an insight into different interpretations of recent economic trends. In particular, the review shows that the global economy was by no means as stable as suggested by many observers, and thus, given the warning signs, the crisis should have come as no surprise. That said, the crisis was largely unexpected and due to its complex roots, it continued to puzzle policymakers, economists and other commentators as it unravelled and sucked in at first banks and companies, and then economies across the globe. The collapse in the real economy has had devastating consequences for households as a result of rising unemployment and surging poverty. At the same time, some countries have been affected more than others due to differences in initial conditions (state of economy, labour market, fiscal space, institutional framework) and exposure to direct and indirect impact of the crisis via credit and trade channels.

This volume seeks to help shed light on some of these issues in the context of both advanced and developing economies. The chapters are presented in two parts: Part I deals with the impact of the crisis in terms of economic and labour market outcomes, while Part II addresses policy responses. In Part I, chapter 2 provides an overview of the crisis in terms of causes, consequences and policy responses. Chapter 3 focuses on how the crisis has affected developing economies, which is further addressed in chapter 4 with respect to the impact on labour markets in these countries. Chapter 5 shifts attention to the impact of the downturn on labour markets in advanced economies, particularly in terms of youth and other vulnerable segments of the population. In Part II, chapter 6 offers an in-depth discussion on macroeconomic policies and how they can be used to support an employment-led recovery, while chapter 7 focuses on the need for fiscal and policy space in developing countries in order to cope with external shocks. The last chapters address the role of labour market and social policies as part of the response to the crisis (chapter 8) and the crucial role of social dialogue in coping with the adjustment costs unleashed by global economic volatility (chapter 9). The volume concludes with chapter 10, which draws attention to the intellectual momentum for a new consensus on a post-crisis policy paradigm. It suggests a menu of policy options that has the potential to secure sustainable, employment-led recovery.

The chapters: a reader's guide

Part I

Chapter 2: The 'Great Recession' of 2008–09: Causes, Consequences and Policy Responses

This chapter provides a comprehensive overview of the Great Recession of 2008–09. In particular, it addresses the causes, consequences and policy responses witnessed across the globe. As stressed by this chapter, the main factors behind the Great Recession were loose monetary policy and low interest rates, global current account imbalances, the underestimation of risk, and lax regulation. The remainder of the chapter focuses on the impact of the crisis in terms of both the economy as a whole and the labour market more specifically. In this context, this chapter provides a summary of key factors behind the vulnerability of countries to the impact of the crisis. Next, the chapter reviews policy responses taken by governments around the world to mitigate the impact of the crisis, addressing both the overall stimulus packages and the more targeted labour market and social policies. Finally, a discussion on economic recovery is outlined, which stresses that for many economies, including the United States, there is still a long way to go, particularly with respect to the situation in the labour market.

Chapter 3: The Global Recession of 2008–09 and Developing Countries

The chapter presents new evidence to show that developing countries have not been impacted equally by the global financial crisis. It constructs a typology of developing countries in terms of their income levels and structural characteristics to suggest how varied the impact of the crisis is on short-run growth performance at the national level. The chapter highlights the challenge of tracing the impact of the 2008–09 global economic downturn on real wages, employment and poverty because of the paucity of relevant and timely data. The chapter also reviews the policy responses undertaken by the various developing countries.

Chapter 4: The Employment Challenge in Developing Countries during Economic Downturn and Recovery

This chapter revisits a sizeable literature that has spawned a debate on the manner in which labour markets adjust to economic downturns in developing economies. One influential view maintains that labour markets in developing economies usually demonstrate 'real wage flexibility', that is, real wages adjust downwards to absorb external shocks. Hence, 'quantity adjustments' in the context of downturns entailing a rise in unemployment is relatively unimportant in developing country labour markets. This chapter draws on country-specific experiences from past crises (such as the Argentinean crisis of 1999–2001 and the Asian financial crisis of 1997) as well as the global recession of 2008–09 to argue that one cannot generalize on the nature of labour adjustments to external shocks. Labour markets respond to recessions in a variety of ways entailing changes in real wages, participation rates, unemployment, hours worked and the composition of employment. The chapter also contends that the well-documented lags in employment recovery from global and regional recessions depend on the extent to which economic downturns are cyclical or structural in nature. The chapter notes that designing appropriate policy responses to usher in employment-led recovery depends upon a proper comprehension of the labour market adjustment process.

Chapter 5: The Impact of the Global Financial Crisis on Labour Markets in OECD Countries: Why Youth and Other Vulnerable Groups Have Been Hit Hard

Building on chapter 4, this contribution explores the ramifications of the global economic and jobs crisis for the labour market from an OECD perspective. This chapter stresses that there has been tremendous variation in how labour markets have been affected, which is due to differences in economic factors and institutions, along with the impact of government policies on the adjustment process. Beyond this aggregate picture, the downturn of 2008–09 has had different implications for various segments of the population as defined by such characteristics as gender, age, education, contractual status, race and country of origin. These traits render individuals more vulnerable to a recession because of either long-term barriers they face in the labour market or because of their overrepresentation in a sector that is more strongly affected by changes in macroeconomic conditions. The analysis presented in this chapter show that, in general, it has been men, particularly younger men, individuals with a low level of educational attainment, and those on temporary contracts who have borne the brunt of the downturn in advanced economies. At least in the case of the European Union (on aggregate), migrant workers have in fact fared better than nationals. Moving to the situation for youth, the chapter argues that the outcome is complex, but in the majority of cases young men seem to have been more adversely affected by the job losses engendered by the economic downturn. This can be attributed to a range of factors, including the fact that recessions affect male-dominated industries (such as construction) more than others. It highlights the policy implications that follow from such a sectoral analysis.

Part II

Chapter 6: The Rise and Fall of Macroeconomic Policy – Pre- and Post-Crisis Perspectives

This chapter argues that the oil price shock of the 1970s and the stagflation that followed led to a paradigm shift in the realm of macroeconomic policy. Concerns with inflation control and fiscal and financial stability superseded the attainment of full employment as a core macroeconomic policy goal that one associates with the 'golden age' of Keynesian economics of the pre-oil shock era. The author draws on cross-section and time-series data (covering more than two decades prior to the crisis for a fairly large sample of countries) to show that the basic tenet of conventional macroeconomics and inflation targeting that the attainment of stability per se will lead to growth, employment and poverty reduction has not materialized. In terms of prescribing alternatives that will enable policymakers to engineer a jobs-led recovery, the chapter suggests that the mandate for macroeconomic policy managers at the national level, that is, the central bank and finance ministry, needs to change. This would entail formally endorsing the attainment of 'full and productive employment and decent work for all' (Millennium Development Goal 1, target 1b) within a framework of price stability and fiscal sustainability as the mandate of macroeconomic policy managers.

Chapter 7: The Perennial Quest for Fiscal and Policy Space in Developing Countries

This chapter proceeds from the premise that developing economies cannot rely on the 'trickle-down' benefits from globally coordinated fiscal actions. They need policy space to enact fiscal stimulus packages. This reveals a structural issue of the capacity of developing economies to engage in counter-cyclical policies. It is possible to enhance both fiscal and policy space in sustainable ways. This means a renewed commitment to domestic resource mobilization, the reorientation of economic policies and better preparedness to cope with global downturns. In particular, developing countries with access to global capital markets should be wary of the dangers of 'liability dollarization' that can severely hamper national policy choices. The chapter suggests that developing countries need global and regional cooperation in order to harness new resources on a significant scale to assist them to cope with external shocks and global economic downturns.

Chapter 8: Labour Market Policies in Times of Crisis

This chapter offers an analytical dissection of the role of labour market policies in mitigating the impact of economic crises on the labour market. These policies play an important complementary role to macroeconomic measures in terms of supporting labour demand, improving the match between demand and supply, providing income support and other forms of social protection, and targeting vulnerable groups that may not benefit from mainstream policy measures. Using illustrations from a cross-section of high- and middle-income countries, the chapter discusses the advantages and disadvantages of specific policies in the wake of the global recession of 2008–09. In general, the policy response to the crisis should build on existing measures, match the objectives, and weigh up the relative costs and benefits of different interventions. As a result of financial and technical constraints, the set of options available to high-income countries is far larger than for emerging and developing economies. For this reason, such countries will require assistance to implement policies. Over the medium and long term, governments should aim to develop a comprehensive and integrated policy and institutional framework that will enable them to better respond to the labour market implications of an economic downturn. This in turn will require better monitoring and evaluation of policies to ensure they are effective in times of crisis.

Chapter 9: Coping with Crises: Easing the Burden of Macroeconomic and Structural Adjustments through Social Dialogue

This chapter argues that global and regional recessions inevitably trigger adjustments costs that can be rather asymmetric in their nature. Some industries and regions get hit harder than others. Some members of the workforce (such as young men and migrants) are more adversely affected than others. Attenuating the asymmetric nature of adjustment costs require a consultative and negotiated approach – or 'social dialogue' – at the micro, meso and macro levels. The participation of workers' and employers' organizations, together with the representatives of governments, will help shape more effective policy responses to the crisis that are supportive of employers while protecting workers' rights. Left unattended, the adjustment costs of global and regional recessions can unleash political and social tensions. The chapter uses this framework to sift through the evidence, at both the enterprise and national levels, to evaluate the extent to which both developing and developed countries have used the instrument of social dialogue to ease the burden of macroeconomic and structural adjustments engendered by the 2008–09 global recession as well as other crises in the past. The chapter suggests that the pattern is complex, with some countries faring better than others.

Chapter 10: The Way Forward

The concluding chapter weaves together the diverse, but interrelated, issues into a summary of key findings. It reflects on the extent to which the 2008–09 global recession marks a turning point in the intellectual evolution of ideas on global development. It argues that, despite a predilection among some for upholding the *status quo ante*, there is indeed an intellectual momentum for a new consensus on a post-crisis policy paradigm. What might such a post-crisis policy paradigm look like? The chapter offers a menu of policy options that have the potential to secure sustainable, employment-led recovery. This will entail a portfolio of tried and tested policies that range across macro- and microeconomic dimensions. These policies are aligned closely with the ILO's Decent Work Agenda and Global Jobs Pact that was endorsed by the 98th Session of the International Labour Conference held in June 2009 and by the G20 Leaders Summit in September 2009. The chapter argues that the implementation of a range of macro- and microeconomic policies to engineer sustainable recovery at the national level needs to be complemented by global and regional cooperation. The chapter notes that other multilateral agencies, such as the World Bank and Asian Development Bank (ADB), have advanced ideas in the wake of the Great Recession of 2008–09 that are largely aligned with the agenda of 'fair globalization'.

Notes

1. Rampell (2009) traces the evolution of the term and points out with some irony that it has also been used to describe all postwar recessions. Reinhart and Rogoff (2009b) refer to the crisis as the 'Second Great Contraction'. A note on the nomenclature used in this chapter. The terms 'global financial crisis' and 'global economic crisis' (2007–09), and the 'Great Recession' of 2008–09 are utilized interchangeably in this chapter.
2. See IMF (2009i).
3. See also Bezemer (2009b) 'Why some economists could see the crisis coming', *Financial Times*, 7 September 2009.
4. See Easterly (2001).

5. See the Remarks by Governor Ben Bernanke at the meeting of the Eastern Economic Association, Washington, DC on February 2004, http://www.federalreserve.gov/BOARDDOCS/SPEECHES/2004/20040220/default.htm. See also Baker (2007), Bernanke (2004), Blanchard and Simon (2001), and Reinhart and Rogoff (2009b).
6. See Laeven and Valencia (2008), IMF (2009i) and Reinhart and Rogoff (2008a,b). Pollin (2009: 1), drawing on the seminal work of Charles Kindleberger, makes the point that '... from 1725 onwards, financial crises have occurred throughout the Western capitalist economies at an average rate of about one every eight and a half years'.
7. There is much literature on the Asian Financial Crisis. See, for example, Lee (1998).
8. As Garnaut and Huang (2007: 9) put it: 'Global growth looks set to exceed 5 per cent in 2007 for the fourth successive year – higher than the 4.9 per cent average of the 'Golden Age' from 1950 to 1953. China is now at the centre of what could turn out to be the strongest period of global economic growth the world has seen – a 'Platinum Age'.
9. Michael Bruno, a former World Bank Chief Economist, observed: 'The 1960s look like the golden age of development'. See Bruno (1995: 9).
10. See Lin (2008) who highlights the surge in external financing of global growth over the 2002–07 period, but does not emphasize its lack of sustainability.
11. See, for example, IILS (2008), ILO (2008b), ILO (2009), Ghose et al. (2008).
12. See the 2007 editorial by the OECD on the 'globalization paradox' and the statement by Holzmann (2006) on behalf of the World Bank.
13. On Indonesia, see Dhanani, Islam and Chowdhury (2009: chapter 4). On South Africa, see Verick (2010) and on Turkey, see Yelden and Ercan (2009).
14. See IMF and World Bank (2009) Global Monitoring Report, Washington DC, p. 1. As the report puts it: 'For poor countries, this is a crisis upon crisis. It comes on the heels of the food and fuel crises. The triple jeopardy of the food, fuel, and financial crises is pushing many poor countries into a danger zone, imposing rising human costs and imperilling development prospects'. See also R. Islam and Buckley (2009).
15. See the statement of the World Bank's President in April 2008, http://go.worldbank.org/5W9U9WTJB0.

Part I

2
The Great Recession of 2008–09: Causes, Consequences and Policy Responses

I. Islam and S. Verick

Introduction

The historical perspective provided in chapter 1 on the decades leading up to the financial crisis shows that the global economy was by no means as stable as had been suggested by many observers. That said, the crisis was largely unexpected and due to its complex roots, it continued to puzzle policymakers, economists and other commentators as it unravelled and sucked in at first banks and companies, and then economies across the globe. The collapse in the real economy has had devastating consequences for households as a result of rising unemployment and surging poverty. At the same time, some countries have been affected more than others as a result of differences in initial conditions (state of economy, labour market, fiscal space, institutional framework) and exposure to direct and indirect impact of the crisis via credit and trade channels.

After enduring the trauma and turbulence of the global recession of 2008–09, most countries are slowly entering a phase of economic recovery. Consequently, attention is shifting to concerns about exit strategies and the increasing demands of tackling the crisis-induced fiscal deficit and government debt. At the same time, a premature withdrawal of monetary and fiscal stimulus would endanger the recovery and have further negative implications for the labour market. In any case, the challenge is to ensure that the world experiences a jobs-led recovery rather than a jobless one, which typically characterizes the economic rebound following a deep recession.

It is from this standpoint that this chapter provides a summary of the causes, consequences and policy responses of governments to the global financial crisis. The succinct account of these issues highlights both the severity of the crisis and the diversity in its impact on both advanced and developing economies. Finally, the chapter considers the recovery phase that began in mid-2009 and the potential risks that remain.

Rates, risk, regulations and global imbalances: factors behind the global financial crisis

Leading up to the crisis there were many tell-tale signs that should have set off alarm bells. The vast majority of academics, officials and investors ignored the signals and rather made profuse claims about a new era. There was a general euphoria about the conditions in the global economy with many commentators claiming that 'this time is different', using the phrase (and title) adopted by Reinhart and Rogoff (2009a). As argued by this study, there are, however, many similarities between the US subprime crisis and previous banking crises such as the massive surge in housing and equity prices, the growing current account deficit and rising level of (private) debt. At the same time, the exposure of lenders and investors was complicated by the securitization of mortgages (through the mortgage bank securities and collateral debt obligations), which created considerable uncertainty in financial markets as the crisis unfolded. This in turn resulted in a sudden reversal of risk perceptions (from risk seeking to risk aversion).

Understandably the causes of the crisis have become a major topic of discourse among both academics and policymakers. The debate surrounding this issue has generally focused on the role of market failure in precipitating the crisis, namely the catastrophic performance of the financial market that was in stark contrast to the theoretical proposition that it is efficient (that is, prices in the stock and bond markets instantly and accurately reflect all available information at the time). This calls one of the core tenets of capitalism into question. At the same time, most contributions to the ongoing post-mortem analysis of the crisis recognizes that government failure has played a major role in allowing banks and other financial institutions to capitalize on loopholes in the regulatory system to increase leverage and returns. In terms of government policy, Taylor (2009) stresses that the excessively loose US monetary policy fuelled the credit boom, while others such as Elmendorf (2007) conclude that interest rates were not too low. In addition to these dimensions, the debate has considered both the contribution of domestic issues (US financial regulation and monetary policy) and global imbalances (the glut of savings flowing from surplus countries to deficit economies).

Overall, drawing from a comprehensive review of crisis-related studies,[1] four core, but interrelated, factors can be identified: interest rates, global imbalances, perceptions of risks and regulation of the financial system.

Loose monetary policy versus global imbalances

Any post-mortem of the first decade of the twenty-first century cannot avoid the role that past US administrations have played in shaping it. When faced with a recession in 2001 following the bursting of the so-called 'dot.com' bubble, the US monetary authorities aggressively reduced the policy interest rate to unprecedented levels and thus fuelled a debt-financed consumption boom that led the way in boosting global aggregate demand. Interest rates in the United States stood at just 1 per cent in 2003 (Figure 2.1). This ensured that the 2001 recession was shallow and short-lived, but it paradoxically sowed the seeds of the global recession of 2008–09.[2] In this respect, Taylor (2009) argues that over the period 2001–06, the Federal Reserve's policy was too loose, resulting in interest rates that were far lower than suggested by the Taylor rule, which in fact was the largest deviation since the 1970s.[3] In contrast, Elmendorf (2007) argues that interest rates were only 'a little too easy for too long,

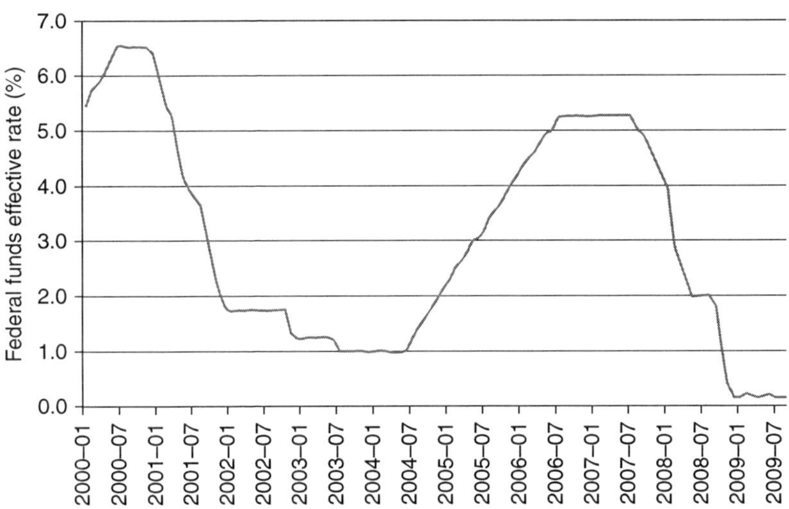

Figure 2.1 US interest rates were too low following the bursting of the dot.com bubble (monthly Federal funds effective rate)

Source: http://www.federalreserve.gov/releases/h15/data.htm.

Note: Federal funds effective rate; the monthly effective federal funds rate is a weighted average of rates on brokered trades.

but the adjustments that appear optimal in hindsight would not have fundamentally altered the housing cycle and related developments' (Elmendorf 2007: 3). In any case, by focusing on a narrow definition of price stability, monetary policy in the United States and elsewhere failed to tackle the ballooning bubble in asset markets.

Looking at the long end of the market, yields on US government bonds (Treasury Bills) were also unusually low during the pre-crisis period.[4] The low interest environment in the United States persisted because oil exporters in the Middle East and export powerhouses – led by China – developed a prodigious appetite for building up foreign exchange reserves in US dollar-denominated assets (typically low-yield US government bonds). Thus was bred the so-called 'global imbalances' that entailed the juxtaposition of 'excessive savings' by surplus countries (led by China) and 'excessive consumption' by deficit countries (led by the United States). Proponents of the global imbalances thesis could argue that such imbalances were unsustainable and would have unravelled at some point even if the US sub-prime market did not implode by mid-2007.

In the years leading up to the crisis, a number of economists expressed their concerns that the large current deficit in the United States was unsustainable. Based on previous current account-driven crises, many commentators felt that the US deficit of more than 5 per cent was a signal of a potential crisis. Roubini and Setser (2004) even warned of the likelihood of a global crisis unless these imbalances were reduced. In emerging economies, current account crises typically occurred when there was a loss of confidence and a reversal of capital flows (a 'sudden stop', leading to sharp depreciation of the currency) (Edwards 2004). However, in the case of the crisis of 2007–09, there was no reversal of capital flows to the United States and thus the US dollar did not collapse as predicted by some economists.

What, then, is the link between the global financial crisis and the imbalances leading up to 2007? In this respect, it is argued that the flows of capital from China and other exporting countries fed into the US housing bubble and credit boom along with its depressing effect on bond yields. For this reason, mortgage rates remained low in the United States even after the Fed started tightening monetary policy in 2004 (Baily et al. 2008). In addition, foreign borrowing directly funded both investment in US companies and the mortgage debt instruments that were at the centre of the subprime disaster. Overall, during the decade preceding the crisis, credit indeed grew most strongly in deficit countries, which was only possible to maintain through the ever-increasing flows of capital from surplus economies (Astley et al. 2009).

The search for higher yields, underestimation of risk and lax financial regulation

Low interest rates and yields on government bonds ultimately encouraged investors to search for higher-yielding assets. Yields on emerging market or corporate bonds also narrowed relative to T-bills, thus leading investors to search for higher returns; hence, the demand for mortgage-backed securities. In the United States lenders took advantage of low interest rates to expand their activities, but having exhausted creditworthy borrowers, they turned to riskier segments of the market (subprime, alt-A and other non-standard loans).[5] These efforts at financial innovation were enabled by lax regulation of the financial system and also propelled by the desire of the political authorities to enhance home ownership rates among disadvantaged and low-income groups. The main sequence of events is summarized in Table 2.1.

The combination of profit-maximizing behaviour and the desirable social goal of enhancing home ownership created the setting for the emergence of so-called 'subprime' housing market in the US. Such 'subprime' borrowers who would not be regarded as credit-worthy under normal prudential standards were deemed to be profitable and worthy business targets by yield-seeking lenders and investors. Special investment vehicles (SIVs) were pressed into service and kept off the balance sheet, which allowed financial institutions to increase leverage and returns on their investments. Thus, mortgages that were in the past the domain of the traditional banking system could now be traded in open markets both within the US and outside its borders, beyond the scope of regulatory measures.

The development of new complex financial products outside the scope of existing rules proved to be a major regulatory failing (Table 2.1). The central elements of this failure were: inadequate capital requirements on products such as the collateral debt obligations (CDOs); inadequate use of ratings and the way credit rating agencies themselves were regulated; and the incentives for risk-taking generated by structured remuneration arrangements (i.e. bonuses) (Astley et al. 2009; Baily et al. 2008; Bean 2009; Obstfeld and Rogoff 2009).

The underestimation of risk, lax financial regulation and low returns on riskless assets contributed to fuelling the excessive leverage and investment in risky assets, namely the mortgage-backed securities. Subprime mortgages were at the centre of the crisis but were by no means the cause.

The trigger: bursting of the US housing bubble

Against this backdrop, the trigger for the crisis unsurprisingly was the US housing market. After the Federal Reserve started increasing interest

Table 2.1 The steps to financial crisis during the US subprime meltdown

Step	Risks
1. Household borrows from the originator (broker or lending institution)	• Asymmetric information – broker did not fully know the credit worthiness of the borrower • Lax lending standards further deteriorated in 2004 and 2005 ('teaser' interest rates, no equity loans, no documents) • In some states of the US, the mortgage contract is 'without recourse to the borrower' – i.e. households can walk away from mortgage
2. Originator sells the mortgage to another financial institution	• Perverse incentives – Since the risk was sold on, originators had the incentive to sell as many mortgages as possible (the 'originate-to-distribute' model)
3. Financial institutions issue mortgage-backed securities (MBS)	• MBS issuers (particularly the government sponsored enterprises, Fannie Mae and Freddie Mac) transferred thousands of loans to structured investment vehicles (SIVs), an off-balance sheet special purpose vehicle (SPV), which allowed these institutions to avoid capital requirements (allowing greater leverage). These SIVs had to be brought back onto the balance sheet once securities were downgraded after the crisis started. • Securities were separated into senior, mezzanine (junior) and non-investment grade (equity) tranches, but effective tranching relies on the assumption that proper risk analysis on the underlying assets was done (which was not the case). • Mortgages were selected from geographically diverse areas but the risk of correlated default was much higher than predicted. • Securitization increased rapidly since 2001, which was based on the growth in sub-prime and Alt-A loans.
4. Private financial sector issues collateralized debt obligations (CDOs)	• CDOs issuers purchased different tranches of MBS and pooled them together with other asset-backed securities (backed by such assets as credit card, auto, business, and student loans) • CDOs 're-securitized' securities, allowing further re-distribution of risk (and hence, adding further complexity), converting some of them into new senior AAA-rated securities • Investment banks were not supervised like commercial banks and thus were not required to adhere to capital requirements. These banks could borrow short term and hold risky longer-term assets with low levels of capital or reserves.
5. Growth in credit default swaps (CDS)	• CDO issuers purchased CDS, which enabled them to receive AAA ratings. These transactions were not regulated as they occurred in the over-the-counter market

Sources: Astley et al. (2009) and Baily et al. (2008).

rates, the delinquency rate on home loans began to rise in 2006 before gaining momentum in 2007 (Astley et al. 2009). This led to the failure of a number of US mortgage lenders. Over 2007, hedge funds were hit hard by the defaults and the subsequent unwinding of the subprime market. However, the real problem was that banks and other investors around the globe were exposed to this situation, but because of the complex nature of the financial products, particularly the collateral debt obligations, could not quantify the size of their exposure and losses. Consequently, in mid-2007, financial institutions started to hoard liquidity, which led to a freezing of the market for asset-backed commercial paper. The credit crunch had begun. This in turn led to a further increase in perceptions of risk and decrease in lending, which was greatly exacerbated by the failure of Lehman Brothers in September 2008.

The global economic and jobs crisis: the diverse nature of its impact on national economies

The financial crisis that started in the United States in mid-2007 eventually spread around the world to both advanced and developing economies, resulting in the worst recession since the Second World War. Despite the severity of the crisis, there has been a great deal of diversity in how countries have been affected by the downturn in terms of both magnitude of economic contraction and subsequent deterioration of the labour market. This section reviews this variation in the impact in the context of countries' initial conditions and transmission channels.

The economic consequences of the global financial crisis

The United States was the epicentre of the crisis and its economy was hit directly by the meltdown in the subprime mortgage market along with the repercussions of the financial crisis and the ensuing credit crunch. As a consequence, the US economy fell into recession in December 2007 and is estimated to have shrunk by 2.7 per cent in 2009.[6] However, this contraction is smaller than most G20 countries and smaller than the average for advanced economies (–3 per cent) (Figure 2.2).

An important theme of this chapter is that while this downturn may be the worst since the Second World War, the ensuing impact of the crisis on economies across the globe has by no means been the same. Indeed, diversity is a hallmark of the Great Recession of 2008–09. Since the United States went into recession at the end of 2007, most advanced economies have joined the ranks, particularly those exposed through financial and later trade channels. But at the same time, others, particularly in the Asia region (namely China and India but also Australia), have avoided a major

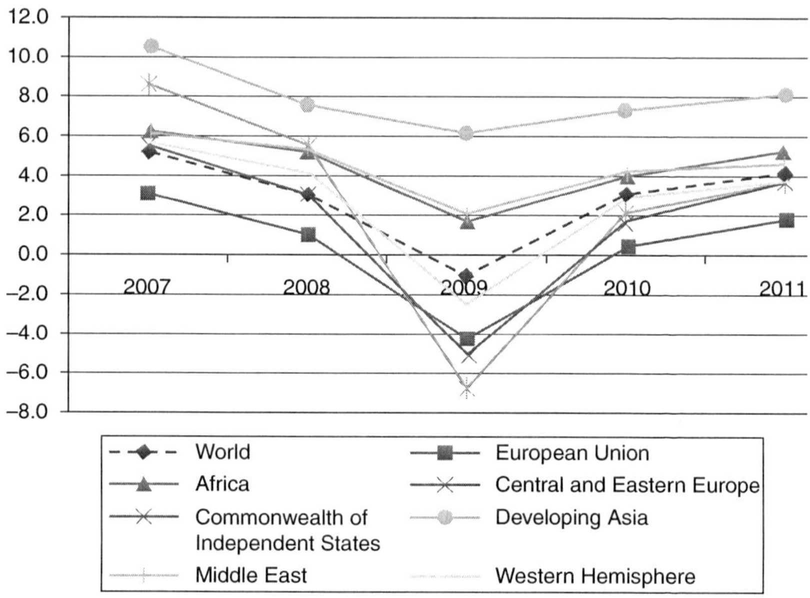

Figure 2.2 Economic growth across the world, real GDP growth (annual % change)
Source: IMF World Economic Outlook Database October 2009, data accessed 24 February 2010.

contraction, despite their integration with the global economy. A number of low-income countries such as Ethiopia and Uganda also continued to grow strongly despite the downturn (Figure 2.3).

Indeed, in contrast to some of the earliest predictions, the impact of the crisis on developing countries has been far from universal. The most severely affected are middle-income countries, especially in Central and Eastern Europe and the Commonwealth of Independent States (Figure 2.3). This has been driven by the combination of the credit crunch and domestic imbalances such as large current account deficits and housing bubbles (the two being not unrelated). The countries estimated to have contracted by the greatest margin include Lithuania, Latvia, Armenia, Estonia and Ukraine, which all experienced a decline in GDP of 14 per cent or more in 2009 (Figure 2.3). These are depression-like contractions. The overall similarities between the 'Great Depression' of the 1930s and the 'Great Recession' of 2008–09 are presented in Box 2.1.

Due to its links with the United States, most of Latin America fell into a deep recession (a contraction of 2.1 per cent in 2009), although there is a considerable variation within the region. Mexico has been hit hardest and is estimated to have contracted by 7.1 per cent in 2009. In comparison, Brazil grew by 0.1 per cent (World Bank 2010).

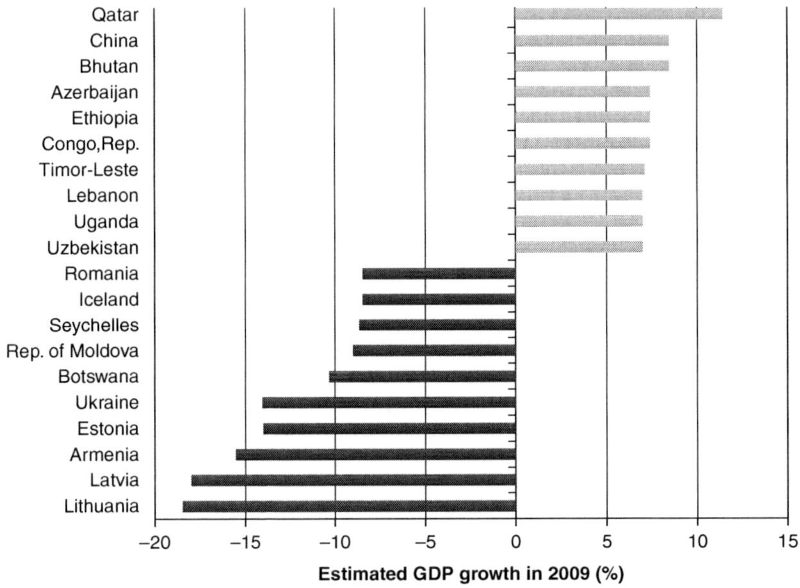

Figure 2.3 The fastest-growing and contracting countries in 2009
Source: IMF World Economic Outlook Database October 2009, accessed on 4 February 2010.
Notes: GDP growth figures for 2009 are estimates. Afghanistan is excluded due to its specific economic circumstances.

Most low-income countries, however, evaded a recession, but the slowdown in growth witnessed in these countries nonetheless has negative implications for poverty. Overall, the smaller, more open economies have been hit harder, while the larger emerging economies have been supported by domestic demand and government spending. China and India have notably continued to grow strongly during the crisis.

Greater diversity in the impact of the crisis on the labour market

Moving from the variation in the contraction of output to the impact on the labour market reveals that there is even more diversity in outcomes across countries (see chapter 5 for further details). In OECD countries, the unemployment rate increased from 5.7 per cent in the third quarter of 2007 to 8.6 per cent in the third quarter of 2009, representing a rise of 10.1 million individuals without jobs.[11] The five hardest-hit OECD countries in terms of a surge in the unemployment rate from 2007Q3 to 2009Q3 are Estonia (+10.9 percentage points), Spain (+10.3 ppts), Ireland (+8.1 ppts), United States (+4.9 ppts) and Turkey (+4.6 ppts). The average increase in the OECD is 2.9 percentage

Box 2.1: From the Great Depression of the 1930s to the 'Great Recession' of 2008–09

It is by now *de rigueur* to refer to the global recession of 2008–09 as the worst since the Great Depression of the 1930s. Certainly, the world economy contracted for the first time since the end of the Second World War. In addition, some scholars have noted that: (1) the rate of contraction in global trade between its peak in 2007 and April 2008 was worse than the Great Depression; (2) the rate of global industrial production declined at a faster rate between mid-2007 and the first four months of 2008 than during the 1930s; (3) the proportionate decline in global stock market wealth was rather dramatic by the standards of the Great Depression.[7] One estimate suggests that household wealth in the United States declined by 17 per cent in 2007–08, while it declined by a mere 3 per cent in 1928–29.[8] Viewed from such perspectives, one can suggest that the notion of the 'Great Recession' is justified. On the other hand, it would be naïve to argue that, in terms of the duration of the recession and the sheer impact on jobs and livelihoods, the Great Recession of today is equivalent to the Great Depression of yesterday, despite the shared nature of the prefix. During the 1930s, the decline in industrial production lasted for three years. This is certainly not the case today.[9]

Unemployment reached 25 per cent in the United States during the trough of the 1930s. In both 2008 and 2009, even the worst-affected economies did not exhibit unemployment rates in that range. Indeed, comparative evidence suggests that job losses during the global economic crisis of 2008 and 2009 were lower than in previous recessions in the postwar period. This does not necessarily mean that the labour market consequences of the global recession of 2008 and 2009 were marginal. For a variety of reasons – and especially in the industrialized world – job retention rates by firms have been particularly pronounced. What this means is that, unless there is broad-based recovery, millions of jobs continue to be at risk.[10]

points. At the same time, a number of countries have experienced a mild impact on the labour market in terms of rising unemployment. In Poland and Germany, the unemployment rate has in fact decreased over this period (by 1.2 and 0.7 percentage points, respectively). In others such as Austria, the Netherlands, Republic of Korea and Slovakia, the change in unemployment rate has been marginal.

In addition to looking at unemployment, there has been considerable variation in the adjustment of working hours, wages and employment across countries (see chapter 5). For example, as was much discussed during the crisis, employment in Germany has adjusted by a small margin, while hours have decreased more than in most European countries (lower left corner). In Germany's case, this was driven by employers' concerns of holding on to skilled workers, which was in turn supported by a subsidized reduced working time scheme (*Kurzarbeit*) (see chapter 8). In contrast, adjustment to both employment and hours has been above average in countries with more flexible labour markets such as the Czech Republic, Latvia and the United Kingdom. In the majority of European countries, adjustment has taken place in both employment and hours to a moderate degree. This diversity in employment and working time adjustment across European countries is due to differences in economic factors (sectoral impact, transmission channels) and institutions (such as the degree of unionization, wage flexibility, dismissal protection legislation), along with the impact of government policies on the adjustment process (for example, the reduction in working hours through work-sharing schemes).

Beyond looking at these more aggregate dimensions, the impact of the global financial crisis can also be disentangled in terms of how it has affected vulnerable segments of the population. In this respect, five dimensions can be identified, which define the groups that were hit hardest during the global downturn: gender, age, educational attainment, type of employment contract, race and country of origin. There are, of course, other dimensions that determine outcomes in the labour market, such as disability status, but these are harder to measure.

Figure 2.4 depicts changes in employment in the European Union over the crisis period for men, youth, the unskilled, workers on temporary contracts and migrant workers. Two different trends can be discerned in these figures. Firstly, employment has contracted more for young people, individuals with low levels of educational attainment and workers on temporary contracts. Secondly, the employment of foreign-born workers in the EU decreased by 2.4 per cent between the third quarter of 2008 and the third quarter of 2009 (although it is still higher than the level at the end of 2007). That said, employment of these workers was increasing at a faster rate when the crisis hit Europe in the second half of 2008.

In developing countries, it is more difficult to form strong conclusions on the impact on the labour market due to the lack of up-to-date data. In the aftermath of previous crises, laid-off workers in developing countries have been typically forced to take up employment in the urban informal or rural economies (i.e. a reversal of rural–urban migration flows), which act as absorbing sectors during economic downturns.[12] As also witnessed during previous downturns, real wages can decline in developing countries, resulting in rising poverty (for example, in Indonesia following the East Asian financial crisis).

Based on the available figures, the labour market impact of the global financial crisis in developing countries includes both rising unemployment and changes in other labour market outcomes. Middle-income countries such as Mexico and Turkey have experienced a severe economic contraction over 2009, resulting in rapidly increasing unemployment. In the case of South Africa, one of the hardest-hit African countries, the recession of 2009 has translated more into rising discouragement than unemployment.[13] At the same time, employment in the informal sector in South Africa contracted over most of the crisis period, which contradicts the general assumption that this sector absorbs laid-off workers. Informality in Indonesia was on a downward trend before it started increasing in response to the impact of the crisis.

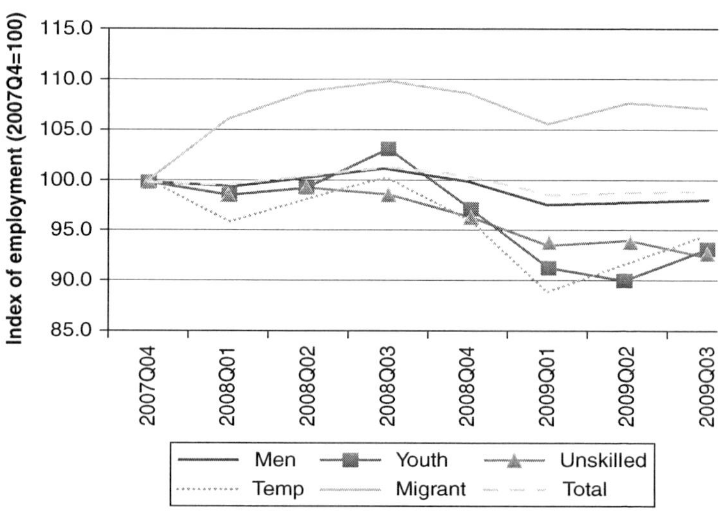

Figure 2.4 Adjustment in employment across different segments of the population, European Union (27 Member States), 2007Q4–2009Q3

Sources: EUROSTAT Labour Force Survey Database, http://epp.eurostat.ec.europa.eu/portal/page/portal/employment_unemployment_lfs/data/database; authors' calculations.

Notes: The figures presented are the aggregate level of employment in the 27 member States of the European Union, which have been converted into an index (2007Q4=100); Youth = employment level of individuals aged 15 to 24; Unskilled = employment level of individuals with pre-primary, primary and lower secondary education – levels 0-2 (ISCED 1997); Temp = number of employees on temporary contracts; Migrant = employment level of foreign=born workers.

The share of informal employment in Indonesia stood at 63.1 per cent in February 2007, which continued to fall, reaching 61.6 per cent in February 2008.[14] The share has since grown to 62.1 per cent, which reflects that the impact of the crisis has been relatively mild in comparison to other middle-income countries, particularly those located in Latin America, Central and Eastern Europe, and the CIS region. Although data are not yet available on household income, poverty has most likely increased in badly affected countries.

Mitigating the effects of the crisis and securing a sustainable recovery: the effectiveness of policy responses

As the global financial crisis unravelled, governments across the globe increasingly recognized the severity of the downturn and the urgency to intervene in order to avoid a catastrophic collapse of the financial markets and the real economy. The response has consisted of three main interventions: (1) bailouts of the financial sector and injections of money into the financial system to maintain the flow of credit; (2) cutting interest rates to stimulate borrowing and investment; and (3) extra fiscal spending to shore up aggregate demand (including automatic stabilizers such as unemployment insurance benefits). These measures have sought to prevent further economic deterioration and keep workers in jobs where possible or help create new jobs to provide opportunities for the unemployed. Overall, this response has contributed to avoiding a far more severe downturn, although the effectiveness of packages has varied considerably across countries. In this context, this section summarizes both the macroeconomic and labour market policy responses.

Macroeconomic policies, stimulus packages and the composition of policy interventions: an overview

Systemically important nations, especially from the developed world, have engaged in historically unprecedented expansionary monetary policy, entailing both aggressive reductions in policy rates and quantitative easing. This has been combined with the assumption of contingent liabilities on behalf of the banking system (especially through deposit guarantee schemes) and massive support – running into trillions of dollars – for beleaguered financial institutions. At the same time, policymakers across the world held the view that monetary and financial policies alone could not cope with the global recession of 2008–09. A United Nations Development Programme (UNDP) study maintains that there are now 48 countries for which there are reliable data on fiscal stimulus packages.

Collectively, the fiscal stimulus packages account for 3.9 per cent of world GDP (as measured in 2008) and 4.8 per cent of their national GDPs. Twenty out of the 48 can be classified as developing countries.[15]

The UNDP study highlights the point that social protection expenditures account for a relatively modest proportion of the announced fiscal stimulus packages – about 25 per cent of the total – but does not analyze the composition of the range of policy interventions. An important ILO study fills this gap by highlighting the composition of policy interventions in 54 countries which includes a mix of developed and developing countries and G20 members. The ILO study (2009a) examines policy interventions in four broad areas: stimulating labour demand, supporting jobs, job-seekers and unemployed; expanding social protection and food security; using social dialogue and protecting rights at work. The general conclusion is that some interventions (such as additional public expenditure on infrastructure and extending credit to small and medium-sized enterprises) have been more popular than others (such as providing enhanced protection to migrant workers). Table 2.2 complements this effort by delineating how policy interventions have varied across different thematic areas (macroeconomic policy, social protection measures and so on) in a sample of 20 regionally representative low- and middle-income countries. As can be seen, some policy interventions have been used more frequently than others. A majority of countries in the sample have engaged in expansionary fiscal and monetary policies and support for small and medium-sized enterprises. Much less effort has been expended in boosting income and employment protection and in taking account of the particular circumstances of vulnerable groups (informal economy workers, young people and migrant workers).

While analyses of the composition of policy interventions are useful, it is necessary to comprehend how effective such interventions have been in coping with the global recession. An in-depth knowledge of the efficacy of country-specific policy interventions is missing, but an illustration is offered of two cases from the G20 countries – the United States and Indonesia – that have enacted fiscal stimulus packages. The former was the most publicised and has been subjected to multiple evaluations. The launch of the latter was supported by an official evaluation. In both cases, the outcomes have been modest – see Box 2.2 on the United States and Box 2.3 on Indonesia.

What does the evidence show in terms of the collective ability of the G20 to close the output gap? In a report prepared for the G20 Leaders Summit held on 24 September 2009, the ILO estimated that the overall size of the fiscal expansion measured as a proportion of GDP (including

Table 2.2 A typology of policy responses to the global recession of 2008–09 in 20 low- and middle-income countries, December 2009

Policy area	Specific interventions	Frequency (%)
Monetary and financial policy	Interest rate reductions	75
	Quantitative easing	40
	Deposit guarantee schemes and other measures to protect the financial sector	75
Fiscal policy	Overall tax and expenditure adjustments	65
	Public investment in infrastructure	100
Exchange rate/ capital account	Exchange rate depreciations	40
	Export financing or tariff reduction	45
Income and employment protection	Efforts to limit layoffs	30
	Unemployment benefits	25
	Employment guarantee schemes	20
	Minimum wages	40
Social protection	Cash and in-kind transfer programmes	45
	Additional social expenditure	65
Increasing employability	Training and re-training	45
	Public employment services	20
Group-specific initiatives	Informal economy workers	10
	Youth	10
	Migrant workers	30
	Public sector employees	20
Sector-specific initiatives	Support for SMEs	70
	Support for key export sectors	20
	Support for 'green' jobs	10

Source: Compiled from online media reports and country-specific websites. The information was collected between August 2009 and December 2009.

both discretionary expenditure and automatic stabilizers) can, at best, offset 43 per cent of the employment gap engendered by the current recession in the G20 countries (ILO 2009a). This conclusion is supplemented by exploring the impact and implications of the composition of fiscal stimulus packages that have been adopted.

What guidelines should policymakers follow in determining the composition of fiscal stimulus packages? One approach is to use ex-post values of fiscal multipliers by type of policy measures, which can be broadly categorized as spending and revenue measures. The objective is to use these ex-post values or benchmarks to allocate resources in such a way that the policy interventions maximize the fiscal multipliers.

There is a sizeable literature embodying estimates of fiscal multipliers by type of measures. These estimates have been compiled by the IMF

Box 2.2: The US fiscal stimulus package: an assessment

The US fiscal stimulus package – known as the American Recovery and Reinvestment Act (ARRA) – was enacted into law on 17 February 2009. Its original size was US$825 billion to be spread over 2009–11. It was subsequently reduced to US$787 billion after protracted political negotiations in Congress and the Senate. If one takes out the outlays on the State Fiscal Stabilization Fund and state fiscal relief, the size of ARRA at the federal level stands at US$531 billion. The majority of this amount (53 per cent) can be attributed to tax cuts. 23 per cent account for government purchases and the balance is taken up in the form of transfers.

There are now multiple evaluations (two of which are official versions) of ARRA that enable one to compare the projected job creation rates from the fiscal interventions with what has actually been accomplished so far. The US administration expected that ARRA would create 3.5 million jobs by the end of 2010. This was well within the range of estimates offered by others (example Congressional Budget Office, Levy Institute). What strikes one is the variation in the range of estimated impact of ARRA on employment. They range from a modest 300,000 jobs created to 1.5 million jobs created by the third quarter of 2009. This has to be contrasted against the fact that the labour market has shed 8.4 million jobs since December 2007. The latest estimates suggest that over the next three years 11.1 million jobs would have to be created to restore the pre-crisis unemployment rate. It thus seems fair to conclude that ARRA has had a modest outcome in the specific sense that it staved off a much bigger surge in unemployment and probably avoided a depression, but did not come close to restoring full employment.

There are several likely explanations for the modest outcome. One possibility is that the US administration's initial forecasts about the depth and duration of the recession, and its expected impact on the labour market, were rather optimistic. This perhaps influenced the size of the fiscal policy response and made it less ambitious than it otherwise would have been. One 'back-of-the envelope' calculation (Baker, 2009) suggests that the current employment and output gap can only be bridged by a fiscal stimulus package that is more than three times larger than ARRA. Some leading economists (example, Paul Krugman and Laura Tyson) have lent their voices to calls for a new round of fiscal stimulus. It also appears that the rate of disbursing the allocated monies to various projects has been quite slow. So far, only about 30 per cent of the committed funds for 2009 have been spent. Even by 2010, 75 per cent of ARRA funds are scheduled to be utilized. Concerns have been raised about the current composition of ARRA. One study (Zandi, 2009) shows that the mean values of fiscal multipliers range between 0.30 and 0.49 for (permanent) tax cuts, but they are substantially higher for government purchases and transfers (between 1.38 and 1.73). Hence, one can justify the claim that the '... government could have achieved ... more at the same cost by skewing the stimulus package towards outlays rather than tax cuts' (Zacharias et al. 2009).

Sources: Andrews, E.L. (2009) 'Doubts About Obama's Economic Recovery Plan Rise Along With Unemployment', *New York Times*, 6 July; Baker, D. (2009) 'Stimulus Arithmetic', *The Guardian*, 13 July; Burtless, G. (2009) 'Faulty Economic Forecasts or Faulty Policy Evaluation? The Difference is Important', *Brookings*, 20 July; Congressional Budget Office (CBO) (2009) 'Estimated Macroeconomic Impacts of the American Recovery and Reinvestment Act of 2009', 2 March; Council of Economic Advisers (CEA) (2009) 'Estimates of Job Creation from the American Recovery and Reinvestment Act of 2009', Washington DC, May; Romer, C. (2009) 'From Recession to Recovery: The Economic Crisis, the Policy Response, and the Challenges We Face Going Forward', Testimony before the Joint Economic Committee, 22 October; Recovery.gov, 'Timeline', 20 July; Zacharias, A *et al.* (2009) 'Who Gains from President Obama's Stimulus Package... and How Much?', *The Levy Economics Institute of Bard College*, Special Report, 12 June; Romer, C. and Bernstein, J. (2009) 'The Job Impact of the American Recovery and Reinvestment Plan', Washington DC: *Obama-Biden Transition Project*, 9 January; Zandi, M. (2009) 'The Economic Impact of the American Recovery and Reinvestment Act', *Moody's.com*, 21 January; Bivens, J. (2009) 'How we know the recovery package is helping', Economic Policy Institute, 29 October, www.epi.org; Shierholz, H. (2010) 'Job market stuck on pause', Economic Policy Institute, 5 March, www.epi.org.

and OECD. A simplified version is presented in Table 2.3, which illustrates that the mean values of fiscal multipliers are highest for capital expenditure and lowest for corporate tax reductions. In general, spending measures have higher multipliers than tax measures. As noted in Khatiwada (2009), financial rescue efforts have been significantly larger than fiscal spending.

Box 2.3: The Indonesian fiscal stimulus package: an assessment

Official projections suggest that the global economic crisis will reduce the Indonesian economic growth rate to 4.0–4.7 per cent in 2009 from a pre-crisis growth rate that reached above 6 per cent per annum in 2007 and 2008. The Indonesian government has responded to the projected growth slowdown with a combination of financial, monetary and fiscal policies. A fiscal stimulus package has been enacted (with effect from 1 March 2009), amounting to 1.4 per cent of GDP.

Tax cuts represent approximately 79 per cent of the overall fiscal package of Rp 73.3 trillion. They consist of reductions in both indirect taxes and income taxes. The balance is directed towards infrastructure expenditure (Rp 12.2 trillion) and direct subsidies (Rp 4.8 trillion). Thus, a modest amount has been allocated towards enhancing job-creating public expenditure. It is widely acknowledged that tax cuts are not as effective as job-creating public expenditure or a scaled up social protection system in dealing with the consequences of a systemic global economic downturn.

An official estimate claims that 93 per cent of the earmarked expenditure was accomplished by end-2009 and that an estimated 1 million short-term jobs were created. A 'simulation' exercise was also undertaken by the Indonesian government to work out how the unemployment rate will behave with expansionary fiscal policy and without it. The exercise that was undertaken demonstrated that fiscal expansion along the lines described here would contain the rise in the unemployment rate to 8.3 per cent in 2009. In the absence of the fiscal interventions, the 'simulation' exercise shows that unemployment will rise to 8.9 per cent. Had the pre-crisis growth rates prevailed, the aggregate unemployment rate would have declined to 7.4 per cent. These estimates suggest that the impact of the fiscal stimulus package is modest.

Sources: Ministry of Finance (2009) *The 2009 Revised Budget Fiscal Stimulus Programme: Mitigating the Impact from the Global Crisis and States Budgets 2008 and 2009*, Republic of Indonesia; Soesastro, H. (2009) 'After the London G20 Summit', *Jakarta Post*, 11 April; Islam, I. and A. Chowdhury (2009) 'Global Economic Crisis and Indonesia', *Jakarta Post*, 5 May.

The policy message embedded in Table 2.3 is that governments enacting fiscal stimulus packages should concentrate on spending measures rather than tax cuts. Furthermore, within the category of spending measures, governments should focus on capital expenditure, such as investments in employment-intensive infrastructure. This will yield higher dividends in terms of the impact on output and jobs for any given size of fiscal expansion. A simple numerical example that draws on the parameters in Table 2.3 can be used to substantiate this point.

Consider country X. Assume that policymakers decide to go for a 'diversified' approach, that is, they adopt a fiscal policy design entailing a mix of tax cuts (say, 60 per cent of the overall fiscal stimulus package) and spending measures (say, 40 per cent of the overall package). Assume too that the size of the discretionary fiscal stimulus is US$100 billion for a given period. The (weighted average) value of the fiscal multiplier is 0.71, yielding a projected increase in GDP of US$71 billion over the relevant period. Assume an alternative scenario in which policymakers, based on their knowledge of fiscal multipliers, decide to adopt a 'concentrated' approach in which fiscal resources are directed entirely towards supporting capital expenditures. In this case, the value of the multiplier is 1.1, yielding a projected increase in GDP of US$110 billion over the relevant period. The 'concentrated' approach yields a projected increase in GDP that is approximately 1.5 times higher than the 'diversified' approach, although the size of the discretionary fiscal expansion remains constant.

The above example is admittedly contrived and relies on rather simple stimulus arithmetic. The reality is certainly more complex. Fiscal

Table 2.3 Fiscal multipliers by type of measure

Type of fiscal measure	Mean values of multipliers
Capital expenditure	1.1
Other expenditure	0.65
Tax cuts	0.45
(source)	(Spilimbergo et al. 2009: 3 for IMF)
Government expenditure	1.1
Corporate tax cuts	0.3
Personal income tax cuts	0.5
Indirect tax cuts	0.5
Reductions in social security contributions	0.4
(source)	(OECD 2009c: 114)

Note: These multipliers are derived from studies of high-income economies.

multipliers rely on a range of factors and are shaped by country-specific circumstances. In general, small, open economies have smaller multipliers than economies with large domestic markets. Developing countries have smaller multipliers than developed countries. Furthermore, fiscal multipliers are not immutable values – they can vary under changing economic circumstances. One could argue, for example, that the recession of 2008–09 has made the debt-constrained private sector (households and firms) rather cautious about the future and preoccupied with meeting their debt obligations. This could cause a decline in their propensity to consume and invest. This implies that tax rebates are likely to be saved by the private sector more than would be the case in normal circumstances. This will thus reduce the potential of tax measures to boost aggregate demand.[16]

On the other hand, given that the global financial crisis of 2007 was largely unanticipated, it is unlikely that governments across the world would have a large portfolio of 'shovel-ready' projects that can be readily activated. Infrastructure programmes (building roads and bridges, investing in social housing, refurbishing school buildings, expanding IT infrastructure, etc.) take time to design and deliver. They can also be driven by political imperatives. Ideally, they need to go through a reliable tendering and procurement process and should be subjected to cost–benefit analyses. Given such pragmatic constraints, it might well be the case that some – or even many – governments opt for tax cuts more than spending measures, or at least a 'diversified' approach.

What have governments in the G20 and elsewhere done in terms of the composition of fiscal stimulus packages over 2008–09? Figure 2.5 shows the share of tax cuts in the policy packages of G20 countries. The average is 33 per cent, but some countries have a high proportion of tax cuts in their discretionary fiscal policy packages: Indonesia, the United Kingdom, Germany, the Russian Federation and Brazil stand out, with the share of tax cuts ranging from 68 per cent to 100 per cent of their policy packages.

The implications of the above findings for developing nations that fall outside the G20 is that they cannot rely on the 'trickle-down' benefits from a globally coordinated fiscal stimulus undertaken by the G20. If the present is any guide, the indirect benefits of collective fiscal action by systemically important nations are unlikely to accrue on a timely and a large enough scale to make a difference to the economic circumstances of the developing world. In any case, many developing countries lack the necessary repertoire of labour market and social protection policies to protect the poor and vulnerable from the deleterious consequences of the global recession.

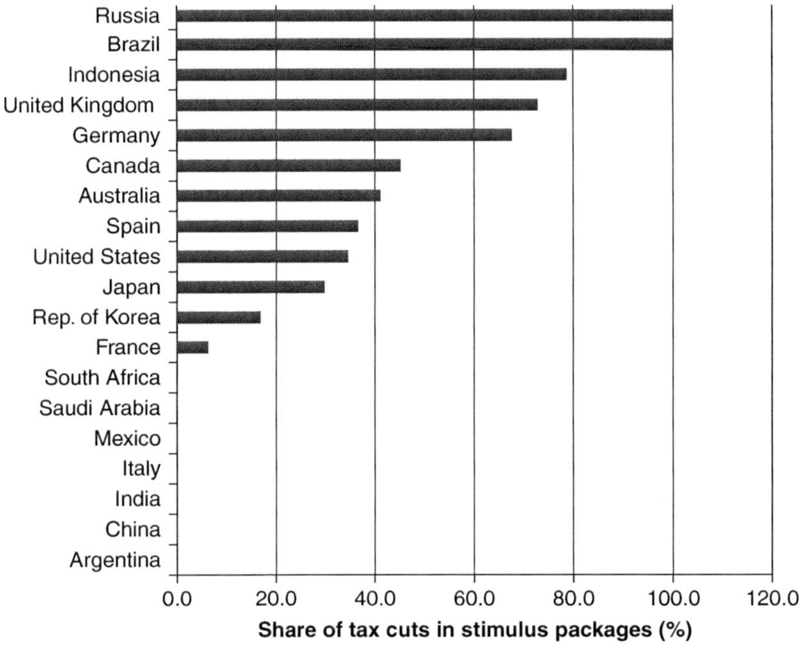

Figure 2.5 Share of tax cuts in stimulus packages in G20 countries
Source: Derived from Table 3, Jha (2009).

Has the 'diversified approach', entailing a mix of tax cuts and spending measures, been effective? Ex ante evaluations, based on five major studies (see Table 2.4), seem to suggest that the 'diversified' approach, in conjunction with the overall size, has had some impact on the output and employment gap engendered by the recession of 2008–09, but it has not been adequate enough. In sum, the analysis presented here supports the contention that the economic stimulus packages in the G20 countries has only partially offset the output and employment gap created by the global economic recession, a point also made by Khatiwada (2009).

It thus appears that developing countries need direct support in enacting fiscal stimulus packages. One exercise, drawing on the experience of sub-Saharan Africa, points out that an aid-financed fiscal expansion of US$50 billion will be needed for the region to remove an estimated output gap of US$40 to US$50 billion.[17] The composition of the fiscal intervention is important. An aid-financed public investment in infrastructure is the best option, provided it is well-designed and

Table 2.4 Summary of key findings on fiscal stimulus packages

Agency	**Sample coverage**	**Estimated size of fiscal expansion (as % of GDP)**	**Key findings**
IILS (2009)/ Khatiwada (2009)	G20 + 12 countries	1.7	* Overall size inadequate relative to what is needed * Composition does not maximise employment impact * Model-based simulation suggests that biggest employment impact from labour-intensive public * expenditure programs * Model-based simulation suggests that delay in implementation reduces ability to close 'jobs gap'
Brookings	G20	1.4	* Size falls short of benchmark set by IMF * Composition varies significantly and not geared towards maximising size of fiscal multipliers * Frontloading in many cases, that is, fiscal expansion mostly in 2009
IMF (1)	Nine 'largest economies'	3.4	* Although size appears large, impact not significant enough to offset output gap * Diversified approach (mix of tax cuts and spending) * There is a +ve relationship between output gap and size of fiscal expansion (higher output gap leading to higher fiscal expansion) * Initial conditions constrain size of fiscal expansion
IMF (2)	G20	1.5	* Although sizeable increase in output and employment, overall impact still not significant enough to offset output gap * Diversified approach, but evidence that infrastructure spending has biggest impact on growth * There is a +ve relationship between output gap and size of fiscal expansion (higher output gap leading to higher fiscal expansion) * Initial conditions constrain size of fiscal expansion

(*continued*)

Table 2.4 Continued

Agency	**Sample coverage**	**Estimated size of fiscal expansion (as % of GDP)**	**Key findings**
OECD	OECD economies	3.4	* Although size appears large, impact not significant enough to offset output gap * Diversified approach, but evidence is that 'spending multipliers' bigger than 'tax multipliers' * -ve relationship between 'automatic stabilizers' and size of fiscal expansion

Sources: IILS (2009), IMF (2009c,d), Khatiwada (2009), OECD (2009c) and Prasad and Sorkin (2009).

well-managed. This strategy contributes to the long-run growth potential of the region and also confers benefits to the donor countries by increasing demand for their goods and services.

Labour market and social policies as part of the response to the crisis

In addition to the role of macroeconomic policy, specific labour market measures also play a role in mitigating the impact of the crisis on workers, helping reduce the lag between economic growth and job creation, as well as preventing the risk of unemployment persistence, long-term unemployment and human capital deterioration. Formulating appropriate policy interventions requires recognizing how the labour market adjusts as a result of the credit squeeze and collapse in aggregate demand, which is discussed further in chapter 5. In this respect, the degree and form of adjustment will depend on the magnitude of the crisis in their country and region, and the level of labour market flexibility, which is influenced by the institutional arrangements in the labour market (such as wage setting institutions, unionization, employment protection legislation, and so on).

In light of the various labour market adjustment mechanisms discussed above, the labour market policy response to the crisis has centred around four main areas: maintaining and increasing labour demand; improving the match between demand and supply; providing income support; and targeting of vulnerable groups.

Drawing on the findings of a range of recent surveys on the policy response to the global financial crisis of 2008–09 (see chapter 8), a large number of high-income countries have considered policy measures that address the different goals of active labour market policies (ALMPs).[18] The most commonly used intervention in these advanced economies is training for both those threatened by layoffs and the unemployed (including work experience and apprenticeship initiatives) (27 countries), followed by work sharing (24 countries), increased resources for public employment services, including job search assistance measures (20 countries), and job/wage subsidies (20 countries). The least-implemented intervention in this group of countries is public works programmes (six countries), which is not very surprising given the limited effectiveness of this intervention in such labour markets.

Overall, the use of labour market policies in terms of scope and diversity declines with the income level of countries, which reflects the financial and technical constraints hindering the response of these governments. Nonetheless, a range of policies have been utilized in low- and middle-income countries, in some cases in a similar fashion to more developed nations. As discussed in chapter 8, the most utilized policy response in the middle-income group is training (with 25 countries) followed by job search assistance, entrepreneurship incentives and public works programmes. There are far fewer low-income countries implementing such policies in response to the crisis. In general, low- and middle-income countries tend to rely on labour market policy measures that do not require complex institutional structures and social dialogue. Nonetheless, some governments are turning to more innovative policies that have not been widely used before such as providing subsidized training for threatened workers.

From recession to recovery

Economic recovery only slowly taking hold

Towards the end of 2009, a variety of indicators showed that the worst of the global financial crisis was over in most countries. Stock markets have recovered from their nadir that was evident in March 2008 and also exhibit far less volatility than at the height of the crisis (World Bank 2010). Third quarter figures for GDP did indicate that most OECD countries technically exited recession (besides Greece, Hungary, Iceland, Spain and the United Kingdom).[19] At the same time, there is evidence of an incipient asset price boom in some countries (for example, in the housing sector in China). Later in 2009, trade and industrial production statistics suggested that a recovery was underway. Figures on manufacturing activity in China, Europe, the United States, and other badly hit countries indicate that the global recovery was beginning to strengthen at the start of 2010. Most notably, US industrial activity reached its highest level since August 2004.

Looking at the recovery from a more comprehensive perspective reveals that despite the return to positive economic growth late in 2009, most advanced economies are still in a vulnerable situation, particularly when judged from the standpoint of the welfare of workers. As reported in Table 2.5, 20 OECD countries have technically exited recession by the fourth quarter of 2009 (out of 30 countries). The Czech Republic, Germany, Italy and Portugal grew in 2009Q3 before growth stalled in the last quarter of 2009, reflecting the fragile nature of the recovery. Overall, growth in the European Union has slowed down (from 0.3 per cent in 2009Q3 to 0.1 per cent in 2009Q4). Expansion in the United States and Japan appeared to gather pace, although some of this has been argued to be driven by the 'inventory effect' (i.e. business have run down stocks and have started replenishing their inventory), which will not continue to be an engine of growth over coming quarters.[20]

Of the countries that emerged from recession at the end of 2009, gross capital formation has only expanded in Australia, Canada, Iceland, Mexico, Norway, Republic of Korea, Switzerland, Turkey and the United States, which does not bode well for the longer-term growth prospects in other countries. Output growth in a majority of economies (80 per cent) has been supported by an expansion in exports, which emphasizes the important contribution of the rebound in global trade to the recovery.

Labour market remains in crisis

The real test of the recovery is not whether the economy in aggregate is back on track but whether there are signs of improvement in the labour market. In this respect, unemployment continues to rise in the vast majority of OECD countries, having peaked only in Australia, Japan, Mexico, Republic of Korea and Poland (out of the 20 countries that have emerged from recession), and even in these countries, it is still too early to proclaim that the crisis in the labour market is over.

A fuller insight into the state of the labour market can be gained by looking at the flow data (not just stocks). In this respect, layoffs peaked early in 2009 before returning to pre-crisis levels. This trend is evident in both the data on monthly layoffs at the company level in different sectors as reported by the media between December 2008 and September 2009 (Figure 2.6), and official figures on flows in the US labour market

Table 2.5 Identifying recovery in OECD countries as of the fourth quarter of 2009

	Component of GDP registered positive growth in 2009Q3/Q4 (compared with previous quarter, seasonally adjusted)					*Unemployment peak reached as of 2009Q3/Q4 (quarterly data, seasonally adjusted)*[b]
Country	**Total GDP**	**Private cons.**	**Gov. exp.**	**Gross capital form.**	**Exports**	**Unemployment rate**
Australia	Yes	Yes	Yes	Yes	Yes	Yes
Austria	Yes	Yes	Yes	No	Yes	No
Belgium	Yes	Yes[a]	Yes[a]	No[a]	Yes[a]	No
Canada	Yes	Yes	Yes	Yes	Yes	No
Czech Republic	No	No[a]	Yes[a]	No[a]	Yes[a]	No
Denmark	Yes	Yes	No	No	No	No
Finland	No	Yes	Yes	Yes	Yes	No
France	Yes	Yes	Yes	No	Yes	No
Germany	No	No	No	No	Yes	Yes
Greece	No	Yes[a]	Yes[a]	No[a]	No[a]	No[a]
Hungary	No	No[a]	No[a]	No[a]	Yes[a]	No
Iceland	Yes	Yes	No	Yes	Yes	No
Ireland	Yes[a]	No[a]	No[a]	No[a]	No[a]	No
Italy	No	Yes[a]	No[a]	Yes[a]	Yes[a]	No
Japan	Yes	Yes	Yes	No	Yes	Yes
Korea, Rep. of	Yes	No	No	Yes	No	Yes
Luxembourg	Yes[a]	Yes[a]	Yes[a]	No[a]	Yes[a]	No
Mexico	Yes	Yes[a]	Yes[a]	Yes[a]	Yes[a]	Yes
Netherlands	Yes	No	Yes	No	Yes	No
New Zealand	Yes[a]	Yes[a]	Yes[a]	No[a]	No[a]	No
Norway	Yes	Yes	Yes	Yes	Yes	No[a]
Poland	Yes	Yes	Yes	No	Yes	Yes
Portugal	No	Yes[a]	Yes[a]	Yes[a]	Yes[a]	No
Slovakia	Yes	Yes	Yes	No	Yes	No
Spain	No	Yes	No	No	Yes	No
Sweden	No	Yes	Yes	No	No	No
Switzerland	Yes	Yes	Yes	Yes	Yes	No
Turkey	Yes[a]	No[a]	Yes[a]	Yes[a]	Yes[a]	No[a]
United Kingdom	Yes	Yes	Yes	No	Yes	No[a]
United States	Yes	Yes	Yes	Yes	Yes	No

Source: OECD.Stat Extracts, http://stats.oecd.org/Index.aspx; author's calculations.
Notes: GDP = C + G + GCF + X - M (+change in inventories and residual)
a – Figures are for 2009Q3.
b – 'Yes' = The unemployment rate has fallen by more than 2% from the previous quarter.

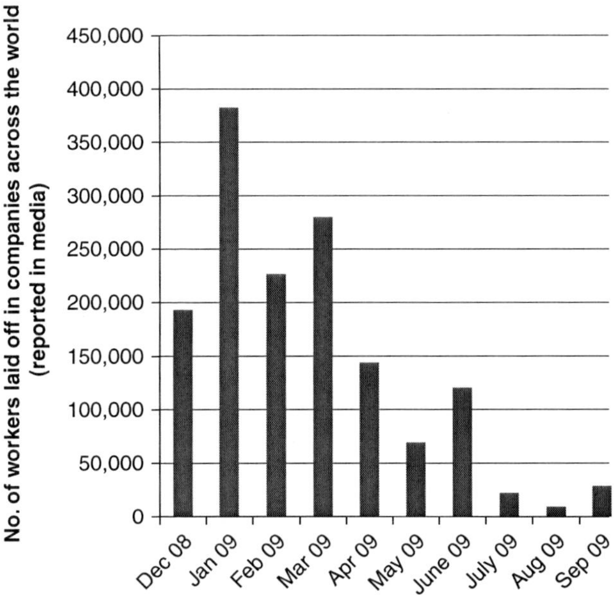

Figure 2.6 Announced layoffs peaked early in 2009, monthly data (December 2008 to September 2009)
Source: compiled from various ILO's 'Financial Crisis News Alerts', December 2008 to September 2009 (media-announced layoffs), http://www.ilo.org/intranet/english/support/lib/about/financialcrisis.htm.

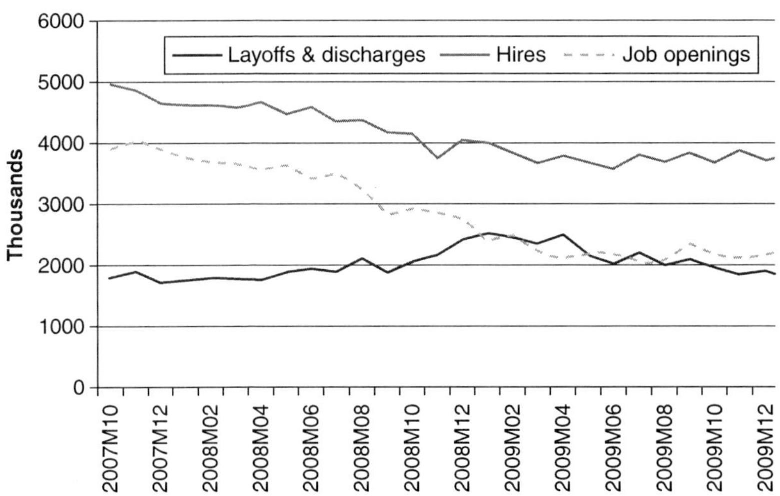

Figure 2.7 Layoffs and hires in the United States during the crisis, monthly data (December 2007 to January 2010)
Source: Bureau of Labor Statistics (Job Openings and Labor Turnover Survey (JOLTS)), http://data.bls.gov:8080/PDQ/outside.jsp?survey=jt.
Notes: Figures are for the US private sector; data accessed 22 March, 2010; data is seasonally-adjusted. Figures for January 2010 are provisional.

(Figure 2.7).[21] In the case of media-announced layoffs (which tended to be within large companies), the peak occurred in January 2009 when almost 382,000 pending dismissals were announced globally. In the United States, total monthly layoffs in the non-farm sector reached a maximum of 2.5 million in the same month before declining from mid-2009.

However, while layoffs are an important indicator of labour market distress, they only reveal part of the story. More specifically, although layoffs add to the pool of unemployed, it is the reduced number of job opportunities and the subsequent collapse in hiring that drives the unemployment rate once the economy has bottomed out. This is clearly evident in the United States as shown in Figure 2.7: monthly hires fell from 5.035 million in December 2006 to 3.715 million in December 2009, which is a far greater margin than the rise in layoffs over the crisis period. Moreover, there is no evidence that either job openings or hires in the United States have started to improve, which would offer much stronger evidence of a jobs recovery in the world's largest economy.

In addition to the short-term labour market dynamics, rising long-term unemployment is a real concern for many crisis-affected countries. For instance, in the United States, a country used to shorter spells of unemployment, 41.2 per cent of the unemployed have been out of a job for more than six months (January 2010), up from only 22.4 per cent in January 2009.[22] Although in general there is no clear post-crisis trend in the European Union, a number of Member States are already experiencing rising long-term unemployment rates. For example, in Spain, the share of the long-term unemployed (unemployed for 12 months or more) has surged from 19.4 per cent in the last quarter of 2007 to 29.3 per cent in the same quarter of 2009.[23]

These labour market realities confirm the view that as of the beginning of 2010, the recovery is still in its infancy and there is a long way to go before the situation improves for not just Wall Street but also 'Main Street' in terms of sustained job creation. For this reason, labour market policies should continue to play a complementary role in responding to the crisis, so concerted efforts are required to prevent long-term unemployment and to help individuals remain attached to the labour force and find a job. More specifically, governments should consider the following key priorities during the recovery phase:

- Continue to keep workers in jobs through such labour market policies as work-sharing schemes (depending on the pace of economic recovery);

- Utilize job/wage subsidies along with tax credits to encourage employers to start taking on new staff. To minimize deadweight costs, these measures should target individuals who are vulnerable to becoming long-term unemployed or losing contact with the labour force, such as youth and the low-skilled (see chapter 5 for a discussion on the most vulnerable groups); and
- Strengthen re-employment policy, i.e. job search assistance, training and related measures, that improve the employability of the unemployed, which will reduce the risk of long-term unemployment and discouragement, avoid that skills of workers become obsolete, and facilitate any structural changes in the labour market.

Risks to recovery

Stimulus withdrawal versus debt consolidation

Though there has been considerable discussion about the risk of a 'double-dip' recession in light of the role the stimulus packages have had in generating economic growth, most forecasters, including the IMF and World Bank, are not predicting a return to a negative global figure.[24] Nonetheless, the risk of a further deterioration remains and growth is not likely to continue as strongly in 2010 as witnessed in the latter half of 2009. Europe appears to be of greater risk of a 'double dip' than the United States. Therefore, a premature withdrawal of the stimulus would jeopardize the nascent recovery and could push economies back into recession, further prolonging the impact of the crisis for a number of years to come, particularly on labour market and social outcomes.

At the same time, fiscal deficits and debts have serious long-term implications for economic growth and government spending on areas such as pensions and social services, which was in any event being challenge by an ageing population. As reported by Reinhart and Rogoff (2009a), real government debt increases for three years following a banking crisis with an average debt increase of more than 86 per cent. According to IMF estimates, the budget deficit reached 12.5 per cent of GDP in the United States and 11.6 per cent in the United Kingdom in 2009. In the case of the United Kingdom, the deficit is expected to peak at 13.2 per cent in 2010. As a consequence, total net government debt in both of these countries is projected to increase over the next five years reaching 84.9 per cent (US) and 91.8 per cent of GDP (UK) by 2014. Other countries facing mounting problems with public debt include Greece, Ireland, Italy, Japan Portugal and Spain, although in some cases, high levels of debt pre-dated the crisis (Greece, Italy and Japan). Overall, those countries that had the biggest credit booms and asset bubbles have had to increase their public spending by the largest amounts (Cecchetti et al. 2010).

Against this backdrop, there is still considerable uncertainty about how governments will be able tackle debt levels partly because growth is not going to return quickly to pre-crisis levels, and partly because the impact of a rapidly ageing population will increasingly put a strain on the fiscal purse. Therefore, given that many countries are in 'uncharted territory' (at least in terms of living memory), a lively debate on fiscal consolidation has unsurprisingly taken hold. In the United Kingdom, for example, it has resulted in a very public exchange between academics on the timing of debt reduction.[25] This debate in the United Kingdom is a specific manifestation of the global debate between those who argue for the need to engage in fiscal consolidation immediately and those who argue that a 'big bang' approach to fiscal consolidation might even derail the anaemic recovery that currently seems to be underway.[26]

At the same time, developing countries face an uncertain future. As predicted by the World Bank in *Global Economic Prospects 2010*, the crisis is likely to result in higher borrowing costs and lower levels of credit and capital flows to developing countries, which will in turn hamper efforts to bring growth levels back up to pre-crisis levels (World Bank 2010). This study estimates that trend growth in developing countries will be reduced by between 0.2 and 0.7 percentage points over the next five to seven years. This prediction suggests that many of the world's poorer countries are facing the prospects of another 'Lost Decade'. This pessimistic view hinges very much on the role of China, and to a lesser extent India, in the post-crisis global economy.

Correcting global imbalances

In addition to these country-level issues of labour market recovery, stimulus withdrawal and debt levels, the much-discussed global imbalances remain a concern. While savings rates have indeed risen in crisis-affected countries, it is not clear how these economies will develop into ones that are less consumption-driven. A long-term reduction in consumption that is not offset by an increase in other sources of growth (exports, investment) will only put the country on a lower growth path, i.e. a permanently lower level of economic output. Consumption in these countries has already been battered by the recession and losses in household wealth. This argument also applies to economies that contributed to the global liquidity boom prior to the crisis, namely the export-led economies of China, Germany, the Middle East and other emerging countries. For these countries to undergo a transformation to an economy driven by domestic consumption is also far from straightforward and will be a delicate task that requires global coordination.

While the massive stimulus provided by low interest rates, the injection of funds into the financial system and fiscal spending was crucial in preventing a more calamitous downturn, there are signs that these measures are contributing to the growth of new bubbles. Sachs (2009) claims that the measures taken by the Obama administration, Congress and the Federal Reserve have sought to 're-create' a consumption-driven bubble, rather than coming up with a new strategy of economic governance and macroeconomic policy. In addition to this view, the housing bubble in China, which was driven in part by stimulus measures to increase credit, is a major worry for the stability of the weak global economy, which is becoming increasingly dependent on China. For this reason and also those stated above, the potential for further uncertainty and downside risks is very much dependent on what happens in the Chinese economy over the coming years.

Getting the incentives right in the financial system

Solving the regulatory failures in the financial system is complex as it involves both the correction of the use of leverage to invest in risky assets (where a lot of the risk was concealed) and a reduction of the incentives provided by bonuses for short-term profit over long-term sustainability. Those banks that survived the crisis have turned in record profits in 2009, having benefited from government bailouts (both direct and indirect) and the massive injections of liquidity into the financial system, along with the decrease in competition (a market without the likes of Bear Stearns, Lehman Brothers and Merrill Lynch). A number of investment banks have generated large increases in income. The most profitable, Goldman Sachs, reported a record net profit of US$13.4 billion in 2009.[27] Against this backdrop, as Sachs (2009) argues, the incentive structure has not changed radically. Therefore, the challenge is to develop a regulatory system that will prevent the similar risk-taking behaviour witnessed in the lead up to the subprime crisis.

Concluding remarks

This overview chapter has covered several themes. The first focused on the factors behind the emergence of the global financial crisis in 2007, namely loose monetary policy, global imbalances, the underestimation of risk and lax financial regulation. Next, the chapter highlighted how economies around the world have been affected, resulting in millions of job losses. Beyond this aggregate picture, the impact of the crisis is rather diverse, reflecting differences in initial conditions, transmission channels and vulnerabilities of economies, along with the role of government policy in mitigating the downturn. In terms of the policy response, this chapter stresses that macroeconomic stimulus measures and labour market policies have been utilized in both advanced and developing economies. Nonetheless, these policies have only partially offset the crisis; in some cases they have been more successful in helping governments avoid either a severe economic contraction or at least a rapid deterioration in the labour market.

Finally, the chapter underscores that while the recovery phase has commenced, a number of risks remain that could derail improvements in economies and hinder efforts to ensure that the recovery is accompanied by job creation. The main risks to the recovery relate to the premature withdrawal of the stimulus packages, the continuing and emerging imbalances (both globally and domestically) and the challenge of setting an appropriate level of regulation for the financial sector to avoid some of the mistakes that were made leading up to the start of the crisis in 2007. The path to recovery will be protracted and uncertain, and, ultimately, will hinge on whether China (and to some extent, India) can continue to drive global growth.

How the post-crisis era is shaped by policy authorities across the world will depend to a considerable extent on how the past is interpreted. If one uncritically embraces the notion of a global 'platinum age' that prevailed in the 2000s, and if the Great Recession of 2008–09 is regarded as an unfortunate but aberrant event, then the harsh lessons of past policy inadequacies will not have been learnt. In paving the way forward, it is necessary to jettison the mindset of 'business as usual', rethink existing policy paradigms and provide the foundations of sustainable recovery. This will mean an acknowledgement of progress in the pre-crisis period but also recognition of the manifold employment and labour market challenges that continue to confront the community of nations. In any case, considerable efforts are required to ensure that the post-crisis landscape is not one of persistent unemployment and working poverty. The remainder of this volume tackles these issues in greater depth before providing recommendations that address this challenge of delineating the post-crisis world.

Notes

1. See, for example, the contributions in the special issue of the Critical Review by Acharaya and Richardson (2009), Stiglitz (2009c) and Taylor (2009), along with Astley et al. (2009), Baily et al. (2008), Fox (2009), Garnaut (2009), Krugman (2009a,b), Obstfeld and Rogoff (2009), IMF (2009a), Posner (2009), Reinhart and Rogoff (2009b), Sheng (2009) and Stiglitz (2010).
2. As argued by Reinhart and Rogoff (2009a,b), the bursting of the dotcom bubble resulted in a relatively mild recession because it had not been accompanied by an unsustainable increase in debt levels.
3. The Taylor rule prescribes how a central bank should adjust its interest rate policy instrument in response to changes in inflation and macroeconomic activity. In particular, the rule implies that the real short-term interest rate should be determined according to three factors: (1) where actual inflation is relative to the targeted level; (2) how far economic activity is above or below its full employment level; and (3) what the level of the short-term interest rate is that would be consistent with full employment. See, for example, Orphanides (2007).
4. See US Treasury data, http://www.ustreas.gov/tic/ticsec2.shtml.
5. See Baily et al. (2008) for a detailed description of these issues.
6. See the IMF World Economic Outlook Database October 2009.
7. Eichengreen and O'Rourke (2009) 'A Tale of Two Depressions', 1 September, www.voxeu.org.
8. Romer (2009) 'From Recession to Recovery: The Economic Crisis, the Policy Response, and the Challenges We Face Going Forward', Testimony before the Joint Economic Committee, 22 October.
9. Eichengreen and O'Rourke (op. cit.).
10. See IILS (2009) *The World of Work Report*, Chapter 1, Geneva: ILO.
11. See OECD labour force survey data, http://stats.oecd.org/Index.aspx?DatasetCode=LFS_SEXAGE_I_R.
12. See, for example, the case of the East Asian Crisis in Fallon and Lucas (2002).
13. See Verick (2010).
14. See Indonesia's Badan Pusat Statistik, www.bps.go.id.
15. See Zhang, Thelen and Rao (2010).
16. One way in which tax cuts might be made more effective is to target them towards low-income and liquidity-constrained households. One should also acknowledge that the reduced propensity to spend by the private sector during a crisis for precautionary reasons will also lower the value of fiscal multipliers pertaining to government expenditure.
17. Barrel et al. (2009).
18. See Cazes et al. (2009). For similar analysis, see ILO (2009a) and OECD (2009a).
19. See figures from the IMF's World Economic Outlook Database, October 2009, http://www.imf.org/external/pubs/ft/weo/2009/02/weodata/index.aspx.
20. See 'Manufacturing surges back', *Financial Times Europe*, Tuesday, 2 February 2010, and Economist Intelligence Unit (EIU) 'World economy: unsustainable recovery', *ViewsWire*, 20 January 2010.

21. The firm-level figures were estimated from data reported on a bi-weekly basis in the Financial Crisis Alert Series (FCNA) compiled by the International Labour Office since mid-December 2008. In all, information was available on 417 companies across the world.
22. See http://www.bls.gov/news.release/empsit.t12.htm.
23. See EUROSTAT's database, http://epp.eurostat.ec.europa.eu/portal/page/portal/employment_unemployment_lfs/data/database.
24. See IMF Survey Magazine, 18 January 2010, athttp://www.imf.org/external/pubs/ft/survey/so/2010/NEW011810A.htm, and World Bank (2010).
25. On 14 February 2010, Professor Tim Besley and 19 co-signatories called for an acceleration of fiscal consolidation in a letter to the *Sunday Times*. See http://www.timesonline.co.uk/tol/comment/letters/article7026234.ece. In response, Lord Skidelsky and 67 other economists responded in a letter to the Financial Times on February 18 calling for a focus on increasing economic growth rather than a premature reduction in the deficit and level of public debt, see http://www.ft.com/cms/s/0/84b12d80-1cdd-11df-8d8e-00144feab49a.html.
26. See Corden (2009) for a lucid overview of this global debate.
27. See http://www.ft.com/cms/s/0/2e3f4f46-e316-11de-b965-00144feab49a.html?nclick_check=1.

3

The Global Recession of 2008–09 and Developing Countries

N. Majid

Introduction

The aim of this chapter is to make a general assessment of the impact of the 2008–09 recession on the developing world. The recessionary shock to developing countries is circumscribed by the ways in which developing and advanced economies were economically connected to each other *prior* to the recession. In other words, if it is true that the source of the recession is located primarily in the advanced economies then it should follow that the short-run limits of this crisis for the developing world are set by the very 'integration' of the world during its last phase of globalization. Thus, the first round potential negative impacts ought to be from lost trade *from* the developing world to advanced economies; and capital inflows and remittances *to* the developing world from the advanced economies. This is because in the last three decades there have been significant increases in South–North trade (especially in manufacturing exports from some developing countries to advanced economies[1]); increases in certain types of North–South capital flows; and because of (skilled) migration from developing to advanced economies – increased remittances as well. Negative growth and stagnation in advanced economies is likely to adversely affect these flows and produce contagion in developing countries.[2]

Given the limited availability of current data many of these expectations cannot be illustrated easily. Overall, developing countries are clearly less affected by this recession than advanced countries; from the point of view of the developing world the impact of the recession is more differentiated. This is because the expansionary process of globalization over the past three decades did not have a uniform impact on the developing world. A few large and often highly populous (significantly although not exclusively Asian) countries have grown and taken advantage of the trade-led integration of the world, while others have done so to a lesser extent.[3] The economies that have done well on trade-led growth are on average also more affected by decreased demand from advanced economies but they are also perhaps more able to deal with the growth shocks partly because of their gains in the preceding period of globalization. On the other hand, the developing economies that were relatively excluded from the globalization process (particularly low-income countries) are also affected by this crisis, but in a different way. While these economies did not gain through the process of (manufacturing) trade-led growth like other parts of the developing world, they did receive significant (official) capital flows and remittances. Reversal of these flows, which are likely with the recession in advanced economies, could be adverse for the future development of these economies.

In the following sections we will first identify the growth impacts of the crisis. We then go on to speculate on the welfare and employment effects of this crisis in developing countries. Then we proceed to examine each of the aforementioned mechanisms of contagion (capital flows, remittances and trade) through which this impact is likely to be felt. It will be argued that while these mechanisms are not exclusive, there is a hierarchy of relative importance with regard to each of these mechanisms in the developing world if we distinguish two parts of it – the poorest or the least developed part and the medium-income part in which most emerging developing economies can be placed.

Based on past evidence and the limited information that is current and available, four stylized facts can be established about the impact of the recession in developing countries. First, that relative to the richer (industrialized, transition and high-income developing) countries of the world, growth in the core developing world is decelerating but can be expected to be generally positive. This is a crucial point and has implications for future employment and welfare in the developing world. Second, it is the medium-income developing countries that will face a greater growth shock compared to least developed or poorest developing economies. Third, the more important transmission mechanism of the shock in medium-income developing economies is going to come via a loss in trade. Fourth, the impact in the poorer developing economies is driven potentially more by a drying up of aid and declining remittances, although this has not yet materialized in a number of countries. Finally, based on these stylised facts pertaining to contractions in growth, trade, capital flows and remittances, we shall try and draw up some conclusions regarding general policy directions for meeting future challenges in the developing world.

The impact of the crisis on growth in developing countries

The greatest impact of the global recession of 2008–09 is more evident in richer countries of the world, as that is where the crisis has originated. Figure 3.1 shows that the greater the GDP per capita of a country the greater were its chances of experiencing low or negative growth in 2008–09. The graph illustrates the effects of the recession in the developing world. While it is still early to say what will happen in developing countries in the future, it is important to base one's expectations on the illustration below.

As far as country group aggregates are concerned, Table 3.1 clearly shows a few things. First, comparing the numbers in the two columns it is obvious that there is universal *deceleration* in growth. Second, moving from richer to poorer economies, negative growth dominance turns into positive growth dominance. Per capita growth in 2008–09 amongst core developing economies will be around 2.4 per cent for the medium-income countries group and 2.1 per cent for the least-developed group. The growth is a little higher for the manufacturing exporters group. In contrast, industrialized, transition and other high-income countries are generally experiencing negative growth.

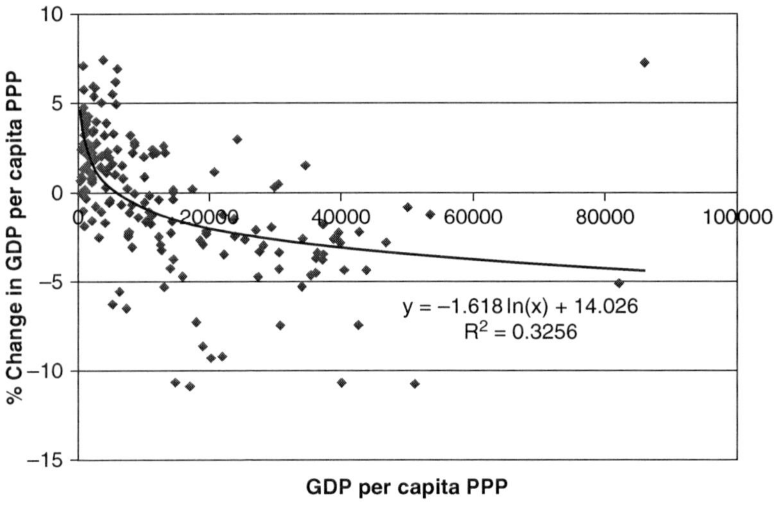

Figure 3.1 The distribution of the impact of the crisis, 2008–09
Note: Data source IMF (2009a). All data from this source are based on the information available in this data set at the time of downloading in July 2009. A number of 2009 figures are estimates. The regression equation is: Y = −1.62***Ln(x) + 14.03; R-squared = 0.33. Number of observations = 181. The x-coefficient is significant at the 99 per cent confidence level.

Table 3.1 Percentage change in GDP per capita for country groups

	2007–08	2008–09
Industrialized	2.3	–3.4
Transition-CIS	7.7	–4.2
Transition-CEE	6.5	–1.8
Other high-income	3.4	–4.8
Developing-petrol exporters	5.1	0.4
Core developing countries, of which		
Medium-income	7.4	2.4
LDC	6.7	2.1
of which manufacturing exporters	7.6	2.7
All countries	**4.1**	**–1.7**

Source: Calculations based on data from IMF (2009a).
Notes: Core developing economies consist of medium-income countries and LDCs. For further details, see Majid (2010) and Ghose et al. (2008).

Table 3.2 Frequency of countries with negative growth rates in GDP per capita (PPP)

	Count of countries with negative year-on-year growth	
	2007–08	2008–09
Industrialized	1/23	22/23
Transition-CIS	0/12	6/12
Transition-CEE	2/16	14/16
Developing-petrol exporters	1/17	5/17
Other high-income	1/20	14/20
Developing-medium income	0/44	19/44
Developing-LDC	1/48	10/49
Total	6/181	90/181

Source: Calculations based on data from IMF (2009a).

While positive growth economies do dominate the developing world, there is a significant minority of economies in the developing world that are also going into negative growth.[4] Table 3.2 gives a comparative count of economies going into negative growth in 2008–09. The 29 negative growth countries amongst the core developing economies are spread across the least-developed and medium-income country groups, but are proportionately greater in the latter.

Therefore, the dominant form of the crisis in developing countries is growth deceleration with positive year-on-year growth rather than growth deceleration with negative year-on-year growth. In contrast to industrialized, other high-income and transition countries this is the central difference. The implications of the difference between growth deceleration that leaves change in GDP per capita positive and growth deceleration that leaves change in GDP per capita negative are obvious and considerable. However, this does not mean that there is reason to be complacent about the impact of the recession on the developing world. As noted, there is a universal deceleration in growth, and developing countries are adversely affected by this deceleration.

One feature of the growth process of the last few decades was a global convergence of per capita incomes across the nations of the world.[5] An obvious question to ask today is whether this recession is going to impact the process of global integration that preceded the crisis. We can see that on a standard measure of international inequality, (using the projected growth rates by the IMF for 2009 and 2010) we still get a continued post-crisis convergence in the world economies.[6] Figure 3.2 shows that the population-adjusted Gini coefficient across per capita incomes of the countries of the world is still declining, although it may be expected to do so at a slower rate after the crisis. Moreover even with the exclusion of the three large globalizers, China, India and Brazil, the trend is the same after 2000. It remains to be seen if a reversal comes about in the immediate future.

The upshot of our assessment of the impact of the global recession in developing countries is that it has slowed down growth in the developing world, just as it has done in the industrialized economies but on average per capita growth has not turned negative in most developing countries. Overall, the least developed economies are relatively

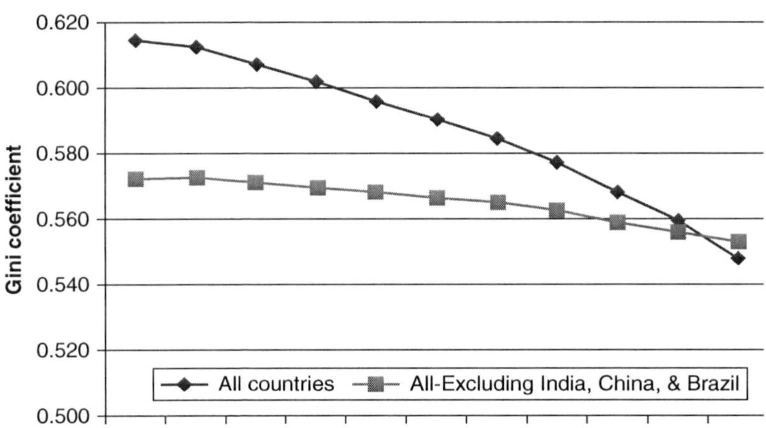

Figure 3.2 Population weighted international inequality: Gini coefficients
Source: IMF (2009a) World Economic Outlook Database, April 2009.
Note: Population weighted Gini for All-Countries Group has 148 countries (coverage = 93 per cent of the world population).

less affected by the growth deceleration than are medium-income developing economies, where most of the successful globalizers of the preceding decades can be placed. Moreover, while global integration or convergence of per capita incomes across all countries of the world has slowed down post-crisis, it also has not reversed direction.

General expectations on poverty, income distribution and unemployment in developing countries

Since social insurance systems are weak in most developing economies, one important effect of a deceleration in growth may well be on the change in livelihoods of the labour force – for both the poor and non-poor parts of it. In fact, the weakness of social insurance systems is precisely the reason why there exist workers in developing economies who live below the poverty line but are nonetheless in 'employment' as a part of survival strategies.[7] Actual survey data on poverty rates are, however, irregular and pre-date the crisis. For example, there were no comparable survey-based estimates of poverty for any developing country for 2008 or 2009 in the World Bank's online POVCAL database on poverty at the time of writing this chapter.[8] Thus it is not possible to say on the basis of actual survey data as to what has happened, post-crisis, to poverty or to the working poor in any particular developing country. This means that estimates have to be based on extrapolating the past under simplifying assumptions. If we assume a robust growth–poverty reduction inverse relation – and this is where part of the problem lies – then 'on average' in positive growth developing countries (regardless of the fact that growth is decelerating over time), poverty rates should in principle still decline.[9] The reason why expectations on poverty rates by using growth rates are difficult to form is because the strength of the relationship between poverty reduction and economic growth, as the latter is and ought to be measured, is weak. Figure 3.3 below plots changes in GDP per capita (PPP) and changes in poverty rates for 60 episodes of changes in poverty from the latest World Bank data.[10]

The association is modest, but the idea that declines in the poverty rate will slow down as the economy slows down are plausible.[11] However and importantly there is little that can be said about the behaviour of the poverty rate when growth turns negative – there are 10 historical cases of negative growth in the POVCAL database using our selection criteria for episodes – the situation that obtains in 29 core developing countries today. In short, while it is obvious that even positive per capita income growth is only often and not always associated with declining poverty rates, what is also quite clear is that there are more recent

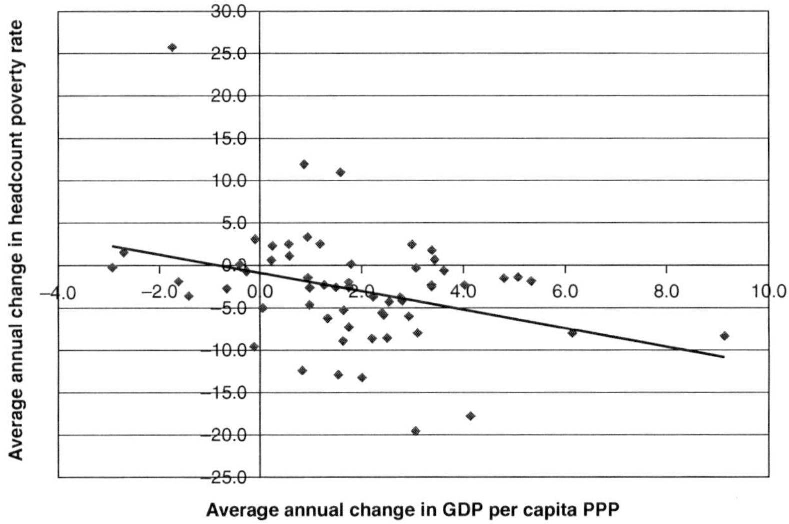

Figure 3.3 Episodes of change in poverty rate and change in GDP per capita for core developing countries
Source: World Bank POVCALNET, World Bank World Development Indicators Online.
Note: See Majid (2010) forthcoming. The regression equation is:
$Y = -1.0855*(x) - 0.8142$; Number of observations = 60; R-squared = 0.12
The x-coefficient has greater than a 99 per cent confidence level.

historical episodes in the developing world with declining poverty rates and negative growth than those of increasing poverty rates and negative growth.[12] Consequently, speculating on the poverty impacts of growth deceleration with negative year-on-year growth in developing countries is even more problematic than doing the same for decelerating but positive growth economies. If one ignores most of these problems and goes with the inverse growth–poverty rule of thumb, growth contractions in developing countries ought to slow down the achievement of poverty-related MDGs.[13]

As far as income distribution is concerned there are further complications. If we accept the argument and supporting statistics that growth in the past decades in developing economies has been distribution-neutral (as that is exactly what was needed to argue that growth is robustly poverty reducing) then whether there is a growth slowdown with positive growth or for that matter negative growth, we should have no systematic expectation on changes in inequality.[14] In particular, in negative growth economies (as in some developing countries today and in most advanced economies) we should not *necessarily* expect worsening income distribution. In fact the position on the basis of 'received wisdom' ought to be an agnostic one.

Now we can look at the data on the same 60 pre-crisis core developing country episodes from the World Bank POVCAL dataset. Contrary to the view that growth is distribution neutral,[15] in considering the simple association between change in GDP per capita and change in the Gini coefficient, which is the most standard measure used to measure income distribution, we get a positive relationship. It suggests that if one is to form an expectation, it is that inequality would on average increase with positive growth in developing countries.[16] There is evidence to suggest that GDP per capita growth in developing countries in general tends to increase inequality as opposed to evidence which suggests that it does nothing systematic to it.[17] Since most developing economies are in a position of decelerating but still positive growth, the expectation that inequality will increase will be appropriate but that is because the majority of developing economies are not in negative but still in positive growth! In other words, inequality can be expected to increase in most developing countries because they have been less affected by recession and not more!

Reported data, at the time of writing this chapter, on unemployment rates in developing countries also precede the crisis in most cases.

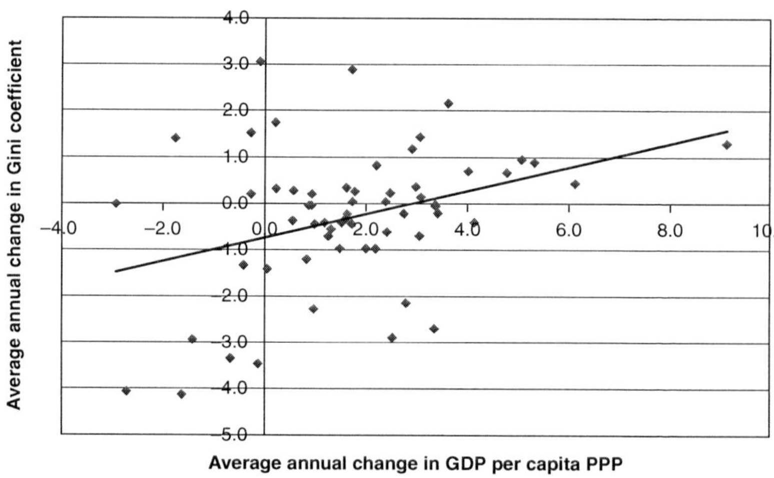

Figure 3.4 Episodes of change in the Gini coefficient of income distribution and change in GDP per capita for core developing countries

Source: As Figure 3.3.

Note: Majid (2010) forthcoming. The regression equation is:
Y = 0.255(x)* − 0.746; Number of observations=60. R-squared=0.12; *-The x-coefficient is significant at the 99 per cent confidence level.

Table 3.3 Selected unemployment rates – developing countries

Country	**% Change in unemployment rates 2008–09**
Chile*	22.39
Turkey*	18.34
Ecuador*	18.33
Malaysia*	11.11
Sri Lanka	7.84
Colombia*	6.25
Egypt	4.11
Brazil*	3.83
Peru	3.28
South Africa*	1.07
Mauritius	–2.44
Venezuela*	–4.20
Morocco	–5.88
Uruguay	–6.04
Philippines*	–6.25

Sources: ILO LABORSTA and national sources.
Notes: A. Not all data is available for each country for all months. Only months with available data for both 2008 and 2009 were used for this estimate. The numbers below indicate the number of months used to calculate the average. The period of comparison always begins with January and does not skip any month, i.e. period of comparison = 3 means that unemployment rates from January, February, and March are calculated in the averages for 2008 and 2009. The Philippines uses the months of February to April. Chile-6; Colombia-6; Ecuador-6; Egypt-3; Malaysia-3; Mauritius-3; Morocco-6; **Peru-6; **Philippines-3; Puerto Rico-4; **South Africa-6; **Sri Lanka-3; Turkey-2; Uruguay- 4; Venezuela-4.
B. Puerto Rico, Turkey, Uruguay and Venezuela are ILO verified data. The other countries are from country statistical official websites.
C. * connotes negative growth economies in 2008–09.

Among developing countries, there are only 17 countries for which unemployment rates extended into a period in 2009. Sixteen countries are medium-income countries and one is a petroleum exporter. There is no current unemployment data for the least developed economies. The limited evidence suggests that there has been an adverse impact on unemployment rates.[18] Increasing unemployment rates are clearly more pronounced in countries that experienced negative growth in 2008–09. This issue is discussed further in chapter 4.

The *general* impact of this recession on workers in the developing world is a slowdown in the rate of poverty reduction. In some of those instances where countries are contracting for a prolonged period, there may be an increase in poverty rates, but this is also not as obvious as it may appear, for reasons discussed above. As far as the unemployment rate is concerned, one can expect adverse effects not only in negative growth economies but also in those economies that show export declines and decelerating (but positive) per capita growth.[19]

Capital flows to developing countries and the crisis

One of the main fears stemming from the global recession pertains to capital flows, in particular the anticipated difficulties for open developing economies to access international capital for trade, development finance and balance of payments support. Large-scale borrowing by advanced economies from the pool of internationally available funds for global lending could well raise the future costs of finance in developing countries.[20] It is too early to say how these constraints will evolve for developing economies in the future and to see in any detail how the recapitalization of parts of the financial sector by advanced economy governments and the size of stimulus packages in them, will impinge on the terms of developing-country borrowing. Most developing countries face the prospect of an increasing cost of financing new loans and maintaining international obligations whose timeliness is critical, on the one hand, and emerging budgetary constraints because of tax and revenue losses on the other. Coupled with limited reserve capacities, these problems will definitely limit their ability to aggressively intervene in order to address the growth decelerations they face.[21]

The problems emerging from higher costs of borrowing in an environment of scarcer capital and growth deceleration will be important in the immediate future and it will also have an effect on monetary policy and revival strategies in the developing world. This problem of terms and timeliness of credit access needs to be distinguished from the broader discussions on private capital flows in developing economies that have been taking place in the last two decades, where the growth context was often a positive and expansionary one as opposed to a recessionary one. There is a vast literature on the subject of the costs and benefits of private capital flows (and especially FDI) in developing countries. However, in net terms and as a percentage of national income (as opposed to individual inflow components in absolute terms), it is likely that the global recession is going to lead to a reduction in the net inflow of international capital to developing economies. In order to take a view on what this likely contraction in capital flows may do in developing countries we need to first have a realistic overview of its pre-crisis levels and distribution between official and private components, and bear in mind that the situation these data describe obtained in general conditions of buoyant growth expansion preceding the crisis. It is also important to bear in mind here that the question being posed concerning the quantum of net inflows is separate from the question concerning the growth effects of regulatory regimes that facilitate or control capital flows. It is true that in the decades preceding the crisis, there was very sharp growth of private capital flows globally, including to some developing countries, while official flows (bilateral and multilateral loans and grants) stagnated.[22] After the Asian financial crisis of the 1990s,[23] there is little disagreement in developing countries that there are volatility risks associated with highly liberalized capital market regimes.[24]

Turning to least-developed economies, the data presented in Table 3.4 below show that overall net foreign inflow of capital as a percentage of GDP was considerable in the case of the least-developed countries

Table 3.4 Net foreign capital inflows as share of GDP for selected countries,[a] 2000–07 (percentages)

	Foreign direct investment (FDI)[b]	**Portfolio equity**[c]	**Private loan**[d]	**Official flow**[e]	**Total**
	(1)	(2)	(3)	(4)	(5)
Medium-income developing	2.7	0.7	–0.3	– 0.1	3.0
Least-developed	3.1	0.1	0.2	8.3	11.5

Sources: Col. 1: UNCTAD, Foreign Direct Investment database (http://www.unctad.org/Templates/page.asp?intItemID=3199&lang=1); Cols. 2, 3 and 4: World Bank, Global Development Finance database; data on GDP are from World Bank, World Development Indicators database.

Notes: [a] Based on data for the following 86 (core) developing countries:

Medium-income developing: Argentina, Bolivia, Botswana, Brazil, Cameroon, Chile, China, Colombia, Costa Rica, Côte d'Ivoire, Dominican Republic, Ecuador, Egypt, El Salvador, Ghana, Guatemala, Honduras, India, Indonesia, Jamaica, Jordan, Kenya, Lebanon, Malaysia, Mauritius, Mexico, Mongolia, Morocco, Nicaragua, Pakistan, Panama, Papua New Guinea, Paraguay, Peru, Philippines, South Africa, Sri Lanka, Swaziland, Thailand, Tunisia, Turkey, Uruguay, and Viet Nam.

Least developed: Angola, Bangladesh, Belize, Benin, Bhutan, Burkina Faso, Burundi, Cambodia, Cape Verde, Central African Republic, Chad, Comoros, Democratic Republic of Congo, Djibouti, Eritrea, Ethiopia, Gambia, Guinea, Guinea-Bissau, Haiti, Lao People's Democratic Republic, Lesotho, Liberia, Madagascar, Malawi, Maldives, Mali, Mauritania, Mozambique, Nepal, Niger, Rwanda, Samoa, Senegal, Sierra Leone, Solomon Islands, Sudan, Togo, Uganda, United Republic of Tanzania, Vanuatu, Yemen and Zambia.

[b] Net FDI inflow is defined as inflow minus outflow.

[c] Portfolio equity flow includes country funds, depository receipts and direct purchase of shares by foreign investors, inflow minus outflow.

[d] Net inflow of private loans is new public and publicly guaranteed debt and private non-guaranteed external debt to private creditors minus principal repayments and interest payments on past debt.

[e] Net official inflow is new debt from international organizations (multilateral loans) and loans from governments (bilateral loans) to official creditors plus official grants minus principal and interest payments on past debt to official creditors.

in the period 2000–07 (11.3 per cent of GDP) and that this inflow was based significantly on foreign aid (8.3 per cent). This is where effective declines can be expected. There has been a shift in the contribution of FDI in least-developed economies from the 1990s, which is in good part due to South–South investment (e.g. Chinese FDI in Africa).[25] For this reason, one should not expect a significant impact of reduction in FDI in some of these poorer economies.[26] In any event the main point here is that in many of these least-developed economies where official flows were significant, savings rates were often lower than investment rates, and official flows despite the inefficiencies associated with them, are likely to have nurtured investment. In medium-income developing countries, on the other hand, the overall net inflow of foreign capital as a share of GDP was not so high and was also concentrated in a few countries. The fact is that pre-crisis net foreign capital flows to medium-income economies have only been around 3 per cent of GDP on average for the period 2000–07.

So the rapid growth of cross-border capital flows in the pre-crisis period was not associated with extraordinarily high net inflows of foreign private capital (as a percentage of national income) into developing countries. Unlike private flows, official flows to least-developed economies, on the other hand, have been much larger, and it is the potential declines on such flows that ought to be of the greatest concern.

Turning to the crisis period, the World Bank report on *Global Development Finance 2009: Charting Global Recovery* estimates that net private capital inflows to developing countries fell from $1.3 trillion in 2007 to $707 billion in 2008, and are projected to fall further – to $363 billion – in 2009. As for the inflow of FDI to developing countries, although there was some growth in 2008, a sharp decline of 30 per cent was projected for 2009. Since FDI is an important source of investment in several medium-income developing countries, such a sharp fall in its flow is certain to have an adverse effect on their growth.

Migration and remittances

The widespread liberalization of international trade and capital flows since the mid-1980s have stood in contrast with the relative lack of liberalization of international migration. This was the situation prior to the crisis. The movement of people across national frontiers was and remains severely restricted. In fact general restrictions on the movement of persons were more severe during the period of 'globalization' preceding the global financial crisis, than they were in the era of closed economies in the 1960s and the 1970s. While total migration from developing countries from the point of view of their own labour forces

Table 3.5 Adult migrants from developing to developed countries as a share of adult population in developing countries, 2000 (percentages)

	All migrants	**Migrants by level of education**		
		Low	**Medium**	**High**
Medium-income developing	1.06	0.62	2.33	8.09
Least-developed	0.59	0.25	4.19	14.80
Developing	1.01	0.57	2.40	8.38

Sources: Derived from OECD Database on immigrants and expatriates (http://www.oecd.org/document/51/0,2340,en_2649_33931_34063091_1_1_1_1,00.html) and Barro and Lee (2000).
Notes: See Ghose et al. (2008). Developing countries refer to medium-income developing and least developed countries taken together. High level of education refers to "completed tertiary education", medium refers to 'completed upper secondary education' and low refers to 'completed lower secondary education'.

is low, there is a disproportionately high share of relatively skilled out migration from developing countries.[27]

For most developing countries, while international migration has had no significant effect on the size of total labour forces, the migration of high-skilled workers from developing to developed countries has been very substantial, and may well have restrained the growth of skill-per-worker (and average labour productivity) in sending countries. This is a special feature of migration from the developing to the advanced world during recent decades. It is estimated that in the case of medium-income developing countries, about 8 per cent of their adult population with tertiary education was working in developed countries in 2000. In the case of the least-developed countries, this percentage was higher, and we estimate that about 15 per cent of the adult population with tertiary education had migrated to developed countries. So essentially while total outmigration from developing countries has been limited, it has had a definite high skill bias. Clearly future skilled migration from the developing world is likely to be affected negatively as the recession deepens in advanced economies and this may affect remittances.

Figure 3.5 shows that it is specifically in the least-developed economies that remittances were around 5 per cent of GDP in 2007. In the medium-income country category, the percentage of remittances as a percentage of GDP is under 2 per cent of GDP. Therefore, like official foreign capital flows, it is in the least-developed economies, where dependence on remittances as a percentage of national income is high. Official flows and aid taken together constitute over 13 per cent of GDP in the poorest economies of the world.

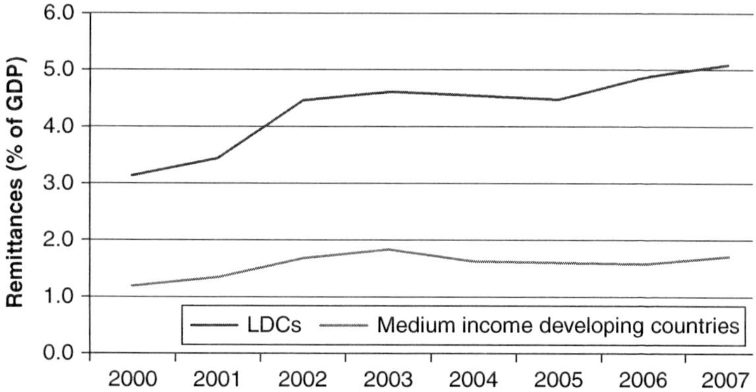

Figure 3.5 Remittances as a percentage of GDP, 2000–07
Source: Calculations and graph based on World Development Indicators Online database.
Notes: The 2000–2007 average on remittances as a percentage of GDP for all core developing countries is 1.7 per cent, of which the LDCs account for 4.5 per cent and the medium-income countries for 1.6 per cent. For the High manufacturing exporters this average is also 1.6 per cent of GDP. The graph is based on 59 countries of which 26 are least developed and 33 are medium income developing countries.

There are two implications of this that need to be considered as new data become available. First as the impact of recession is felt by existing migrants in advanced economies, their remittances to home countries may be affected adversely (see chapter 5 for evidence of this impact). Second, if the recession or stagnation lasts for a long time in advanced economies then in the longer run, this may even be the cause of some reversal in brain drain. Clearly in countries from where the migration is of low-skilled workers and in particular to other developing as opposed to industrialized economies remittances should be less adversely affected. This is as far as expectations go, based on the pre-crisis situation.

Although covering only 11 economies, available data for the post-crisis period show that on average non-Asian economies have been more likely to face the remittance constraint, but the evidence is limited. The data only include two LDC economies, each of which shows an increase in remittances between 2008 and 2009. These are both Asian economies. In general, there is a regional pattern where Asian economies are less impacted while the Latin American economies are more adversely affected by remittance loss, which is the result of the large numbers of migrants working in the United States.[28] While the initial post-crisis focus from a developing-country perspective ought to concern job losses of skilled migrants in advanced economies and its effect on their home remittances, if the recession moves to those higher-income (especially petroleum exporting) developing

Table 3.6 Average remittances in selected economies (US$ million)

	2008 Average	2009 Average	Change 2008–09
Pakistan	564.2	695.2	131.08
Bangladesh	744.1	853.1	108.95
Nepal	191.6	228.0	36.33
Philippines	1,340.2	1,374.7	34.52
Kenya	57.9	49.1	–8.79
Honduras	218.4	200.6	–17.75
Dominican Republic	259.1	240.8	–18.33
El Salvador	323.1	302.0	–21.13
Jamaica	166.1	137.2	–28.93
Guatemala	356.8	322.9	–33.96
Mexico	2,063.2	1,831.2	–232.03

Sources: Migration and Remittances Team, Development Prospects Group, World Bank, http://www.worldbank.org/prospects/migrationandremittances, http://go.worldbank.org/G7EKFMM9B0. July 2009.
Notes: Data from the same months of 2008 and 2009 were averaged and then the difference between the two is reported in the column 'Change 2008–09'. Data for the first six months of 2008 and 2009 was available for: Guatemala, El Salvador and Pakistan; the first five months: Bangladesh, Honduras, Mexico and Nepal; the first four months: Kenya and the Philippines; the first three months: Dominican Republic and Jamaica.

economies where unskilled labour migration from the South has taken place then remittances losses will be more widespread.

Trade contraction and the crisis

One clear impact of the financial crisis has been on global trade. Compared to the situation before the crisis the world is now effectively less open (Figure 3.6). In spite of the common deceleration in GDP per capita growth, the difference between advanced and developing countries has been the negative and positive growth rates of GDP per capita. Therefore, examining change in trade as a percentage of GDP in relation to change in GDP per capita is unlikely to reveal the true impact of trade loss in driving the recession. Examining change in absolute trade volumes and change in GDP per capita reveals this more clearly. Figure 3.7 shows that a change in GDP per capita in the recession period has indeed been associated with a change in total trade volumes. The figure also clearly shows that trade volumes have declined in the vast majority of countries across the world. Late in 2009, trade recovered quite strongly, though it is too early to say how robust it will be throughout 2010.

As far as core developing economies are concerned, the relationship is also as expected (Figure 3.8), but it differs from the global picture in that

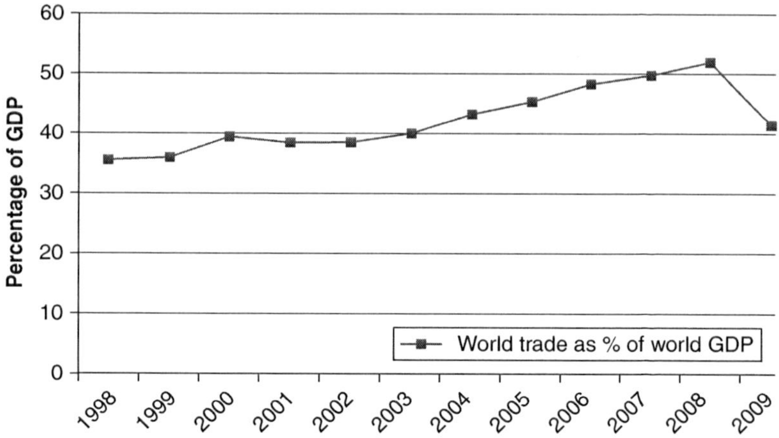

Figure 3.6 Global trends in openness

Sources: Data for trade are from DOTS database IMF (2009b) and for GDP from IMF (2009a).

Note: The graph is based on aggregates of 103 countries that covered 82 per cent of the world's population in 2008. The 2009 trade as a percentage of GDP is an estimate. This was calculated by summing the global trade volumes for 2008 Q1 and 2009 Q1 respectively and calculating the per cent change. This percentage change number was multiplied by the total 2008 trade volume (for the sample) and then divided by the total 2009 GDP (estimated by the IMF) to derive trade as a percentage of GDP.

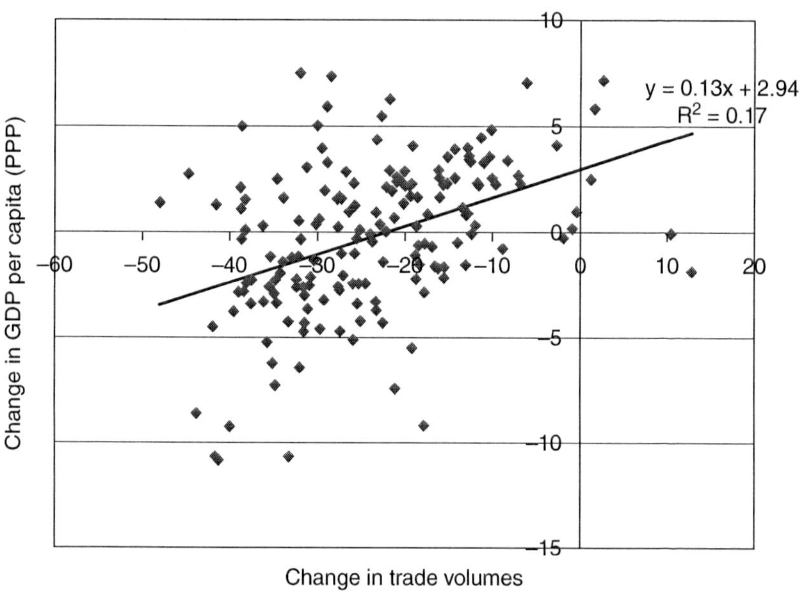

Figure 3.7 Change in trade volumes vs. change in GDP 2008–09, all countries of the world

Source: IMF (2009a).

Note: Change in GDP per capita (PPP) = (2.938)** + (0.133)** Change in Trade volumes. Number of observations = 170, R-square = 0.17.

** In front of the coefficient denotes that the coefficient is significant to the 95 per cent level.

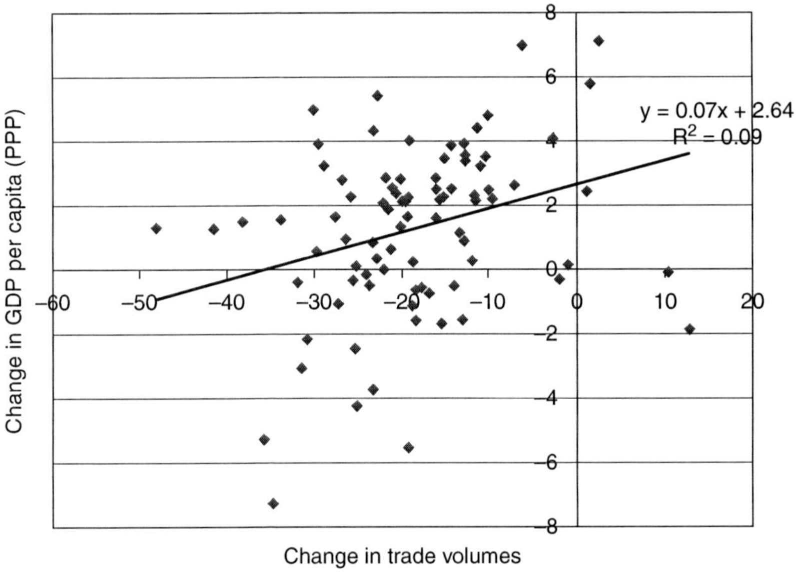

Figure 3.8 Change in trade volumes vs. change in GDP 2008–09, core developing countries (LDC and MIC)
Source: As Figure 3.7.
Notes: Change in GDP per capita (PPP) = (2.641)** + (0.074)** Change in trade volumes. Number of observations = 85, R-square = 0.09.
** In front of the coefficient denotes that the coefficient is significant to the 95 per cent level.

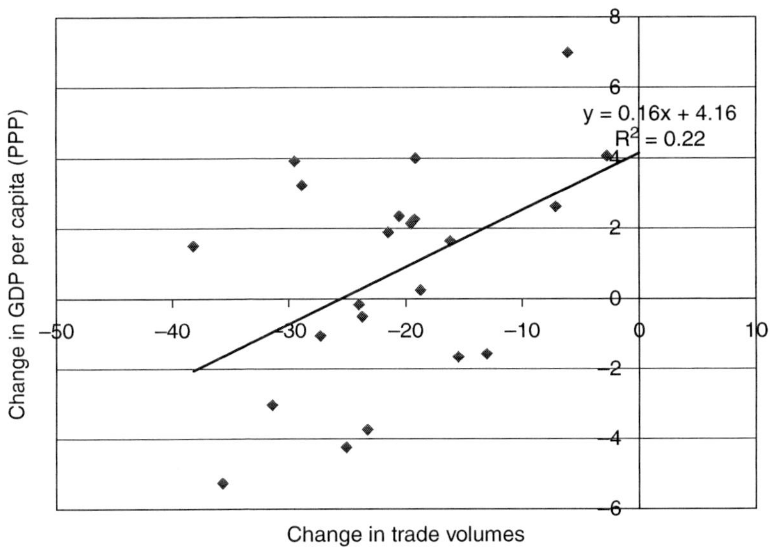

Figure 3.9 Change in trade volumes vs. change in GDP 2008–09, core developing country manufacturing exporters only
Source: As Figure 3.7.
Notes: Change in GDP per capita (PPP) = (4.157)* + (0.163)* Change in Trade volumes. Number of observations = 22, R-square = 0.22; * In front of the coefficient denotes that the coefficient is significant to the 99 per cent level.

it is comparatively weaker. The third point concerns the main globalizer developing countries that have increased their manufacturing exports over the past few decades. We find the relationship to be the strongest for the high manufacturing exporter group of developing economies (Figure 3.9).

Overall, the trade-based vulnerability to a growth shock is clearly greater in those countries that were at the forefront of globalization (medium-income economies). It is also clear that some of these economies seem to have been able to adjust, while others have fallen into both negative growth and a trade contraction. Moreover, the analysis suggests that the specific trade effect impacts the medium-income economies (on average) more, while it is the remittance and aid effect that is likely to impact the least developed economies (on average) more.

Responding to the slowdown in growth

We are yet to see in any detail how the recapitalization of parts of the financial sector and the size of stimulus packages in advanced economies will itself impinge on the terms of developing-country borrowing. This matter will affect international financing in all developing economies in times to come. Disbursed grants and aid, as suggested, may also be lower and slower in materializing in many cases and this will have a greater impact upon the poorer developing economies. The same is true for the relative impact of declining remittances. The least-developed economies will be affected more in respect of aid and remittances because they are more dependent on these flows.

The situation in medium-income economies is somewhat different from that observed in the least-developed economies. These economies were also affected by critical short-run credit access problems, but it is also the case that these countries faced separate foreign exchange constraints because of revenue loss through contractions in the volume of trade. In this situation, the reserves that developing countries have had at their disposal will circumscribe their ability to take action. The greater

Table 3.7 Core developing countries counts with total reserves in relation to months of imports: average of 2005, 2006 and 2007

	Reserves greater than 7 months of imports	**Reserves greater than 4 months of imports**
Developing-medium income	10/44	23/44
Developing-LDC	2/34	20/34
Total	20/111	62/111

Source: IMF (2009a).

the reserves the greater will be the national policy space for response. Although information on reserves for 2009 is not available at the time of writing, it is quite clear that even prior to the onset of the crisis, very few developing countries were in reasonably strong financial positions to undertake large-scale interventions. Generally, the level of reserves in developing countries, barring a few, is low. Table 3.7 shows the number of countries whose reserves were greater than a given number of months of imports before the crisis. It suggests that capacities to undertake prolonged interventions were only limited to a few countries. In short, many countries face the prospect of an increasing cost of financing international obligations on the one hand, and budgetary constraints due to tax and revenue losses on the other. Given limited reserve capacities, these problems will definitely limit their ability to aggressively intervene in order to address the crises they face. The issue of policy space is further explored in chapter 7.

It was suggested in the foregoing discussion that some medium-income economies may be in a better position than others to withstand the growth contractions compared to others. We have also suggested above that it is the globalizer developing economies that are the most likely to be affected by contractions in trade. However, there is considerable variation in their ability to respond to the slowdown in growth. While some of these economies are amongst the worst affected by trade losses, some of these are also economies that have accumulated reserves. In fact, it would seem that a better reserves position in these economies is associated with smaller contractions in growth. Given the severe data constraints one can only illustrate these matters in a cursory manner. However, it is interesting that Figure 3.10 below, for 23 globalizer economies for which there were data available, shows that the higher the reserves the greater the chances were that an economy had been in positive growth in 2008–09. In fact, it can be seen that countries that had more than six months reserves tended to avoid negative growth altogether.

The other cushion as far as the globalizer developing economies is the size of their domestic markets. In other words, there are economies amongst the globalizers that have enhanced trade significantly, but their domestic or non-tradable economy in comparison to the size of the tradable economy is still quite large. There are other countries where enhanced trade has altered the structure and orientation of the economy making them much more vulnerable to trade shocks. In times of growth loss it is the former type of economies that ought to have greater room to re-focus development efforts in the face of contractions in their export markets. Therefore not only is the share of trade in GDP an indicator of

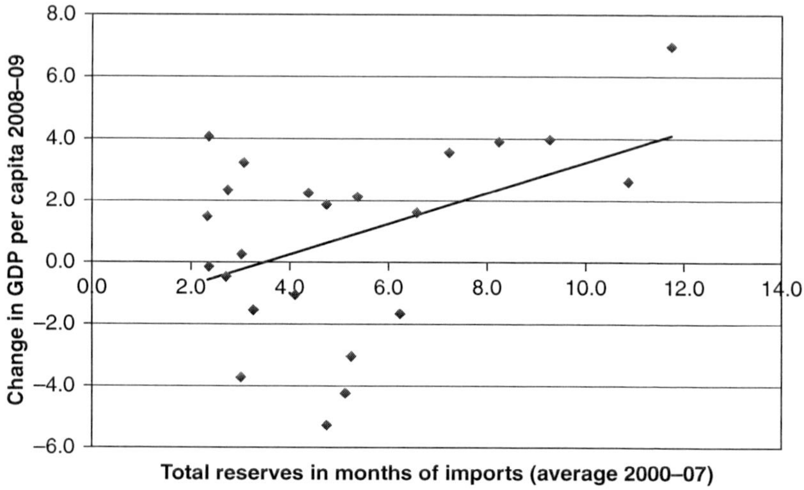

Figure 3.10 Developing country globalizers: low reserves on average may reduce ability to withstand the trade shock
Source: World Bank, World Development Indicators Online, IMF (2009a).
Notes: Change in GDP per capita (PPP) = *(0.50) Average reserves in import months + ** (1.75); Number of observations = 23; $R^2 = 0.20$.

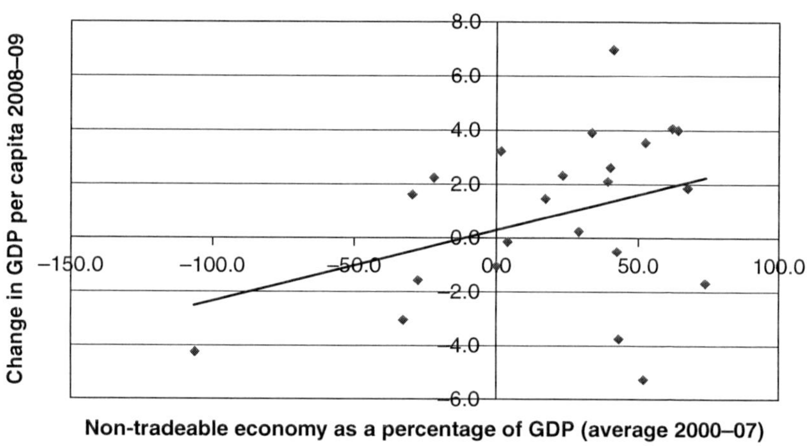

Figure 3.11 Developing country globalizers: larger domestic economies on average may help respond to the crisis
Source: As Figure 3.10.
Notes: Change in GDP per capita (PPP) = (.026)* Non traded economy as a percentage of GDP. Average + 0.303**; Number of observations = 23; R-squared = 0.132. The proxy for the size of the non traded economy is the 100 − trade as a percentage of GDP averaged over 2000–07. Economies with very high trade GDP ratios (more than 100 per cent) would get negative values here.

'openness' but its inverse is also a measure of the size on the non-traded economy. Figure 3.11 shows a positive relationship between the average level of the non-traded economy as a percentage of GDP amongst high manufacturing exporters and their recent 2008–09 change in GDP per capita. It is also plausible on this basis to suggest that on average larger non-tradable sectors cushion the contraction. The case of India illustrates how resilience can be achieved through strong domestic demand.

Concluding remarks

This review has highlighted what the data from 2008–09 tell us about the impact of the global financial crisis on developing countries. The situation in these countries is serious because even a deceleration in growth can have adverse consequences. However, overstating the adversity ultimately constitutes an obstacle to diagnostics as well as solutions. In general, the impact of the crisis on the developing world can be summarized as follows:

- The majority of core developing economies experienced decelerations of growth with positive as opposed to negative year-on-year growth. Deceleration with positive growth has adverse consequences (especially for financing future economic development), but it is unambiguously better than deceleration with negative growth.
- This is a critical point because it has serious implications for our expectations with regards to welfare loss in these economies as well as on the international distribution of income. In a situation where current and actual survey-based information on poverty and inequality is virtually non-existent and on unemployment rates very limited, one must speculate with extreme care.
- The impact of the crisis on the future costs of international borrowing is a cause for worry and this is likely to be a generalized concern across the developing world. It is, however, clear that the likely decline in official capital flows as the result of debt pressures on advanced economy governments, and falling remittances because of job losses and the decreased demand for skilled migrant labour in advanced economies, will impact the least-developed economies relatively more than medium-income developing economies.
- Trade contraction is also universal in developing countries. However, the economies that are particularly affected by this contraction are precisely those dominantly medium-income economies that were at the forefront of the pre-crisis era of globalization, some of whom may have more fiscal space to intervene than others. In other

words, amongst the globalizer developing economies, which have accumulated healthier reserves and have relatively larger domestic economies, have in general been able to withstand the transmitted shock of the recession better than others.

In terms of central policy objectives, the focus of the least-developed economies ought to be on evolving strategies that minimize remittance loss from advanced economies as well as the loss in effective aid flows. In contrast, the central policy objective for medium-income economies should be on minimizing the loss from trade. These are clearly difficult objectives to pursue as they are tantamount to suggesting that policy objectives for developing economies ought to be those that reverse the very adverse impacts that the recession is having on them. But that is the point. Clearly, the industrialized economies of the world, despite having been harder hit by the crisis (because of regulatory and institutional failure in them), also have responsibility for redress towards those far poorer economies that shoulder no responsibility for the slowdowns in their growth.

It is also the case that within the developing world the relatively better-off economies ought to evolve collective frameworks for recovery that also include the poorest and least-developed nations. For the least-developed economies it is unclear how they will help themselves as their dependence upon external (official) flows has historically been high. Clearly, if there is a decline in disbursed aid then advanced economies will not exactly be increasing their help to the poorest in the world. The same is true to the extent that remittances of migrants originating from least-developed economies contract, concerning which the space for policy action in advanced economies is more limited.

As far as trade is concerned, amongst developing countries there is an obvious danger of increased competition in shrinking global markets that can lead to 'beggar-thy neighbour' consequences. There is consequently a need for market diversification and deepening upon the part of developing economies. In particular, there is a need to enhance South–South trade through regional and subregional arrangements on the one hand, and taking measures to deepen domestic markets on the other.

The other trade policy focus is in the remit of advanced economies. Continued protectionism in advanced economies against imports from the South can only prolong adverse effects on unemployment as well as the working poor in the South. Dismantling structures of protection would benefit both the least developed and medium-income economies. While some trade-offs between unemployment in advanced economies and trade growth in developing economies may obtain here,[29] a genuine attempt at a coordinated response to a fair global recovery requires this. Advanced economies are committed to a standstill on protection; ideally, they need to have targets to reduce protection. However, it is unlikely that we shall see too many advances on this front today, if they did not come about before the recession. The area in which advanced economies may still be expected to do something is on the facilitation of developing-country trade, including short-term trade credits. From the point of view of developing countries, while there is no harm in hoping that the latter hopes will be met, depending upon them to happen would perhaps be too optimistic.

Notes

1. See Ghose (2000); World Bank (2004).
2. Most developing country financial sectors were not complex enough to accommodate the type of instruments that were directly responsible for the reckless behaviour that led to the market failures that triggered the recession. See, for example, Stiglitz (2009a) for details. Those developing countries that had more developed financial sectors perhaps learnt dearly from the Asian financial crisis (see Lee (1998) for an overview) in the 1990s to build regulatory firewalls around their banking sectors.
3. ILO (2004a).
4. In 64 out of 93 core developing countries in our sample we expect positive growth in 2008–09. There is a near universal deceleration in growth even in these positive growth developing economies.
5. Of course, if per capita incomes are not population weighted or the majority population developing countries (the globalizers) are excluded from the sample an increase in global inequality can be shown.
6. It is, of course, well known that international inequality measures do not take into account national inequality because they assume the average income of a country is representative. See Milanovic (2009) for discussion of global inequality measures that take in to account national inequality. The global inequality and international inequality indicators are based on different concepts and are not comparable. We are concerned here with differential growth rates across nation states in the context of the crisis. The trend on the same indicator of international inequality in Milanovic (2009) is the same as the trend reported here.
7. Majid (2001). This is also why in core developing economies unemployment rates are often much lower than poverty rates.
8. http://iresearch.worldbank.org/PovcalNet/povcalSvy.html.
9. See Ghose et al. (2008, chapter 5) and Majid (2010).
10. The selection of poverty episodes is from the new World Bank POVCAL data. We have selected episodes core developing economies by applying the following rules: (1) leaving out the cases where the gap between the initial and terminal periods is less than four years, (2) choosing, wherever data for more

than two periods are available, initial and terminal periods in such a way as to minimize the possibility of deriving misleading trends, (3) choosing a single time-period or "spell" for each country even though multiple "spells" could have been chosen for many, and (4) leaving out the cases in which the incidence has been and remains very low (2 per cent or less). The resulting sample of is of 60 country episodes. The sample increases to 69 countries when we include non-core economies, which are essentially transition economies that still meet the other selection criteria. For details on the data see Majid 2010.

11. In fact they get considerably weaker if we take the whole sample of 70 country episodes that include transition economies.
12. Of the 11 core country episodes with negative GDP per capita growth in the POVCAL sample, selected on our aforementioned criteria, seven have shown a decline in poverty rates. In fact there is an asymmetry between the negative and positive growth economies. These are: Burundi (1992–2006), Malawi (1998–2004), Swaziland (1995–2001), Central African Republic (1993–2003), Niger (1992–2005), Madagascar (1993–2005) and Mauritania ((1993–2000). See Majid (2010).
13. Chen and Ravallion (2009) argue that global poverty rates will continue to fall (from 42 per cent to 39 per cent) in 2009, while the pre-crisis trend would have reduced poverty to 38 per cent. The numbers given for the "new poor" will be 64 million.
14. World Development Report 2006. Actually here too, there is no relationship worthy of comment if the proxy for growth is the survey mean. See Majid (2010).
15. Dollar and Kraay (2002).
16. Interestingly the strength of this relationship is not any different from the one between growth and poverty in Figure 3.4.
17. See Majid (2010) for reasons why the expectation that growth in developing countries increases inequality is plausible.
18. It is important to point out that in the case of most developing economies where effective social insurance and automatic stabilisers are absent the employed by definition include the working poor. Therefore unlike the case of advanced economies, using the employment elasticity of growth to estimate impact of a slowdown in employment from a recession tells us little about improvements or adversity in the labour market. This is especially true for large developing countries like China, Brazil and India on which using such elasticities is a temptation. The only employment elasticity that makes sense in a developing economy context is one for manufacturing sector.
19. The mechanism of increasing unemployment in successful globalizer medium income economies is likely to be one in which exports losses initiate a reduction in demand in the formal parts of the economies that are connected to the exports sectors. These multipliers would vary across different economies, but it should be noted that direct employment effects on tradable parts of typical developing economies are in themselves low percentages of country labour forces. It will be shown below that trade loss is a central mechanism through which the recession is transmitted to developing countries.
20. See projections made by the World Bank in its Global Economic Prospects 2010 (World Bank 2010).

21. It is not clear how this constraint will manifest itself but it may well end up in a situation where (unreformed) international lending institutions begin encouraging pro-cyclical financial conservatism in developing economies while encouraging counter cyclical monetary policy in advanced economies. Given that most developing countries have faced some growth deceleration, their ostensible stances on investment revival already suggest the possibility of other pressures. One indicator for which we have 2009 data for some developing countries is the discount rate (IMF 2009a). The discount rate is an interest rate a central bank charges depository institutions (i.e. commercial banks) that borrow reserves from it. It is therefore a summary measure of the stance that government's monetary authority takes with respect to facilitating lending by commercial banks. In times of crisis, it can be taken as proxy to gauge government policy to encourage investment. Between January 2008 and January 2009, while 6 out of 7 advanced economies in the sample show a decline in discount rates, it is only 10 out of 43 core developing countries than show a decline in this rate. What is particularly noteworthy is that in the 20 negative-growth developing economies for which we have data, the discount rate is declining in only 4 cases. This is in sharp contrast to advanced countries, which are also negative growth economies, and where trends in discount rates suggest pro-cyclical stances.
22. See, for example, Ghose et al. (2008).
23. See Lee (1998).
24. With hindsight the longer run question in developing countries in this regard concerns the growth benefits of a liberalised capital market regime versus growth losses due to its volatility. The circumspection regarding its so called unquestionable benefits began a few years ago. See Stiglitz (2009a) and the references therein to shifting positions within the IMF.
25. See UNCTAD (2007a).
26. There is some firm-level evidence in Tong and Wei (2009), for emerging economies based on pre crisis data of 2000–06, that shows the volume of capital flows has no effect stock prices changes for manufacturing firms. The same research also shows that credit constrained firms, which are more dependent on external capital flows, are more vulnerable compared to those dependent on FDI investment. This is tantamount to showing that while the amount of capital inflow is of no consequence to change in stock prices, the composition of capital inflow matters. The strong version of the argument for economy wide growth benefits of FDI flows however requires the demonstration of more than its relative advantage vis-à-vis other private capital for credit constrained firms in emerging economies.
27. See Ghose et al. (2008).
28. On a monthly trend, while there seems to be a dip in the latter part of 2008, most economies for which data exist seem to be recovering after that dip. However, there are more countries with remittances lower in the most recent month for which data are available compared to September 2008. The picture does not change significantly if we examine these trends as a percentage of the 2008 GDP. We do not have enough data for the countries (LDCs) where we know remittances are a much higher percentage of GDP.
29. See Majid (2008) for references and a discussion on this topic.

4
The Employment Challenge in Developing Countries during Economic Downturn and Recovery

R. Islam

Introduction

Fluctuations in economic activities are quite normal in market-based economies. However, such fluctuations may become severe and take the form of a crisis. Indeed, both the volatility of economic growth and the frequency of severe fluctuations in growth that warrant the use of the term 'crisis', appear to have increased during the past three decades compared to the earlier decades. An ILO report (2004b) shows that during the period 1980–2000, the degree of volatility of GDP growth and per capita GDP growth has been higher than that observed during the period 1960–80. Lustig (2000) mentioned that, during the period 1990–98, there were over 40 cases in Latin America alone in which per capita GDP fell by 4 per cent or more. During the Asian economic crisis of 1997–98, a number of countries of East and South East Asia experienced sharp declines in the levels of economic growth. Sharp economic downturns experienced by several central Asian countries during their period of economic reforms in the 1990s also assumed crisis proportions (Torm 2003). The global economic recession of 2008–09 caused downturns in economic activities in a large number of developing countries.

However, crises beginning in the financial and economic world do not remain confined to their places of origin; they are soon transformed into crises in the labour markets, thus affecting the lives of workers and households that depend upon them.[1] The labour markets, in turn, may adjust in different ways – through variations in quantity (viz., increases in unemployment), changes in the type of employment (for example, moving towards more part-time or flexible labour arrangements, shift of workers to informal segments of the economy, and so on), and adjustments in wages.

Depending upon the seriousness of the situation, public policy aimed at stimulating declining economies may also include measures to minimize the adverse impact on labour markets. But such stimulus measures are usually time-bound, and once an economy starts to recover, macroeconomic considerations of inflation and budget deficit lead to the termination – and even the reversal – of anti-cyclical measures. What often goes unnoticed is that while the impact of economic downturns is rapidly transmitted to labour markets, recovery in the labour market usually comes with a lag. Some examples may be helpful in illustrating this point.

Reinhart and Rogoff (2009b), citing 15 historical cases (covering both developed and developing countries) of banking crises and unemployment cycles, points out that unemployment has been seen to keep rising for almost five years after the beginning of a crisis. In the case of the US recession of 2001 (which was not very deep and did not last long), economic recovery started in 2002, but the unemployment rate kept rising until 2003 (hitting 6 per cent) and has not yet returned to the pre-recession level of 4 per cent. The unemployment rate fell to 4.6 per cent in 2007 before it started to rise.[2] Data on Indonesia (Islam 2003a) show that the unemployment rate kept rising until 2002, although GDP growth became positive in 2000. As for the recession of 2008–09, the unemployment rate in the United States rose above 10 per cent, and it may take several years before it returns to the 2007 level.[3]

One important point to note about the lag in labour market recovery is the country-level variation. For example, in the case of recovery from the Asian economic crisis of 1997–98, Thailand's labour market recovered with a lag of one year while Indonesia's took five years (Reinhart and Rogoff 2009b). There could be different reasons for the lag in labour market recovery, depending upon the situation in which the crisis started. From the point of view of policies, it would be important to not only monitor the impact of a crisis on employment and the labour market, but also to examine specific aspects of an economy that hinge on labour market recovery and may cause delays.

The main focus of the present chapter is on the mechanisms through which labour markets adjust to the impact of economic crisis in the context of developing countries and on factors that might be responsible for a lag in labour market recovery or a jobless recovery. The chapter points out that labour markets adjust through a combination of price and quantity mechanisms, and that unemployment and underemployment may increase even when wages are flexible. Another aspect of the chapter is the analysis of the time lag between economic and labour market recovery in terms of the nature of job losses during downturns.

The chapter is organized as follows. First, an analytical framework is presented for examining the manner in which labour markets adjust to economic downturns and for understanding why labour markets respond to economic recovery with a lag. Secondly, the chapter presents two illustrations of how labour markets adjust to economic downturns, and of lags in labour market recovery following an economic crisis and recovery. In doing so, we revisit the debate on the relative importance of various adjustment mechanisms, viz., employment and wages. We also bring out the importance of looking at the economic factors that are important in analysing the lag in the labour market recovery. Third, the chapter looks at the impact of the global economic crisis and recession of 2008–09 on labour markets in selected developing countries and presents a preliminary (given the fact that it is still too early to have a full picture) analysis of the types of adjustment that is taking place. The stimulus measures being implemented by various countries are examined from the point of view of their suitability to address the issue of lag in labour market recovery.

Economic downturns and labour market adjustment: an analytical framework

Alternative ways in which labour markets adjust to economic downturns

There are two broad ways in which the labour market of a country can adjust to economic downturns that cause sharp declines in labour demand: by lowering wage rates and by reducing the level of employment (which, respectively, could be referred to as price adjustment and quantity adjustment). The latter could also have different variants. For example, rather than a simple reduction in the level of employment an economy (and its enterprises) may resort to measures like changing the nature of contracts (e.g., from regular to temporary), hours of work, and so on. Adjustment could also be made through changes in the structure of employment, e.g., through a shift from formal/modern sectors to informal/traditional sectors, or a shift from regular wage employment to self-employment. Some of the latter could also have implications for the level of earnings (if not the wage rate as such) of workers. In addition, adjustment could be made through a combination of the different means mentioned above. Figure 4.1 provides a stylized description of how the adjustment mechanisms through variations in wage and employment levels could work.

The basic framework adopted here is that of Lewis (1954) which assumes a dualistic economy consisting of a modern sector and a traditional sector.[4] We consider situations with or without the existence of surplus labour. It is assumed that labour demand in the traditional sector is not directly affected by the downturn, but the sector plays the role of absorbing the workers that may be retrenched from the modern sector. Figure 4.1a depicts the above situation and the alternative adjustment mechanisms. While Figures 4.1a and 4.1b represent the modern sector (respectively, with and without surplus labour in the economy), Figures 4.1c and 4.1d represent the traditional sector (respectively, with and without surplus labour).

Consider the modern sector of an economy with the existence of surplus labour which is depicted in Figure 4.1a. D_1 and S_1 represent the demand and supply of labour before the fall in demand for labour while D_2 represents the demand curve after the fall in labour demand as a result of economic recession. If wages are rigid at OW_0, the decline in demand would lead to a contraction of employment from OL_0 to OL_2. However, if wages are flexible and decline to OW_1, employment does not have to fall to OL_2; it would fall to OL_1. In this case, the labour market adjusts through a combination of wage and employment reduction rather

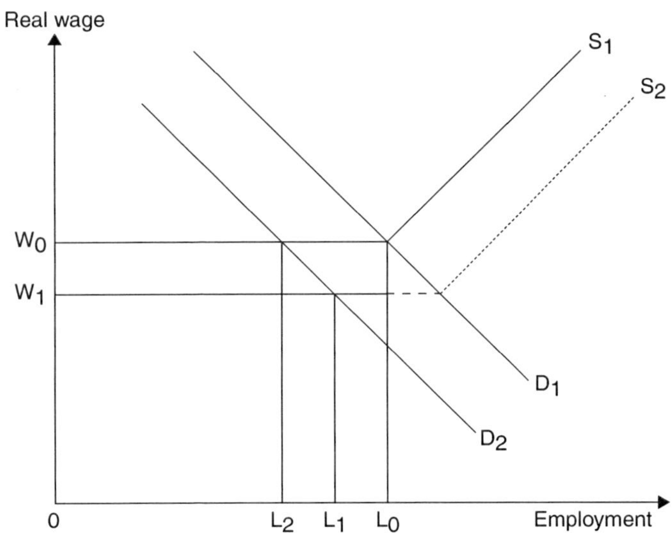

Figure 4.1a Labour market adjustment to a fall in labour demand: modern sector in an economy with surplus labour

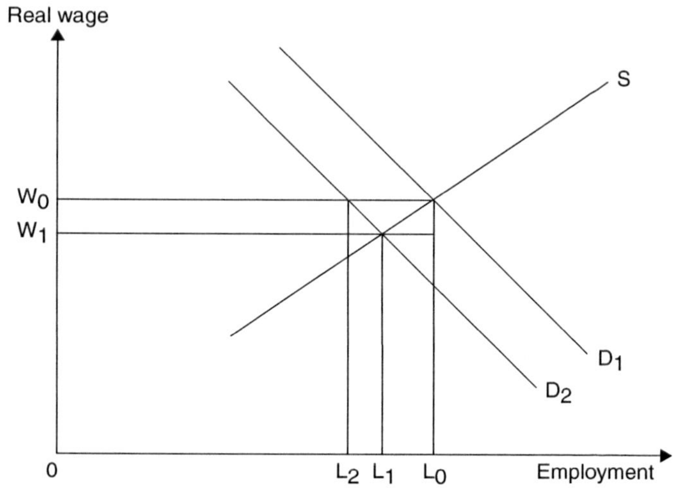

Figure 4.1b Labour market adjustment to a fall in labour demand: modern sector in an economy without surplus labour

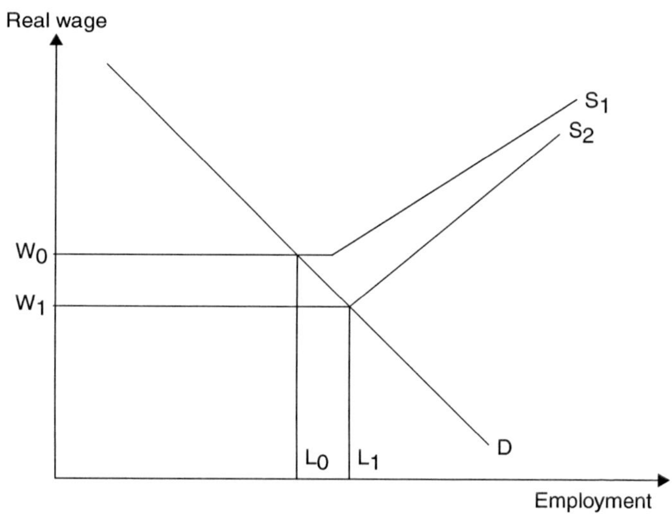

Figure 4.1c Labour market adjustment to a fall in labour demand: traditional sector in an economy with surplus labour

than employment reduction alone. The same is shown in Figure 4.1b for the modern sector of an economy in which there is no surplus labour. The supply curve is upward sloping throughout, and depending upon the existence of wage flexibility, adjustment could be entirely

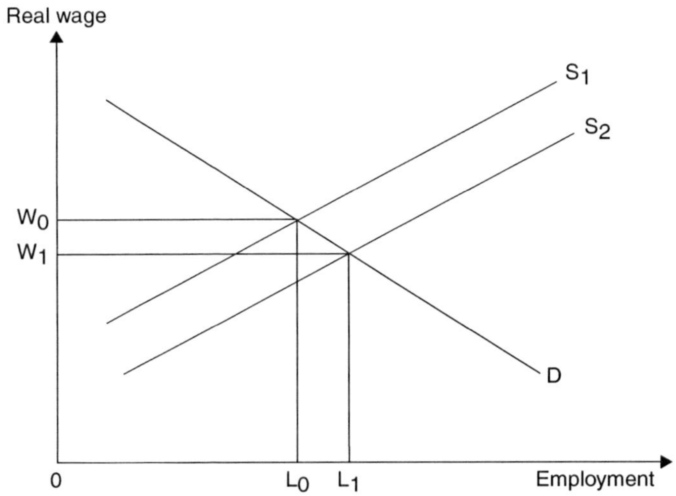

Figure 4.1d Labour market adjustment to a fall in labour demand: traditional sector in an economy without surplus labour

through the employment route or through a mix of employment and wages.[5]

Figures 4.1c and 4.1d depict the situation of the traditional sector as a result of the fall in the demand for labour in the modern sector. As mentioned above, employment in the modern sector is likely to decline even if wages are flexible and some part of the adjustment takes place through the wage route. In the absence of social protection measures such as unemployment benefits, those who lose jobs in the modern sector are most likely to end up in the informal parts of the economy. As a result, the supply curve for labour in the traditional sector shifts to the right as shown by S_2. Employment in the traditional sector increases from OL_0 to OL_1, but wages decline to OW_1.

To sum up, with or without surplus labour in the economy, the result of a fall in labour demand in the modern sector is likely to be a combination of falls in both wages and employment (unless one of them is rigid). The impact of the fall in labour demand is likely to spill over to the traditional sector where there would be an increase in the supply of labour, and an increase in employment is likely to be accompanied by a decline in wages.

It needs to be mentioned here that the framework outlined above does not take into account many other ways in which labour markets in developing countries adjust to a sharp fall in the demand for labour.

The other mechanisms include a shift to part-time work, a change in the composition of employment type (e.g., from wage employment to self-employment), a change in the type of contract (e.g., from regular to fixed-term), migration from urban to rural areas and from one region of a country to another, and dropping out of the labour force.[6]

Why does labour market recovery follow economic recovery with a lag?

There are some easily understandable reasons to explain why recovery in labour markets follows economic recovery with a lag. One such reason is the uncertainty that prevails for a period when an economy recovers from recession. During that period, it would be natural for enterprises to respond to increased demand for products by raising productivity rather than by adding to the workforce. The deeper the recession, the more uncertain is likely to be the initial period of recovery; and hence the longer may be the time before firms start hiring again.

Another reason for the lag in labour market recovery could be the change in the approach to enterprise management that is made possible by a recession. In modern market-based economies where there has been an increase in volatility in economic activities, enterprises may be looking for opportunities to change the structure of operations; and a recession may offer them that opportunity. For example, an enterprise may opt to shift towards a leaner structure in terms of regular staff and increase its dependence upon the hiring of temporary staff to meet demand, so that it has more flexibility in terms of payroll costs. Every recession creates an opportunity for enterprises to introduce changes in management style that are considered to be more in line with the prevailing economic environment. Indeed, the experience of post-Asian crisis labour market transformation in the countries of East and South East Asia indicates this kind of changes in the labour market resulting in a slower growth of employment than witnessed before the economic downturn.[7]

Third, counter-cyclical measures adopted during economic downturns usually involve expansionary monetary policy, one of whose major mechanisms is the reduction in interest rates. That may lead to a change in the relative prices of factors of production in favour of capital, thus creating an incentive for entrepreneurs to adopt capital-deepening measures. That in turn may reduce the requirement for labour and cause a decline in the labour requirement during the period of recovery.[8]

In addition to the reasons mentioned above, there could be factors that are more fundamental to an economy and the downturn that it experiences which could have implications for the speed of response of the labour market. One such factor requires an understanding of the nature of the adjustments that are likely to take place in an economy and its labour market during a recession. Adjustments required and made by an economy (and its enterprises) during a recession can be of two types: cyclical and structural.[9] The cyclical adjustments refer to changes that are made when the fall in demand simply reflects the downward phase of a business cycle, and are expected to be reversed as the economy recovers. In such a situation, enterprises simply adjust quantity of output; retrenchments of workers are temporary, and re-hiring is expected to start when the volume of production rebounds. In contrast, structural adjustment refers to changes that are required when the decline in economic activities is not only a matter of quantitative adjustment to the falling segment of the business cycle, but one that is more fundamental, reflecting a change in the *pattern* of demand, technological change, and the reorganization of production. The latter kind of change could lead to a permanent fall in demand and warrant a reallocation of the factors of production, including labour. When this kind of adjustment takes place in an economy, retrenchments are likely to be of a permanent kind because even when the economy comes to an upturn, production and hiring may not resume in the same lines of activities. Old industries may decline, and new ones may emerge; hiring may take place in new industries, and hence the same workers may not be re-hired.

It should be clear from the above distinction between cyclical and structural adjustments that while job losses during the former are likely to be temporary, they are unlikely to be so in the second type of situation. There may, of course, be a lag between the resumption of production and that of hiring even when adjustment is cyclical for the reasons mentioned earlier, but the lag could be longer when the nature of the adjustment is structural. And the overall lag with which labour markets recover would be a function of the relative weight of the structural versus cyclical adjustments in various sectors of an economy. Labour market recovery would be slower if more layoffs are structural (and hence, permanent) in nature. On the other hand, if many of the layoffs are cyclical (and hence, temporary) in nature, the labour market recovery could be quicker. Hence, from the point of view of explaining the lag in job recovery during economic recovery, it would be important to examine the type of adjustment that is taking place in an economy during the recovery period.

Labour market adjustment during downturn and recovery and the social consequences: some case studies

The issues discussed in the earlier section, viz., the different ways in which labour markets adjust to a fall in demand for labour, and the lag between economic and labour market recovery, can be illustrated by re-visiting the experience of economic downturns and recovery in some countries. Here we pick up two countries, Argentina and Indonesia, both of which experienced deep economic downturns during recent times: Indonesia in 1997–98 and Argentina during 1999–2002. But there are important differences in the manner in which their labour markets adjusted and in the time lag involved. A re-visiting of these experiences may be helpful in understanding how the labour markets in developing countries might adjust to the impact of the global economic crisis of 2008–09, a question to which we turn in the next section.

Argentina

It may be recalled that, in the early 1990s, against the backdrop of huge external debt and hyperinflation, Argentina had introduced a dollar-based economy. While that led to a decline in inflation, unemployment and the debt burden continued to grow. The growth in GDP began to decline around the mid-1990s and was negative in 1999. The recession continued until 2002, with GDP growth becoming positive only in 2003. The overall unemployment rate continued to rise, reaching nearly 20 per cent in 2002. Growth of employment was either negligible or negative during the period of recession. But unemployment started declining quickly once the economy rebounded. In fact, employment growth followed GDP growth quite closely (Figure 4.2). The experience of the manufacturing sector was very similar – with negative growth in both output and employment during the period 1999–2002, and a quick recovery in both since 2003.

As for wages, Figure 4.3 presents an interesting picture. Real wages did not decline during the first two years of the crisis. But in 2002, there was a relatively sharp decline in real wages. However, they recovered quickly in 2003 following economic recovery (alongside a high rate of growth of employment). And from that year, real wages continued to rise.

Two conclusions on labour market adjustment in Argentina can be drawn fairly easily from the above account. First, the labour market adjusted mainly through quantity (i.e., decline in employment growth and increase in unemployment) rather than the price (viz., adjustment

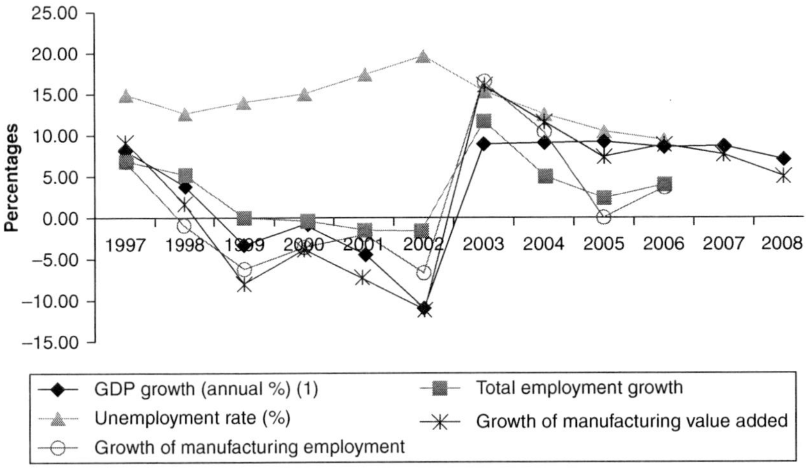

Figure 4.2 Growth and employment in Argentina
Source: World Bank, WDI 2009 online; EIU, Country Report May 2009; ILO, KILM, 5th edition.

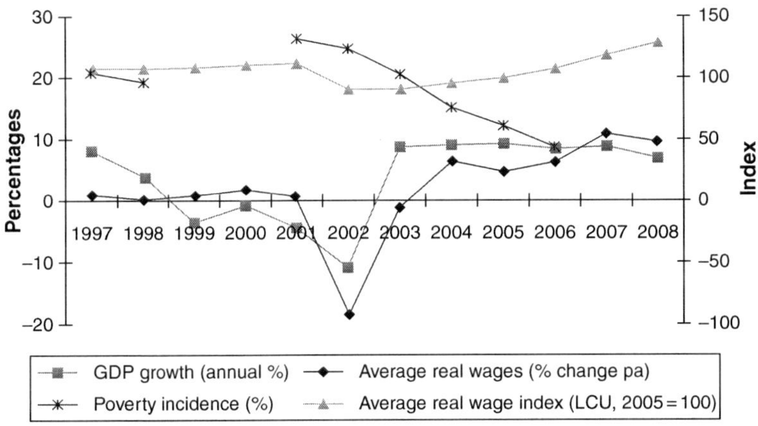

Figure 4.3 GDP growth, wages and poverty in Argentina
Sources: EIU, WorldData online for wages; M. Gonzales-Rozada, and Menendez, A. (2002) 'Why has Poverty and Income Inequality increased so much? Argentina 1991–2002', Princeton Univ., New Jersey, United States for poverty incidence in 1997, 1998 and 2001; Encuesta Permanente de Hogares (EPH), INDEC in Objetivos de Desarollo del Milenio; Argentina 2007 for poverty 2002–2006; World Bank, WDI 2009 online for GDP growth.

in real wages) mechanism. Second, when recovery started, the lag between output growth and employment growth was not very long. In fact total employment growth exceeded GDP growth in the first year of recovery (viz., 2003). In manufacturing, employment growth in that

Table 4.1 GDP growth, employment, wages and poverty in Argentina

Years	GDP growth (annual %)	Total employment growth[b]	Unemployment rate[b] [e]	Manufacturing		Average real wage index (LCU, 2005 = 100)	Average real wages (% change pa)	Poverty incidence
				VA growth	Employment growth[b]			
1997	8.11	6.63[d]	14.90	9.15	6.68[c]	107.20	0.90	20.6[h]
1998	3.85	5.35[d]	12.80	1.85	−0.94[c]	107.50	0.30	19.3
1999	−3.39	0.08[d]	14.10	-7.93	−6.28[c]	108.30	0.70	n.a.
2000	−0.79	−0.28[d]	15.02	-3.82	−3.66[c]	110.10	1.70	n.a.
2001	−4.41	−1.43[d]	17.40	-7.36	−2.03[c]	110.90	0.70	26.3
2002	−10.89	−1.56[d]	19.60	-10.96	−6.75[c]	90.80	−18.10	24.8[g]
2003	8.84	11.72[e]	15.40	15.97	16.61[e]	89.80	−1.10	20.5[i]
2004	9.03	5.12[e]	12.63	11.98	10.52[e]	95.50	6.40	15.0[i]
2005	9.18	2.37[e]	10.58	7.46	−0.05[e]	100.00	4.70	12.2[i]
2006	8.47	4.17[f]	9.46	8.87	3.75[f]	106.30	6.30	8.7[i]
2007	8.65	n.a.	n.a.	7.64	n.a.	117.90	10.90	n.a.
2008	7.00[a]	n.a.	n.a.	5.02[a]	n.a.	129.20	9.60	n.a.

Sources: World Bank, WDI 2009 online for GDP growth and manufacturing growth, unless otherwise indicated.
Unemployment rate, total employment (computed from); employment in manufacturing (computed from) ILO, KILM, 5th edition from EIU, Country Report May 2009; WorldData; A. Menendez, and M. Gonzales-Rozada (2002) 'Why has Poverty and Income Inequality Increased So Much? Argentina 1991–2002', Princeton Univerity, New Jersey, USA for poverty incidence in 1997, 1998 and 2001; Encuesta Permanente de Hogares (EPH), INDEC in Objetivos de Desarollo del Milenio, Argentina 2007 for poverty figures in 2002–06.

Notes:
[a] From EIU, Country Report May 2009; for manufacturing value added growth, it is the average of the quarterly values.
[b] Age 10+.
[c] Reference period: April and November. Geographic limitation: 28 urban agglomerations.
[d] Reference period: average of April and November. Geographic limitation: Greater Buenos Aires.
[e] Reference period: second semester. Geographic limitation: 28 urban agglomerations.
[f] Reference period: second semester. Geographic limitation: 31 urban agglomerations.
[g] Figures of 2002 are those of May.
[h] 1996.
[i] Second semester.
For 1997, 1998 and 2001, the measure of poverty used is calculated on a household basis and is equal to $P=N-1\Sigma(1-xi/z)\ 1(xi<z)$ where xi is the total household income, z is the poverty line and is equal to 0. This poverty measure is the headcount ratio (P0), which indicates the percentage of households that are below the poverty line. The poverty line, z, is computed using the methodology established by the INDEC in its official estimates. The procedure consists in estimating the value of a basic food basket (BFB) that takes into account consumption habits and covers during a month the protein and calories requirements for an adult man between 30 and 59 years old. From this BFB a total basic basket (TBB) is constructed by adding non-food goods and services. This is done through an expansion of the BFB using the inverse of the Engel's coefficient which is defined as the relationship between food expenditures and total expenditures.

year equalled output growth. Thus, while the downturn caused widespread job losses, recovery brought the jobs back.

Indonesia

It may be recalled that the East Asian economic crisis began in Thailand with a sharp devaluation of the currency and a collapse of equity prices and stock markets that followed massive reverse flows of foreign capital.[10] The contagion effect of those developments spread quickly to several countries in East and South East Asia including Indonesia, the Republic of Korea, Malaysia and the Philippines. In Indonesia (as well as in the other affected countries), economic growth declined in 1997, and in 1998, the economy contracted sharply (GDP declining by 13.13 per cent in Indonesia). Employment growth – overall as well as in the manufacturing sector – also declined sharply in those years. Even when economic recovery started (i.e., after 1999), employment growth remained quite flat (see Figure 4.4). In fact, employment growth never went back to the kind of growth achieved by the economy during the 1980s and early 1990s.

Of course, real wages also declined very sharply in Indonesia in 1998. But that can be ascribed more to the hyperinflation experienced by the economy in that year than to an adjustment in actual wages. It may be

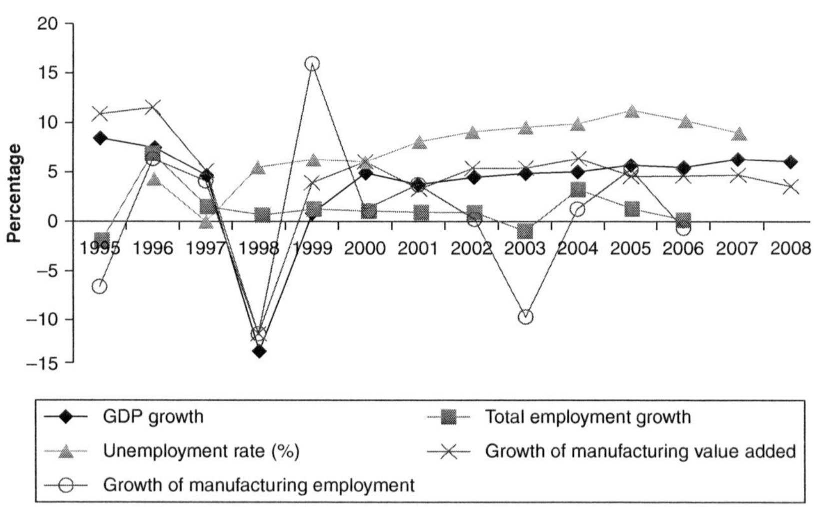

Figure 4.4 Growth and employment in Indonesia
Source: World Bank, WDI 2009 online; EIU, Country Report May 2009; ILO, KILM, 5th edition.

recalled in this context that the consumer price index for workers rose to 213 in 1998 (compared to the base of 100 in 1997).[11] The decline in real wages witnessed in 1998 was therefore hardly surprising. However, as prices started stabilising, real wages also started to rise, returning to the pre-crisis level by 2002 (Figure 4.5).

The story of labour market adjustment to the economic crisis in Indonesia will not be complete without the mention of other important mechanisms that came into play. There was a significant change in the structure of employment. For example, employment in agriculture increased by about five million (which was 6 per cent of the labour force),[12] and much of that was supply-driven. Indeed, in the areas where there was an increase in the level of total employment, much of that increase was accounted for by the increase in employment in agriculture. Second, the share of wage employment declined. This share, which was rising gradually before the crisis (thus indicating a trend towards the formalization of the economy) and had reached 35 per cent by 1997, declined to 32 per cent in 1998. Correspondingly, there was an increase in the share of self-employment and informal forms of employment. These adjustments helped to preclude the possibility of a bigger decline in the open unemployment rate. Another adjustment mechanism operating in the

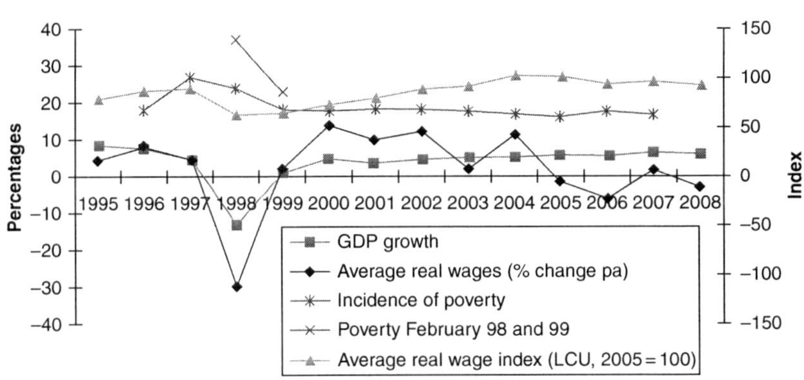

Figure 4.5 GDP growth, wages and poverty in Indonesia
Source: EIU, WorldData online; World Bank, WDI 2009 online: BPS Statistik http://www.bps.go.id.ILO, Jakarta and Geneva (2002). 'Employment Policies for Poverty Reduction during Indonesia's Economic Recovery'; Islam, I. (2002) Poverty, Employment and Wages An Indonesian Perspective, ILO: Geneva for poverty in 1996–2000 and 2002; Heriawan and Imawan, Provision of Macro and Micro Data for Anti-poverty program in Indonesia: Challenges and Responses; ILO, Globalization, flexibilization and working conditions in Asia and the Pacific, edited by Lee and Eyraud, Chandos Publishing, 2008; www.ggdc.net.

Table 4.2 GDP growth, employment, wages and poverty in Indonesia

Years	GDP growth	Total employment growth[b] [c]	Unemployment rate[b]	Manufacturing		Average real wage index (LCU, 2005 = 100)	Average real wages (% change pa)	Incidence of poverty
				VA growth	Employment growth [b] [c]			
1995	8.40	−2.34	n.a.	10.88	−6.58	79.10	4.40	n.a.
1996	7.64	6.98	4.44[c]	11.59	6.38	85.90	8.50	18.00
1997	4.70	1.57	n.a.	5.25	4.10	89.50	4.20	27.00
1998	−13.13	0.72	5.45[c]	−11.44	−11.42	62.70	−29.90	37.00[g] 24.00[f]
1999	0.79	1.30	6.29[c]	3.92	15.93	64.00	2.00	23.00[g] 18.00[f]
2000	4.92	1.14	6.07	5.98	1.23	72.70	13.60	17.60[e]
2001	3.64	1.07	8.10	3.30	3.67	79.70	9.70	18.20
2002	4.50	0.92	9.06	5.29	0.20	89.50	12.20	18.20
2003	4.78	−0.94	9.50	5.33	−9.77	91.10	1.90	17.50
2004	5.03	3.23	9.85	6.38	1.31	101.40	11.20	16.70
2005	5.69	1.31	11.24[c]	4.60	5.26	100.00	−1.30	15.90
2006	5.51	0.24[d]	10.28[c]	4.59	−0.64[d]	94.00	−6.00	17.80
2007	6.32	n.a.	9.10[c]	4.66	n.a.	95.50	1.60	16.60
2008	6.10[a]	n.a.	n.a.	3.65[a]	n.a.	92.80	−2.90	n.a.

Sources: World Bank, WDI 2009 online for GDP growth and manufacturing growth, unless otherwise indicated; Unemployment rate, total employment (computed from); employment in manufacturing (computed from) ILO, KILM, 5th edition from EIU, Country Report May 2009; WorldData.
BPS Statistik http://www.bps.go.id, ILO, Jakarta and Geneva (2002). '*Employment Policies for Poverty Reduction during Indonesia's Economic Recovery*'.
Islam, I. (2002) *Poverty, Employment and Wages: An Indonesian Perspective*, ILO: Geneva for poverty in 1996–2000 and 2002; Heriawan and Imawan, Provision of Macro and Micro Data for Anti-poverty program in Indonesia: Challenges and Responses presented in the Seminar on Measuring Critical Social Issues: Experiences and Challenges, New York 22 February 2008 for poverty in 2005–07.
Total number of poor is taken from Lee and Eyraud (2008).
Data on population are from Groningen on: www.ggdc.net.

Notes:

[a] From EIU, Country Report May 2009; for manufacturing value added growth, it is the average of the quarterly values.

[b] Age 15+.

[c] Reference period: May.

[d] Reference period: February.

[e] This figure is from 'Employment Policies for Poverty Reduction during Indonesia's Economic Recovery' (2002), EMP/RECON, ILO.

[f] 1998 and 1999 figures are those of December and August respectively.

[g] February figures.

For poverty incidence, figures of 1996–2000 and 2002 are based on the 'new' poverty standard based on 1998 data according to which the December 1998 poverty line was 96,959 rupiahs for urban areas and 72,780 rupiahs for rural areas.

In 2001, 2003 and 2004, the poverty line in Indonesia is calculated on the basis of the expenditure necessary to maintain a daily intake of 2100 calories and to meet other basic needs.

Figures of 2001, 2003 and 2004 are obtained by dividing the total number of poor by the total population.

Indonesian labour market was the reverse migration of workers from urban to rural areas (which was reflected in the rise in employment in agriculture).

The conclusions for Indonesia (regarding the adjustment of the labour market to a severe economic downturn) are as follows. First, labour market adjusted through both the quantity (i.e., employment/unemployment) and price (i.e., real wages) mechanisms.[13] Indeed, given that the decline in real wages was a reflection of hyperinflation experienced by the economy, it may even be argued that quantity adjustment was the more dominant factor. The fact that open unemployment did not increase very sharply should not lead one to conclude that quantity adjustment was less important. Indeed, as mentioned above, while open unemployment did register some increase, the Indonesian labour market also adjusted through structural change: from non-agriculture to agriculture and from formal to informal sectors. A second observation that can be made on the basis of the Indonesian data concerns the lag with which the labour market recovered. Although the economy returned to healthy growth in 2000 (GDP growth was 4.9 per cent), employment growth was much slower (only 1.1 per cent). And the low and fluctuating employment growth continued throughout the period of economic recovery and growth in Indonesia. In fact, in two years (2003 and 2006), the manufacturing sector recorded negative employment growth although output in the sector had healthy growth of 5.3 and 4.6 per cent respectively in those years. Thus, the experience of Indonesia during the recovery from the Asian economic crisis can be described as a classic case of jobless recovery and growth.

Observations on the debate on labour market adjustment

The above conclusions regarding the experience of labour market adjustment in Argentina and Indonesia do not lend support to those found in Fallon and Lucas (2002) and McKenzie (2004). The former, for example, concludes, on the basis of an analysis of the experience of seven countries (viz., Indonesia, Republic of Korea, Malaysia, Thailand, Argentina, Mexico and Turkey) that experienced economic crisis during the 1990s, that 'the dominant labour market effect of the financial crises of the 1990s was a cut in real consumption wages, rather than in employment or hours of work, though unemployment did emerge' (p. 41). The experience of Argentina and Indonesia described above shows clearly that the impact, especially in Indonesia, was broader than simply the emergence of unemployment, although open unemployment also continued to increase and reached double-digit levels during the period of recovery and growth.

Based on an analysis of the experience of Argentina during the crisis of 1999–2002, McKenzie (2004) comes to the following conclusion: 'The finding of Fallon and Lucas (2002) that real wage cuts are the main impact of financial crises is therefore found to hold not only in manufacturing but also for workers as a whole in Argentina' (p. 721). He draws this conclusion even after mentioning that 'by October of 2002, urban open unemployment had reached 21.7 per cent of the economically active population' (p. 722), and that 'overall labour demand ... in March 2002 was 40% less than in November 2001, and 59% less than for the previous March' (p. 734). He also says: 'We observe an increase in job exits and a decrease in job entry' (p. 735). However, he seems to base his final conclusion on the observed change in the source of income of households. He reports: '73% of the average fall in total real household income is due to real wages falling for workers remaining in the same job, whereas only 10% is due to losses from household members exiting from their jobs' (p. 753). The data (presented above), however, show that apart from a decline in one year, real wage growth has been positive throughout the period of the crisis, and it is the unemployment rate that increased when GDP growth plummeted. Thus, at least in the case of Argentina, it is not at all clear whether dominance of price adjustment would be the right conclusion.

What explains the lag in Indonesia's labour market recovery?

Mention has already been made above of the lag with which employment recovery followed economic recovery in Indonesia. In Argentina, on the other hand, unemployment declined soon after output began to recover, and growth in employment (both overall and in manufacturing) followed output growth quite closely. How does one explain this divergence in the performance of labour markets in the two countries? At least a tentative explanation can perhaps be found in terms of the distinction drawn in an earlier section between structural as opposed to cyclical types of adjustment that might take place in an economy during recession. A closer look at what happened in Indonesia's economy (especially in its manufacturing sector) just before, during and immediately after the economic crisis of 1997–98 throws some useful light on this issue. A few points may be worth noting in that regard.[14]

First, significant changes had been taking place in the structure of manufacturing industries of Indonesia even before the eruption of the crisis in 1997. For example, growth in the output of major labour-intensive industries like textiles and wood had declined sharply during the period 1993–97 compared to the trends in 1989–92. And that trend continued even when the economy began its recovery in 2000. During the period 2000–04, the growth in the textiles, wood and food industries was well below the growth rates achieved in the 1980s and 1990s. In fact, the only industry that achieved a double-digit growth rate during 2000–03 was chemicals (which is not a labour-intensive sector).

Second, the decline in the growth of labour-intensive industries in Indonesia is a reflection of the decline in the growth of exports of their products. The shares of labour-intensive industries such as food, textiles and wood products, in total exports declined during 2000–03 compared to 1993–97. On the other hand, there was an increase in the share of chemical, transport equipment and machinery, and miscellaneous manufacturing. Thus, the structure of Indonesia's exports had undergone a significant change away from labour-intensive manufacturing.

Third, Indonesia's major labour-intensive industries (e.g., textiles, garments and footwear) suffered a decline in the growth of labour productivity which, in turn, led to the loss of international competitiveness and decline in export growth in these sectors.[15]

On the whole, it is evident that the economic crisis and downturn experienced by Indonesia during 1997–98 was associated with major structural changes in the economy (especially in the manufacturing sector). As a consequence, a large proportion of the job losses that took place must have been structural (rather than cyclical) in nature. As traditional labour-intensive industries like textiles, garments, footwear, wood products, etc. were no longer growing at nearly the same rate as before the crisis, workers who lost jobs from those sectors were finding it difficult to get rehired.

In contrast, there has been no major change in the structure of the manufacturing sector in Argentina during the crisis of 1999–2001. There has, of course, been some decline in the share of labour-intensive sectors like textiles and garments (Table 4.3). But the share of food manufacturing and leather products (which are also at the labour-intensive end of the scale) increased to make up for the decline in that of garments and textiles. In terms of growth of output, both the latter registered healthy performance during 1997–2002.

Given the contrasts between the experiences of Argentina and Indonesia during their recovery from economic downturns, it is unsurprising that the lag in labour market recovery in the former was much shorter than in the latter. Changes in the structure of the manufacturing

Table 4.3 Manufacturing industry in Argentina, 1997–2001

Code	Share in total manufacturing (%)			Growth rates (%)	
	1997	2001	2002	97–01	97–02
D	100	100	100	−4.16	3.54
15	24.31	27.57	30.21	−1.01	7.24
16	1.09	1.65	0.95	5.49	4.20
17	4.39	3.34	2.42	−9.52	−6.54
18	2.34	1.91	0.77	−10.19	−14.85
19	2.24	1.81	2.49	−7.73	5.23
20	0.93	0.83	0.72	−7.23	−2.17
21	3.13	4.09	4.55	1.69	10.05
22	5.54	4.77	2.42	−8.09	−10.10
23	3.65	7.92	6.26	14.86	19.45
24	15.70	17.51	19.32	−1.46	7.50
25	4.59	3.96	4.41	−7.67	1.25
26	4.36	3.51	2.38	−9.23	−6.83
27	5.63	5.50	10.04	−4.13	13.17
28	4.61	3.90	2.66	−7.81	−5.98
29	4.96	3.60	2.84	−12.21	−7.16
30	0.04	0.06	0.02	15.22	−1.52
31	1.96	1.49	1.09	−11.45	−8.40
32	1.26	0.62	0.43	−17.76	−16.24
33	0.58	0.49	0.41	−8.04	−3.91
34	6.57	3.89	4.88	−17.41	−4.02
35	0.72	0.45	0.20	−16.03	−18.17
36	1.40	1.13	0.53	−9.09	−12.57

Sources: INDEC (National Institute of Statistics and Census of Argentina), Annual Industrial Survey on http://www.indec.mecon.ar/principal.asp?id_tema=4835; World Bank, WDI 2009 online for the manufacturing deflator.
Notes: The deflator used for the data of 1997–2001 is calculated based on data from World Bank. In 2002, the data presented by INDEC were already adjusted by an index of prices combined of IPIM and of CPI services. Growth rates are computed by a regression.

sector in Indonesia that were taking place at the time it was hit by the economic crisis of 1997–98 made a major difference to what happened to employment during the recovery period.

The social consequences

Irrespective of the mechanism of labour market adjustment to the economic crises in Argentina and Indonesia, the social consequences, especially in terms of the impact on poverty, are unambiguous. In both countries, there were sharp short-term increases in the incidence of poverty. In Argentina, after a period of increase in poverty during the crisis of 1995, there was an improvement in that the incidence of poverty

Table 4.4 Employment by occupational category (Argentina)

Categories / Years	Wage & salaried workers (employees) (%)	Total self-employed workers (a + b) (%)	Employers (a) (%)	Own-account workers (b) (%)	Contributing family workers (%)	Not classified (%)
			Argentina[a]			
1995[c]	70.6	27.9	5.2	22.7	0.0	0.0
1996[d]	70.7	27.5	4.7	22.9	1.7	0.1
1997[d]	71.7	26.7	4.6	22.1	1.5	0.1
1998[d]	72.1	26.5	4.6	22.0	1.3	0.1
1999[d]	72.4	26.2	4.5	21.7	1.4	0.0
2000[d]	72.3	26.4	4.8	21.7	1.2	0.1
2001[d]	71.8	27.1	4.4	22.7	1.1	0.0
2002[d]	71.6	27.2	3.8	23.4	1.1	0.0
2003[d]	73.6	24.6	3.8	20.9	1.7	0.1
2004[d]	74.1	24.5	4.1	20.4	1.4	0.0
2005[d]	74.5	24.3	4.1	20.2	1.2	0.0
2006[e]	75.8	23.1	4.1	19.0	1.1	0.0

			Indonesia[b]			
1997[f]	35.5	46.0	1.7	44.3	18.5	0.0
1998[f]	32.9	47.6	1.7	45.9	19.5	0.0
1999[f]	33.1	48.6	2.9	45.7	18.3	0.0
2000[g]	32.8	47.0	2.3	44.8	20.1	0.0
2001[h]	29.3	44.7	3.1	41.6	19.4	6.7
2002	32.3	50.2	3.0	47.2	17.6	0.0
2003	31.0	48.7	2.9	45.8	20.3	0.0
2004	31.9	49.6	3.2	46.5	18.5	0.0
2005	33.6	48.4	3.0	45.3	18.0	0.0
2006	33.9	49.2	3.0	46.2	16.9	0.0
2007	34.0	48.7	2.9	45.8	17.3	0.0

Source: ILO, KILM, 5th edition.

Notes:

(a) Age 10+.

(b) Age 15+.

(c) Reference period: October. Geographic limitation: Greater Buenos Aires.
Data are derived from micro-sources.

(d) Reference period: Average of May and October. Geographic limitation: 28 urban agglomerations.
In 2003, the methodology has been revised; thus the data may not be strictly comparable.

(e) 31 urban agglomerations.

(f) Contributing family workers refer to 'unpaid workers' with no family qualification specified.

(g) Reference period: August. Geographic limitation: excluding Maluku Province.
Contributing family workers refer to 'unpaid workers' with no family qualification specified.

(h) Reference period: August. Contributing family workers refer to 'unpaid workers' with no family qualification specified.

had declined from 20.6 per cent in 1996 to 19.3 per cent in 1998. However, the figure increased sharply during the crisis of 1999–2002 – from 19.3 per cent in 1998 to 26.3 per cent in 2001 (Gonzales-Rozada and Menendez 2002).

There was a sharper impact on poverty in Indonesia. Before the crisis, that country (along with others like Malaysia and Thailand) was cited as a success story for the rapid rate of poverty reduction. The incidence of poverty (based on the national poverty line) had declined from 40.1 per cent in 1976 to 28.6 per cent in 1980 and to 11.3 per cent in 1996 – the year before the crisis (Islam 2002). But there was a reversal of this declining trend after 1996, and poverty increased sharply in both 1997 and 1998. Due to a change in the definition in 1996, the figure for that year was revised upwards to 18 per cent. And according to that new definition, poverty increased to 27 per cent in 1997 and to 37 per cent in February 1998. However, as the hyperinflation of 1998 eased, the incidence of poverty also started to decline – falling to 23 per cent in February 1999, and then to 18 per cent in August 1999 (Table 4.2). However, the incidence of poverty remained at that level until 2002 although economic recovery began much earlier. Moreover, even though the incidence of poverty began to decline after 2002, the rate of decline has been relatively slow.

One explanation for the sharp rise in the incidence of poverty witnessed in Indonesia in 1997 and 1998 is in terms of a distinction between transient poverty and the long-term behaviour of income/consumption poverty and the existence of a large segment of the population just above the poverty line. When there is an external shock of a severe nature (e.g., the shock caused in Indonesia by a combination of job loss or move to a job with lower earnings and hyperinflation), transient poverty can hit those people who are usually just above the poverty line. In such a situation, a shock may affect their income/consumption at least for a short period and push them into a position of poverty. It has been shown empirically that during the period of the crisis, the number of people in poverty in Indonesia is extremely sensitive to the change in the poverty line: a 10 per cent increase in the cost of living of the people could result in an almost 7.5 per cent increase in the headcount measure of poverty (Dhanani and Islam 2002).[16]

It is well known that labour market flexibility (in terms of the ease with which workers can be hired and fired and wages could be adjusted to the market situation) in the countries of East and South East Asia is often mentioned as a positive feature that makes them more attractive as destinations for investments and conducting business. However, a combination of flexibility and very weak (or virtual absence of) social protection made it difficult for countries like Indonesia to preserve the gains they had made in reducing poverty during periods of economic prosperity.

Wage flexibility manifested itself not so much in the absence of minimum wage legislations as in the actual market outcomes. Indonesia (and other countries of East and South East Asia, e.g., Republic of Korea, the Philippines and Thailand) did have minimum wage legislation before the crisis. And yet real wages were seen to be quite flexible (thus reflecting the fact that wage adjustments could not keep pace with price increases). A similar observation can be made about regulations governing the termination of employment. At the time it faced the economic crisis in 1997, Indonesia had no specified notice period for termination – although there was a stipulated severance pay. In any case, such provisions and regulations were not implemented very effectively (Khan 1994).

Another important element that could make a difference in reducing the vulnerability of workers when an economy goes through a crisis is social protection. And in that respect, Indonesia (or for that matter other countries affected by the crisis in 1997–98) had little to talk about. In fact, until the early 1990s, there was little other than protection from illness, workplace accident, disability and certain minimal provisions in the event of death (ILO 1997). The only notable form of social protection was the state-run provident fund designed mainly to provide retirement benefits. And retrenched workers could withdraw their balance of accumulated savings from the fund. But the coverage of this was also limited: only 12 per cent of the employed in Indonesia (Lee, 1998).

The global financial crisis of 2008–09 and its impact on labour markets in developing countries

As stressed above, the developing regions and countries of the world have been affected by the global financial crisis of 2008–09 in varying degrees. The variation reflects the structure of their economies, the degree of dependence on exports, and the destination of their exports. Some data on these aspects are presented in Tables 4.5 through 4.9. A few points emerge – at least tentatively – from the data presented in these tables.

First, amongst the broad regions, Latin America was the most severely affected region while Africa and Asia were relatively unscathed. This perhaps reflects the degree of dependence of many countries of Latin America on exports to the United States. Second, there is a good degree of inter-country variation within regions. For example, while Asia in general has been less affected, the decline in GDP growth has been quite

Table 4.5 GDP growth rates (actual and projections) (per cent per annum)

Countries \ Years	2003	2004	2005	2006	2007	2008	2009
World and developed countries							
World	3.6	4.9	4.5	5.1	5.2	3.2	−1.3
United States	2.5	3.6	2.9	2.8	2.0	1.1	−2.8
Japan	1.4	2.7	1.9	2.0	2.4	−0.6	−6.2
France	1.1	2.2	1.9	2.4	2.1	0.7	−3.0
Germany	−0.2	1.2	0.8	3.0	2.5	1.3	−5.6
United Kingdom	2.8	2.8	2.1	2.8	3.0	0.7	−4.1
EU	1.5	2.6	2.2	3.4	3.1	1.1	−4.0
Developing countries							
Africa	5.5	6.7	5.8	6.1	6.2	5.2	2.0
Developing Asia	8.2	8.6	9.0	9.8	10.6	7.7	4.8
Latin America*	2.2	6.0	4.7	5.7	5.7	4.2	−1.5

Source: International Monetary Fund, World Economic Outlook Database, April 2009.
Notes: 2009(P): Projection by IMF in April 2009; * Include some Caribbean countries.

sharp in the export-oriented economies of Indonesia, the Republic of Korea, Malaysia and Thailand. China and India also suffered substantial declines in GDP growth. Within Africa, South Africa appears to have been the worst hit, while Kenya and Nigeria have also suffered sharp declines in growth. Clearly, countries like Ethiopia and Uganda, which are less export oriented, have experienced relatively lower declines in growth. In Latin America, countries like Ecuador and Mexico are not only more export oriented, they are also more dependent on the United States for their export markets. And those two countries also suffered very sharp declines in GDP growth. South Africa's dependence on the US export market increased substantially during the period 1995–2006.

The decline in economic growth naturally had an impact on the employment and labour market situation. Ever since the onset of the economic recession in late 2007, the media has been replete with reports of job losses, especially in the developed countries, but not confined to them alone. In addition to job losses, there are also reports of other forms of labour market adjustments, e.g., increase in part-time employment, leave without pay, postponement of wage adjustment, etc. While data on employment and unemployment are available on an up-to-date basis for the developed countries, that is not the case for most developing countries. In many of these countries, labour force surveys (which are the major source of data on unemployment and

Table 4.6 GDP growth (actual and forecast) for selected developing countries

Countries \ Years	2003	2004	2005	2006	2007	2008	2009(P)
			Asia				
Bangladesh	5.8	6.1	6.3	6.5	6.3	5.6	5.0
China	10.0	10.1	10.4	11.6	13.0	9.0	6.5
India	6.9	7.9	9.2	9.8	9.3	7.3	4.5
Indonesia	4.8	5.0	5.7	5.5	6.3	6.1	2.5
Korea, Rep. of	2.8	4.6	4.0	5.2	5.1	2.2	−4.0
Malaysia	5.8	6.8	5.3	5.8	6.3	4.6	−3.5
Pakistan	4.8	7.4	7.7	6.2	6.0	6.0	2.5
Philippines	4.9	6.4	5.0	5.4	7.2	4.6	3.8*
Sri Lanka	5.9	5.4	6.2	7.7	6.8	6.0	2.2
Thailand	7.1	6.3	4.6	5.2	4.9	2.6	−3.0
Viet Nam	7.3	7.8	8.4	8.2	8.5	6.2	3.3
			Africa				
Ethiopia	−3.5	9.8	12.6	11.5	11.5	11.6	6.5
Ghana	5.2	5.6	5.9	6.4	6.1	7.2	4.5
Kenya	2.8	4.6	5.9	6.4	7.0	2.0	3.0
Nigeria	10.3	10.6	5.4	6.2	6.5	5.3	2.9
South Africa	3.1	4.9	5.0	5.3	5.1	3.1	−0.3
Tanzania	6.9	7.8	7.4	6.7	7.1	7.5	5.0
Uganda	6.5	6.8	6.3	10.8	8.6	9.5	6.2
			Latin America				
Argentina	8.8	9.0	9.2	8.5	8.7	7.0	−1.5
Brazil	1.1	5.7	3.2	4.0	5.7	5.1	−1.3
Chile	4.0	6.0	5.6	4.6	4.7	3.2	0.1
Colombia	4.6	4.7	5.7	6.9	7.5	2.5	0.0
Ecuador	3.6	8.0	6.0	3.9	2.5	5.3	−2.0
Mexico	1.7	4.0	3.2	5.1	3.3	1.3	−3.7
Peru	4.0	5.0	6.8	7.7	8.9	9.8	3.5
Uruguay	0.8	5.0	7.5	4.6	7.6	8.9	1.3
Venezuela	−7.8	18.3	10.3	10.3	8.4	4.8	−2.2

Sources: International Monetary Fund, World Economic Outlook Database, October 2008; April 2009.
Notes: *Projection made in October 2008; 2009(P): Projection by IMF in April 2009.

employment) are not carried out every year. Even when they are carried out every year, there is usually a time lag between the survey and the date when the data are available. In a situation like this, a picture of the employment and labour market situation can be drawn only on the basis of scattered (and sometimes anecdotal) evidence. It may, however, be useful to start by looking at some projections made by the ILO.[17]

Table 4.7 Exports of goods and services as a percentage of GDP

Countries \ Years	2000	2007
	Asia	
Bangladesh	14	22
China	23.3	40.1*
India	13.2	21
Indonesia	41	29
Korea, Rep. of	40.8	46
Malaysia	124.4	112
Pakistan	13.4	14
Philippines	55.4	39
Sri Lanka	39	29
Thailand	66.8	68
Viet Nam	55	76
	Africa	
Ethiopia	12.5	13
Ghana	48.8	36
Kenya	21.6	23
Nigeria	54.3	39
South Africa	27.9	30
Tanzania	n.a.	n.a.
Uganda	11.2	13
	Latin America	
Argentina	10.9	24.7*
Brazil	10	13
Chile	31.6	48
Colombia	21.5	19
Ecuador	37.1	34
Mexico	30.9	32
Peru	16	27
Uruguay	19.3	29
Venezuela	29.7	29

Source: World Bank, WDI online.
Notes: *2006.

Projections of employment and unemployment made by the ILO present a rather gloomy picture. At the global level, according to the ILO estimates, the total numbers unemployed in 2009 could have increased by between 29 million and 59 million (depending on the scenario used), with a middle scenario pointing to an increase of 39 million. That would imply an increase in the rate of unemployment from 5.7 per cent in 2007 to somewhere between 6.5 and 7.4 per cent. And that would be

Table 4.8 Annual average growth rates of exports

Countries \ Years	1995–2000	2000–2007
	Asia	
Bangladesh	9.82	11.15
China	16.57	17.99
India	9.85	14.80
Indonesia	0.13	8.03
Korea, Rep. of	14.80	11.05
Malaysia	7.55	6.63
Pakistan	−1.38	9.68
Philippines	2.63	6.87
Sri Lanka	6.65	5.07
Thailand	7.11	6.78
Viet Nam	11.76	16.96
	Africa	
Ethiopia	11.99	11.55
Ghana	10.33	4.22
Kenya	−0.79	7.27
Nigeria	1.99	9.58
South Africa	4.43	3.71
Tanzania	0.84	10.23
Uganda	8.80	11.52
	Latin America	
Argentina	6.37	7.21
Brazil	6.52	9.17
Chile	7.61	6.41
Colombia	5.87	5.09
Ecuador	2.33	7.21
Mexico	12.48	5.64
Peru	8.26	8.52
Uruguay	−17.95	22.37
Venezuela	2.18	−0.85

Source: EIU, WorldData.
Note: Computed with a regression with constant data based on the year 2005.

something that the global economy has not witnessed for a number of decades. In that sense, the world is today confronted not just with an economic crisis but also a crisis of jobs which in turn could result in a full-blown social crisis.

According to available data (including the results presented in chapter 5), it is the developed countries that are going to be the hardest

Table 4.9 Destination of exports (as a percentage of total exports)

Countries	EU		United States		Japan	
	1995	2006	1995[b]	2006	1995	2006
			Asia			
Bangladesh	44.8	46.8	34.0	25.0	3.3	1.1
China	13.6	19.6	17.6	21.0	19.1	9.5
India	27.5	21.1	18.3	17.0	7.0	3.0
Indonesia	15.2	12.2	14.7	11.5	27.1	19.4
Korea, Rep. of	13.3	15.3	19.9	13.3	13.0	8.1
Malaysia	14.4	12.8	21.6	18.8	12.5	8.9
Pakistan	31.0	22.2	16.8	21.0	6.8	1.1
Philippines	17.7	18.5	36.9	18.3	15.8	16.5
Sri Lanka	32.4	28.9	36.9	27.7	5.3	2.5
Thailand	16.1	13.8	18.7	15.0	16.6	12.6
Viet Nam	12.6	19.8	3.3	21.2	26.0	12.3
			Africa			
Ethiopia	50.9	30.8	6.9	7.2	12.7	7.8
Ghana	58.3	45.2	13.0	6.7	4.3	2.6
Kenya	35.7	28.6	3.4	8.3	0.7	0.6
Nigeria	33.2	23.0	41.0	48.8	1.0	1.6
South Africa	29.6[a]	35.9	5.2[a]	11.8	5.0[a]	12.1
Tanzania	n.a.	n.a.	n.a.	n.a.	n.a.	n.a.
Uganda	86.0	48.1	3.7	3.1	1.8	0.9
			Latin America			
Argentina	21.4	17.5	7.7	8.9	2.1	0.9
Brazil	28.4	22.5	19.9	17.8	6.7	2.8
Chile	27.1	26.8	15.1	15.6	17.6	10.5
Colombia	28.9	16.3	45.6	35.8	3.8	1.3
Ecuador	20.0	11.7	43.3	53.6	2.7	1.0
Mexico	4.3	4.1	86.1	84.7	1.2	0.6
Peru	30.5	17.9	19.9	24.1	9.1	5.2
Uruguay	21.2	20.0	6.7	12.1	0.9	2.6
Venezuela	9.1	9.2	51.7	46.2	1.5	0.4

Source: UNCTAD, Handbook of Statistics, 2005, 2008.
Notes: [a] Customs Union; [b] United States and Canada.

hit by open unemployment, although the developing countries are not going to be spared. Within the developing world, the impact is going to vary, depending on a variety of factors, such as the degree of interlinkage with the global economy through the channels of trade, capital flows and flows of labour and remittances as mentioned above. ILO projections indicate that open unemployment will increase more in the countries of East and South East Asia compared to those in sub-Saharan Africa.

ILO has also made projections of the likely lag between economic recovery and that of labour markets under alternative assumptions of the strength of the economic recovery and the success of the stimulus packages. The projections indicate that the lag could range from three to six years or more, depending upon the situation. For example, if the recovery in output is weak and its job content is also weak, recovery in the labour market could take six years or longer. But if policies to counteract the recession and stimulate growth in output are focused on maximizing the job content of recovery, the lag in labour market recovery could be reduced to three years (ILO 2009d).

In order to get an insight into the full range of ways in which labour markets in the developing countries are adjusting to the global economic crisis, it would be necessary to go beyond the projections made at the regional/subregional level and look at what is happening at the country level. Of course, the most common pattern is quantity adjustment, i.e., the retrenchment of workers. And that in turn would lead to an increase in the rate of open unemployment. However, as mentioned earlier in this chapter, this is not the only (or even the main) mechanism through which labour markets adjust to economic fluctuations in developing countries. It would, therefore, be important to take a more comprehensive look at how the labour markets are adjusting to the economic downturn of 2007–09. Although country-level data needed for such an analysis are not readily available, an examination of the scattered data that are available may provide one with some idea of the possible direction and type of adjustments that are taking place.

Quantity adjustment

In **China**, for example, as early as November 2008 officials had started to express concerns about the labour market.[18] The Ministry of Human Resources of China announced that as of 31 December 2008, 8.86 million urban residents were registered as unemployed – 556,000 more than at the end of the third quarter of the year.[19] Reports in early 2009 mentioned that 20 million migrant workers returned to their home villages and towns.[20] Even if some of them find alternative employment in their places of original residence, it appears that a large number may end up as either unemployed or at best underemployed in various marginal occupations in rural areas and small towns. However, China's return to strong growth in 2009 should help these laid-off workers find new forms of employment.

In **India**, a sample survey carried out by the Ministry of Labour and Employment shows that about half a million workers have lost their jobs during October–December 2008.[21] The decline in employment has affected contract workers more than direct workers. However, more recent figures indicate that employment has since recovered: employment increased by 497,000 during July–September 2009 (over April–June 2009). This further strengthened in October–December 2009 when employment in these sectors increased by a further 638,000, reflecting the resilience of the Indian economy.

A study on **Indonesia** mentions that no single day goes by without news of the layoffs of workers.[22] There are also reports of retrenchments (40,000 jobs) that took place in the last two months of 2008 and of the likely retrenchments in the construction and textile sectors.[23] Although unemployment has continued to decrease over the period of the crisis, the share of informal employment in total employment has increased by 0.8 percentage points from August 2008 to February 2009, reaching 62.1 per cent of total employment. The increase is even higher for female employment: around 1.3 percentage points against 0.5 for male employment. In the context of a rising labour supply, this means that the number of informal workers increased by about 2 million (of which 1.36 million were female workers) from August 2008 to February 2009.[24]

In the **Philippines**, a country that has a large number of workers working abroad, there is an apprehension of a decline in the flow of workers going overseas. And in the domestic labour market, the number employed in agriculture and manufacturing has already gone down, leading to a rise in open unemployment from 6.25 per cent in 2007 to 6.81 per cent in 2008.[25]

Likewise, official data on **Thailand** shows that the share of employment in manufacturing fell from 15.1 per cent in the third quarter of 2007 to 13.8 per cent in the third quarter of 2008.[26] Another study on Thailand indicated that the second quarter of 2009 would see a rise in unemployment and underemployment.[27]

Within Asia, **Bangladesh** emerges as a country that has not been affected so severely by the global economic recession of 2008–09. So, the overall impact on the labour market does not appear to be very pronounced. And yet there are some indications of quantity adjustments.[28] While the overall rate of open unemployment is not rising substantially, with the reduction in the growth rates in manufacturing being offset to some extent through higher levels of growth in the agricultural sector, rates of underemployment are likely to increase. At the sector level, some of the sectors that have been affected – for example, textiles, and jute goods – have witnessed the retrenchment of workers. A survey of entrepreneurs reveals that 8.3 per cent of them have resorted to laying off workers and another 5.6 per cent had to close down their production units. A further 11.1 per cent said that they would lay off workers if there was a deepening of the recession. Likewise, 11.1 per cent said they would close down production units in the event of a worsening of the situation. New recruitment in major export-oriented sectors like garments has slowed down considerably. So, it seems that the quantitative mechanism of adjustment in the labour market is active even in a country which has not been so seriously damaged by the recession.

As a result of its strong links with the global economy, **South Africa** was hit hard by the crisis, which has exacerbated the longer-term structural problems affecting its economy and labour market.[29] Consequently, the country fell into a recession in the fourth quarter of 2008; estimates indicate that that GDP growth in 2009 will be –2.1 per cent. Overall, the number of South Africans employed has fallen from 13,729,000 in the second quarter of 2008 to 12,855,000 in the third quarter of 2009, which has been driven by layoffs, particularly in the wholesale and retail trades, and the repair, manufacturing and agricultural sectors. Initially, the fall in employment levels in South Africa did not translate to an increase in official unemployment. In fact, the unemployment rate for the whole population only increased from 23.1 per cent in 2008Q2 to 23.6 per cent in 2009Q2. Later in 2009, the situation did deteriorate further with the unemployment rate jumping to 24.5 per cent in 2009Q3 (before dropping marginally to 24.3 per cent in 2009Q4). The main effect of the crisis-induced recession in South Africa, however, has been rising discouragement rather than a surge in official unemployment.

In **Mauritius**, exports declined by 10.5 per cent and tourist arrivals declined by 20 per cent during 2007–08. As a result, open unemployment has increased. Figures suggest that 7 per cent of the jobs in textile and other manufacturing sectors were lost in the first quarter of 2009 alone.[30]

Price adjustment (changes in real wages/earnings)

In addition to adjustment through increased unemployment, adjustment is also taking place through the price mechanism, i.e., either through a decline or a freezing of real wages. Again, it is too early to get concrete data on a systematic basis; but there are sufficient indicators to show that this mechanism is also being used by the labour market to adjust to the fall in demand for labour resulting from a decline in outputs. In **India**, the survey mentioned earlier shows that nominal earnings during the last quarter of 2008 declined by 3.45 per cent per month (though earnings did increase later in 2009).[31] Given the rate of inflation prevailing during that period, it is most likely that real wages declined.

In **Bangladesh**, there has been no reduction in money wages; but the survey of entrepreneurs mentioned above reveals that workers' fringe benefits have been cut back. Moreover, given the slowdown in the growth or negative growth in some export-oriented sectors, the rate of capacity utilization may have declined, leading to a decline in the hours of work, and consequently, the take home pay of workers. If one adds the rate of inflation to all of that, it is impossible to rule out the possibility of a decline in real wages. And the survey of entrepreneurs mentioned earlier reveals that 3.7 per cent of them would resort to a wage cut in the event of a further deepening of the recession. During "focused group discussion" with workers, they expressed their willingness to work at a reduced wage rate for a short period instead of facing retrenchment (Rahman et al. 2009).

In **Mauritius**, the salaries of those whose have retained their jobs have been frozen for an indefinite period.

The above are just a few examples of labour markets adjusting through the price (i.e., real wage/earnings) mechanism. For many countries, the lack of data on real wages and earnings on an up-to-date basis makes it difficult to say anything about the use of this route for adjusting to the impact of the economic recession. But even the fragmentary evidence available points to the simultaneous use of both quantity and price adjustment in the labour markets of developing countries.

Adjustment through changes in the composition of the labour market

As in the wake of previous economic crises, the economic recession of 2008–09 led to important changes in the composition of the labour markets in developing countries. In India, the survey carried out by the Ministry of Labour Employment (mentioned earlier) showed that in 2008 the rate of decline in employment (or retrenchment) was six times for contract workers compared to regular workers. Thus, a vast majority of those who lost their jobs are in the informal segment within the formal sectors. Moreover, they belonged to the manual category, had lower levels of skills and received lower levels of remuneration (Kannan 2009a). There is a similar experience in Bangladesh where workers retrenched from the jute goods sector belonged primarily to the category of temporary/contract workers (Rahman et al. 2009).

By contrast, informal sector employment in South Africa contracted over the course of most of the crisis, from 17 per cent of total employment in the second quarter of 2008 to 15.5 per cent in the third quarter of 2009 (Verick 2010).

The phenomenon mentioned above (of temporary workers being laid off first) points to at least two interesting aspects of the labour market. First, when an economy goes through a period of expansion, the labour market adjusts by taking in more workers on a contract basis so that the workforce can be adjusted easily at times of downturn. And when the downturn comes, they are the ones to be retrenched first, the result of which may not even show up in figures of open unemployment. Secondly, workers hired on a contract basis and thus belonging to the informal category may go down further in that segment in terms of the quality of jobs and earnings when laid off from the formal sectors.

Another change that is taking place in the composition of the labour market is a reverse movement towards agriculture and other activities based in rural areas and the movement of workers from one region to another within the same country. The former is clearly happening in Bangladesh and China. In Indonesia, as a result of the decline in commodity prices and the resulting decline in the growth of the plantation sector, there has been a large-scale return of workers from Kalimantan and Sumatra to Java (Djaja 2009).

Policy responses at the national level and their possible implications for labour market recovery

Following standard policy prescriptions for tackling economic downturns, various countries adopted policy measures aimed at stimulating their economies and coming out of the downturn.[32] As outlined in chapter 2, they typically consisted of monetary policy measures like cutting interest rates and fiscal measures of various types to provide tax concessions and other benefits to entrepreneurs in an effort to help them remain competitive and to consumers to stimulate their demand. The assumption behind such measures was that they would help the economy to recover and with that would come employment. An examination of the contents of the policy responses (popularly referred to as stimulus packages) adopted during 2008 and the early part of 2009 reveals a number of interesting aspects.[33]

First, only 1.8 per cent of the total spending was allocated to direct employment-related measures while the rest represented tax cuts, transfers, infrastructure spending and other spending. One can, of course, understand that the amount spent on infrastructure is likely to have a strong positive effect on employment (especially if labour-based approaches are used).

Second, examples of labour market initiatives in response to the crisis indicate that in a few countries, there was something in terms of allocation for public sector jobs or infrastructure spending. But on closer examination, it would appear that some of that allocation was either made independently of the crisis (e.g., for the National Rural Employment Guarantee Programme of India) or are relatively small in magnitude (see chapter 8).

Third, such allocations were not based on a careful understanding of the nature of the job losses experienced by various countries. However, as mentioned earlier, the time needed for recovery in the labour market would depend to some extent at least on that; and the general allocation for job creation schemes (or on infrastructure that could create jobs) may serve as a temporary palliative without having a sustained effect on labour market recovery. In order to facilitate the latter kind of recovery, it would be essential to base policy responses on an understanding of the nature of the job losses and to focus policy support to sectors with growth and employment potential whenever a structural change in the economy appears likely.

Unfortunately, given the present state of knowledge and the availability of data, not much can be said about the nature of job losses (i.e., whether they simply represent a cyclical phenomenon or whether there are structural factors associated with them). However, it may still be useful to consider a few issues that may have some relevance for the question at hand. First, after decades of trumpeting the virtues of export-led growth, discussion on development suddenly woke up to the possibility of domestic markets acting as an alternative driver of growth. This occurred as several countries experienced double-digit declines in their export growth, raising the question of whether or not the export-dependent economies could adjust to a situation in which consumers in the developed world were no longer sustaining the growth in market demand. Making domestic demand the main driver of growth would of course imply a major reorientation of growth strategy. For one, consumers in China, India or Viet Nam may not demand the same goods as their counterparts do in the United States and other developed countries. Moreover, the strength and pattern of domestic demand in developing countries would depend upon the growth of incomes of average households which, in turn, would be influenced by their pattern of growth and the distribution of income. Not only would a substantial change in them take time, but it is also likely to have implications for the growth in employment.

In the above context, it may be useful to note that when developing countries move to higher levels of development, one often finds that consumer demand is boosted through the use of credits and subsidies. But it is usually the demand for consumer durables that is supported by such measures; and the employment outcome of the growth of such demand is not necessarily very positive. Credit-driven growth in domestic demand in China and India provides examples of such patterns of growth.[34] On the other hand, if domestic demand were to be strengthened on a broader basis, it would be necessary to put in place a strategy of growth that stimulates growth of incomes in rural areas and amongst the vast numbers in the ranks of middle- and lower middle-income groups in the urban areas. But the policy package needed for engendering such a growth strategy and their implications for employment are matters that are yet to be worked out.

In the meantime, some countries are adopting measures with the aim of initiating some change in their pattern of growth. Indonesia, for example, is talking about changing the share of the domestic market for some of their major industries such as garments and footwear. And the stimulus package adopted by the country provided for a subsidy to these two sectors (Hailu 2009c). From the point of view of the employment implications of the growth of these two industries, a stimulus to their growth would certainly appear to be pro-employment. However, given the weak demand for their products in the international market, such a policy measure may simply help maintain the level of profit of the entrepreneurs, unless of course demand for the products in the international market is highly price elastic.

Malaysia, in its stimulus programme, focused on developing new industries (Pilling 2009). If that involves moving away from the strategy of labour-intensive industrialization which has been the hallmark of development and industrialization in Malaysia, recovery in the labour market will naturally be slow.[35]

There is another factor that may have an adverse effect on the employment–output relationship during the period of recovery, and thus cause a delay in recovery in the labour market; and that has its source in the stimulus programmes themselves. As mentioned already, it is quite common to lower interest rates in order to boost economic activities during a recession. Unless there are measures to reduce the cost of labour to the entrepreneurs (e.g., through a subsidy on wages), the use of monetary policy may lead to a distortion in the relative price of labour and capital and encourage the use of capital by making it artificially cheaper. In India, for example, even before the economic downturn of 2008–09, a variety of measures to encourage investment had led to an artificial lowering of the cost of capital relative to labour. And a further lowering of interest rates in the wake of the global economic recession must have aggravated the situation. Likewise, the government of Indonesia provided direct subsidy for the purchase of machinery under the Machinery Revitalisation Programme (Hailu 2009c). Neither of these two countries is known to have any measure to encourage the use of labour in industries.

The content of a stimulus programme may unwittingly contain measures that may encourage a growth pattern that is not very employment-intensive. In China, for example, the list of industrial sectors that would benefit from government support includes steel, automobiles, machinery, shipbuilding, textiles, electronics and petrochemicals. It is quite clear from this list that apart from textiles and electronics, the sectors are at the capital-intensive end of the industrial scale. It is unsurprising that independent observers within China itself are voicing concern about the danger of a jobless recovery (Riskin 2010).

Concluding remarks

The present chapter presents a framework for analyzing the various ways in which labour markets in developing countries adjust to a fall in demand for labour caused by economic downturns. The framework takes into account the existence of modern and traditional sectors and considers situations in which surplus labour may or may not be present. The analysis points out that adjustment in the modern sector could take place through a combination of quantity and price adjustment, i.e., through increases in unemployment and underemployment as well as declines in real wages and earnings. The impact of the fall in labour demand is likely to spill over to the traditional sector where there would be an increase in the supply of labour, and an increase in employment is likely to be accompanied by a decline in wages. Apart from these two broad mechanisms, the structure of labour markets could also change in response to the fall in labour demand. The relative importance of the various mechanisms may, of course, vary from country to country depending upon the level of development and the factors causing the economic downturn.

The present chapter also notes that recovery in labour markets can follow economic recovery with a lag, the length of which could vary from country to country depending upon the nature of the job losses (i.e., whether the phenomenon is simply cyclical or structural), and the nature of policy responses adopted by various countries.

The framework mentioned above is applied first to previous recessions in two countries, viz., Argentina and Indonesia. Those two countries went through economic crisis and downturn in the recent past (during the periods 1999–2001 and 1997–98, respectively), and it is found that labour markets adjusted through a combination of higher unemployment/underemployment and declines in real wages. In Indonesia, in addition to the quantity and price adjustments, there were also a number of changes in the structure of the labour market. One important difference between the two countries is the time lag involved in the recovery of the labour market following economic recovery. While recovery in the case of Argentina was fairly rapid, it took much longer in the case of Indonesia. And the hypothesis put forward in the present chapter to explain this difference is that the economic downturn in Indonesia was accompanied by changes in the structure of the economy (especially in the manufacturing sector) which led to job losses that were simply not cyclical in nature. As a result, when the economy recovered, old jobs were not replaced. In the case of Argentina, there was no such structural change during the economic crisis of 1999–2001. The difference between the two experiences mentioned above may provide useful lessons for an understanding of the likely lag in labour market recovery when countries emerge from the economic downturn of 2008–09.

Coming to the impact of the economic downturn of 2008–09, an overview of some country experiences indicates that while the immediate response of the labour markets is quantity adjustment (i.e., increases in unemployment and underemployment), price adjustment (i.e., decline in real wages and earnings) is also taking place. Furthermore, changes in the structure of labour markets (as seen in Indonesia and in other Asian countries during the crisis of 1997–98) also seem to be taking place, although full information on such aspects is still not available.

The review of country experiences mentioned above already indicates (even though some of the information is anecdotal and scattered) the possibility of structural changes taking place in various economies which, in turn, may have implications for the time needed for recovery in the labour markets. The possibility of such structural changes is greater in economies that are at higher levels of development and were in any case poised for a transition to a different stage of development and are now required to look for new drivers of growth (for example, a shift from export-oriented to a more domestic-oriented demand base for their products). China, India, Indonesia and Malaysia are notable examples of such countries. The stimulus packages adopted by such countries may be successful in aiding the process of economic recovery in the short term. In some cases (for example, in China), increases in public investment, especially in infrastructure, may help to boost the labour market to some extent. But recovery in the labour market as a whole and its sustainability is likely to be influenced significantly by the structural changes that these economies may be undergoing during the process of economic recovery. In contrast, in countries that are unlikely to witness major structural changes in their economies, the jobs lost during the economic downturn of 2007–09 may be more of a cyclical phenomenon, and hiring may restart soon after the export orders return to the usual levels. Countries like Bangladesh, Cambodia and Viet Nam may be in that category.

The preliminary analysis of the policy responses made by various countries indicates a possibility that relative factor prices may be becoming distorted in favour of the use of capital rather than of labour. To the extent that happens, the impact on employment and labour market recovery will naturally be negative. Such measures range from simple reductions in interest rates to subsidies on capital use, interest paid, and for the replacement of machinery. Unless such subsidies are counteracted by incentives for the use of labour, policy responses may have little impact in terms of hastening the pace of labour market recovery. Likewise, stimulus programmes focused mainly on capital-intensive industries may also not be very helpful for a recovery in the labour market.

Notes

1. By now, there is a sizeable body of literature on the impact of economic crises on employment and labour markets in developing countries. See, for example, Betcherman and Islam (2001), Fallon and Lucas (2002), IILS (2009), Islam (2003a), Lee (1998), McKenzie (2004) and Manning (2000).
2. The data quoted here are from the website of the US Bureau of Labour Statistics, www.bls.gov.
3. In an interview with the weekly magazine Newsweek on 18 May 2009, the US Treasury Secretary Timothy Geithner said that the economy is stabilizing but that unemployment will continue to rise, and that hiring tends to lag behind other improvements in the economy.
4. For use of similar frameworks, see Fields (1994) and Manning (2000).
5. It needs to be noted that a reduction in wages may have an adverse effect on employment via demand depression.

6. These other mechanisms of labour market adjustment may operate in developed countries as well. For example, during the economic recession of 2008–09, recourse to part-time employment and irregular contracts, and dropping out of labour market were common in developed countries as well.
7. In the Republic of Korea, for example, during the economic crisis of 1997–98, the number of 'daily workers' started rising soon after the decline in the first quarter of 1998, while the number of 'regular workers' continued to decline throughout 1998. The proportion of part-time workers increased significantly (from 7.2 per cent to 9.3 per cent) during 1997–98. See Kang et al. (2001).
8. This argument is based on the assumption that the choice of technology is influenced by relative factor prices. One may, however, point to the possibility of re-switching of technologies and the adoption of similar technologies at different factor prices. But the point being made here is that while different measures may reduce the price of capital, often there is nothing to encourage the use of labour. This point will be elaborated further (in the section on policy responses) with empirical evidence in the context of the economic crisis of 2008–09.
9. This distinction was made by Groshen and Potter (2003) in the context of their analysis of jobless recovery in the United States from the recession of 2001.
10. There is a large body of literature on the causes of the crisis. A good analysis is provided by Lee (1998).
11. These data and data on real wage index are from ILO (1999).
12. This figure and other data mentioned in this paragraph are from Islam et al. (2001).
13. Betcherman and Islam (2001) came to the same conclusion based on the experience of Indonesia and other countries of East and South East Asia.
14. The observations made in the next three paragraphs are based on data presented in Islam and Chowdhury (2009c).
15. It may be worthwhile to mention here that one study points out that 'External factors rather than internal factors such as rising wage rates were responsible for the declining competitiveness of traditional Indonesian exports' (Dhanani, 2000, p. 5, quoted in Islam and Chowdhury, 2009c).
16. Illustrative calculations of the elasticity of poverty incidence with respect to the level of poverty line for selected countries of Asia shows that even in countries with relatively lower incidence of poverty (e.g., Sri Lanka and Thailand), large numbers of people remain vulnerable to transient relapses into poverty when faced with severe external shocks that affect their incomes. See Islam (2003b).
17. Data provided in the following paragraph are from ILO (2009b).
18. 'China Vows to Focus on Jobs as Unemployment Rises', *International Herald Tribune*, 20 November 2008.
19. Reported in *The Daily Star* (Bangladesh), 21 January 2009.
20. Reported in *International Herald Tribune*, 2 February 2009, and *The Economist*, 31 January–6 February 2009. See also Chang Hee Lee, 'National Policy Responses to the Financial and Economic Crisis: The Case of China'. Undated draft, ILO-ROAP, Bangkok.
21. See the various editions of Report on 'Effect of Economic Slowdown on Employment in India' produced by the Labour Bureau, Ministry of Labour & Employment, Government of India, http://labourbureau.nic.in/reports.htm.

22. Djaja (2009).
23. ILO ROAP, op. cit.
24. Data from Indonesian Bureau of Statistics, www.bps.go.id.
25. Yap (2009).
26. Reported in ILO ROAP, op. cit.
27. Jitsuchon and Siamwalla (2009).
28. Data presented in these paragraphs are from Rahman et al. (2009).
29. See Verick (2010).
30. Ibid.
31. Government of India, Ministry of Labour and Employment (2009).
32. It needs to be noted in this context that the ability of a country to adopt counter-cyclical fiscal policy and the size of the fiscal stimulus adopted depend on the fiscal space that it has. On this see, Islam, I. (2009).
33. For more details, see (IILS, 2009). The figures quoted in this paragraph are based on data from 22 countries – 10 advanced and 12 developing and emerging countries.
34. In China, for example, the government's stimulus programme includes 13 per cent subsidy in rural areas on the purchase of appliances like televisions, refrigerators, washing machines, air conditioners and computers. See 'Market Watch', *Beijing Review*, 25 June 2009. Such a subsidy-driven consumption boost may not produce an employment-intensive recovery. Likewise, a credit-financed and inequality-driven boom in consumption demand is mentioned as a factor responsible for an increase in the production of capital-intensive goods resulting in a rise in their share in total industrial output. On India, see Chandrasekhar and Ghosh (2008).
35. Of course, given the level of development that has already been achieved by Malaysia, it can afford to (and perhaps should) shift gear and move to a different path of growth. But this transition can be smoothened by preparing the labour market for the purpose, e.g., by introducing appropriate measures of social protection and active labour market policies.

5

The Impact of the Global Financial Crisis on Labour Markets in OECD Countries: Why Youth and Other Vulnerable Groups Have Been Hit Hard

S. Verick

Introduction

The global financial crisis of 2007 quickly spread from the housing and credit markets in the United States to the rest of the world, resulting in the worst global recession since the Second World War. As a consequence of the downturn, millions of workers have been laid off, while for those lucky enough to hold on to their jobs, many have experienced cuts in hours worked, wages and others benefits as enterprises seek to reduce labour costs in order to remain afloat. In the *Global Employment Trends* for January 2010, the ILO estimates that unemployment reached 212 million in 2009, an increase of 34 million over the figure for 2007 (ILO 2010). According to the OECD, the downturn has pushed more than 15 million workers into unemployment since the end of 2007 (OECD 2009a). Although most countries had technically exited recession by the end of 2009, unemployment rates across the world are likely to stay stubbornly high for some time to come, long after the economy has recovered fully.

This is naturally a generalization of the impact of the global financial crisis on the labour market, which, as indicated in chapter 2, has in fact varied considerably across (and within) countries depending on the structure of the economy, institutions in place and how policymakers have responded. Similar to previous crises, this downturn has had different implications for various segments of the population as defined by such characteristics as gender, age, education, contractual status, race and country of origin. These traits render individuals more vulnerable to a recession because of either the long-term barriers they face in the labour market or their over-representation in a sector that is more affected by changes in macroeconomic conditions.

Understanding how the labour market has been impacted by the crisis on aggregate and how specific segments of the population have been hit harder are both crucial pieces of information for policymakers. In particular, this type of breakdown is necessary in order to design targeted policy responses, which aim to reduce the risk of long-term unemployment and discouragement (where individuals give up job search). For this reason, this chapter aims to provide an in-depth analysis of the diverse employment impact in OECD countries, which complements the developing-country focus of chapter 4.

The remainder of this chapter is structured as follows: the next section provides an overview of the labour market impact of the global financial crisis in OECD countries. First, the chapter summarizes how specific segments of the population have been hit harder. This is followed by a discussion of the specific vulnerability of young men and women to unemployment. The chapter then proceeds to a discussion of the drivers of youth unemployment trends before turning to concluding remarks.

The overall impact of the crisis on OECD labour markets

In OECD countries, the unemployment rate has increased on average from 5.7 per cent in the third quarter of 2007 to 8.6 per cent in the third quarter of 2009.[1] The five hardest-hit OECD countries in terms of a surge in the unemployment rate from 2007Q3 to 2009Q3 are Estonia (+10.9 percentage points), Spain (+10.3 ppts), Ireland (+8.1 ppts), the United States (+4.9 ppts) and Turkey (+4.6 ppts). At the same time, a number of countries have experienced only a mild impact on the labour market in terms of rising unemployment. In Poland and Germany, the unemployment rate has in fact decreased over this period (by 1.2 and 0.7 percentage points, respectively). In others such as Austria, the Netherlands, Republic of Korea and Slovakia, the change in unemployment rate has been marginal.

Analysing output and unemployment adjustment jointly provides a mapping of OECD countries that reflects both the diversity and complexity of the crisis. As captured by Table 5.1 and Figure 5.1, Norway has averted both a severe economic contraction and labour market impact, while others including Austria, Germany, Republic of Korea, the Netherlands, and Poland have avoided a major deterioration in the labour market despite a greater fall in output. The majority of OECD

		Mild labour market impact	Medium labour market impact	Severe labour market impact
		Δunemployment rate of less than or equal to the 25th percentile (percentage points)	*Δunemployment rate of more than the 25th percentile and less than the 75th percentile (percentage points)*	*Δunemployment rate of more than the 75th percentile (percentage points)*
Mild economic contraction	*ΔGDP growth rate of less than or equal to the 25th percentile (percentage points)*	Norway (–5, 0.6)	Australia (–3.3, 1.5) Cyprus (–4.9, 1.7) Denmark (–4, 2.3) France (–4.7, 1.6) Greece (–4.8, 0.8) Portugal (–4.9, 1.8)	Canada (–5, 2.6) United States (–4.8, 4.9)
Medium economic contraction	*ΔGDP growth rate of more than the 25th percentile and less than the 75th percentile (percentage points)*	Austria (–7.3, 0.1) Croatia (–10.7, 0.2) Germany (–7.8, –0.7) Rep. of Korea (–6.1, 0.5) Netherlands (–7.8, 0.5) Poland (–5.8, –1.2)	Belgium (–5.8, 0.9) Czech Rep. (–10.4, 1.8) Finland (–10.6, 1.7) Hungary (–7.9, 2.3) Italy (–6.7, 1.5) Japan (–7.7, 1.7) Luxembourg (–10, 2.4) Malta (–5.8, 0.8) Mexico (–10.6, 2.3) Switzerland (–5.6, 1) United Kingdom (–7, 2.4)	Spain (–7.4, 10.3) Sweden (–7.4, 2.6)
Severe economic contraction	*ΔGDP growth rate of more than the 75th percentile (percentage points)*	Bulgaria (–12.7, 0.4) Romania (–14.7, –0.2) Slovakia (–15.1, 0.3)	Slovenia (–11.5, 1.3)	Estonia (–21.2, 10.9) Iceland (14.1, 4.6) Ireland (–13.5, 8.1) Latvia (–28, 12.5) Lithuania (–27.4, 9.5) Turkey (–11.2, 4.7)

Sources: IMF WEO Database, OECD Labour Force Survey Database, EUROSTAT Labour Force Survey Database; author's calculations.

Notes: Figures for GDP growth in 2009 are estimates (see IMF WEO Database October 2009). Δ = change from period t–1 to t. The figures presented in the parentheses are the change in GDP growth rate (percentage points) and the change in the unemployment rate (percentage points).

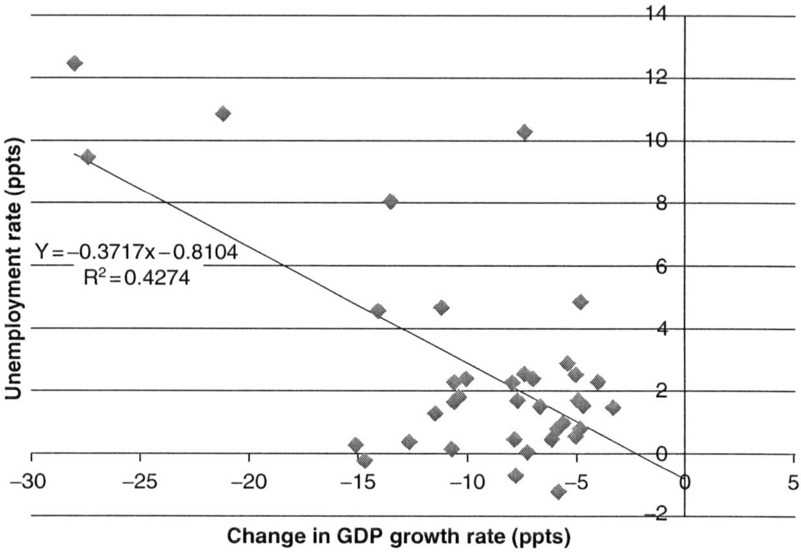

Figure 5.1 The relationship between economic contraction and deterioration in the labour market, OECD countries, 2007Q3–2009Q3
Source: See Table 5.1.

countries, however, lie somewhere in the middle. As illustrated by Figure 5.1, these data suggest that for every 1 percentage point decrease in the GDP growth rate, the unemployment rate increases by 0.37 percentage points.[2]

Adjusting to a labour demand shock

As addressed in chapter 4, there are three main channels for adjustment to external shocks in labour demand at the firm level: working time (hours worked), number of workers and wages/non-wage benefits.[3] In general, firms tend to adjust hours of work more rapidly than the number of workers because of cost considerations and the need to retain workers (due to firm-specific capital) (also known as internal adjustment). The sensitivity of working hours to the business cycle also varies across sectors depending on the importance of these factors (OECD 2009a). Cutting wages and the other benefits of remaining workers may reduce labour costs, but has an adverse social impact. That said, nominal wages tend to be rigid due to institutional reasons and because employers are reluctant to cut wages.[4] Ultimately, a sharp drop in economic activity leads to dismissals, mass layoffs, plant closures, and hiring freezes (external adjustment), which all contribute to rising unemployment that has been described above.

During the global financial crisis, there has been considerable variation in the adjustment of working hours, wages and employment across countries in response to the shock to demand and credit crunch. As captured in Table 5.2, adjustment in the manufacturing sectors of European countries can be categorized on the basis of two dimensions (employment and working hours). This relationship is presented using sectoral data as a proxy for changes made at the firm level.[5] In the resulting matrix, eight sets of countries emerge. For example, as discussed on many occasions during the crisis, employment in Germany has adjusted by a small margin, while hours have decreased more than in most European countries (lower left corner). In Germany's case, this was driven by employers' concerns about holding on to their skilled workers, which was in turn supported by a subsidized reduced working time scheme (*Kurzarbeit*) (see chapter 8). In contrast, adjustment to both employment and hours has been above average in countries with more flexible labour markets such as the Czech Republic, Latvia and the United Kingdom. In the majority of European Countries, adjustment has taken place in both employment and hours to a moderate degree.

This diversity in employment and working time adjustment across European countries is the result of differences in economic factors (sectoral impact, transmission channels) and institutions (such as the degree of unionization, wage flexibility, dismissal protection legislation), along with the impact of government policies on the adjustment process (for example, the reduction in working hours through work-sharing schemes).

Analysing wage adjustment since the onset of the crisis in 2007 is more complex due to a number of factors: lack of data on earnings for 2009; comparison between changes in nominal and real wages; and differences between adjustment in hourly wages and weekly/monthly wages. Nonetheless, based on the available data, it is possible to derive a number of tentative conclusions regarding wage adjustment during the global financial crisis. Firstly, data for OECD countries suggests that nominal hourly earnings have not fallen in most countries. At the same time, growth in nominal wages has slowed since late 2008.

Secondly, in many cases real wages have risen because of either a fall in prices (as occurred, for example, in the United States) or a slowdown in inflation (disinflation) (as, for instance, in the European Union). In the case of the United States, the real average hourly earnings were decreasing over the pre-crisis period due to an increase in consumer prices (Figure 5.2). Since the onset of the recession, prices had fallen rapidly, and consequently, real hourly earnings have increased. This trend in the United States illustrates the importance of movements in prices for the

Table 5.2 Adjustment of employment and working time in the manufacturing sector, selected European countries, 2008Q3–2009Q3

		Strong hours adjustment	**Moderate hours adjustment**	**Weak hours adjustment**
		Percentage change in actual weekly working hours less than or equal to the 25th percentile	*Percentage change in actual weekly working hours more than the 25th percentile and less than the 75th percentile*	*Percentage change in actual weekly working hours more than the 75th percentile*
Strong employment adjustment	*Percentage change in employment less than or equal to the 25th percentile*	• Czech Republic (–13.6, –2.4) • Latvia (–24.4, –1.9) • United Kingdom (–15.8, –1.9)	• Denmark (–16.1, –1.0) • Ireland (–13.8, –1.5) • Lithuania (–14.8, –1.5) • Slovakia (–14.3, –0.8) • Spain (–16.1, –0.7)	
Moderate employment adjustment	*Percentage change in employment more than the 25th percentile and less than the 75th percentile*	• Austria (–7.5, –1.9) • Estonia (–13.0, –3.2)	• Bulgaria (–8.2, –1.5) • Finland (–11.4, –1.0) • France (–7.6, –1.0) • Hungary (–9.6, –1.5) • Netherlands (–9.5, –0.7) • Romania (–10.0, –1.2) • Slovenia (–11.4, –1.5)	• Belgium (–8.4, –0.3) • Croatia (–11.6, 0) • Cyprus (–9.2, 0.5) • Sweden (–11.7, 0.3)
Weak employment adjustment	*Percentage change in employment more than the 75th percentile*	• Germany (–6.1, –3.4) • Malta (0.4, –3.3)	• Italy (–6.5, –1.7) • Poland (–5.3, –0.7)	• Greece (–5.2, –0.5) • Luxembourg (0, 4.0) • Norway (–6.2, 0.3) • Portugal (–4.7, 1.0)

Source: EUROSTAT Labour Force Survey Database, http://epp.eurostat.ec.europa.eu/portal/page/portal/employment_unemployment_lfs/data/database; authors' calculations.

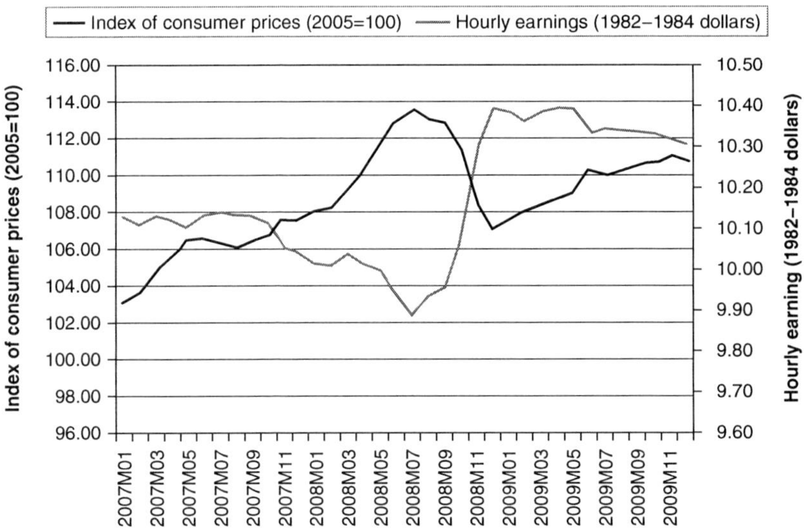

Figure 5.2 Changes in consumer prices and real hourly wages in the United States during the crisis, 2007–09 (monthly data)

Sources: Bureau of Labor Statistics, Current Employment Estimates database (hourly earnings); EUROSTAT database of harmonized index of consumer prices (HICP) (index of consumer prices).

Notes: Data are monthly for the period January 2007 to December 2010. Hourly earnings are in 1982–84 US dollars, averaged over the entire private sector.

real wage (i.e. variation is driven more by the denominator) and that the crisis has in fact contributed to a correction in the pre-crisis fall in real hourly wages that was caused by rising inflation (and stagnant nominal wages), particularly in 2008. At the same time, it should be noted that household incomes in many countries have been hit through the reduction in working hours, unless it has been subsidized – as is the case in many European countries (which only partly subsidize lost income). Overall, once the necessary data become available, it will be possible to draw more conclusive findings on wage adjustment.

How the global financial crisis has affected employment levels of different segments of the population

Moving beyond the aggregate picture, the impact of the global financial crisis on labour markets in OECD countries can be disentangled in terms of how it has affected vulnerable segments of the population. In this respect, a number of key dimensions can be identified: gender; age; educational attainment; contractual status; race; and country of origin.[6] There are, of course, other dimensions that determine outcomes in the labour market, such as disability status, but these are harder to measure or analyse using the available data.

The different dimensions of vulnerability explored in this chapter include both predetermined individual characteristics (gender, race, age) and those that reflect outcomes (educational attainment, contractual status, and migration decisions). It is also important to recognise that these dimensions are interrelated: for example, gender influences educational attainments, which in turn has an impact on outcomes in the labour market. In this chapter, the notion of vulnerability relates to the likelihood of experiencing worse outcomes in the labour market vis-à-vis the average or most resilient segment of the population (usually prime-age males). Moreover, most of the focus here is on vulnerability to increases in unemployment and decreases in employment, rather than longer-term disparities. This is an important distinction as evident by the discussion on gender: though clearly women typically face greater challenges in the labour market, men bear the brunt of recessions due to their higher representation in badly-affected sectors. This is, however, not a case of direct discrimination.[7]

In terms of the situation for specific groups, the global financial crisis has in general hit men harder in advanced economies, particularly younger men.[8] For example, since the fourth quarter of 2007, the unemployment rate in European Union's 27 Member States increased by 6.2 and 4.1 percentage points for young men and women (aged less than 25), respectively, while it rose by a lower margin for prime-age men (2.8 points) and prime-age women (1.4 points). The comparative changes in employment for these groups also reflect the more pronounced deterioration for young men and, to some extent, young women (see Figure 5.3). This phenomenon is not a case of 'reverse' discrimination; rather, it is due to the fact that young men were working in sectors that were badly affected by the global downturn such as construction and manufacturing. In addition, young people entering the labour market have been competing for fewer vacancies with older individuals who have lost jobs but nonetheless have higher levels of experience and skills. These aspects are the focus of later sections.

Secondly, workers with lower levels of education have been more vulnerable to losing their jobs since the onset of the crisis. This is again due to their over-representation in sectors that have been badly affected, particularly construction.[9] This can also be explained by the reluctance of

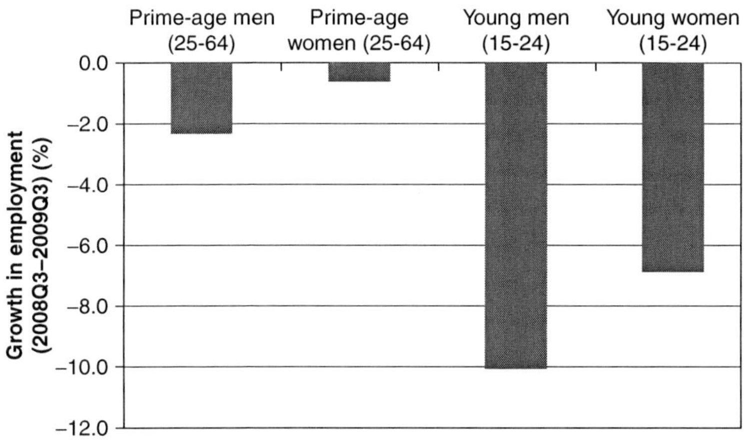

Figure 5.3 Decline in employment by gender and age, European Union (27 Member States), 2008Q3 to 2009Q3
Source: EUROSTAT Labour Force Survey Database, http://epp.eurostat.ec.europa.eu/portal/page/portal/employment_unemployment_lfs/data/database; authors' calculations.

employers to fire highly skilled workers during a downturn because of the costs involved in hiring, which were on the increase prior to the global financial crisis as a consequence of a growing skills shortage. This situation is evident in both the European Union and the United States. In the case of the United States, employment of individuals who did not complete high school has fallen by 15.5 per cent from the first quarter of 2007 to the fourth quarter of 2009 (Figure 5.4). In comparison, individuals with a high school education fell by 8.1 per cent, while it in fact rose by 2.4 per cent for those with a college degree.

Contract status also plays an important role in determining the vulnerability of workers to a downturn. Even prior to the crisis, precarious contracts were on the rise in a number of countries, particularly in Europe (for example, the increase in temporary work in Germany). Once the crisis hit, employers first resorted to cutting back on those staff employed on temporary contracts, a policy that is far cheaper and more rapid than attempting to make redundancies of permanent staff who are protected by legislation or collectively bargained agreements. For this reason, temporary workers dominate such sectors as construction, which are volatile and require a considerable degree of flexibility. For instance, in Spain, which had before the onset of the crisis the highest proportion of temporary workers in the European Union, the share of these workers in total employment fell from 30.1 per cent in

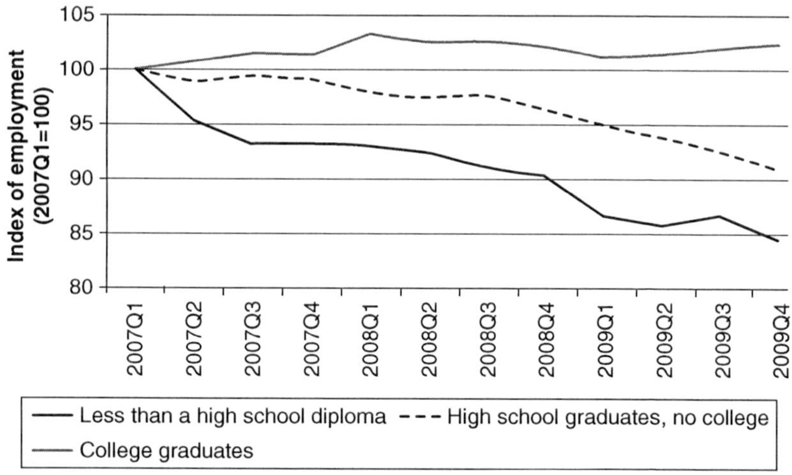

Figure 5.4 Educational attainment and the impact of the global financial crisis on employment in the United States, 2007Q1 to 2009Q4
Source: US Bureau of Labor Statistics Current Population Survey; author's calculations.
Notes: Data are seasonally adjusted.

the fourth quarter of 2008 to 25.1 per cent in the last quarter of 2009. The main challenge for policymakers is that these workers have limited access to social protection measures such as unemployment insurance.

Another group that has been particularly vulnerable are migrant workers, not just in countries that have a high proportion of these workers – such as in the Middle East – but also in high-income countries. For example, non-western Dutch immigrants experienced a greater increase in the unemployment rate during the global financial crisis than Dutch-born citizens (around 3 percentage points from 2008Q3 to 2009Q3 compared to 1.2 percentage points) (Central Bureau of Statistics 2009). On aggregate, the evidence is more mixed. The employment of foreign-born workers in the EU decreased by 2.5 per cent between the third quarter of 2008 and the third quarter of 2009 (although it is still higher than the level at the end of 2007) (Figure 5.5). That said, the employment of these workers was increasing at a faster rate in the period leading up to the crisis, so the subsequent fall was greater. At the same time, employment has grown for citizens of other EU countries (27 Member States) (by 1.8 per cent), while it has fallen for citizens of non-EU countries (by 5.2 per cent). In Spain, where many migrants were working in the construction sector and agriculture, the impact on foreign workers has been far greater, particularly on those from outside the EU. Between 2008Q3 and 2009Q3, employment

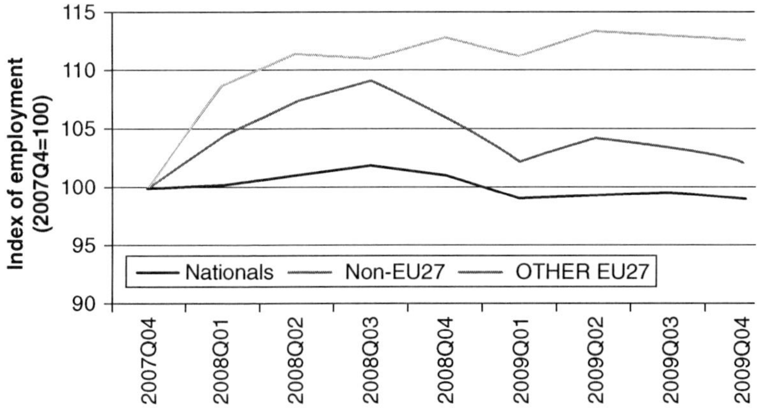

Figure 5.5 Migrants and the global financial crisis in the European Union, 2007Q4 to 2009Q3

Source: EUROSTAT Labour Force Survey Database, http://epp.eurostat.ec.europa.eu/portal/page/portal/employment_unemployment_lfs/data/database; authors' calculations.

Notes: Non-EU27 = citizens of countries outside the European Union 27 Member States; Other EU27 = citizen of another country within the European Union.

of Spanish citizens fell by 10 per cent. In comparison, the number of non-EU citizens employed dropped by 13.5 per cent or 286,000 (–1.2 per cent for citizens from other EU Member States). In the fourth quarter of 2009, the employment of non-EU citizens fell even further (over 112,000 alone in just these three months).

Departing from this disaggregated view, it is also crucial to consider the overall implications for household welfare, which is in turn a function of the individual characteristics discussed above (for example, members of poor households are more likely to have low levels of educational attainment). In this context, recent evidence indicates that poor households in the United States have borne a disproportionately large burden. According to Sum and Khatiwada (2010), US households in the lowest decile (those earning $12,160 or less) were experiencing on average an unemployment rate of 30.8 per cent in the fourth quarter of 2009, in comparison to just 3.2 per cent for households in the top decile (those earning $138,700 or more). A similar disparity is found for underemployment (individuals working part-time because of economic reasons). Sum and Khatiwada (2010: 13) conclude: 'A true labour market depression faced those in the bottom two deciles of the income distribution, a deep labour market recession prevailed among those in the middle of the distribution, and close to a full employment environment prevailed at the top. There was no labour market recession for America's affluent.'

This overview reveals a number of insights into which segments of society have been most vulnerable to the global recession. Primarily, these figures show that it has been men, particularly younger men, individuals with a low level of educational attainment, and those on temporary contracts who have borne the brunt of the downturn in advanced economies. In some countries, migrant workers have been clearly more affected than nationals.

Why youth have been hard hit by the crisis

As is made evident above, youth in advanced economies, especially young men, have suffered more since the onset of the global financial crisis in 2007. For this reason, the remainder of the chapter is devoted to a further analysis of the impact of the crisis on young men and women in these countries and to explaining why this has been the case.

Youth around the world are especially vulnerable to marginalization in the labour market because they lack skills, work experience, job search abilities and the financial resources to find employment (United Nations 2003; ILO 2006). As a consequence, young people are more likely to be unemployed or employed on more precarious contracts. This is the case even during good economic times. In the midst of a severe recession, youth find it increasingly difficult either to acquire a job as a new entrant in the labour market, particularly as a consequence of hiring freezes, or to remain employed since they are more likely to be laid off than workers with more seniority. Overall, youth unemployment rates are far more sensitive to the business cycle than witnessed for the adult population (OECD 2008). As discussed in Verick (2009), an analysis of the impact of earlier financial crises in Finland, Japan, Norway, Spain and Sweden reveals that youth were more vulnerable to rising unemployment than the prime-age population. Moreover, the increased gap between youth and adult unemployment rates remains even after the economy has begun to recover.

Governments are rightly concerned about rising levels of youth unemployment not only because of the direct economic costs, but also due to the social impact of joblessness as manifested by increased crime, mental health problems, violence, drug-taking and social exclusion.[10] Moreover, spells of unemployment, particularly those of a longer duration, can lead to scarring effects in terms of a higher likelihood of being unemployed later in life and a wage penalty (Bell and Blanchflower 2009).

To identify a heightened vulnerability to the impact of the crisis, this section compares trends in the unemployment rates for young men and women aged under 25 to the situation for men aged 25 and older (prime-age men), who serve as a reference group since they typically experience the fewest barriers in a given labour market.[11] Youth unemployment rates are often reported as a ratio to the adult rate to indicate the degree of labour market marginalization experienced by young people.[12] However, this ratio can in fact decrease during a period of crisis. For example, in Finland, the ratio of young male to prime-age male unemployment rates decreased from 3.75 prior to the financial crisis of 1990 to 1.96 during the midst of the downturn in 1993. Looking at the ratios would suggest that the situation of young men vis-à-vis prime-age males has improved, which was not the case. Rather, the unemployment rate of Finnish prime-age men was increasing from a very low initial condition. For this reason, the focus in this chapter is on the absolute increase in unemployment rates, which is more indicative of the situation as illustrated below.

Another issue to be aware of is that unemployment rates change not only because of entry to or exit from unemployment, but also due to changes in labour force participation. If segments of the population exit the labour force altogether, this will also affect the unemployment rate. For example, if laid-off workers chose not to search for a job because of enrolling in a course, deciding to have a family or discouragement, this will contribute to a reduction in the size of the labour force, and hence, a fall in the denominator of the unemployment rate, leading to an increase in the figure.[13] This is particularly relevant for women.

Based on this approach, Figure 5.6 displays the change in the monthly unemployment rate (seasonally adjusted) of young men and young women since December 2007. The change in unemployment rates is calculated as the difference between the minimum rate reached after December 2007 and the latest monthly figure. By using a country-specific minimum (trough in the unemployment rate), the measure used in this chapter accounts for variation in the business cycle and a differential impact of the crisis on economies. The sample of countries presented in Figure 5.6 includes 27 European Union Member States (Austria, Belgium, Bulgaria, Cyprus, the Czech Republic, Denmark, Estonia, Finland, France, Germany, Greece, Hungary, Ireland, Italy, Latvia, Lithuania, Luxembourg, Malta, Netherlands, Poland, Portugal, Romania, Slovakia, Slovenia, Spain, Sweden and the United Kingdom) along with Australia, Canada, Croatia, Norway, Turkey and the United States.[14] Data for the percentage point change in the unemployment rate of young

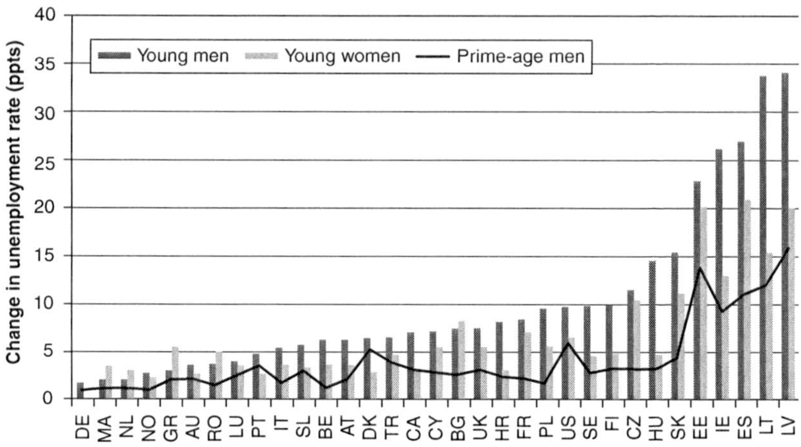

Figure 5.6 Changes in seasonally adjusted unemployment rates in Europe, Australia, Canada and the United States
Source: Australian Bureau of Statistics (accessed 1 February 2010), EUROSTAT Employment and Unemployment (Labour Force Survey) database (accessed 1 February 2010), and Statistics Canada (accessed February 2010); author's calculations.
Notes: Young men and women are those aged less than 25, while prime-age men are aged above 25. The latest month is November 2009 for all countries except Belgium, Cyprus, Denmark, Estonia, Greece, Italy, Latvia, Lithuania, Romania, Slovenia, Turkey and the United Kingdom (September 2009); Norway (October 2009) and Australia (December 2009). Unemployment rates are seasonally adjusted. The change in unemployment rates is calculated as the difference between the minimum monthly rate reached after December 2007 and the latest monthly figure. See Table A5.1 in the Appendix for full country names.

men, the initial unemployment rate (trough) and date for the trough are presented in Table A5.1 in the Appendix.

Confirming the trends witnessed in previous crises, the main message of Figure 5.6 is that unemployment rates have increased in all countries. As before, the increases for youth have outstripped the rise in unemployment among prime-age men. Overall, since December 2007, the unemployment rate in the European Union member countries had increased by 6.1 and 3.5 percentage points for young men and women, respectively, while it rose by a lower margin (2.1 percentage points) for prime-age men. Altogether, an additional 2.2 million young men and 1.2 million young women have become unemployed in the European Union, Australia, Canada, Croatia, Norway, Turkey and the United States since the start of the crisis in December 2007. In a number of countries, the number of unemployed youth has more than doubled within an 18-month period. In terms of the timing of these trends, in almost half of the countries in the sample, the unemployment rates for youth reached a trough before the end of the first quarter of 2008 before starting on an upward trend (see Table A5.1 in the Appendix).

As expected, these averages mask considerable heterogeneity across countries in terms of the relative changes in unemployment rates. There is in fact great variation in how unemployment has responded to the economic downturn: the change in the unemployment rate for young men ranges from an increase of 1.7 percentage points in Germany to a mammoth increase of 34.1 percentage points in Latvia. Based on the trends presented in Figure 5.6, a number of general groupings can nonetheless be made:

1 In general, in terms of increasing unemployment rates, youth have been hit much harder than prime-age men. Young men have more often than not experienced larger increases in unemployment rates than young women, although this does not detract from the fact that the latter often have higher initial rates of unemployment. Unemployment rates have been increasing faster since mid-2008.
2 In the five countries most affected by the crisis, Lithuania, Estonia, Latvia, Spain and Ireland, unemployment rates have surged by at times unprecedented levels. In these countries, the rate for young men has increased by more than 20 percentage points in less than 18 months, reflecting rapid economic contraction. In these countries, the increase in unemployment rates for young women exceeded that of prime-age men. In three Eastern European countries, the Czech Republic, Hungary and Slovakia, the increase has exceeded 10 points.
3 A large number of countries are in the middle range, including Luxembourg, Denmark, the United Kingdom, Portugal, Turkey, Canada, Slovenia, France, the United States, Hungary, Finland and Sweden, which have all witnessed increases in the unemployment rate of young men of more than five percentage points.
4 In Germany, Malta, the Netherlands and Norway, the change in unemployment rates have been relatively 'mild'. In these four countries, the unemployment rate amongst young males increased by three percentage points or less since December 2007.
5 In five countries, Malta, the Netherlands, Greece, Romania and Bulgaria, young women have experienced a greater increase in unemployment than young men, which contrasts with the rest of the sample. In general, the gender difference is larger for the harder-hit countries.

Germany, the United Kingdom and the United States

In addition to these overall characteristics of the sample, it is informative to reflect on the situation of the largest economies in this group, namely the United States, Germany and the United Kingdom. The trends in the unemployment rates of young males in these three countries are mapped out in Figure 5.7.

These trends show that the unemployment rate among young men has risen far more rapidly in the United Kingdom and the United States. In the United States, the unemployment rate for this group increased from 12.1 per cent in April 2008 to 21.8 per cent in November 2009 (an increase of 9.7 percentage points). In the United Kingdom, the rate has increased from 15.4 per cent in December 2007 to 22.8 per cent in September 2009. In comparison to the United Kingdom and the United States, unemployment started to increase in Germany only in August 2008. Moreover, the rise in unemployment rates in Germany has been so far modest despite the collapse in global trade flows and the severe contraction of the Germany economy in 2009. The rate for young German men rose by a mere 1.7 points from August 2008 (from 10.2 to 11.9 per cent).

Together with the evidence from previous crises as discussed in Verick (2009), these trends confirm that it is young workers who are the most

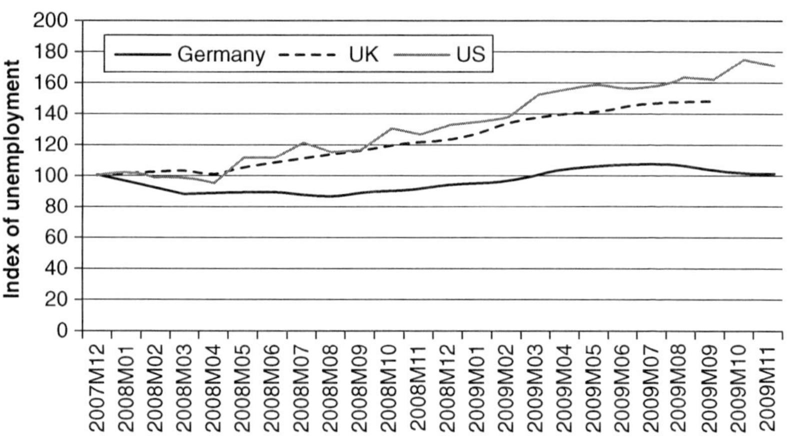

Figure 5.7 Unemployment trends in Germany, the United Kingdom and the United States

Source: EUROSTAT Employment and Unemployment (Labour Force Survey) database; author's calculations.

Notes: Young men and women are those aged between 15 and 24, while prime-age men are aged between 25 and 54. Monthly data are seasonally adjusted. The index of unemployment equals 100 in December 2007.

vulnerable to increasing rates of unemployment – something that is borne out by the global financial crisis of 2007–09. At the same time, it should also be stressed that the impact of this latest global crisis varies considerably across countries with a few – such as Lithuania, Latvia, Estonia, Spain and Ireland – being severely affected, while others – including Germany and the Netherlands – have yet to display adverse outcomes in their respective labour markets. In the next section, an attempt is made to understand this variation in the labour market impact of the global financial and economic crisis.

Explaining the impact of the global financial crisis on youth unemployment rates

The considerable variation in the impact of the global financial crisis on youth unemployment requires further investigation, particularly as a deeper understanding of this situation has important policy implications for governments around the world. In this section, a number of possible explanations are explored, namely the relationship between changes in unemployment rates and the level of economic contraction, the sectoral composition of employment and institutional setting in terms of employment protection and the utilisation of less protected contracts. The focus in this section is on explanations for changes to unemployment rates of young men given that this is the group that has experienced the largest increases since the start of the downturn.

Firstly, given that labour demand is dependent on aggregate demand, a collapse in the latter will have direct implications for the former. As discussed above, the precise magnitude of this impact will depend upon unemployment elasticities, which vary across countries. The latest estimates for growth in 2009 reveal that there is a large variation in the expected contraction of economies. Gross domestic production in the Baltic States (Estonia, Latvia and Lithuania) is estimated to have declined by more than 14 per cent in 2009. In Ireland, GDP is projected to have fallen by 7.5 per cent. Looking at the correlation between the change in economic growth and unemployment rates for the sample, it is evident that unemployment rates have unsurprisingly increased more in countries suffering a larger collapse in economic growth, such as the ones mentioned above (Figure 5.8). The implied unemployment elasticity is high (close to 1), which is higher than found for the total population as presented in Figure 5.1. However, once the five main affected countries (the Baltic States, Ireland and Spain) are dropped from the sample, there is in fact no evidence of the expected negative

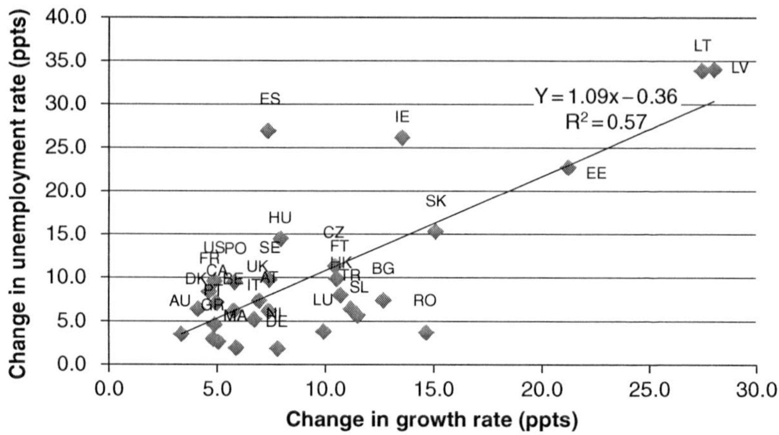

Figure 5.8 The relationship between economic contraction and changes in unemployment rates for young men

Source: EUROSTAT Employment and Unemployment (Labour Force Survey) database and International Monetary Fund World Economic Outlook Database October 2009; author's calculations.

Notes: The change in unemployment rates is for young men aged 15–24 from the trough reached after December 2007 to latest month available (see notes for Figure 5.6 above). The change in growth rates is the difference between GDP growth rates in 2007 and 2009, where the 2009 figure is an IMF estimate. The sample consists of AT, AU, BE, BG, CA, CY, CZ, DK, EE, FI, FR, DE, GR, HR, HU, IE, IT, LV, LT, LU, MA, NL, NO, PL, PT, RO, SK, SL, ES, SE, TR, UK, US. See Table A5.1 in the Appendix for full country names.

relationship between change in growth and unemployment rates (the fitted line in fact becomes slightly negative).

In light of failing to find a robust relationship between changes in economic growth and unemployment rates, it is important to delve deeper behind the impact of the collapse in aggregate demand on unemployment rates. As a next step, this section considers the relationship between the sectoral composition of employment and subsequent changes to rates of youth unemployment. In line with previous crises, specific sectors are contracting more than others because of their exposure to the financial dimension of the downturn (reversal in flows of capital and freezing of credit channels) and the trade impact (fall in exports). The construction sector, in particular, benefited greatly from the boom years as easy credit helped to fuel a housing bubble, while the strong demand for exports boosted the manufacturing sector in many industrialized countries. Since the start of the crisis, the collapse of the housing bubble has resulted in a massive contraction of the construction sector. The ensuing global recession and fall in trade has had a severe impact upon the manufacturing sector. This situation implies that the unemployment rate of young men should have increased more in countries in which these sectors were major employers of this group.

Evidence for this explanation is mixed, however. As displayed in Figure 5.9, there is a strong positive relationship between the share of young men employed in the construction sector in 2007 (i.e. prior to the crisis), and the subsequent increase in unemployment rates (the sample excludes Australia, Canada and the United States). The largest shares of young men employed in construction are in the five countries most affected by the crisis (the Baltic States, Ireland and Spain). In these countries, the share of young men employed in construction in 2007 ranges from 27.7 per cent in Lithuania to 33.7 per cent in Estonia. Without these observations in the sample, there is a weakening of the statistical relationship presented in Figure 5.6.

In comparison, the correlation between the increase in unemployment rates and the share of young men in manufacturing is not as strong, even after the five main outliers are excluded from the sample.[15]

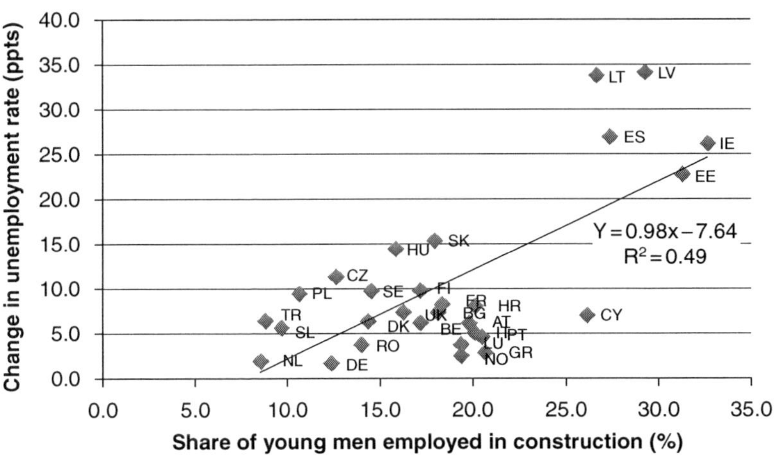

Figure 5.9 The relationship between share of employment in construction (2007Q3) and changes in unemployment rates of young men since December 2007

Source: EUROSTAT Employment and Unemployment (Labour Force Survey) database; author's calculations.

Notes: Sample of countries includes: AT, BE, BG, CY, CZ, DK, EE, FI, FR, DE, GR, HR, HU, IE, IT, LV, LT, LU, NL, NO, PL, PT, RO, SK, SL, ES, SE, TR, UK. See Table A5.1 in the Appendix for full country names.

Linking the sectoral composition to the impact of trade, there is some evidence that the unemployment rates of young men have increased faster in countries where manufactures accounted for a large proportion of merchandise exports, but this holds only once the five outliers have been removed.

Another potentially important factor is the share of youth in temporary employment, which by definition are not as well protected as regular jobs. This is an illustration of the relationship between the different vulnerability dimensions discussed above. On average, 41 per cent of young men in the European Union have jobs which are classified as temporary employment. Spain, in particular, is a country in which a large number of young people have been traditionally employed on temporary contracts: in 2007, 63 per cent of young Spanish men were employed on a temporary basis. As underscored above, unemployment is likely to have risen faster in countries where this share is higher since it is easier for employers to lay off workers on such contracts. However, although the correlation between these two variables is (weakly) negative, this is driven again by the outliers (Figure 5.10).

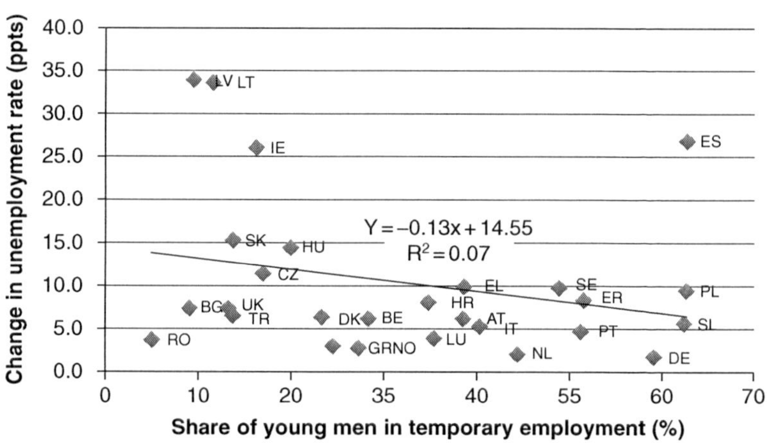

Figure 5.10 The relationship between share of young employed men in temporary employment and changes in unemployment rates of young men since December 2007

Source: EUROSTAT Employment and Unemployment (Labour Force Survey) database; author's calculations.

Notes: Sample of countries includes: AT, BE, BG, CZ, DK, FI, FR, DE, GR, HR, HU, IT, LU, NL, NO, PL, PT, RO, SK, SL, ES, SE, TR, UK. Temporary employees are expressed as a percentage of the total number of employees for young men aged 15–24 (%) as of 2007. See Table A5.1 in the Appendix for full country names.

Continuing with labour market institutions, employment protection legislation (EPL) is often claimed to be a major factor behind the high levels of unemployment in certain European countries. In the context of the crisis, it is expected that countries with more stringent EPL would experience a smaller increase in the unemployment rate of young men. However, the point here is not to find evidence that labour market institutions such as EPL have a negative impact of adjustment. Rather, it is the opposite: it is precisely these institutions that can potentially help countries to avoid massive increases in unemployment such as witnessed in the Baltic States.[16]

Using the OECD indicators for 2008, there does indeed appear to be a negative relationship between the change in young male unemployment rates and the overall employment protection index, although it is still by no means large (R^2=0.03) (Figure 5.11). This negative correlation is slightly stronger once the outliers of Estonia, Ireland, and Spain are removed (data are lacking for Latvia and Lithuania). Overall, it is difficult to derive a clear generalization as there are countries with rigid employment protection – such as Greece, Norway and Germany – that are experiencing smaller increases in unemployment. On the other hand, there are countries with similar levels of protection –

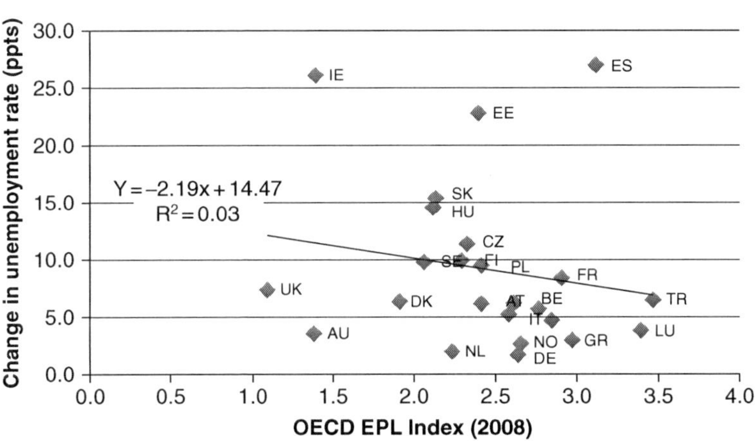

Figure 5.11 The relationship between employment protection legislation and changes in unemployment rates of young men since December 2007
Source: EUROSTAT Employment and Unemployment (Labour Force Survey) database and OECD Indicators on Employment Protection 2008; author's calculations.
Notes: Sample of countries includes: AU, AT, BE, BG, CA, CZ, DE, DK, EE, ES, FI, FR, GR, HR, HU, IE, IT, LU, NL, NO, PL, PT, SK, SE, TR, UK, US. See Table A5.1 in the Appendix for full country names.

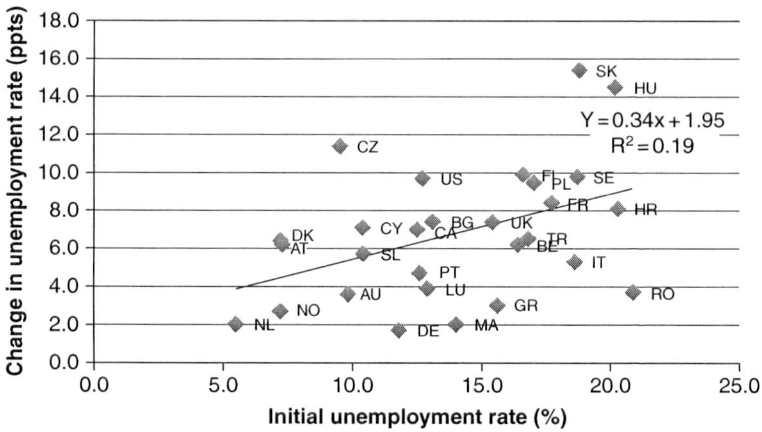

Figure 5.12 Initial conditions and changes to unemployment rates of young men during the crisis

Source: EUROSTAT Employment and Unemployment (Labour Force Survey) database; author's calculations.

Notes: The change in unemployment rates is for young men aged 15–24 from the trough reached after December 2007 to latest month available (see notes for Figure 5.3 above). Sample consists of AT, AU, BE, BG, CA, CY, CZ, DK, FI, FR, DE, GR, HR, HU, IT, LU, MA, NL, NO, PL, PT, RO, SK, SL, SE, TR, UK, US. See Table A5.1 in the Appendix for full country names.

such as Spain – that are nonetheless going through a much more severe adjustment in the labour market. There are similar contrasts at the other end of the employment protection spectrum.[17]

Prior to the start of the crisis, young male unemployment rates varied considerably in the sample of countries used in this chapter.[18] Using country-specific troughs (i.e. the lowest rate as of or reached after December 2007), the rates range from 5.2 per cent in Netherlands to 18.7 per cent in Sweden. As illustrated in Figure 5.12, there is a strong positive correlation between the initial unemployment rate and the subsequent change (excluding the five outliers of the Baltic States, Ireland and Spain). This implies that young men have been more affected in countries which were already experiencing high levels of unemployment. The initial level itself is the outcome of a range of factors, including structural causes of youth unemployment (for example, lack of skills/skills mismatch and poor education levels of young men).

Concluding remarks

The global financial crisis of 2007–09 resulted in the worst global downturn since the Second World War, leading to millions of job losses and a deterioration in working conditions. Though most of the badly affected countries technically exited recession at the end of 2009, history shows that after synchronized and global crises, such as the global financial crisis, unemployment rates across the world are likely to stay stubbornly high for some time to come. In the Global Employment Trends for January 2010, the ILO estimates that unemployment reached 212 million in 2009 – an increase of 34 million over the figure for 2007 (ILO 2010). According to the OECD, since the end of 2007 the downturn had pushed more than 15 million workers into unemployment (OECD 2009a).

Beyond this aggregate picture, the labour market impact of the crisis has varied considerably across (and within) countries depending on the structure of the economy, the institutions in place and the ways in which policymakers have responded. The five hardest-hit OECD countries in terms of a surge in the unemployment rate from 2007Q3 to 2009Q3 are Estonia (+10.9 percentage points), Spain (+10.3 ppts), Ireland (+8.1 ppts), the United States (+4.9 ppts) and Turkey (+4.6 ppts). The average increase in the OECD is 2.9 percentage points. At the same time, a number of countries have experienced a mild impact on the labour market in terms of rising unemployment. In Poland and Germany, the unemployment rate has in fact decreased over this period (by 1.2 and 0.7 percentage points, respectively). In others such as Austria, the Netherlands, Republic of Korea and Slovakia, the change in unemployment rate has been marginal.

During the global financial crisis, there has also been considerable variation in terms of the adjustments to working hours, wage levels and employment across countries in response to the shock to demand and the credit crunch. Data for OECD countries suggest that nominal hourly earnings have not fallen in most countries, which is in line with the findings of the literature on downward wage rigidity. At the same time, growth in nominal wages has slowed since late 2008. Secondly, real wages have in many cases risen because of either a fall in prices (for example, the United States) or a slowdown in inflation (disinflation) (for example, European Union). This diversity in employment, working time and wage adjustment across European countries is due to differences in economic factors (sectoral impact, transmission channels) and institutions (such as the degree of unionization, wage flexibility, dismissal protection legislation), along with the impact of government policies on the adjustment process (for example, the reduction in working hours through work-sharing schemes).

Furthermore, this chapter underscores a number of insights into which segments of society have been most vulnerable to the global financial crisis. Primarily, these figures show that it has been men, and in particular younger men, individuals with low levels of educational attainment, and those on temporary contracts who have borne the brunt of the downturn in advanced economies. In some countries, migrant workers have been affected more by job losses than nationals.

The heightened vulnerability of youth, especially young men, to increasing unemployment during the crisis can be explained in part by a combination of the degree of economic contraction, the sectoral composition of prior employment and institutional structures. Young women do experience increasing unemployment rates often in a similar fashion to young men, and in some countries, they are in fact the group that suffers the most. Moreover, this comes on top of the longer-term barriers young women continually face in the labour market.

In light of this situation, governments should ensure that vulnerable groups are targeted as part of policy interventions such as subsidies, training schemes and job search assistance programmes. Indeed, a majority of OECD countries have done precisely this by targeting measures at youth to mitigate the impact of the economic downturn. This is essential to ensure that these segments of the population do not become long-term unemployed or discouraged, which would reduce their future career prospects and earnings potential. The challenge for policymakers is not to withdraw targeting policies too early and to ensure that the labour market is carefully monitored to identify vulnerable individuals who are 'falling through the cracks' and thus at risk of labour market exclusion. This in turn requires careful consideration of how skills development and other measures would benefit these individuals so that they have a chance to find employment in a new occupation or an expanding sector.

Notes

1. See OECD labour force survey data, http://stats.oecd.org/Index.aspx?DatasetCode=LFS_SEXAGE_I_R.
2. This is line with empirical estimates of Okun's Law. The relationship between economic growth and unemployment rates has been famously described by Okun (1962) in what became known as Okun's Law. Estimates of Okun's statistical relationship for the United States indicate that there is approximately a 2 per cent decrease in output for every 1 per cent increase in unemployment. See also Schnabel (2002).
3. See Cazes et al. (2009) for more details.
4. See the discussion on wage rigidity in Akerlof and Shiller (2009) and Bewley (1999).

5. The observations therefore only represent the net effect of the crisis on employment and hours worked (i.e. stocks as opposed to flows), which are also affected by changes in participation.
6. See European Commission (2009) for a discussion on the differential impact of the crisis on the population.
7. It is well established that women face considerable hurdles in the labour market, as a result of discrimination in hiring and wages. In terms of the latter issue, there is a vast literature on the gender wage gap, which has demonstrated the presence of disparities even after controlling for observable characteristics. For example, empirical evidence from an international meta-analysis reveals indicates that men with similar labour market qualifications as women earn a wage premium of 25 per cent on average and that this wage premium varies considerably between countries (Weichselbaumer and Winter-Ebmer 2005). That said, the situation for women in the labour market has improved over recent decades, particularly in line with the improvements in access to education and training.
8. See Verick (2009) for more details on this issue. It must also be noted that female workers were hit harder than male workers in the export-oriented industries of East Asia. See, for example, Green, King and Miller-Dawkins (2010).
9. As highlighted in OECD (2009a), business-cycle sensitivity of working hours decreases with educational attainment.
10. These direct economic costs include financing unemployment benefits, retraining schemes and other active labour market policies, and the loss in potential output resulting from lower employment rates.
    For a discussion on the costs of unemployment, see United Nations (2003) and Bell and Blanchflower (2009).
11. There are some differences in definitions, though most countries provide data for youth aged 15 to 24.
12. See, for example, ILO (2006).
13. The unemployment rate is defined as the number of unemployed divided by the labour force (unemployed plus employed). According to the ILO definition, the unemployed comprise all persons who during a reference period are without work, currently available for work and are actively seeking employment.
14. Due to the lack of seasonally adjusted disaggregated data, Japan has been excluded from the sample.
15. The figure is available on request.
16. In addition to the role for institutions in shaping the labour adjustment process, governments, as highlighted by the case of Germany, have implemented a range of policies to mitigate the impact of the crisis on the labour market, namely work-sharing schemes that have kept workers in their jobs and have thus helped keep the labour market from deteriorating.
17. At the same time, there isn't a clear relationship between the gross unemployment benefit replacement rate and change in young male unemployment rates, once the outliers of Ireland and Spain are dropped (figure available on request).
18. It is also worth repeating that despite the larger increases in unemployment rates of young men since the start of the crisis, young women often experience higher permanent rates of unemployment.

Appendix

Table A5.1 Initial unemployment rate, date of unemployment trough and changes in unemployment rates since the start of the global financial crisis

		Young men			Young women			Prime-age men		
Full country name	Country code	Initial unemployment rate (trough)	Date of trough	Change since trough	Initial unemployment rate (trough)	Date of trough	Change since trough	Initial unemployment rate (trough)	Date of trough	Change since trough
Austria	AT	7.2	June 2008	6.2	7.1	Jul 2008	2.6	2.6	May 2008	2.1
Australia	AU	8.2	Feb 2008	3.6	7.5	Aug 2008	3.6	3.6	Feb 2008	2.2
Belgium	BE	16.3[a]	Oct 2008	6.2	16.2[a]	Apr 2008	3.6	5.3	Mar 2008	1.3
Bulgaria	BG	13.1	Dec 2007	7.4	7.9	Aug 2008	8.2	4.1	Nov 2008	2.6
Canada	CA	12.1	Jan 2008	7.0	9.4	Dec 2007	3.2	5.0	Feb 2008	3.2
Cyprus	CY	7.9[a]	July 2008	7.1	9.0[a]	Jan 2008	5.4	2.4	June 2008	2.8
Czech Republic	CZ	9.4	Apr 2008	11.4	9.3	Apr 2008	10.4	2.7	Sep 2008	3.2
Germany	DE	10.2	Aug 2008	1.7	8.4	Aug 2008	0.1	6.8	Jul 2008	1.0
Denmark	DK	6.3[a]	Jan 2008	6.4	7.1[a]	Dec 2007	2.8	1.9	May 2008	5.3
Estonia	EE	7.9[a]	Jan 2008	22.8	5.8[a]	Dec 2007	20.1	2.8[a]	Jan 2008	13.8
Spain	ES	17.5	Dec 2007	26.9	22.2	Dec 2007	20.9	5.9	Dec 2007	11.0
Finland	FI	15.9	Mar 2008	9.9	15.4	May 2008	4.7	4.4	Feb 2008	3.3
France	FR	17.3	Feb 2008	8.4	18.2	Feb 2008	7.0	5.7	Apr 2008	2.1
Greece	GR	15.6[a]	Dec 2007	3.0	28.3[a]	Apr 2008	5.5	4.1[a]	Apr 2008	2.1
Croatia	HR	17.3	Oct 2008	8.1	26.8	Apr 2008	3.1	5.1	Jul 2008	2.5
Hungary	HU	17.8	May 2008	14.5	19.7	Oct 2008	4.6	6.1	Feb 2008	3.3
Ireland	IE	10.7	Dec 2007	26.1	7.4	Jan 2008	12.9	4.3	Dec 2007	9.3
Italy	IT	17.8[a]	Jan 2008	5.3	24.4[a]	Jan 2008	3.6	3.9	Dec 2007	1.8
Lithuania	LT	6.2[a]	Dec 2007	33.8	10.0[a]	Dec 2007	15.3	4.0	Dec 2007	12.0
Luxembourg	LU	12.2	Jan 2008	3.9	18.9	Dec 2007	3.5	2.5	Dec 2007	2.3

Latvia	LV	7.8[a]	Dec 2007	34.1	9.1[a]	Dec 2007	19.9	5.3	Dec 2007	15.7
Malta	MA	12.8	Sep 2008	2.0	9.0	Mar 2008	3.4	4.0	Dec 2007	1.2
Netherlands	NL	5.2	Jun 2008	2.0	4.8	Jan 2008	3.0	1.9	June 2008	1.3
Norway	NO	7.0	Jan 2008	2.7	5.9	Jan 2008	2.2	1.7	Feb 2008	1.0
Poland	PL	14.6	Jul 2008	9.5	18.5	Aug 2008	5.5	5.1	Aug 2008	1.7
Portugal	PT	11.9	Apr 2008	4.7	18.6	Oct 2008	2.6	5.6	Dec 2007	3.5
Romania	RO	18.0[a]	Oct 2008	3.7	15.8[a]	Dec 2007	4.9	5.1[a]	Jul 2008	1.5
Sweden	SE	18.7	Dec 2007	9.8	20.0	Dec 2007	4.5	3.8	Dec 2007	2.8
Slovakia	SK	9.0[a]	Oct 2008	5.7	10.4[a]	Jul 2008	3.3	2.9	May 2008	3.0
Slovenia	SL	18.0	Sep 2008	15.4	19.5	Apr 2008	11.1	6.5	Sep 2008	4.4
Turkey	TR	16.0[a]	Apr 2008	6.5	17.9[a]	Apr 2008	4.6	7.2[a]	Jan 2008	3.9
United Kingdom	UK	15.4	Dec 2007	7.4	11.5	Feb 2008	5.4	3.6	Dec 2007	3.1
United States	US	12.1	Apr 2008	9.7	9.8	Apr 2008	6.5	3.7	Dec 2007	5.9

Source: Australian Bureau of Statistics, EUROSTAT Employment and Unemployment (Labour Force Survey) database, and Statistics Canada; author's calculations.
Notes: Young men and women are those aged less than 25, while prime-age men are aged above 25. The latest month is November 2009 for all countries except Belgium, Cyprus, Denmark, Estonia, Greece, Italy, Latvia, Lithuania, Romania, Slovenia, Turkey and United Kingdom (September 2009); Norway (October 2009) and Canada and Australia (December 2009). Unemployment rates are seasonally adjusted. The change in unemployment rates is calculated as the difference between the minimum monthly rate reached after December 2007, the start of the recession in the United States, and the latest monthly figure. [a] = these countries only provide quarterly data and the month listed in Table A1 denotes the first month of the quarter.

Part II

6
The Rise and Fall of Orthodox Macroeconomic Policy: Pre- and Post-Crisis Perspectives

M. Muqtada

Introduction

The World Summit for Social Development held in Copenhagen in 1995, essentially to review the social attainments and progress of the last quarter of the twentieth century, provided, arguably, a significant impetus to the debates on macroeconomic policymaking. During nearly two decades prior to the year of the Summit, most developing countries were largely locked in a 'one-size-fits-all' macroeconomic policy framework that was singularly focused on achieving macroeconomic stability. The now well-documented unsatisfactory economic outcomes and the social costs of the policy reforms that were largely induced by the conditionality of the stabilization-based lending programmes of the Bretton Woods institutions underlined the universal disenchantment at the Summit. The Copenhagen Declaration that came out of the deliberation of the Summit carried a commitment, of more than 80 participating Heads of State and government, to 'promoting the goal of full employment as a basic priority of our economic and social policies'.[1] Such a commitment on full employment was not only an expression of solidarity with all those in poverty and poor working conditions, but also a collective resolve to pursue a development agenda that ensured both economic and social progress. The neoliberal, orthodox macroeconomic policies that upheld that markets (including that of labour) would clear if prices were 'right' came under intense scrutiny. Thus, the Summit, by drawing attention to the dismal social progress during the 1980s and 1990s, and by endorsing a commitment to full employment as a way forward, challenged the reigning macroeconomic strategy of the day.

The full employment objective that was central to macroeconomic policies of the so-called 'golden era' of growth during the 1950s and

1960s disappeared from the macroeconomic agenda during the era of stabilization that followed. Its significance came to be relegated in the aftermath of the oil-price shocks of 1973 and 1979, which triggered a global recession, including a severe debt and foreign-exchange crisis in many Latin American countries. Owing to dwindling resource flows, rising interest rates in international borrowing, and rising debt/GDP ratios, the bulk of the developing countries were caught in a web of macroeconomic imbalances. The Bretton Woods institutions, to which these countries turned to for resources, offered loans that were conditional on (what later came to be known as) 'inflation targeting' and on belt-tightening in the fiscal and current accounts. The Washington Consensus, now well known even to non-practitioners, provided the blueprint of a new development alternative where employment and social progress were predicated on sound macroeconomic fundamentals and allocative efficiency of the market. This called for a major shake-up in the design of macroeconomic policies that in turn warranted pervasive liberalization in both the tradable and non-tradable sectors. Liberalization, which in the 1970s was advanced by the IFIs as an advocacy, soon became conditionality.

Since the early 1980s, this 'macroeconomic prudence' has almost decisively altered the course of employment-centred macroeconomic policies of the previous era, in both developed and developing countries. In the latter countries, during the next two decades, stabilization (and the closely associated structural adjustment programmes to support de-control and liberalization) was held as the central tenet in their economic policy designs. As we noted, this neoliberal mantra was maligned at the Copenhagen Summit, 1995. Moreover, this conservative reforms package was pursued not only during normal times, but also in recessionary periods. Such prescriptions were challenged by the countries hit by the Asian crisis during 1997–98 when pro-cyclical policies only helped to aggravate a regional recession. Yet, this mantra, with a number of modifications, appears to hold sway in the developing countries even today, both in normal periods as well as during crises (as the most recent post-crisis 2008–09 IMF stand-by loan agreements with several countries affected by the 2008–09 crisis would testify).[2]

This chapter critically reviews the macroeconomic experiences of the past three decades to argue the case against orthodox macroeconomics. It then proceeds to suggest that the prevailing orthodoxy in macroeconomics needs to give way to an alternative policy paradigm in which the Copenhagen commitment on full employment, subsequently incorporated as a Millennium Development Goal in 2008, plays a central role. The global recession of 2008–09 reinforces the potency of this proposition.

A brief empirical account

It may be useful to recall the three major 'facts and controversies of the 1990s', as recounted in World Bank (2005): (i) stabilization measures, combined with liberalization were central to the reforms programme; (ii) conventional wisdom held that to achieve greater efficiency required a reduction in the role of the state; and (iii) 'reforms had to be rapid'.[3]

The policy reforms to getting prices 'right' brought in their sweep quite draconian measures fairly rapidly. Thus, during the 1980s and 1990s, most of the developing countries adopted, with a degree of urgency, a series of interrelated policy measures to usher in rapid economic liberalization, particularly in trade. In addition, several 'structural adjustment programmes' were also introduced, essentially intended to rein in the role of the state and public interventions (e.g. privatization, de-control, and so on) and to facilitate market efficiency, including through labour market flexibility, to encourage private sector participation. As we now know, the above measures, which were central to the World Bank/IMF's lending programme, generated huge debates as the outcomes of the measures that were implemented came under scrutiny by the academia as well as the policy planners.[4] These policy reforms and programme measures, which found gradual articulation in a stabilization-focused framework of macroeconomic strategy, had a passionate following among the neoliberal academia. At the same time criticisms and contentions to this approach began to mount as the 'one-size-fits-all' strategy failed to produce tangible signs of sustained growth. Reviewing this extensive literature would be a task on its own. For the empirical record, Easterly (2001) provides a thorough and systematic account of the impact of the policy reforms on growth during the 1970s until the 1990s. The author clearly establishes that actual growth declined, and fell far below what was predicted. He has dubbed this period the 'lost decades' (see also chapter 2 in this volume).

The present author assesses further evidence on the relationships observed between the stability variables and GDP growth based on panel data for 80 developing countries.[5,6] The main findings are as follows:

- nearly two decades of stabilization reforms have in fact reduced the inflation levels in most countries of the world;

- with the exception of a few countries, growth of GDP is observed to be low or inadequate during the 1980s and much of the 1990s;
- despite substantial declines in inflation rate and budget deficit, hence arguably better macroeconomic stability, investment-GDP ratio (I/GDP) has failed to gain momentum;
- I/GDP as a single variable tends to explain growth better than 'stability' variables; and
- Current account deficit is negatively related to growth but not robustly.[7]

Table 6.1 brings out the limited explanatory power of the individual stability indicators. It further confirms the significant role of the investment/GDP ratio in explaining growth, which opens up a host of issues with respect to what, in fact, explains the growth in investment, and why despite all efforts at stabilization, investment failed to pick up. As the experiences of the East Asian growth success have shown us, macroeconomic stability was only one of the objectives of their macro-policy; financial policies and incentives towards resource mobilization as well as focused public interventions helped boost saving and investment in these economies.

As noted above, the defence of, and disenchantment with, the stabilization-focused policy reforms produced debates about the appropriate design of macroeconomic strategy. Often, however, the debates were

Table 6.1 GDP growth and stabilization, 1980–2007

Dependent variable: GDP growth (%)				
Investment/GDP (%)	0.213***			
	(0.028)			
Budget deficit/GDP (%)		0.135*		
		(0.069)		
Inflation (%)			–0.003**	
			(0.001)	
Current Account Balance/GDP (%)				–0.052
				(0.042)
Constant	–0.835	3.769***	3.755***	3.407***
	(0.604)	(0.226)	(0.251)	(0.297)
R^2	0.425	0.056	0.067	0.019
Adj.R^2	0.418	0.041	0.054	0.007
N° of countries	82	68	82	82

Source: Author's calculations based on World Bank, *World Development Indicators 2009* online.

Notes: OLS regression is applied to obtain the above results. Standard errors in parentheses, *** 1%, ** 5%, * 10% level of significance.

diverted away from the core objectives of macroeconomic policy to why the pursuit of stabilization at the country level was not yielding the expected output outcomes. Attention was thus deflected to a consideration of the pace and sequence of stabilization; to rigid labour markets; and, not least, to the lack of good governance. Nonetheless, the long record of low and inadequate growth, and widespread unemployment and poverty, certainly called for a serious review by the authors of these policy reforms.

Macroeconomics of stabilization: static gains vs dynamic efficiency

While there was a growing body of literature that was critical of the policy reforms, an honest self-evaluation from the reforms-enforcing agencies was long in coming. World Bank (2005: 11) produced, arguably, the most intensive self-evaluation. It observes:

> In retrospect, it is clear that in the 1990s we often mistook efficiency gains for growth. The 'one size fits all' policy reform approach to economic growth and the belief in 'best practices' exaggerated the gains from improved resource allocation and their dynamic repercussions, and proved to be both theoretically incomplete and contradicted by the evidence.

The stabilization and structural adjustment policies were indeed directed towards achieving an enabling macroeconomic environment that would likely encourage both domestic and foreign investment, and facilitate long-term capital accumulation and growth. If nearly two decades of such policy reforms have not yielded a return to growth, what precisely have these reforms achieved?[8] As noted, the recent evaluation by the World Bank itself seems to suggest that macroeconomic stabilization policies have often led to static gains, and that not enough attention has been given on how dynamic efficiency would be further reaped.[9] In plain economic terms, this would simply reiterate what critics of the Washington Consensus have maintained, i.e. in most countries a degree of stability has been achieved, but that this has not necessarily led to growth and investment.

One clear, and possibly the most significant, indicator of such stability is the price discipline. There is no doubt that a fairly substantial reduction in the inflation levels has been attained in the developing countries, especially when one compares the 1980s and 1990s with the 2000s (see Appendix Figure A6.1). Whereas during the period 1981–90,

39.2 per cent of countries had an average inflation rate of 10 per cent or more, during the period 2001–08 only 17.9 per cent of countries exceeded this threshold. Indeed, policies aimed at 'getting prices right', chiefly through strict monetary policies and fiscal discipline, have brought about this so-called 'static' gain. Apart from such downward trends in inflation, similar empirical evidence is also available to show fairly tangible declines in budget deficits, and current account deficits – the other two variables that have been the usual targets of stabilization policies.[10]

Should then the debate surrounding the role and outcome of the orthodox macroeconomic policy framework end on the note indicated by the World Bank evaluation; that is, some static gains have been achieved, but these have not necessarily led to the expected returns to investment and growth? There have been a few exceptions. Chile, for example, which during the 1980s and 1990s pursued macroeconomic reforms, attained a fair degree of stability and growth. One must note, however, that the country incorporated additional policies and incentives to encourage savings and investment, boost productivity and exports. Chile was not averse to accepting external capital but introduced capital controls to discourage short-term capital inflows.[11]

Chile's experience during the stabilization reforms era has been more of an exception to the norm.[12] In most of the developing countries, a persistence of the pursuit of stability without acceleration in growth actually implied difficulties in sustaining such stability. While it was amply clear that a higher level of growth and employment generation would require substantially increased resources and expenditures (for example, on physical and social infrastructure), the stabilization measures continued to squeeze the fiscal space for undertaking such expenditures.

Apart from the World Bank's self-evaluation, a key (re-)interpretation of the Washington Consensus is laid out in Besley (2005), which contains a series of essays by policymakers on the interface between policy experiences and analytical discourse.[13] The debate that initially surrounded the stricter orthodox macro policies that accompanied the early years of the Bretton Woods loan conditionality has been reviewed within a broader political economy canvas (that is, incorporating the policy reforms alongside institutional and structural perspective). The following assessment is instructive:

> The structural transformation that is economic development can be achieved only by a sustained process of change based on actors who

> perceive their interests in making that change work through a combination of appropriate public and private incentives tailored to the history and institutions of the country in question. *While some key elements of the Washington consensus would be part of any such strategy, it came up short as a blue print for economic development.*[14]

Despite these caveats, Besley (2005) claims that several of the elements of the Washington Consensus are as valid today as when they were initially conceived.[15] Indeed, there can be little dispute that several of the elements of the Washington Consensus, inasmuch as they seek macroeconomic stability, are useful prescriptions. It is, however, not that policymakers are unaware or ambivalent about stability being a precondition of sustainable growth, for that growth can be hindered by a number of structural and institutional constraints. The critical caution in respect of stabilization, as many have pointed out, is on establishing the appropriate degree of the measures and policy reforms, the adjustments needed, and the sequencing of policies that takes account of country-specific circumstances.[16] More importantly, there is a need to appreciate how macroeconomic imbalances, in practical and pragmatic terms, ought to be reduced: that is, what policy instruments should a developing country, under immense resource constraints, use to reduce the prevailing imbalances. Evidence from country-level experiences is persuasive enough to suggest that throughout the 1980s and 1990s stabilization effectively amounted to 'compression', viz. rapid compression of fiscal expenditures (particularly, development expenditures) to reduce budget deficits; a drastic curtailment of imports to reduce current account deficits; and restrictive monetary policy to contain inflation. Very few countries had, during the early days of stabilization lending, the *policy* or *resource* space to seek alternative routes, such as through raising resource mobilization, expanding exports and productivity.

The consequences of the manner in which stability was achieved eventually led to disenchantment with policy reforms. *The instruments that were used to attain stability had clear trade-offs; the consequences of these trade-offs were not properly assessed or anticipated.* Restrictive monetary policies often led to hikes in interest rates which had an adverse effect on investment; import restrictions, apart from depriving governments of substantial revenues, had an effect on industries and on a country's export capacity; reduction in government expenditures badly affected development and various social transfer programmes, thus inhibiting the growth of physical and social expenditures.[17] In addition, strict adherence to fiscal deficit targets led to a steady decline in public

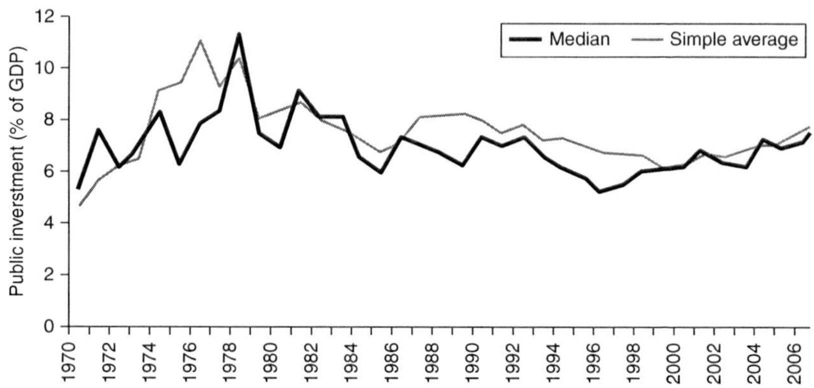

Figure 6.1 Declining public investment in sub-Saharan Africa, 1970–2007
Source: Author's calculations based on WDI 2009 online.
Note: Based on 37 sub-Saharan African countries.

investment. The figure above shows the steady decline during the 1980s and 1990s in median public investment in the sub-Saharan countries (Figure 6.1).

A steady decline in investment, a distinct fall in private consumption and public expenditures, and sluggish export performance – these coalesced to produce a fall in aggregate demand.[18] The price of pursuing the elements of the Washington Consensus both with respect to *targets* pursued, as well as *instruments* introduced to achieve the targets, has been largely a decline in aggregate demand. Dynamic efficiency has been traded off with 'static' gains. In order to stave off crises of the kind mentioned by Besley (2005), the stabilization reforms in the developing countries led to a crisis of a different kind, i.e. a crisis of output and jobs growth. The above thus challenges the rather circumspect self-evaluation of the World Bank by arguing that in many countries the instruments (e.g. inflation and deficit controls etc) that were used to deliver static efficiency gains were themselves the reason for growth failures. In other words, the processes set by the policy reforms, by ignoring the demand side of a country's economic activity, created the *raison d'être* for unsatisfactory growth and employment outcomes.

Resurgence of growth, 2002–07: What lessons for macroeconomic policy?

The beginning of the present century witnessed a distinct turnaround in the growth performance of the majority of countries across all continents. The period 2002–07 in particular has been described by Lin (2008) and others as one of global boom with the emerging economies leading the growth table.

While this period is under intense investigation and while various explanations are being forwarded to explain the sudden surge in growth (e.g. the rise in global trade, FDI and financial flows, the boom in commodity prices, and so on), stabilization protagonists may, equally, claim success in explaining this growth. It may be recalled that attempts to establish a negative relationship between growth and the usual stability variables – that is, inflation, budget deficit and current account deficit – have not been very convincing.[19] Despite mixed results and unsatisfactory experiences,[20] the stabilization doctrine, particularly through 'inflation targeting', continues even today to dominate the macroeconomic policy design in many developing countries.[21] Even after the Poverty Reduction Strategy Papers (PRSPs) came to the centre of the World Bank's concessional lending framework, the Bretton Woods institutions continued to remain focused on stabilization, without much attention to how the overall macroeconomic policy framework would support a poverty-reducing development agenda. In particular, there is country-level evidence to suggest that there could be tension and conflict between the PRSPs, and the two other facilities of the IFIs, viz. PRGF (Poverty Reduction and Growth Facility) and PRSC (Poverty Reduction Support Credit) through which orthodox stabilization measures were pursued.[22]

While for the 1980s and 1990s the causality and/or associational relationship between growth and stability variables are observed to be amorphous, it may be interesting to assess these relationships during the more recent period of growth (i.e. 2000–06). The following two graphs (Figures 6.2 and 6.3) depict the relationship between inflation and growth for a fairly large sample of developing countries for which data are available for the period 2000–06.[23]

Figure 6.2 takes into account all countries that have registered an inflation level of less than 10 per cent, while Figure 6.3 broadens the sample by taking into account a 30 per cent inflation level. These two figures do not provide any strong statistical evidence of a negative relationship between growth and inflation (the coefficients are in fact positive). Muqtada (2009) has argued that these results, at the very least, call for a nuanced view of the role of inflation and growth.[24] Particularly in developing countries with underutilized capacities, growth can be compatible with a moderate rate of inflation; in fact, modest inflation is most likely to help mobilize resources. Historical structural and institutional factors all need to be reviewed in the context of each

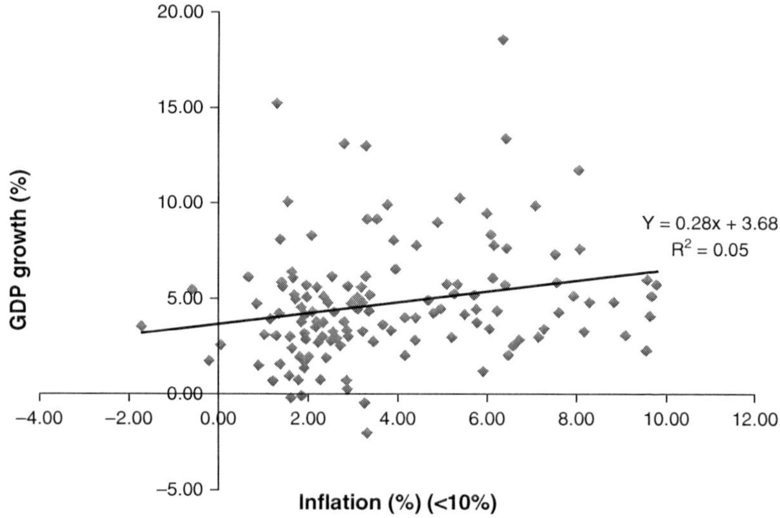

Figure 6.2 Inflation (<10%) and GDP growth, 2000–06
Source: World Development Indicators 2009 Online database.

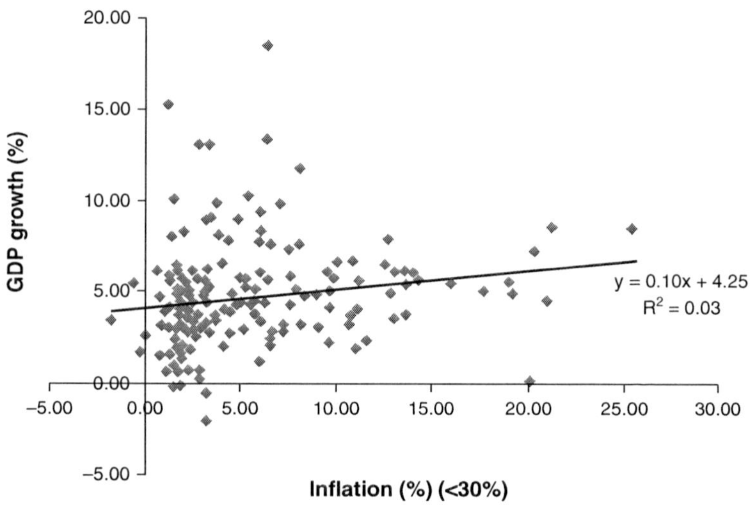

Figure 6.3 Inflation (<30%) and GDP growth, 2000–06
Source: World Development Indicators 2009 Online database.

individual country's stabilization programme before the setting of any restrictive inflation targets.[25] Inflation thresholds, especially in the developing countries, could vary substantially owing to a number of price and non-price factors.

For the same growth period, we have also drawn a scatter plot to assess the relationship between growth and the two other oft-cited stability variables, viz. budget and current account balances, both as a percentage of GDP (Figures 6.4 and 6.5).[26] The relationship in both cases does not reveal a strong positive relationship between growth and these indicators of stability. In fact, other studies tend to suggest that a modest budget deficit may well accompany, rather than hamper, growth, especially when a higher level of growth and poverty alleviation may warrant critical expenditures on infrastructure and social provisions.[27]

Empirical estimates reinforce the arguments made earlier: except a weak negative relationship with budget deficit, growth is seen to be positively related with the observed levels of inflation and current account deficit in the sample countries.[28] According to these estimates, investment is again observed to be the significant explanatory factor of growth.

One may recall that the East Asian economies in their high-growth era of the 1970s and 1980s achieved investment–GDP ratios of more than 30 per cent. This was facilitated as much by macroeconomic stability as by public interventions in incentive structures, and physical and social infrastructures.[29] High savings–investment rates, among other factors, together with a relatively egalitarian growth, helped these economies to achieve full employment and structural transformation.

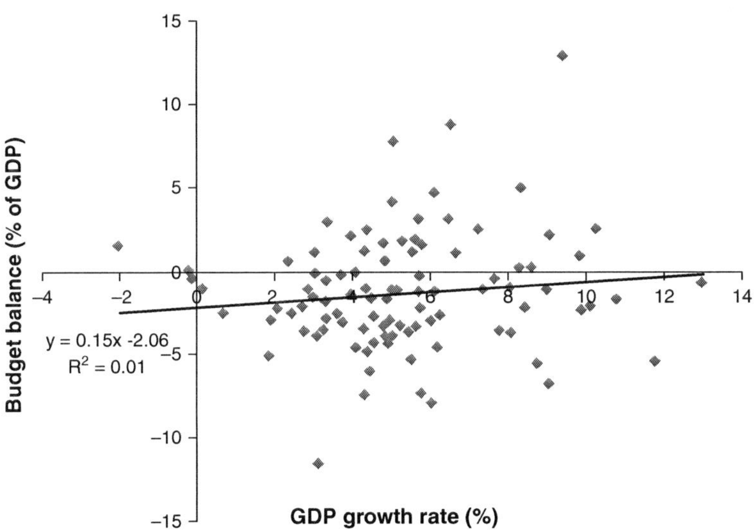

Figure 6.4 Budget balance and GDP growth rate, average 2002–06
Source: The World Bank, World Development Indicators 2009 Online database.

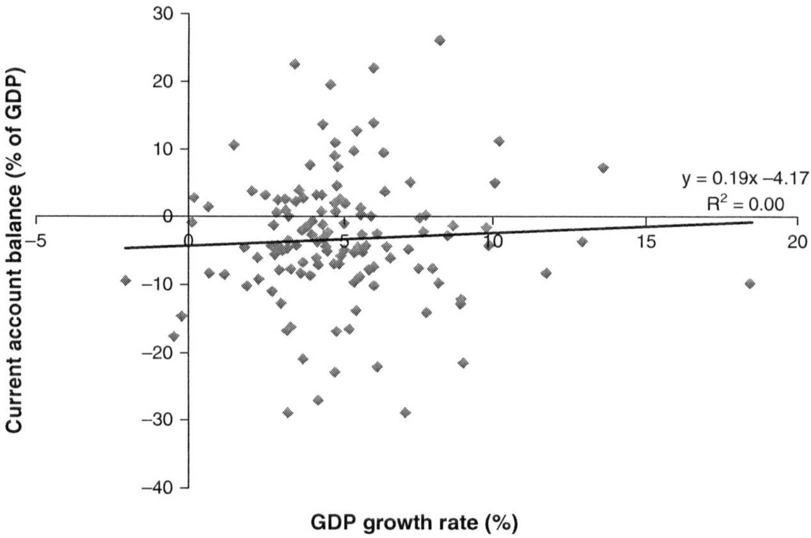

Figure 6.5 Current account balance and GDP growth rate, average 2002–06
Source: The World Bank, World Development Indicators 2009 Online database.

Such achievements would be less forthcoming when stabilization *per se* tends to return a low growth, rates of investment show declining trends, and the savings–investment gap continues to widen.[30] This is precisely what had been happening, especially in Africa during the 1980s and 1990s, i.e. investment/GDP ratio was low, at around 20 per cent, while the savings rate was around 10 per cent (see Muqtada 2009).

Indeed one must note that, during the global boom of 2002–07, or even a few years before, the African economies did grow at a healthy rate. Investments also grew. How far could this be attributed to the *stabilization per se* that took place in many African economies? Without denying that African economies were much more stable at the start of the present decade, than they had been in the past two, one must note that the increase in growth was also strongly associated with the sudden boom in commodity prices, the rise in foreign direct investment, and the availability of resources released through major debt cancellations by the donor countries. Domestic investment rose only slightly but growth seems to have been spurred significantly through FDI, which has grown steadily since the late 1990s and reached a peak of 3 per cent of GDP in 2007.[31] However, the investment ratio, particularly in sub-Saharan Africa, is still well below the levels attained by the East Asian countries during their high-growth period.[32]

While macroeconomic, financial and institutional reforms would be needed to encourage an acceleration of resource mobilization and domestic savings, most African countries are increasingly looking forward to FDI and debt relief. For long-term growth, domestic investment would need to increase secularly. However, as we noted, investment growth would tend to depend on numerous factors, besides the stabilization indicators. This would call for broadening the 'targets' in the macroeconomic policy designs.

Crises and macroeconomic policies

An immediate policy challenge during any major crisis is to bring the macroeconomic framework of the economy in order. Throughout history, crises appear to have induced major changes in existing policy measures to restore macroeconomic balances and confidence in the markets. The rationale has been straightforward, especially since many of the past crises, originating in a particular country, have been induced by (either singly or through a combination of) inflation episodes, currency crisis, bloated public borrowing, or defaults in the balance of payments. With the help of lessons drawn from the Great Depression and recovery, the advanced economies, during subsequent crisis, have tended to follow unorthodox policies, especially through lowering of policy rates and expansionary fiscal policies to restore consumer and market confidence.

The story has, however, been different for the developing countries. During the recent crisis episodes, policymakers, often under the aegis of the Bretton Woods institutions, were advised to follow orthodox pro-cyclical policies to restore macroeconomic stability. Such pro-cyclical policies usually included drastic reductions in public spending to curb budget deficits; hiking interest rates to contain inflation; and compressing imports to reduce current account deficits. In a situation of dramatic declines in GDP, such orthodox attempts to deal with macroeconomic instability could only reduce aggregate demand, thereby often accelerating the negative growth trends.[33] This was indeed the situation in many recent crises: the case of the Asian financial crisis 1997–98 stands out in particular. What apparently started as a currency crisis in Thailand (which had kept its currency pegged to the dollar despite its rapid depreciation) mutated rapidly into a full-scale financial crisis precipitated by a market panic resulting from a rapid outflow of short-term capital.[34] The crisis spread to neighbouring Malaysia, Indonesia and the Republic of Korea which were growing at 7–8 per cent per annum in the preceding years. Even such economies were reduced to near stagnation. During the slump in growth, some of these countries adopted pro-cyclical measures, largely advocated by the IMF, through bank closures, cuts in public spending and the raising of interest rates – which further weighed down aggregate demand. In fact, investment/GDP rates in Thailand declined from 41 to 22 per cent in 1998.[35] It may be recalled that these economies, prior to the 1997–98 crisis, could hardly be faulted for not having sound macroeconomic fundamentals. Fortunately, these economies reversed their policy stances, largely through fiscal stimulus packages and the lowering of interest rates, in order to restore growth. Thus, during economic downturns and recessionary tendencies, the adoption of counter-cyclical measures, including a focused and well-targeted fiscal stimulus, is critical in raising/sustaining aggregate demand, GDP, growth and job creation. This lack of sensitivity in the stabilization policies to how these may affect aggregate demand is not only a shortfall in the orthodox macroeconomic policy framework but is particularly perverse when a crisis-hit country is struggling to recover.[36]

Let us turn to the recent global financial and economic crisis of 2008–09, which came suddenly after an unprecedented global boom period. This crisis, which had been triggered by the house price crash in the United States, had a rapid impact on the country's banking and financial sectors, and spread rapidly to every other sector of the economy. Thanks to the increasing levels of global integration, the crisis spread across the world.[37] This led to adverse employment and labour market outcomes, not only in the advanced countries, but also via several transmission channels, in many in the developing world (see Figure A6.2 in the Appendix for some comparative snapshots of increase in unemployment across the regions). Figure 6.6 shows one example of real world effects of the crisis, that of Mexico.

It is precisely in a scenario in which growth and employment are badly affected that pro-cyclical policies, adopted in the cause of stabilization, are only likely to aggravate the crisis situation. Unfortunately, the Washington Consensus and the conservative macroeconomic policy stance continue to feature strongly in the Bretton Woods advocacy even during this present economic catastrophe. At the G20 London Jobs Summit, the IMF sent out a strong warning to countries to stick to a policy of macroeconomic stabilization, while at the same time acknowledging the necessity for the massive, coordinated fiscal stimulus packages unveiled by the advanced countries.[38] For the latter, these anti-cyclical measures are seen as temporary, time-bound and targeted.[39] Nevertheless, it would appear as 'double standards' should

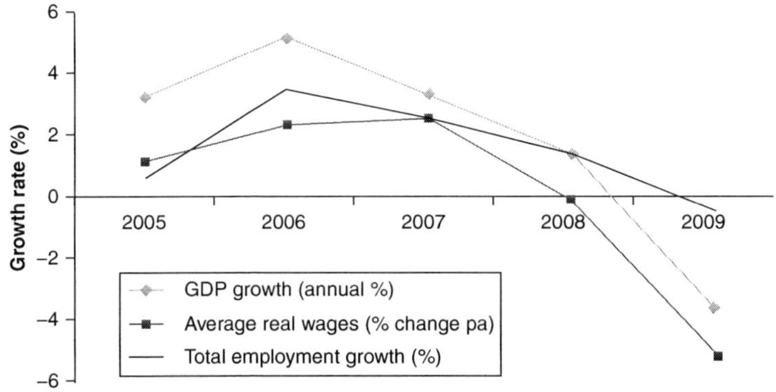

Figure 6.6 Growth, employment and wages in Mexico
Sources: International Monetary Fund, World Economic Outlook Database, April 2009 for GDP growth; EIU, WorldData for average real wages (% change pa); ILO, KILM, 5th edition for total employment 2004–07 and EIU, WorldData for employment 2008, 2009.

the developing world, in the face of a similar growth and jobs crisis, be denied access to such measures. While containing the debt-to-GDP ratio may be relatively easier for the developed countries, ways must be found to support enhancing the fiscal space of developing countries in order to mount a fiscal stimulation of the economy. The various stand-by loan agreements that IMF has reached in the post-crisis period appear to suggest that the orthodox package of stabilization still continues to dominate such agreements. The recent agreement with Pakistan and Ukraine, for example, are cases in point.[40] It must be noted, however, that the crisis has put the IMF and its orthodox policies under the spotlight, and very recently the IMF has come around to acknowledge that a rethink of macroeconomic policy is required (see Box 6.1).

The macroeconomics of crises need to be framed in the context of the nature and causes of the crisis, and about the nature of its effects. The food security crisis, for example, that took place just before the financial crisis in 2008, created high inflation episodes in some countries. Policymakers in some countries were quick to conduct conventional, restrictive monetary policy to contain inflation, when in fact such price increases came about due to external 'supply shocks'. Hailu (2009a) provides a graphic presentation of misplaced policy priorities in the case of Ethiopia.

The recent global financial and economic crisis as faced by the individual countries is an externally induced one, transmitted sharply through such channels as falling trade, financial flows, FDIs, remittances

Box 6.1: IMF's rethinking on macroeconomic policy

A recent staff position paper by Blanchard et al. (2010) provides possibly the first serious introspection by IMF on what has been a long and rigid IMF policy position with respect to macroeconomic strategy. The paper laments that 'we (the IMF) thought of monetary policy as having one target, inflation, and one instrument, the policy rate' (p. 3), thereby acknowledging (and as argued in our chapter) that there can be *multiple targets* in a macroeconomic strategy, and *multiple instruments* to attain these targets. In particular, the paper relents on the singular focus on inflation ('...behavior of inflation is much more complex than is assumed...' p. 7) since macroeconomic stability (i.e. output and price moderation) can be affected by several other factors (see Muqtada 2003). What the paper fails to mention explicitly is the distinction between end-targets and intermediate targets of macroeconomic policy; and that price stability earned through strict monetary policy could not be sustained unless, as Keynes points out, aggregate output/employment was allowed to settle at less than full-employment equilibrium.

The paper thus recognizes the role of fiscal policy as a significant tool, especially in times of crisis when counter-cyclical measures are warranted, and when monetary policy often reaches its limits, as observed in Japan during the 1990s, and now, in the advanced economies during the 2008–09 crisis.

The paper is rather fleeting in the context of macroeconomic options for the developing countries; these are countries where IMF's conditional lending has been a major source of discontent. The paper's call for exploring the consequences of raising the target of policy rate from existing 2 per cent to 4 per cent may appear sensitive to the developed countries but, as we have seen earlier, such inflation targeting will still remain insensitive to the conditions prevailing in the developing countries. In fact, Khan and Senhadji (2001) suggest for the latter group of countries, an inflation threshold of 11–12 per cent beyond which growth will be hampered. We have estimated the following decade-wise table to show (i) the large variations that can exist in the inflation-growth relationship and (ii) to suggest countries (in 2008–09) which obtained around 4 per cent per capita GDP growth had inflation of more than 10 per cent.

The IMF stocktaking fails to acknowledge a distinction between "inflation targeting" and targeting a stable inflation level.

GDP per capita growth growth (annual %)

	INF <3%	**INF≥3% and <5%**	**INF ≥5% and <10%**	**INF ≥10%**
1960–1970	2.9	3.5	3.6	1.5
1971–1980		5.6	2.2	3.2
1981–1990	0.7	2.3	2.0	0.6
1991–2000	2.0	1.9	2.7	0.9
2001–2008	1.9	2.7	3.5	4.0

Source: World Bank, WDI 2009; author's calculations.
Notes: INF = consumer price inflation, annual (%).

Finally, the paper is strikingly silent on the entire question of full employment as an objective (target) of macroeconomic policy, and how output stability could be sustained without appropriately addressing issues related to sustaining/increasing aggregate demand. Nevertheless, the paper marks important first steps in re-evaluating the manner of how the IMF's conditional lending needs to operate.

and ODA. With reduced growth and falling revenues, many developing countries – especially the LDCs in sub-Saharan Africa – would have little fiscal space to initiate a much-needed expansionary macroeconomic policy, not only to address the immediate vulnerable groups, but also to restore growth (see chapter 7 of this volume for more details on fiscal and policy space). This is precisely one consideration where a coordinated global macroeconomic policy could meaningfully address concerns of the developing world, viz. the enhancement of a fiscal space that could help the poor countries to install some instruments of automatic stabilization. It is only the higher-order middle-income countries, especially the emerging economies, which have, contrary to orthodox macro policies, undertaken substantial fiscal spending, based largely on 'reserves' they have built up over the past few years. In these countries, public debts have gone up, and foreign exchange reserves have gone down; depending on the duration and depth of the crisis

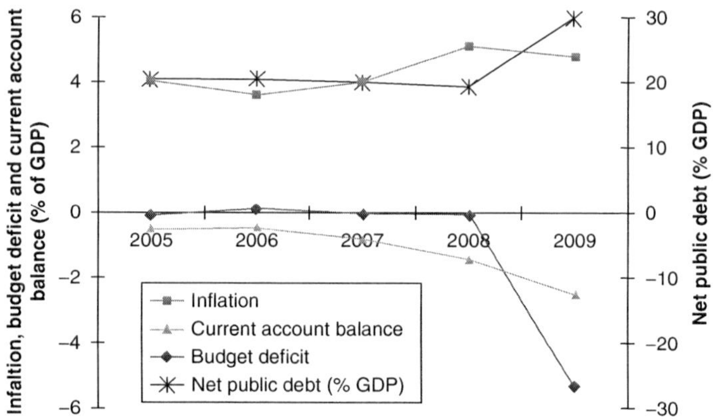

Figure 6.7 Macro fundamentals in Mexico, 2005–09
Sources: EIU, WorldData for budget balance and net public debt; IMF, World Economic Outlook Database, April 2009, for current account balance and inflation.

and its impact, the macro fundamentals of some of these countries are already being threatened.

Again, to take an example from the recent experience of Mexico, Figure 6.7 brings out the 2008 cut-off points, where relative stability has started giving way to crisis-induced macroeconomic *instability*. It is the relative reserve position, the debt–GDP ratio, as well as the pace of recovery that will determine the resilience of these economies. The rest of the developing countries, in the absence of external resources, would have to embark on an aggressive resource mobilization and fiscal consolidation not only to support the weak and fragile labour market and social protection frameworks, but also to finance a job-led recovery. Donor support may be absolutely crucial for some of the poorer countries, who may otherwise be left to tread the more risky route of downsizing aggregate demand.

Towards an employment-focused macroeconomic policy

As we have observed, macroeconomic policy designs in developing countries, often under the 'conditionalities' of loan agreements with the Bretton Woods institutions, had effectively become *uni-dimensional* (that is, largely focused on getting prices right), without adequate consideration being given to the various other targets of a macroeconomic policy framework. Economic growth was seen to be contingent on a country's ability to attain macroeconomic stability, while the various goals of development – such as job generation, labour market outcomes, and social progress – effectively became hostage to such reforms.

The onset of the PRSPs purported to place 'poverty reduction' at the centre of World Bank's lending to heavily indebted countries did not quite rationalize a macroeconomic framework that firmly addressed a poverty-reducing employment-centred growth. Not surprisingly, the PRSP process triggered a complete rethinking of the development strategy. Development was back on the agenda, with the increasing recognition that an employment-friendly growth pattern is the relatively surer way to attain sustained poverty reduction in an economy.[41]

The achievement of full employment, however, is inherently related to a gamut of economic and social policies. ILO (1999) underscores two 'precepts' that would contribute to moving an economy toward full employment: (i) 'achieving economic growth of the type that makes good use of the assets which the poor own (i.e. labour)...'; and (ii) 'any strategy for full employment must be based on a sound macroeconomic framework'. Thus, pursuing and designing a full employment strategy would essentially lie in articulating a combination of economic policies (*including macroeconomic*) and social policies which would fully engage the labour force in expanding productivity, ensure their basic social protection and develop the necessary institutional framework.

It would be only logical to presume that if macroeconomic policies were to be embedded in a country's development strategy, which focused on productive employment generation as the tested path to reduce poverty, then employment would need to be at the centre of macroeconomic policy design. As we observed earlier, in the advanced economies, in the immediate post-Second World War period, the goal of achieving full employment was a key objective in their macroeconomic framework. Only when these economies had achieved nearly two decades of uninterrupted growth, and a situation of near full employment, was there an intensification of the macro policy debate about whether – and to what extent – inflation or employment should become the dominant focus of such policies, such as would keep aggregate supply and demand in balance.[42] As Brown (2002) has pointed out, the roles of macroeconomic and microeconomic policies appear to have reversed over time, i.e. macroeconomic policies, which during the 1950s and 1960s had targeted full employment, shifted during the 1970s and 1980s to targeting inflation and prices. Microeconomic policies which in earlier periods had been used to contain inflation (particularly through the moderation of wages), are now being charged with the responsibility of promoting employment and employability (for example, through active labour market policies). This change in roles of macro policies has to be viewed in the context of the changing assumptions in respect of an individual country's growth and employment situation. The debates about what should be the key objectives of macro policies must not become mired in a rather simplistic ideological positioning. The advanced economies, as seen earlier, are still saddled with unacceptable levels of unemployment. As in the case of EU, although the Maastricht Treaty stipulates stringent stability requirements, high unemployment rates in many countries have kept the debate alive on how measures could be undertaken to enhance aggregate demand, and thereby sustain labour demand.[43] The crisis of 2007–09, which has led to a significant rise in joblessness, has underscored the need for a coordinated, expansionary macroeconomic policy design for the region.[44]

A shift in the key emphases in the macroeconomic policy framework would, of course, imply a shift in the trade-offs desired by a country's policy planners. The critical issue here must be one of *pragmatism* and *policy coherence*. Guidance to macro-design must, therefore, come from a simple, appropriately assessed empirical situation of the individual economy. Over the course of the past six decades, the experiences of macroeconomic policy design, with their variable outcomes, in both the developing and advanced economies, have produced an adequate knowledge base that could inform current policymaking with pragmatic lessons. One such pragmatic lesson appears to be to avoid 'one-size-fits-all' targets since the instruments to achieve these targets could vary from country to country.

In the case of developing countries, where job generation in order to pursue the policy of poverty reduction will continue to dominate the development agenda for quite some time, macroeconomic policy design, without an unambiguous weight to employment objective, would be a 'highly risky method of policymaking'.[45] Lessons can be easily drawn from the experiences of East Asian countries and Chile, where macro-fundamentals were achieved in tandem with macroeconomic and incentive support towards investment and savings, and labour-intensive industrialization and exports. Further, macroeconomic policies also ensured an equity-sensitive growth pattern that helped to support a more rapid pace of poverty reduction.[46] These experiences amply demonstrate the critical role of macroeconomic policies in sustaining macroeconomic fundamentals, as well as in enhancing growth and employment generation. The *uni-dimensional* perception of macroeconomic policies (such as 'inflation targeting'), hitherto practised under the stabilization programme, needs to change. This appears to be the foremost imperative of macroeconomic policy design for the developing countries, especially those with high poverty levels and underutilized labour.

A second imperative of macroeconomic policy, especially as highlighted crucially by the recent crises, is the need to incorporate measures to reduce the volatility of growth, and to offset jobs and income insecurity that it entails. While such volatility can be triggered by external shocks, national policies and institutions need to be in place to ensure protection, especially the most vulnerable groups. Even in the case of some of the relatively strong economies of Asia, the pervasive impact of the 1997 Asian crisis on the world of work exposed a common lacuna, viz. the weak and fragile labour market and social protection frameworks.[47] The huge toll in terms of worker layoffs, loss or reduction of earnings and wages, and so on, forced governments to undertake an array of social safety net measures. The global financial crisis has further underscored the increasing need to establish social security systems[48] in the developing countries. While this has been echoed in various platforms, e.g. at the recent G20 meetings, as well as by multilateral organizations (e.g. World Bank's 'vulnerability fund'), there needs to be a clearly defined national blueprint for how such a system could be developed and financed. Countries with adequate fiscal space, such as China, India and Brazil, have embarked on various safety net and social protection measures, though not along the lines usually adopted in the advanced economies. Although rudimentary in scope and coverage, such social protection systems when internalized in a macroeconomic framework would, in addition to reducing insecurity, tend to act as important regulators of the economy, in particular through sustaining consumption and aggregate demand during recessionary periods. This is, in fact, at the heart of the 'automatic stabilizers' in the macroeconomic policy design of the advanced welfare economies. The poorer developing countries, which during crises usually resort to (often with donor support) discretionary interventions and extensions of existing safety net programmes, need to make their first assessments at what it would take to install a basic social protection system, one that their macroeconomic policy design could incorporate as an approximate automatic stabilizer.

Concluding remarks

The debates about the design of macroeconomic policies have largely been inspired by the ideological divide between demand-side and supply-side approaches to economic performances, in the context of both advanced industrialized countries and developing countries. In particular, the strict version of macroeconomic stability inspired by the Washington Consensus came to be challenged, both by the development strategists, and also by the dismal country experiences of the 1980s and 1990s. The latter, in particular, have echoed the need to formulate a macroeconomic policy framework that would need to be country-specific, and pragmatic, and one that would be embedded in the development strategy of the individual country. Orthodox macroeconomic stabilization policies focused largely on price discipline ('inflation targeting'), leaning on economic levers to ease supply constraints. The fundamental inadequacy of this framework is their lack of understanding of what Krugman (1998) called the 'failures on the demand side of the economy'. For developing countries, in particular, especially those with large surplus labour and poverty levels, a prudent use of monetary and fiscal levers would be needed to address the critical goals of attaining fiscal space for focused public interventions towards enhancing growth, employment generation and social protection. Indeed, such levers also would need to ensure macroeconomic targets that are defined by the economy's toleration limits (of inflation and fiscal deficits).

In the final analysis, a macroeconomic strategy would essentially constitute the individual country's political charter inasmuch as it would require making a collective choice on how it wishes to pursue its development agenda that is defined by the goals of employment generation and poverty alleviation. Its design and implementation would have to take into account the institutional infrastructure and the stakeholders' coalition in the individual countries. Macroeconomic strategy would continue to involve making hard choices on potential trade-offs, such as between employment and inflation; social transfers and fiscal space; and tax policies and incentive structures.

A macroeconomic policy framework would thus entail not only consensus-building among various stakeholders, but also reforms in institutional and decision-making processes towards policy coherence. One way of developing such a consensus is a modified mandate of the macroeconomic policy managers, currently the central bank and finance ministry, to formally endorse the goal of 'full and productive employment and decent work for all' as enshrined in the MDGs.[49] The 'crisis before the crisis',[50] which was characterized by dismal employment and labour market outcomes, as well as the 2008–09 crisis, which has increased the incidence of vulnerable working population, should be powerful reminders why the course of macroeconomic policy design and management needs to change.

Notes

An earlier version of this chapter was published as a working paper by the ILO under the title 'The crisis of orthodox macroeconomic policy: the case for a renewed commitment to full employment', Employment Working Paper No 53, Geneva, 2010.

1. See the text of Commitment 3 of the Copenhagen Declaration and Programme of Action of the World Summit for Social Development, 1995.
2. See Hailu (2009c). A study by Weisbrot et al. (2009) maintains that in 31 out of 41 countries that have financing agreements with the IMF, the conditionalities entailed pro-cyclical macroeconomic policies.
3. For an account of the principles behind these reforms, see World Development Report, 1991; also Williamson (1997).
4. For a defence, see Krueger (1992); Fischer (1993); Bredenkamp and Schadler, eds (1999); critiques from various standpoints include Banuri (1990); Muqtada (2003); I. Islam (2003); McKinley (2001); Stiglitz (1998); Taylor (1988), among others.
5. See Muqtada (2003, 2009).
6. Data taken from WDI database in World Bank (2009).
7. This draws on Muqtada (2009); there is a lot of scepticism expressed with regard to the econometrics, as well as the policy conclusions in respect of such 'growth equations'. Cf. Bazza and Clemens (2009).
8. Cf. Easterly (2001).
9. World Bank (2005).
10. See World Bank (2005); Muqtada (2003).
11. During the era of globalization, developing countries were often strongly urged by IMF and other stakeholders to liberalize their financial sector, and capital account. The Asian financial crisis 1997–98, and the recent recession of 2008–09, exposed the grave risks of such liberalization, unless appropriate domestic regulations, and capital controls (esp. on short-term debts) were not put in place. Ostry et al. (2010) contends that capital controls are necessary in order to shield developing countries from external shocks and financial instability. Malaysia and Chile during the 1980s and China and India in the subsequent period adopted, to their advantage, a cautious approach to capital account liberalization.
12. See Kalter et al. (2004) for an account of how Chile combined stabilization reforms with other economic policies and appropriate institution-building.
13. Also see Williamson's own evaluation of how far the Washington Consensus has been misjudged, in Besley (2005).
14. See Besley (2005). Emphasis added.
15. Ibid.
16. Banuri (1990); Taylor (1988); also World Bank (2005).
17. See McKinley (2001); Ocampo (2002) among many others.
18. World Bank (2005).

19. See Muqtada (2003) for some related estimates.
20. See Bredenkamp and Schadler (1999).
21. For example, see Angeriz and Arestis (2008); also Epstein (2003).
22. See Khan (2006).
23. For a detailed discussion on growth and price stability see Fischer (1993); World Bank (2005); Muqtada (2003); I. Islam (2003); Epstein (2003).
24. See also Khan and Shenhadji (2001).
25. See Banuri (1990), among others on role of institutions and group bargains in controlling inflation.
26. See also Muqtada (2003).
27. See, for example, McKinley (2001).
28. A regression of growth on inflation, budget deficit, current account deficit and investment generates the following estimates (pooled data for 103 countries):

$$\begin{aligned} GDP = {} & 0.347\ (0.27) + 0.128 Inf^{*}\ (2.91) - 0.035 BD\ (-0.54) \\ & + 0.052 CAD\ (1.37) + 0.169 INV^{*}\ (2.93) \end{aligned}$$

    T-values in parentheses; * denotes significance at 5% level.
29. For an identification of the conditions for greater private investment in developing countries, see UN (2001).
30. Griffin (2001) makes a persuasive call for an investment-led growth strategy for Africa.
31. Figure is for Africa, see the African Development Indicators Online database.
32. For a recent assessment of relative issues, see Ndikunama and Verick (2008).
33. See for example Weisbrot (2009); Krugman (1998).
34. See Lee (1998); also for a brief account in the social impact of the Asian crisis.
35. Lee (1998).
36. Krugman (1998).
37. See Lin (2008); also Reinhart and Rogoff (2009a,b).
38. Chair's Report of the London Jobs conference 2009 of the G20 countries (mimeo).
39. Muqtada (2009).
40. See Muqtada (2009); Hailu (2009b) states that IMF's recent stand-by loan agreements with 15 countries contain nearly 224 types of conditionalities, largely in the areas of fiscal reforms; financial liberalization, trade reforms, price liberalization, privatization etc.
41. See R. Islam (2006) for an exposition of the growth–employment–poverty nexus.
42. See the collection of essays in Khan and Muqtada (1997).
43. Ibid.
44. Cf. ILO (1999).
45. See Khan (2006).
46. Cf. World Bank (2005); also see Bhaduri.
47. For a detailed account, see Lee (1998), op. cit.
48. An example is ILO's campaign towards a 'global social floor' (see ILO's Global Jobs Pact in ILO (2009))
49. See Epstein (2003); Muqtada (2003).
50. Cf. ILO/IILS (2009).

Appendix

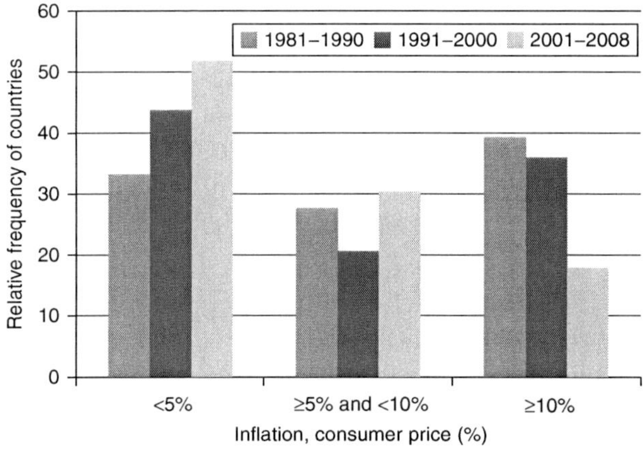

Figure A6.1 Frequency distribution of inflation rates (1980–2006)

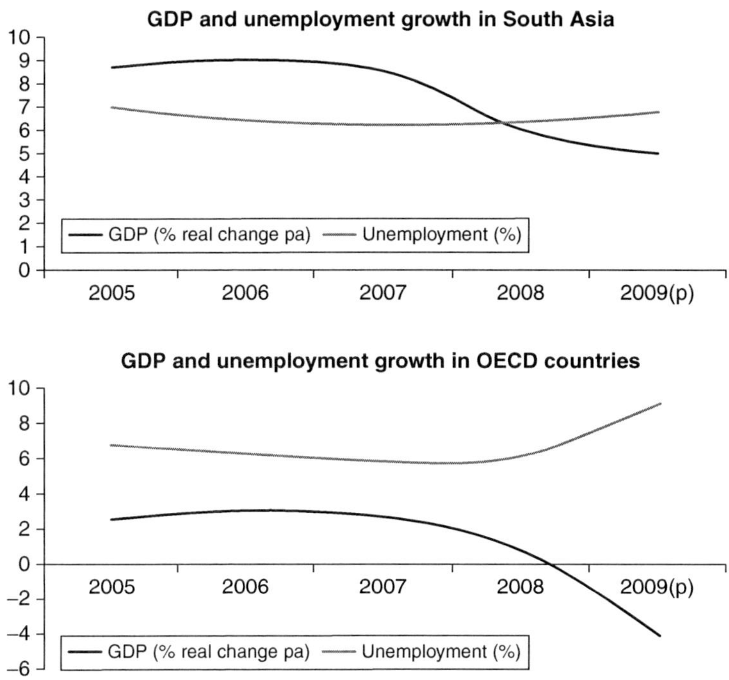

Figure A6.2 (Continued overleaf)

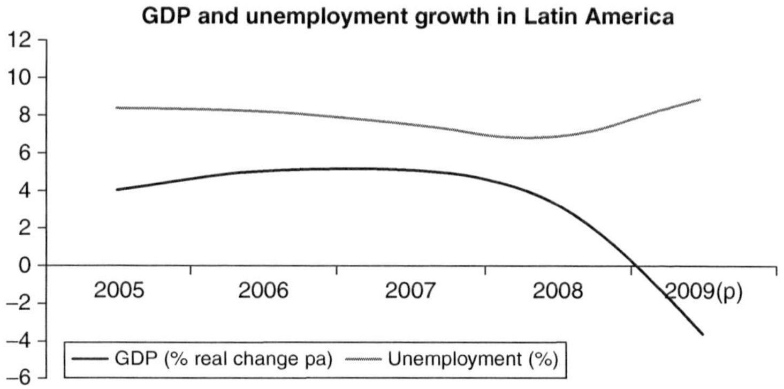

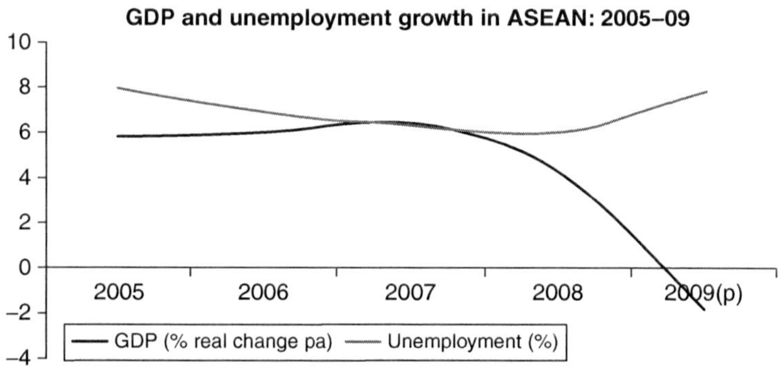

Figure A6.2 GDP and unemployment growth – inter-regional comparisons
Notes: 2009(P): Projection.
Source: EIU, WorldData 2009.

7
The Perennial Quest for Fiscal and Policy Space in Developing Countries

I. Islam

Introduction

A standard lament in the development literature is that many low- and middle-income countries are in an invidious position because of a lack of 'policy' and 'fiscal' space. This has been compounded by the food and energy price shocks that prevailed between 2007 and 2008 and the severe global recession that emerged in 2008 and continued throughout much of 2009. The consequence of the lack of fiscal and policy space in the developing world is that 'there are large asymmetries in global economic policies – counter-cyclical policies are pursued by developed countries, while most developing countries pursue pro-cyclical policies'.[1] Others concur. As is noted in the *Global Monitoring Report of 2009*: '... most developing countries faced with sharply declining growth and consequent major social disruptions lack the resources to mount any fiscal response, and will in fact experience a further erosion of their fiscal space as public revenues fall and external financing dries up'.[2]

Thus, the re-creation of fiscal and policy space for developing countries on a sustainable basis needs to be a central feature of the global development agenda. This chapter starts with an overview of 'principles of good policy design' that are essential in the conduct of economic management both during crisis periods and during normal times. Such principles are equally applicable to both developed and developing countries. It then offers alternative interpretations of fiscal and policy space. It proceeds to highlight how many developing countries are vulnerable to external shocks and fiscal constraints. This serves as a prelude to a discussion of feasible options to enhance fiscal and policy space to fortify the capacity of developing countries to cope with global downturns and external shocks and to secure a sustainable recovery. This will require a combination of national commitment and international cooperation.

Principles of good policy design[3]

As a preamble to the discussion on fiscal and policy space, it is useful to start with a discussion of the principles of good policy design. One can reiterate some well-known guidelines – applicable to both developed and developing countries – that can serve as a basis for good policy design in the context of a crisis as well as in more normal periods. The main message is to avoid or attenuate trade-offs among competing policy goals and to avoid or attenuate circumstances in which particular policy instruments become ineffective. This will enhance the capacity of policymakers to deal with crises and external shocks. From the perspective of labour market policies, these principles also highlight their relevance and limitations as an integral part of crisis-mitigation measures and long-term development strategies. The suggested principles of good policy design are as follows.

- Multiple goals require multiple instruments (the 'correspondence' principle).
- Appropriate instruments should be assigned to relevant goals (the 'assignment' principle).
- Policy initiatives should be feasible and fiscally sustainable (the 'feasibility and sustainability' principle).

Table 7.1 illustrates the 'correspondence' and 'assignment' principle. This is complemented by a brief discussion of the 'feasibility and sustainability' principle. The latter discussion in turn paves the way for a fuller analysis of fiscal and policy space as seen through the prism of developing countries.

From Table 7.1, the key implication is that if the range of policy instruments is not broad enough to match the diversity of goals, then it will lead to unmanageable policy trade-offs. Thus, for example, relying solely on those instruments that can deal with the particular case of formal economy workers will not cater to the specific circumstances of workers in the informal economy. Furthermore, labour market policies cannot fulfil the functions of conditional cash transfers that often deal with the case of the health and education of children that are outside the workforce. Hence, one needs a 'mix and match' strategy.

Table 7.1 Goals, instruments and crisis response package – some examples

Relevant goals	**Appropriate instruments (examples)**
Reduce output gap induced by a downturn	Counter-cyclical monetary, fiscal and exchange rate policies
Enhance access to credit for non-tradable and tradable sectors, especially SMEs	Credit allocation and trade finance
Mitigate employment and real wage impact of business cycles: formal economy workers	Severance pay, unemployment assistance/insurance, work-sharing arrangements
Mitigate employment and real wage impact of business cycles: informal and rural economy workers	Employment guarantee scheme
Enhance employability and redeployment of displaced workers	Training and various 'activation' measures that fall under the rubric of active labour market policies (ALMPs)
Preserve human capital investments of poor and vulnerable HHs	Conditional cash and in-kind transfers + sustained public investment in health, education and infrastructure

Notes: Employment guarantee schemes can also be subsumed under ALMPs. The purpose of making a distinction between employment guarantee schemes and ALMPs as a generic category is that the latter contains elements that are not necessarily targeted towards workers in the informal economy and rural areas.

It is not sufficient just to have a 'mix and match strategy'. It is necessary to ensure that the desired policy instruments can be implemented effectively and that they are fiscally sustainable. One can think of a range of circumstances in which the 'feasibility and sustainability' principle will be impaired. Here are some examples.

- 'Liquidity trap': As is well known, a 'liquidity trap' emerges when the level of aggregate economic activity does not respond sufficiently, even if the interest rate is nominally zero, thus signifying that monetary policy will be ineffective in dealing with downturns. A 'liquidity trap' can also emerge in the context of a 'balance sheet recession', that is a situation where the private sector is debt-constrained and thus cannot respond adequately to the reduced cost of borrowing by increasing the demand for consumption (especially durables and housing) and investment. The global economic crisis of 2008–09 in the advanced economies and emerging economies in some parts of Eastern Europe reflect a 'balance sheet recession'.

- 'Liability dollarization': This is when the liabilities of either the private or public sector are denominated in dollars and the assets are denominated in local currency. In such a situation, policymakers develop a 'fear of floating' and of engaging in expansionary policies. This is discussed more fully at a subsequent stage.
- Synchronized global recession leading to a generalised fall in external demand: Exchange rate depreciations will be largely ineffective. The global economic crisis of 2008 and 2009 reflected a high degree of synchronicity. This is unlike the Asian financial crisis when the crisis-affected economies experienced exchange rate depreciations and could 'export' their way out of a region-wide recession.
- Lack of fiscal and institutional capacity: This afflicts many developing countries. Hence, they cannot engage in counter-cyclical interventions to cope with economic downturns and external shocks even if they have the political will to do so. This means better preparedness by developing countries should happen *before* a crisis inflicts damage on them.

In sum, crisis mitigation measures and economic policies during normal times should take on board the principles of good policy design embodied in the correspondence, assignment, feasibility and sustainability principles. If they are not followed, the responses will be suboptimal.

Dealing with the crisis and securing sustainable recovery: the issue of fiscal and policy space[4]

The discussion of the principles of good policy design serves as a precursor to the analysis of fiscal and policy space in developing countries. As will be seen, there are multiple interpretations of both fiscal and policy space.

Fiscal space: two interpretations

The IMF view of fiscal space: the importance of fiscal sustainability

A prominent IMF economist defines fiscal space as 'the room in a government's budget that allows it to provide resources for a desired purpose without jeopardizing the sustainability of its financial position or the stability of the economy'.[5] The emphasis is thus on maintaining fiscal sustainability. There is no explicit reference to core development goals other than a generic reference to the need to 'provide resources for a desired purpose'.

An alternative view: fiscal space and public investment

Some analysts closely associated with the UNDP have sought to proffer an approach to fiscal space that serves as an alternative to the IMF view.[6] They contend that the approach of the IMF – and of the other Bretton Woods institutions – to fiscal space is dominated by fiduciary concerns about sustainability at the expense of development objectives. This has led in practice to policy advice that focuses on the attainment of short-run fiscal targets (usually using such indicators as debt/GDP ratios and fiscal deficit/GDP ratios). The primary goal of fiscal policy in this alternative interpretation is to mobilize resources to finance public investment to support long run growth and attain the MDGs.

The available evidence suggests that public investment as a share of GDP has fallen, in some cases precipitously, across both low- and middle-income developing countries.[7] This has been detrimental to long-run growth and the attainment of the MDGs.

Why has public investment declined in developing countries? One answer, according to the UNDP-based literature, lies in the first-generation 'structural adjustment programmes' pioneered by the Bretton Woods institutions (BWIs). In the quest to attain fiscal consolidation, the IMF advised developing-country governments to focus on attaining overall fiscal targets. Little attempt was made to distinguish between the composition of the public budget, or current vs capital expenditure, and its overall size. The consequence was that capital expenditure pertaining to spending on infrastructure was cut to meet overall fiscal targets as it is politically difficult to cut current, non-discretionary expenditure pertaining to wages and salaries of civil servants as well as income transfer programmes. The expectation of the BWIs was that private investment would increase to compensate for the shortfall in public investment, but this has not happened.

An alternative view: fiscal space and social protection

As noted, the IMF view of fiscal space attaches priority to the attainment of financial and fiscal sustainability. Rather less attention is given to the fiscal and financial implications of the attainment of key policy goals. UNDP attempts to redress this lacuna by focusing on financing public investment as a route to achieving core development goals. Complementing this effort are two studies, one by the Overseas Development Institute (ODI) and another by ILO that focus on financing a comprehensive social protection system.[8] The ODI study conceptualizes a comprehensive social protection system in terms of two key components: universal child benefits and social pensions. Based on five cases (Congo, Equatorial Guinea, Ghana, Mali and Senegal), two (Congo, Equatorial Guinea) will have fiscal requirements (1 to 2 per cent of GDP) that are affordable.

The ILO study defines a comprehensive social security package that has a broader reach than the ODI study. The key elements of such a package are: (a) basic old age and disability pensions (benefits set at the rate of 30 per cent of GDP); (b) benefits at the rate of 15 per cent of GDP for the first two children below the age of 14; (c) 100 days guaranteed employment at a wage of 30 per cent of per capita GDP for a maximum of 10 per cent of all people of all ages; and (d) essential health care based on one health professional per 300 persons. Using these benchmarks, the study examined 12 countries, of which seven are in Africa (Burkina Faso, Cameroon, Ethiopia, Guinea, Kenya, Senegal, Tanzania) and the rest are in Asia (Bangladesh, India, Nepal, Pakistan and Viet Nam), using projections for the 2010 to 2030 period. The fiscal requirements range from over 10 per cent of GDP (Burkina Faso) to a little over 4 per cent (Guinea).[9] An optimistic message that emanates from the ILO study is that, with a determined effort at domestic resource mobilization, a low-income country such as Nepal can fund 96 per cent of a comprehensive social security package from its fiscal resources.

In sum, both the UNDP and the ODI/ILO studies pay a good deal of attention to the financial and fiscal implications of attaining core policy goals. The challenge is to identify various options for increasing fiscal space in a sustainable fashion. If many developing countries are hampered by poor initial conditions leading to high fiscal deficits and debt service obligations, what is the way out? How does one 'enhance the room in a government's budget' to pursue policy goals within a framework of fiscal sustainability?

Country-specific vulnerabilities and lack of fiscal space: evidence on the scale of the problem and some suggestions for its alleviation

As a preamble to the discussion of the different ways in which one can enhance fiscal space in developing economies, it would be useful to delineate the number of countries that are vulnerable to external shocks and are also subject to fiscal constraints. Tables 7.2 and 7.3 draw on the work of the IMF and World Bank to depict the scale of the problem. To start with, the IMF ranks countries using simulations based on partial

Table 7.2 Distribution of countries by degree of vulnerability to external shocks

	Number of countries	Total number of countries	Percentage of countries
High vulnerability	26	70	37
Medium vulnerability	31	70	44
Low vulnerability	13	70	19

Source: Extracted from IMF (2009c).

Table 7.3 Distribution of countries by fiscal space

	Number of countries	Total number of countries	Percentage of countries
Low fiscal space	35	103	34
Some fiscal space	40	103	39
Adequate fiscal space	28	103	27

Source: Extracted from World Bank (2009c).

equilibrium exercises to assess the immediate impact on the balance of payments and reserves of the assumed shocks to the trade balance (as a result of lower world market prices and export volumes) and to remittances, FDI and aid.[10] For all shocks combined, 70 countries are ranked in three vulnerability categories – high, medium or low – depending upon the impact of these shocks on reserves. The most vulnerable countries are especially sensitive to trade, aid and remittances shocks, while FDI appears to be a less important transmission channel. The results show 81.4 per cent of the sample has either medium or high vulnerability (Table 7.2).

Table 7.3 measures the ability of a country to finance larger fiscal deficits in order to engage in counter-cyclical spending to cope with vulnerabilities. This is linked to a country's ability to harness additional funding domestically and from abroad without jeopardizing macroeconomic stability or debt sustainability. One hundred and three countries are classified as having low, some and adequate fiscal space.[11] In all, 73 per cent of the countries in the sample have either low or limited fiscal space.

The available evidence suggests therefore that a significant proportion of developing countries cannot cope with vulnerabilities because of fiscal constraints. Hence, it is necessary to explore the various feasible ways in which one can enhance fiscal space and thus fortify the capacity of developing countries to engage in counter-cyclical interventions. Here are some suggestions. Illustrations are offered from the African experience to highlight the relevance and efficacy of various options.

1 *Ensure the efficient utilization of existing resources.* There are many cases of countries in the developing world in waste and inefficiency characterizes the use of existing resources. One study on Africa suggests that 'leakages' from existing budgetary allocation can be quite substantial. In Zambia, for example, the 'leakage' from the education budget in 1999–2000 was about 60 per cent.[12]
2 *Engage in private–public partnerships.* One study suggests that there are 'large liquidities in the financial sector of many African economies'.[13] These liquidities could be tapped through a long-term investment fund based on 'voluntary contributions from the most profitable private and public companies'. A related suggestion from this study is the establishment of a microfinance fund based on ODA and voluntary contributions from the banking system. The purpose of the fund is to 'strengthen synergies between the formal and informal financial sectors'.[14] Although this proposal is based on the African experience, it is clear that it has wider applicability.
3 *Encourage capital repatriation.* Capital flight is a perennial problem in many developing countries. Hence, there should be a renewed commitment to (a) encourage capital repatriation and (b) develop mechanisms to reduce the incidence of capital flight in the future. Countries such as Ethiopia, Rwanda and Ghana have shown that it is possible to encourage Diasporas to invest in their country of origin.
4 *Ensure the efficient utilization of remittances.* Many low- and middle-income countries are among the world's top 20 countries in terms of receipt of remittances (as a proportion of GDP). The aim is not just to increase remittances, but to ensure their efficient utilization. This means (a) encouraging the use of formal channels in tapping remittances and (b) increasing the share of remittances allocated to investment. One good example, with respect to (a), is the use of an innovative and cost-effective remittance-related financial services by a bank in Burundi.[15]
5 *Enhance tax-to-GDP ratio in countries with a low tax burden.*[16] This is 'key to creating fiscal space for ... developmental needs'.[17] Higher domestic revenues can serve to insulate a country from the 'Dutch disease' syndrome and unpredictability that can stem from a heavy reliance on external sources of finance. The average tax-to-GDP ratio

increased moderately in sub-Saharan Africa from 15 per cent of GDP in 1980 to 18 per cent in 2005.[18] Most of this increase was driven by natural resource taxes, while non-resource revenues remained stagnant. Furthermore, in low-income African countries, tax revenue is about 14 per cent of GDP which is below the 15 per cent benchmark that is regarded as a reasonable target for low-income countries. This is not an Africa-specific phenomenon. One study finds that the share of revenue in GDP for all low-income countries fell between 1990 and 2004 and is below the 15 per cent benchmark proposed by the IMF.[19] The aim should be the broadening of the tax base rather than increasing particular tax rates. Several factors, stemming from low compliance to international tax competition, underpin this indifferent performance with respect to domestic resource mobilization.

Enhancing fiscal space: some complications

The aforementioned options to increase fiscal space are subject to various complications. Raising the revenue share in GDP is a long-term agenda and requires a resolute commitment to tax reform. The reallocation of public expenditure and the efficient utilisation of existing resources are easier said than done, in view of institutional and political impediments.

The use of deficit financing is an area where the IMF approach to fiscal space has demonstrated a great deal of circumspection. Fiscal deficits can be financed by borrowing from domestic and external sources and by *seignorage* or money creation. The risk of the former is that it can lead to unsustainable debt service obligations, while the risk of the latter is that it can lead to high inflation. Nevertheless, one should avoid the imposition of rigid fiscal rules. Neither theory nor evidence enables one to argue that developing countries should stick rigidly to low fiscal deficits (say 2 to 3 per cent of GDP, regardless of the state of the business cycle). Some degree of deficit financing should be tolerated, especially if the counterpart of such financing is enhanced public investment in growth-promoting infrastructure.

The phenomenon of a low tax-to-GDP ratio in various parts of the developing world is attributable to several factors. Trade liberalization, by reducing tariffs, has eroded a traditional and major source of revenue in developing countries. This 'fiscal shock', amounting to 2 per cent of GDP according to some estimates, has not been adequately compensated by other sources of tax revenue, most notably value-added and income taxes, partly because of limited institutional capacity and partly because of a lack of political will.[20]

High aid dependence in some countries seems to have reduced tax efforts in some developing countries. In a number of African countries, a growing share of current spending is financed by ODA. The share of current expenditure financed by ODA has increased from 16 to 36 per cent over a period of nine years (1997–99 to 2004–06) in Ghana, from 22 to 40 per cent in Tanzania and from 60 to 70 per cent in Uganda.[21] The problem with excessive reliance on traditional sources of external finance is that it exposes a country to a high degree of volatility. Such volatility of aid flows has gone up in recent years and its cost is estimated at 2 per cent of developing country GDP.[22]

There are other elements of the global development agenda whose implications for domestic resource mobilization need to be highlighted. The global agenda on downsizing the public sector, the need to provide tax incentives to attract foreign direct investment and the rise of international tax havens have all worked against the idea of increasing the share of revenue in GDP through the taxation system.

Many low-income countries, and even some middle-income ones, face a so-called 'tax gap' in which their actual tax collection efforts fall well below their potential. This is a major development agenda that deserves renewed attention in light of continuing debates on lack of fiscal space in developing countries.

Policy space: two interpretations

Multilateral trade rules and policy space

There are two broad strands of the idea of policy space. One argues that multilateral rules under the WTO-based international trading system have constrained the capacity of developing country governments to pursue industry and trade policies that are compatible with national aspirations. This thesis is associated with the work of the United Nations Conference on Trade and Development (UNCTAD), but is not the focus of this chapter.[23]

Capital account liberalization, liability dollarization and policy space[24]

A second strand of thinking on policy space – which is the focus of this chapter – stems from the implications of capital account liberalization in developing countries with access to private capital markets. Such access can lead to so-called 'liability dollarization'. In essence, this means that the private sector acquires liabilities in foreign currency, although assets are denominated in local currency. This makes the balance sheet of the private sector highly sensitive to shifts in the exchange rate. Significant exchange rate depreciations can lead to large and negative wealth effects as liabilities increase in value relative to assets. Such wealth effects often cannot offset the positive impact on competitiveness engendered by exchange rate depreciations.

Developing countries with access to private capital markets often experience sharp changes in capital flows. The most conspicuous – and also the most damaging in terms of its impact on real output, employment and wages – are so-called 'sudden stops', when there is an unanticipated cessation of capital flows that are not linked to any systematic policy errors committed by developing country governments. These sudden stops reflect failures and shortcomings in international capital markets.

The presence of liability dollarization – as well as the lack of preparedness – acts as a binding constraint on policy space. Monetary authorities develop a 'fear of floating' and are therefore reluctant to allow the depreciation of the exchange rate and engage in expansionary policies because of the rather large negative wealth effect stemming from liability dollarization.

During the East Asian financial crisis of 1997, several Asian economies also initially tried in vain to defend their quasi-pegged exchange rate regimes. The Argentinean experience of 1998 to 2001, when the government tried to defend the pegged exchange rate system, also highlights the severe constraints on policy space in the presence of liability dollarization.

Enhancing policy space: some suggestions

Developing countries can, in principle, develop the necessary resilience to cope with global downturns and external shocks. As the experience of some successful examples of crisis management in Latin American and Asian countries has shown, there are several ways of attaining such resilience. Here are some suggestions.

- *Avoid or attenuate 'liability dollarization'.* This will entail prudential regulation of the financial system. More specifically, the monetary and financial authorities should carry out surveillance of the balance sheet of the private sector and administer periodic 'stress tests' to ensure balance sheets will be sustainable when faced with the risk of 'sudden stops'. This could be combined with regulatory changes to implement counter-cyclical capital provisioning so that the financial system has adequate reserves to cope with economic volatility.

- *Engage in economic diversification.* Specialization along the lines of comparative advantage is a standard policy dictum. There is, however, the risk that one can rely too much on the tradable sector and thus make national economies vulnerable to declines in external demand. Hence, the current debate on 'rebalancing' growth models. There is evidence, as one of the chapters has shown, that countries that have a relatively large non-tradable sector seem to have more resilience to external volatility.
- *Engage in some degree of 'self-insurance'* by accumulating fiscal resources during 'boom' periods and use such resources to finance expansionary policies or targeted interventions during a downturn. Countries such as Chile and China have shown that self-insurance is possible. It needs to be emphasized that 'self-insurance' schemes, especially when held in the form of low interest-bearing foreign exchange reserves, can be costly and inefficient. Reducing costly and inefficient forms of 'self-insurance' to deal with external crisis requires regional and global cooperation in undertaking reforms to tackle shortcomings in global capital markets. This, however, is a long-term agenda and will take some time to bear fruit.
- *When faced with 'sudden stops', engage in active capital account management by imposing temporary capital controls.* Developing countries should consider some restrictions on capital account convertibility in order to improve its policy space, especially during crisis. Of the 155 countries surveyed in an IMF study, 119 were reported to have imposed some type of restrictions on certain capital account transactions.[25] These restrictions can slow the speed of capital outflows when a country is faced with the possibility of a sudden and destabilizing withdrawal of capital during a time of uncertainty. They can also break the link between domestic and foreign interest rates, so that crisis-hit economies can pursue expansionary monetary and credit policies as a means of growing their way out of debt or a recession without having to worry about possible capital flight and the weakening of the currency. The *2009 Global Monitoring Report,* jointly published by the IMF and World Bank, endorses the idea of capital controls. As it notes:[26]

> Capital restrictions might be unavoidable as a last resort to prevent or mitigate the crisis effects. A few emerging countries have introduced capital controls and other measures to better monitor and, in some cases, limit the conversion of domestic currency into foreign exchange... capital controls might need to be imposed as a last resort to help mitigate a financial crisis and stabilize macroeconomic developments.

Dealing with the crisis and securing sustainable recovery: the role of regional and global cooperation to augment fiscal and policy space at the national level[27]

Dealing with the global financial crisis of 2007–09 and securing sustainable recovery requires a combination of national commitment and regional and global cooperation. It has to be noted that national 'self-insurance' schemes can impose significant opportunity costs on their practitioners – for example, holding billions of dollars in reserves, many times more than the required threshold, as a precaution against global economic volatility, while commendable, also means that countries are foregoing the opportunity to invest scarce resources in activities with prospective high returns. The proclivity to engage in self-insurance at the national level in low- and middle-income countries can be reduced if such countries have ready access to quick-disbursing, low-conditionality sources of external finance. The aim, after all, is to promote 'fair globalization' by resolving, through collective action, a range of common challenges and concerns that cannot be handled by individual nations acting on their own. These include (but are not limited to): (a) reform of the international financial architecture to temper the excesses of financial globalization; (b) the need to deepen the voice and representation of developing countries in global economic governance; (c) the need to attenuate global asymmetry in national policymaking, with developed countries pursuing counter-cyclical policies and many developing countries either unwilling or unable to pursue counter-cyclical policies when faced with externally generated economic downturns.

Proposition (c) is most germane to the issue of fortifying the capacity of the developing economies to respond to the global economic downturn of 2008–09 and its consequences. The G20 Communiqué of 2 April 2009 represents the first major attempt by the global community to tackle the issue. As the Communiqué notes:

> We have... agreed today to make available an *additional* (US$) 850 billion of resources through the global financial institutions to support growth in emerging market and developing countries by helping to finance counter-cyclical spending, bank recapitalization, infrastructure, trade finance, balance of payments support, debt rollover, and social support.[28]

The G20 communiqué of 2 April 2009 promises an injection of US$1.1 trillion into the global economy. This headline-grabbing number appears to be the sum of US$750 billion to augment existing IMF resources, US$100 billion for multilateral development banks (MDBs) and US$250 billion to support trade finance.

This proposal was foreshadowed by a number of suggestions made by multilateral agencies and development practitioners. Some of these suggestions are summarised in Table 7.4.[29] As can be seen, one suggestion offered by Nancy Birdsall was rather close to the mark.

Is the G20 initiative a 'new deal' that will bring the global economy out of the recession and assist developing economies to cope with the crisis? The leaders of the G20 understandably claim that a global solution to a global crisis has been found. The G20 Summit declaration has also received the endorsement of some leading development practitioners.[30] The planned US$1.1 trillion programme (billed as 'support to rescue credit, growth and jobs in the world economy') is added to the existing fiscal stimulus and financial rescue packages announced by the members of the G20 to proclaim that it will raise world output by 4 per cent, which is roughly the estimated output gap of the global level.

An obvious point to be made is that it is misleading to add the US$1.1 trillion to the existing fiscal stimulus and financial rescue packages. Close to 70 per cent of the former represent additional resources for the IMF. This will only have an impact on the ability of developing countries to enhance their resources if they use IMF financial assistance. The irony, as *The Economist* and others emphasize, is that the IMF is finding it difficult to attract many middle-income economies to even use their existing facilities.[31] Some of the quick-disbursing and low-conditionality innovations that have been used by the IMF – such as the flexible credit lines for middle-income countries – are undersubscribed. There were, as at 25 March 2010, only three countries (Colombia, Mexico and Poland) that had made use of the flexible credit line. In addition, the available financial statistics released by the IMF does not allow one to verify how many countries have made use of the 'rapid credit line' that the IMF launched in January 2010 as an innovative, low-conditionality product for low-income economies.[32]

These are largely the result of a so-called 'reputational' effect. Given that the IMF has played a controversial role in past crisis management episodes, and given the onerous conditions that are attached to IMF assistance programs, this reluctance by member states is understandable. Furthermore, such member states can observe that countries that are under current IMF agreements are being subjected to a typical IMF macroeconomic stabilization-cum-adjustment programme, entailing monetary restraint, fiscal austerity and structural reforms.

Table 7.4 Suggestions for an enhanced global financing facility for developing countries: some examples

Proposed by:	**Title**	**Objectives**	**Amount**
IILS (2009)	Global Jobs Fund	To provide stabilization credit separate from traditional IMF package	Unspecified
United Nations (2009a)	• Immediate: untitled • Long term: New Credit Facility	• To support developing countries so that they can engage in counter-cyclical policies • New and sustainable sources of development finance	• 1% of fiscal stimulus packages of G20 (approx. US$22 billion) + existing aid commitments • Amount for new credit facility unspecified
Zoellick (2009b)	Vulnerability Fund	To provide funds to the most vulnerable countries to finance expenditure on social safety nets, infrastructure, SMEs	0.7% of fiscal stimulus packages of G20 (approx. US$15 billion)
Nancy Birdsall (2009)	Untitled	To roll over sovereign debt, existing bank and corporate debt, to finance fiscal deficits, emergency job and food programs	US$1 trillion (US$829 billion of which will go towards emerging, middle-income economies in Asia, Latin America and Eastern Europe; balance for low income countries).

Once the funds allocated to the IMF and trade finance are taken out, the current G20 initiative appears much more modest – amounting to about US$100 billion new monies proposed for the MDBs to finance a variety of initiatives with both short-term and long-term effects. They fall well short of US$500 billion suggested by Nancy Birdsall (see Table 7.4). One study on sub-Saharan Africa suggests that aid-financed, public investment in infrastructure is essential to compensate for the loss of output and sustain long-term growth in the region. This is tantamount to US$50 billion in sub-Saharan Africa.[33] In other words, 50 per cent of the proposed allocations for the MDBs would need to be spent in one region of the developing world alone. To set this number in a broader context, the estimated output loss so far in the developing world is over US$800 billion.[34]

Critics of the G20 initiative make two important points. First, the leaders of G20 failed to come up with fresh and practical ideas to fix the financial system that is at the core of the global economic crisis that started in 2007. Second, they failed to commit themselves to 'spend the hundreds of billions of dollars in additional fiscal stimulus that the world economy needs to pull out of its frighteningly steep dive'.[35]

There is the unresolved issue of the necessary institutional reforms that need to accompany a substantially expanded role for the IMF. Furthermore, what one needs is not just institutional reform, but a move away from a dollar-based international monetary system to a global reserve currency that will make use of multiple currencies of the major trading blocs.[36] The G20 communiqué makes it clear that this is an agenda that will be tackled later (in 2011). Advocates of the reform of the IFIs are understandably disappointed, fearful of the risk that increased resources in an institutionally unchanged IMF might mean 'business as usual'.

Critics of the G20 initiative contend that insufficient attention has been given to the role that regional and local solutions can play in fortifying the capacity of developing countries to cope with the global economic crisis.[37] Some even make the stronger point that regional approaches are desirable, partly because cooperation is easier to engender and partly because geopolitical considerations can afflict the quality of global solutions to a global economic crisis.[38]

What kind of regional initiatives are underway that have some relevance in dealing with today's crisis? In Latin America, there is a Venezuela-led 'Bank of the South' initiative that seeks to develop regionally rooted facilities that can respond to both short-term financing needs and long-term development finance. In East Asia, there are continuing attempts, since the Chiang Mai Initiative of 2000, to develop regional cooperation to enable participating countries to tide over temporary economic setbacks engendered by external shocks. These regional innovations can be seen as attempt to offer opportunities to participating countries to seek access to fast-disbursing, low-conditionality external sources of finance without having to go through the IFIs.[39]

There is considerable scope for 'peer group' learning in the developing world. Developing countries can learn from their peers in nurturing national initiatives to enhance fiscal and policy space. They can seek lessons from successful cases of crisis management without compromising on policy autonomy (such as Malaysia during the 1997 financial crisis).[40] They can learn from successful operations of national stabilization funds (as in the case of Chile).[41] What is important, however, is not to be tempted to regard such national funds as a time-bound operation that is wound up once the global recession is over. This approach is costly and inefficient. The goal of a stabilization fund is to create the necessary 'fiscal space' to sustain investments in human capital and basic infrastructure across business cycles and to scale up programmes pertaining to passive and active labour market policies to cope with external shocks. Such a fund can be financed from excess revenues collected by the government during normal and boom periods. This illustrates once again the critical role that a renewed commitment to domestic resource mobilization can play in enhancing fiscal and policy space on a sustainable basis. The donor community can provide seed funding and technical assistance, but the success of a national stabilization fund in developing countries ultimately depends on national commitment.

Finally, there appears – in the wake of the global economic and jobs crisis of 2008–09 – a renewed interest in the notion of a tax on international financial transactions (TIFT). This is, of course, an old idea first championed by the Nobel Laureate James Tobin (hence the epithet of the 'Tobin tax'). When the idea was first mooted, it was primarily done to identify a fiscal instrument that could temper the volatility associated with cross-border financial flows of a speculative nature without imposing significant efficiency losses.

Subsequent iterations of the notion of a TIFT have also focused on its potential to raise billions of dollars in development finance that could supplement traditional sources of external finance from bilateral and multilateral sources (aid and debt relief) to finance both regional and global public goods. As noted, the problem with traditional sources of development finance is that they are quite unpredictable in nature; they can be mired in onerous conditionality and compromised by geopolitical considerations. Advocates of a well-designed and well-administered TIFT see it as a particularly potent solution for circumventing the complications associated with traditional sources of development finance. Its critics, on the other hand, continue to highlight its impracticality and the risk that a TIFT could kill the proverbial goose (in this case a buoyant financial sector and deepening of financial integration) that lays the golden egg.

It appears that what is important here is the need for the collective political will among systemic nations to undertake the due diligence that would be necessary as a preamble to the application of a TIFT. The widely shared view that iconic financial institutions in the United States, United Kingdom and elsewhere have played a key role in triggering the global recession of 2008 and 2009 have probably created a conducive global environment in which the design and imposition of a TIFT could become part of the international policy agenda. Still, there is no unified view among, say, the G20 nations. The United Kingdom and parts of the EU are prepared to countenance the prospect of a long-term tax on the financial sector, but the United States is less willing to make a commitment. What the G20 leaders came up with at the last leaders summit (24 September 2009) is that the IMF would be required to report back to the G20 leaders on the feasibility of a long-term tax on the financial sector.

Concluding remarks

This chapter examined the notion of fiscal and policy space from the perspective of developing countries. It noted the widely shared view that enhancing fiscal and policy space in developing countries to cope with external shocks and global downturns and to secure sustainable recovery should be a key element of the global agenda. The chapter observed that following principles of good policy design are paramount in avoiding painful trade-offs among competing policy priorities and emphasized that the agenda of fortifying the capacity of low- and middle-income countries to cope with global economic volatility and to respond to the imperatives of long-term development entail a combination of national commitment and international cooperation.

The chapter offered alternative interpretations of fiscal space. The IMF approach highlights the point that any increase in public expenditure and tax cuts either as counter-cyclical measures or as long-term initiatives would need to be conducted within a framework of fiscal sustainability.

The alternative interpretation – associated with the work of UNDP – emphasizes the need to engender fiscal resources to finance public investment, especially in infrastructure, given trends of a secular decline in public investment in many developing countries. The primary goals of such public investment are to sustain long-run growth and support the attainment of the MDGs. At the same time, the chapter highlighted studies by the ODI and ILO that examined the financial and fiscal requirements of funding a comprehensive social protection system. This does not mean that the goal of fiscal sustainability will have to be compromised as there are multiple and prudent options to enhance fiscal space. A key challenge is to increase the mobilization of domestic resources in developing countries. This means that the tax-to-GDP ratio should rise in countries with a low tax burden.

The chapter also offered alternative interpretations of policy space. One pertains to the manner in which multilateral trade rules can constrain policy space, but the issue that is most germane to this chapter stems from the implications of capital account liberalization and liability dollarization. Middle-income developing countries that have access to external private capital markets face the risk of 'sudden stops' in capital flows that can have rather significant adverse effects on output and employment. Liability dollarization can seriously constrain the ability of developing economies to pursue counter-cyclical policies in case of downturns. The chapter suggested how developing economies can deal with this challenge. It would mean avoiding or attenuating liability dollarization, engaging in 'self-insurance' schemes, encouraging economic diversification and imposing temporary capital controls.

The chapter offered an evaluation of the G20 declaration at the London Summit (April 2009) as an example of the extent to which international cooperation is facilitating the capacity of developing countries to cope with global downturns and external shocks and to secure sustainable recovery. It reflected on the views of critics who maintain that the G20 declaration, while promising to harness new resources on a significant scale to assist developing countries, has fallen short in a number of areas. These deficiencies include the lack of a clear template to tackle the reform of global economic governance, the lack of fresh and practical ideas to fix the financial system, the failure to agree to a new round of fiscal expansion to cope with the steep decline in global demand, and the insufficient appreciation of the scope for regional solutions to strengthen fiscal and policy space in developing countries. Developing countries can also learn from each other, most notably from successful cases of crisis management as well as successful operations of national stabilisation funds.

Finally, the chapter noted that there is a renewed interest in the notion of designing and imposing a tax on international financial transactions both as an instrument for tempering financial volatility and also as a new source of development finance. Whether this renewed interest in a tax on international financial transactions will eventually translate into a global reality depends upon the extent to which leaders of the G20 nations can develop a unified approach to respond to the opportunities and challenges that have emerged in the post-crisis era.

Notes

1. Commission of Experts of the President of the United Nations General Assembly on reforms of the international monetary and financial system, 6 January 2009.
2. IMF and World Bank (2009: 5) *The Global Monitoring Report.*
3. The principles cited here draw on the famous work of Jan Tinbergen (1952) and Robert Mundell (1968). Tinbergen noted that to attain a given number of independent targets there must be an equal number of instruments. Mundell (op. cit.: 233–9) developed a 'companion' to Tinbergen's principles by arguing that 'policies should be paired with the objectives on which they have the most influence'.
4. This section draws on Islam and Chowdhury (2009a).
5. Heller (2006).
6. Roy, Heuty and Letouze (2006).
7. See also chapter 6 in this volume.
8. ODI (2009) and ILO (2009e).
9. ILO (2009e).
10. IMF (2009c: 27).
11. World Bank (2009: 3).
12. Gupta and Tareq (2008).
13. UNCTAD (2007b).
14. Ibid.
15. Ibid.
16. The discussion draws on Gupta and Tareq (2008).
17. Ibid.
18. Ibid. See also UNCTAD (2009a).
19. Culpeper and Kappagoda (2007: 12).
20. Ibid.
21. Gupta and Tareq (2008).
22. Kharas (2008). See also Bulir and Hamann (2007) who maintain that aid volatility has increased significantly between 1997–98 and 2000–03 for low-income countries that participated in the 'HIPC' (heavily indebted poor countries) initiative.
23. ODI (2007).
24. This section draws on Cavallo and Izquierdo (eds) (2009).
25. Ariyoshi et al. (2000).
26. IMF and World Bank (2009: 47–8) *The Global Monitoring Report.*
27. This section draws on Islam and Chowdhury (2009b).
28. London Summit – Leaders' Statement, 2 April 2009.
29. See Bergsten (2009), who emphasizes a substantial replenishment of IMF resources. For proposals on enhanced global financing facilities for developing countries that pre-date current versions, see Dervis and Birdsall (2006) and Akyuz (2007).

30. See Sachs (2009).
31. *The Economist* (2009c) 'The IMF: Battling Stigma', 26 March. See also Pomerleano (2009).
32. IMF Financial Activities – 25 March update available at http://www.imf.org/external/np/tre/activity/2010/032510.htm.
33. Barrel et al. (2009).
34. te Velde (2008).
35. *New York Times* (2009) 'The Economic Summit', 2 April.
36. See UNCTAD (2009b).
37. Baker and Walentin (2009).
38. Woo (2008).
39. See Weisbrot (2009) on both the Latin American and East Asian experiments in developing regional sources of development finance. See Woo (2008) for further details on the East Asian experience.
40. Islam and Chowdhury (2000, chapter 7).
41. Islam (2005).

8
Labour Market Policies in Times of Crisis

S. Cazes, C. Heuer and S. Verick

Introduction

As stressed in this volume, labour markets tend to recover slowly after a major financial crisis and usually lag behind economic growth, with unemployment persisting at above pre-crisis levels. For this reason, it is crucial for policymakers to consider various labour market policy (LMP) measures that both mitigate the impact of the crisis on workers and help reduce the lag between economic growth and improvements in the labour market. In turn, these actions depend critically upon appropriate monetary and fiscal measures to boost demand and encourage job creation, which have been a central part of the stimulus packages across the world.

Labour market policies comprise all kinds of regulatory policies that influence the interaction between labour supply and demand. They consist of policies that provide income replacement (usually called passive LMPs) as well as labour market integration measures available to unemployed or those threatened by unemployment (usually labelled active LMPs). Particularly in OECD countries, there has been an increasing effort to 'activate' passive measures in order to enhance the integration of the unemployed and underemployed. The main ALMPs used for this purpose are job search assistance and training. Despite the division in these two policy groups (ALMPs and PLMPs), this chapter refers to LMPs in general, as the grouping is subordinated when designing policy responses. For this reason, this chapter focuses rather on matching policies to specific objectives of policymakers, such as keeping people employed or supporting the unemployed, than on terminology.

Regardless of how policies are labelled, it is important to realize that LMPs can only mitigate the consequences of an economic crisis, such as the global financial crisis of 2007–09. In other words, labour market policies can help workers, employers and communities cope with the consequences of the crisis, but they cannot cure its causes; they can ease the transition between economic cycles, but they are not able to turn a recession into an economic upturn. While the concepts of and policy frameworks for LMPs have been developed mainly in industrialized countries, it does not mean that these policies cannot be applied to other parts of the world. But the economic crisis has tightened the resources constraints, making the LMP response even more challenging for developing economies, especially low-income countries. Ultimately, to design an effective reform or rescue package for a country, LMPs have to be relevant to the overall economic and institutional framework of a country.

Due to the ILO's mandate and its wealth of experience in designing and promoting LMPs, leaders at the G20 Summit in April 2009 called 'upon the ILO, working with other relevant organizations, to assess the actions taken and those required for the future' in order to 'support employment by stimulating growth, investing in education and training, and through active labour market policies, focusing on the most vulnerable'.[1] In this context, this chapter complements other work conducted by the ILO by presenting a comprehensive overview of various labour market policy instruments and sketches the range of options available given countries' institutional and financial capacities. More specifically, the purpose is to provide some insights into how to make the most of short-term LMPs in times of crisis.

The chapter does not intend to review all existing programmes across countries, nor to answer the questions of 'what works' and for 'what groups of the unemployed'; its focus is more on appropriate short-term responses to the crisis and on the possible adjustment and extension of existing policies and programmes. Since new measures and institutional reforms take time to become operational, the experience of the global financial crisis in 2007–09 bolsters the argument that economies need to have permanent, yet adaptable, LMPs and institutions, whose levels and structure vary with the business cycle in order to enable workforce adjustment in a socially acceptable way. Although at the time of writing most countries had technically exited recession, the messages of this chapter are nonetheless relevant to both tackling the increasing and persistent levels of unemployment and to preparing for future crises.

The remainder of the chapter is structured as follows: the next section presents a summary of labour market adjustment mechanisms, before providing a brief discussion on the factors that need to be taken into account when formulating a policy response to the crisis. The following section, making up the main part of the chapter, presents the different policy instruments available to countries to mitigate the impact of the economic downturn on employment and incomes. In this section, country examples are provided in order to illustrate the policy instruments described, drawing largely on the response to the global financial crisis. The final section offers some conclusions.

The role of labour market policies over the business cycle

Channels of adjustment during an economic downturn

Given the large and long-lasting impact of economic crises on jobs, labour market policies play a critical role in responding to the latest downturn. This in turn requires recognizing how the labour market adjusts as a result of the credit squeeze and collapse in aggregate demand, which was discussed in detail in chapters 4 and 5. In this respect, the main immediate challenge facing governments is the subsequent drop in labour demand, rather than addressing frictional and structural problems in the labour market, although the latter will play a role in determining how the crisis translates into unemployment (particularly long-term unemployment) and underemployment.

Indeed, the reaction of employers to the downturn will depend upon the magnitude of the crisis in their country and region, and the degree of flexibility they have in adjusting labour, which is influenced by the institutional arrangements in the labour market (such as wage-setting institutions, unionization, employment protection legislation, etc.). At the firm level, there are two main channels for adjustment to external shocks in labour demand: working time and/or employment (quantitative adjustment) or wages (price adjustment). Adjustments to crises are evident not only in aggregate changes to labour demand, but also in terms of job reallocation within and across sectors. There are also changes to labour supply at the individual and household levels.

As highlighted in chapter 4, in developing and emerging economies, many laid-off workers are often forced to take up employment in the urban informal or rural economies (i.e. a reversal of rural–urban migration flows), which act as absorbing sectors in times of crisis.[2] International migration is also an adjustment mechanism: workers are forced to move to other countries in search of work, or are forced to return to their home country as a consequence of losing their jobs.

Beyond the described mechanisms, there can also be an adjustment process within households, as family members change their labour supply in response to a job loss. During the 1997 East Asian financial crisis, for example, rural households in Indonesia reacted to job losses of males by increasing the labour supply of women. In most of the countries affected by that crisis, adjustment was through a fall in real wages and considerable churning in the labour market (across sectors and into agricultural and informal employment) (see the discussion in chapter 4). The fall in real wages nonetheless resulted in considerable increases in poverty (Dhanani and Islam 2002). Overall, poverty in households increases because: (1) adjustments to labour supply do not make up for losses in employment and wages; and (2) households do not have enough savings or access to other sources of income to smooth consumption, which is being exacerbated by the falling remittances resulting from the global financial crisis.

Goals and principles of labour market policies in times of crisis

In light of the various adjustment mechanisms discussed here and above in chapters 4 and 5, government policies can be implemented to achieve various goals. For example, to reduce layoffs, firms need assistance to adjust to the drop in economic activity, which can be done through various subsidies. One approach is known as work sharing, which has been widely used in industrialized countries during 2008–09. Following a significant economic contraction, these policies, however, can only be partially effective in the sense that they cannot prevent all layoffs, thus leaving an important role for policy interventions that support the unemployed to develop skills and to regain employment. Other measures such as unemployment benefits compensate for the loss of income. The challenge for policymakers is to identify what labour market adjustment is optimal not only for employers but also for society at large. If firms are adjusting too rapidly, governments have a role to play to ensure that adjustment is tempered and in line with the policy goal of keeping unemployment from surging and contributing to a further dampening of economic activity.

In this overall context, the labour market response to the crisis should aim to achieve one or more of the following goals, which centre around four main areas (labour demand, match between demand and supply, income support and targeting):

1 *Support labour demand* by:
  (i) Keeping people in jobs to prevent unemployment and working poverty (i.e. help employers avoid laying off workers through measures to reduce labour costs such as a reduction in working hours or other subsidies)

(ii) Creating new jobs to lift people out of unemployment/underemployment and working poverty (i.e. support laid-off workers and new labour market entrants).

2 *Improve the match between labour demand and supply* by making the unemployed more employable.
3 *Provide income support* to job losers and low-income earners to smooth consumption and prevent poverty.
4 *Target the most vulnerable* segments of society such as youth, older persons, persons with disability, and refugees and migrants, which is a cross-cutting goal relevant to those listed above.

For all of these policy objectives, the main challenge is to develop a suitable LMP package to facilitate recovery without imposing disproportionate burdens on workers, enterprises and public funds. Overall, a number of factors should be taken into account when developing the appropriate policy response. Firstly, since the objective is to develop short-term responses to increasing unemployment and working poverty, the focus of strategies during a recession should be on utilizing and adjusting existing institutions, policies and programmes to ensure that these interventions can be implemented quickly and effectively.

Secondly, labour market policies in times of economic crisis should react to the drop in labour demand, which will vary not only by countries but also across regions within a country. In contrast, policies that aim to improve the efficiency of the labour market are unlikely to deliver any immediate results, although they can play an instrumental role during the recovery to help reduce the lag between economic growth and unemployment rates. Labour market interventions can, therefore, also have a longer-term goal. For instance, as argued by Bell and Blanchflower (2009), special efforts should be made to help youth to prevent the long-term impact of unemployment on their future employment and income prospects. They propose that the UK government supports young people to remain in school and continue to higher education to improve their skills and employability. Such measures will increase their employment chances once the economy has recovered.

Thirdly, it is crucial to understand the changes to job and worker flows in the labour market in order to design the most appropriate policy responses. For example, as witnessed in previous recessions, the rise in unemployment in countries such as the United States is driven to a great extent by the fall in hiring rather than the much-publicized rise in layoffs, which was indicated in chapter 5, a point also made by Hall (2007). Overall, although layoffs add to the pool of unemployed, it is the reduced number of job opportunities and the subsequent collapse in hiring that drives the unemployment rate once the economy has bottomed out. Based on this picture of the labour market during a crisis, policymakers in the United States should focus more efforts on supporting employers to create jobs and hire new staff (which is indeed the main issue of the later stimulus measures announced by the government).

Finally, though ALMPs are a potentially important weapon in the fight against unemployment and poverty, evaluation studies indicate mixed results about their effectiveness.[3] Earlier evaluations of ALMPs in Europe and the United States focused mostly on the short-run employment effects of programmes. Some key messages from this literature are that job-search assistance is relatively effective in the short run and job subsidies generally increase employment chances but may entail significant direct and indirect (deadweight) costs (and hence, should be targeted).[4] In terms of ALMPs targeting youth, evidence from evaluation studies has been rather discouraging. As reported in Martin (2000), the evaluation of youth programmes reveals that: 'One of the most disappointing conclusions from the evaluation literature is that almost all evaluations show that special measures are not effective for disadvantaged youths' (Martin 2000: 95).

More recent studies reveal stronger positive effects of ALMPs once a longer-run perspective on the impact is taken. For example, training measures, which are the most widely-used ALMP in the crisis context, are more beneficial for participants over the longer term with respect to employment and earnings outcomes (Kluve 2006; Lechner and Wunsch 2009). More relevant to the situation countries are currently facing, the conclusions of Lechner and Wunsch (2009) indicate that there are positive medium- to long-run employment effects of German training programmes (in a pre-crisis period), while these benefits are stronger in times of high unemployment. Therefore, such training schemes can act as a counter-cyclical measure, with expenditure increasing with the unemployment rate.[5] In terms of ALMPs during previous recessions, the results of Forslund and Krueger (2008) for Sweden in the 1990s suggest that training and other policies in place at the time did not mitigate the impact of the severe crisis and resulting recession that hit the country in that decade.

As illustrated by Figure 8.1, expenditure on ALMPs varies considerably among OECD countries. Using the 10-year average for the period leading up to the crisis (1998–2007), these statistics indicate that Denmark, Sweden, the Netherlands, Belgium, Germany, and France all

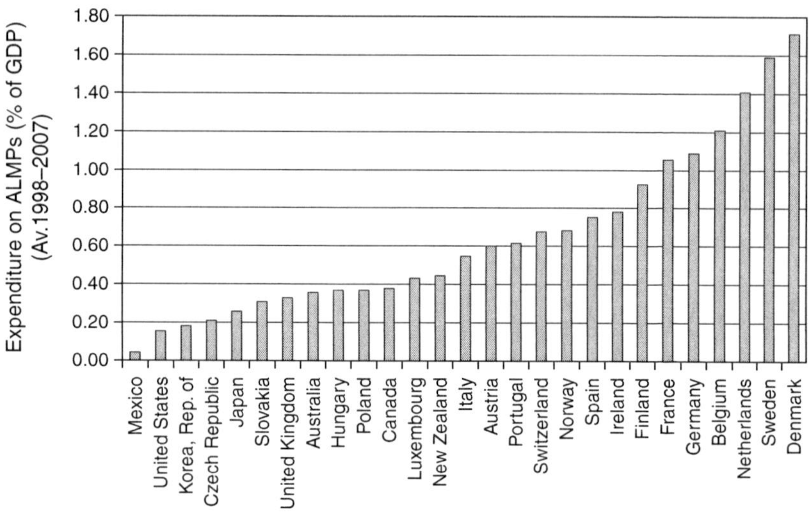

Figure 8.1 Spending on ALMPs in OECD countries, average 1998–2007
Source: OECD at http://stats.oecd.org/Index.aspx?DatasetCode=LFS_SEXAGE_I_R.

spent on average more than one per cent of GDP per annum on these interventions. In non-European OECD countries, the spending on ALMPs was far lower. These figures provide an indication of the varying importance of ALMPs as a policy tool and crisis-response measure in high-income countries.

One key remaining question is whether ALMPs can be effective in an economy generating very few (formal) vacancies as is the case in the majority of developing countries. Moreover, since most findings on the effectiveness of ALMPs are based on programmes in advanced economies, it is difficult to extrapolate these studies to the situation in low- and middle-income countries. At the same time, the potential benefits are much larger in poorer countries, including the the avoidance of conflict (for example, by helping young people to find a job).

That said, the evidence on the impact of policies in developing countries, especially in low-income countries, remains scarce, and thus it is difficult to extrapolate these results to all labour markets around the globe. For this reason, every effort should be made to consider the relative costs and benefits of measures before embarking on their implementation. A major challenge in this respect is that while costs usually can be directly quantified, benefits such as avoidance of unrest and encouragement of social cohesion, which are very important in low-income countries, are difficult to quantify. To shed some light on these issues, the main advantages and disadvantages of policy responses discussed below are highlighted in the text and in Table A8.1 in the Appendix, which also displays the financing sources, the role in targeting groups and highlights potential constraints for developing countries (especially low-income countries).

The key message of Table A8.1 is that although there are a range of different LMP tools available to governments, they all require a certain institutional and financial capacity of governments to fund and successfully implement interventions. Policies that maintain labour demand can be particularly expensive as they require compensation for workers. For example, work sharing is a scheme where employers reduce the number of hours worked to avoid the laying off of staff, which reduces labour costs and helps them to survive a period of low demand. In most European countries, work sharing is subsidized by the state to prevent a loss in income for workers. In addition, subsidies entail indirect costs such as deadweight losses, which arise because employers take advantage of these measures although they would have kept workers on without any financial assistance. Measures that support the unemployed such as job search assistance or training require an effective public employment service and providers of training. Despite the best institutional set-up, these policies can, however, be ineffective in a period where demand is low and firms are not hiring as discussed above.

Labour market policy response to the global financial crisis of 2007–09

Before examining the specific categories of LMPs used to tackle the labour market impact of the global financial crisis, it is useful to have an overview of the measures and programmes that have been introduced by governments since the onset of the downturn. Although it is difficult to collect full information on policies across the globe, available studies and responses reported by governments, summarized in Figure 8.2 and Table A8.2 in the Appendix, provide some important insights into the main tools adopted by governments. The responses reported here draw from various studies that assess policy decisions in 79 OECD and non-OECD countries from Europe, North America, Latin America, Asia, Oceania, Middle East and Africa.[6] It should be stressed that this information is by no means complete and that some policies were only announcements and were not necessarily implemented.

As illustrated in Figure 8.2, a large number of high-income countries have considered policy measures that address all four policy categories

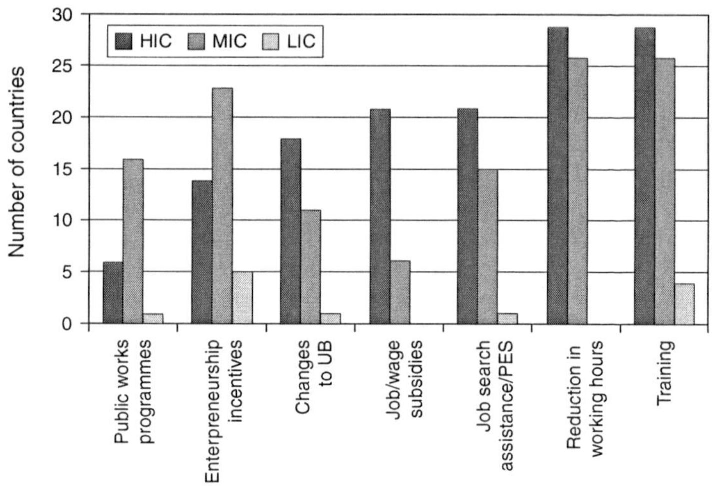

Figure 8.2 National labour market policy responses to the global financial crisis of 2007–09

Source: See Table A8.2 in the Appendix.

Notes: HIC = high-income countries; MIC = middle-income countries; LIC = low-income countries, which are grouped according to the World Bank's classification of countries, see http://go.worldbank.org/D7SN0B8YU0. UB = unemployment benefits schemes.

considered in this chapter. The most commonly used intervention in high-income countries is training for both those threatened by layoffs and also the unemployed (including work experience and apprenticeship initiatives) (27 countries), followed by work sharing (24 countries), increased resources for public employment services including job search assistance measures (20 countries), and subsidies (20 countries). The least-implemented intervention in this group of countries is public works programmes (five countries), which is unsurprising given the limited effectiveness of this intervention in such labour markets. In terms of security provided by passive labour market policies, 17 high-income countries have made changes to unemployment benefits schemes (usually extensions of coverage and broader eligibility criteria).

Overall, the use of labour market policies in response to the global financial crisis is declining with the income level of countries, which reflects the financial and technical constraints hindering the responses of these governments. Nonetheless, a range of policies have been utilized in low- and middle-income countries, in some cases in a similar fashion to that observed in more developed nations. As displayed in Figure 8.2, the most utilized policy response in the middle-income group is training (with 25 countries), followed by job search assistance, entrepreneurship incentives and public works programmes. Interestingly, 11 of these countries are using a reduction in working hours to support employers in response to the downturn, although not all these interventions are subsidized. There are far fewer low-income countries implementing such policies in response to the crisis. Those listed in Figure 8.2 are mostly focusing principally on entrepreneurship incentives (Cambodia, Kenya, Nepal, Tanzania and Viet Nam) and training (Bangladesh, Cambodia, Kenya and Viet Nam). In general, low- and middle-income countries tend to rely on LMP measures that do not require complex institutional structures and social dialogue. Nonetheless, some governments are turning to more innovative policies that have not been widely used before such as providing subsidized training for threatened workers, which is highlighted by the Mauritian case mentioned below.

Supporting labour demand

Maintaining labour demand during a severe crisis is a priority for governments because of the costs of unemployment and the impact of joblessness on further dampening aggregate demand, which can lead to a recessionary spiral as more people lose jobs and consume less. Supporting labour demand involves firstly keeping workers in jobs. However, layoffs have been unavoidable in many cases, particularly in sectors that contract sharply during a recession such as construction and export-intensive sectors. In this case, other labour market policies can help create new jobs to provide employment opportunities for laid-off workers and new entrants in the labour market, though these can be less effective during such a downturn. These schemes can also assist with the reallocation of labour to sectors with a higher growth potential (together with training measures considered below), though this is difficult during a deep recession when few sectors are growing.

Keeping people in jobs

In order to keep workers in their jobs, employers need support to make adjustments to their labour demand and costs without resorting to layoffs. As witnessed during the global financial crisis, governments around the world have bailed out companies, especially financial institutions and automobile manufacturers. Beyond such financial measures, the main LMP tools available for this kind of internal adjustment include reducing working hours, also called work sharing, and providing on-the-job training during slack periods when output has been reduced.

These measures help to sustain labour demand and reduce labour costs for employers without having to resort to dismissing workers.

Work sharing involves the reduction of working hours together with a reduction in wages, which may be subsidized by governments to ease the burden on workers. This scheme is typically limited to a specific period and is often combined with training measures: once economic conditions have improved, workers are meant to go back to the original contracted working time. When the reduction in working hours is subsidized through government revenue, workers' incomes are not reduced; however, in some cases, compensation is not fully proportional to the reduction of hours worked, resulting in a loss of earnings. By reducing labour costs in the short term, this approach supports employers adjust working hours rather than resorting to the adjustment of employment levels. This helps retain skilled workers, which are costly and difficult to hire during better economic times, as witnessed in the boom years leading up to the crisis. For workers, work sharing schemes provide workers with job and income security, and if combined with training, skills development.

Prior to the onset of the global downturn in 2008, work sharing schemes existed in a number of industrialized countries such as Austria, Belgium, France, Germany, Japan, the Netherlands, Republic of Korea, Switzerland and the United States (in certain states). Following the onset of the crisis, a number of countries, among them France and Germany, have extended their work-sharing schemes, known respectively as *chômage partiel* or *Kurzarbeit*, in terms of duration and level of subsidy for the employee or the employer. The maximum duration of the German scheme was increased progressively as the crisis developed and now stands at 24 months (as of May 2009).[7] The German work-sharing scheme *Kurzarbeit* has played an important role in preventing unemployment in Europe's largest economy. Official figures show that as of March 2009, 1.26 million workers were covered by this scheme, up from only 155,000 a year earlier (Bundesagentur für Arbeit 2009). Canada also extended its Work-Sharing Program to 52 weeks from a previous level of 38 weeks (Messenger 2009).

The objective of on-the-job training is longer term as it seeks to enhance the human capital of workers to improve productivity, which is possible because of a reduction in capacity utilization within the company. The challenge for employers is that such measures represent long-term human capital investment and actually require additional resources to cover the costs of training (unless subsidized by the government). Very often, these two policies – a reduction in working hours and on-the-job training – are combined to provide a package that benefits both employers and workers, particularly when the government subsidizes such schemes.

For instance, in March 2009 employers and unions in the Swedish manufacturing sector reached an agreement on a temporary reduction in working hours along with the provision of training. This agreement allows employers to reduce hours worked by employees by 20 per cent (unsubsidized), which can be replaced by participation in training programmes. Volvo has already taken advantage of this agreement, helping the company keep 1,000 workers who otherwise would have been dismissed (Lovén 2009).

If a reduction in the quantity of hours worked is not possible, other measures to reduce labour costs can offer employers support in maintaining employment – for example, by offering wage subsidies or lowering social contributions. These measures can also be used to hire the unemployed and hence be seen as part of the set of policy measures listed below in terms of creating new jobs. The advantage of these schemes is that they can maintain the same wage levels for workers (in case of the reduction of non-wage labour costs), while reducing the cost for employers. At the same time, these measures are very costly for governments, particularly because such policies can be difficult to phase out and entail potentially significant deadweight losses. Moreover, unless governments can finance the reduction in social security payments, cuts in social contributions will have long-term ramifications for the viability of social security funds.

In developing countries, measures such as reducing working hours are difficult to implement because of their costs, although depending on whether or not a social security system is in place, a subsidized reduction of working hours can be less expensive than the payment of unemployment benefits and the further consequences of increased unemployment. Alternatively, unsubsidized measures would result in reduced wages for workers, who are often living near or below the poverty line, and thus the measure would subsequently have long-lasting negative consequences for the welfare of these workers and their families. Overall, these policy options lose some relevance in countries where the formal economy may only represent 10 per cent of workers and where labour costs are not a major constraint for employers. In addition, such interventions require constructive social dialogue, which is often absent.

Despite these challenges, middle-income countries such as Mauritius have looked for ways to keep people in jobs. In May 2009, the Government of Mauritius announced that its National Employment Foundation will run a 'Work cum Training' scheme to enable companies in the manufacturing and tourism sectors, facing a reduction in their turnover, to send their employees on training instead of laying them off.[8] The government is providing Rs 300 million for the scheme and expects to save some 6,000 employees from retrenchment while at the same time improving their skills.[9] Training will be provided for up to two days a week and will run for a maximum period of 18 months until December 2010.

Creating new jobs

During the global financial crisis, many firms have had no choice but to dismiss workers or close down entirely as reflected by the fall in employment in advanced economies (see chapters 2 and 5). The response of governments to such a situation involves a comprehensive set of macroeconomic, sectoral and employment policies to boost demand and economic growth, in which labour market policies play a relatively minor role. Nonetheless, specific labour market policies can be utilized by governments to create jobs – these include wage subsidies, cuts to employer social contributions and public works programmes. These measures can potentially support employers to abandon hiring freezes and start employing new workers. As highlighted above, the failure for firms to hire workers is the main reason why unemployment rates have surged in countries such as the United States.

As already mentioned, measures to reduce labour costs such as wage/hiring subsidies or the lowering of social security contributions make it more attractive to hire new workers, thus creating new jobs. As reported by the OECD, a number of countries have responded to the crisis by establishing or expanding programmes to subsidize wages or reduce social contributions for new hires, often targeting vulnerable populations such as youth (OECD 2009a). For example, Australia introduced a new wage subsidy for employers who hire laid-off apprentices and trainees: The $AU145.6 million *Securing Apprenticeships* scheme aims to keep out-of-trade apprentices and trainees connected to the workforce after becoming laid off prior to the end of their training period.[10]

In contrast to providing incentives through wages, public works programmes directly create paid employment through labour-intensive projects such as road construction, maintenance, irrigation infrastructure, reforestation and soil conservation. These programmes provide some sort of safety net for the poor, rather than offering a long-term solution to the lack of employment opportunities. Public works are considered self-targeting, because non-eligible beneficiaries are reluctant to take up such menial work, typically remunerated at below-market wages (Kanyenze et al. 2000). In general, these programmes are more relevant for developing countries, particularly in terms of supporting vulnerable groups such as youth and those living in rural areas (Auer et al. 2008). The advantage of these schemes is that in addition to providing some sort of income for poor people, they can help to improve the local infrastructure and the environment, which in turn has longer-term economic and social benefits (a 'double dividend'). The challenge for such programmes is the cost and difficulties in creating sustainable livelihoods for participants once the programme has finished. Moreover, these interventions require an institutional set-up that ensures an effective use of resources in terms of maximizing the programme's impact and reducing leakage of funds.

Recognizing the potential benefits of such schemes, South Africa established in 2004 the Extended Public Works Programme (EPWP) with the aim of 'creating at least 1 million work opportunities, of which at least 40% of beneficiaries will be women, 30% youth and 2% people with disabilities'.[11] A second phase launched in 2009 seeks to increase the number of beneficiaries to 2 million full-time equivalent jobs. EPWP beneficiaries participate in a range of infrastructure, economic, environmental and social projects.

The National Rural Employment Guarantee (NREG) scheme in India has received considerable attention, particularly because it enshrines a right to employment and provides a wage floor for the rural poor.[12] The NREG Act was enacted in 2005 building on a previous initiative in the state of Maharashtra (the Maharashtra Rural Employment Guarantee Programme). Adopting a rights-based approach, the NREG scheme confers the right of employment for up to 100 days per year in public works programmes per rural household. Thus, the government is acting as the employer of last resort, providing work to those who are unable to gain employment elsewhere. The NREG scheme should help India to mitigate the impact of the crisis on the rural poor, which underscores the importance of having safety nets in place supported by existing institutions and policies to be able to respond to an economic shock. Recognizing the role of these programmes during the crisis of 2007–09, the Government of India announced as part of its stimulus package additional resources for such schemes as the NREG (ILO 2009a; Kannan 2009b).[13]

Also from the perspective of the crisis of 2007–09, a number of countries have announced public works programmes. For example, the Republic of Korea announced that it would offer 250,000 temporary jobs to the vulnerable and unemployed. These beneficiaries will be involved in repairing and maintaining public facilities and other manual labour, and will earn 830,000 won a month for a 40-hour week over a period of six months.[14]

Improving the match between labour demand and supply by making the unemployed more employable

If layoffs cannot be avoided, it is important for countries to also orient their labour market policies on increasing the employability of those laid off and improving the match between demand and supply. Such matching policies are important over medium- and long-term horizons with job reallocation taking place: even in times of crisis, jobs are being created, so it is crucial to help the unemployed find jobs and keep vulnerable individuals such as youth out of long-term unemployment. The main labour market policies used for this purpose are job search assistance, training, work experience and apprenticeship programmes, and entrepreneurship support.

The objective of job search assistance (JSA) is to improve the chances of an unemployed person finding a job through such activities as the assessment of skills, counselling, training on presentation and job search strategies, and identifying vacancies. Typically, these activities are provided by public employment services (PES), although there are increasingly a large number of private providers that assist the unemployed with job searches. JSA interventions are particularly relevant to youth who lack the necessary skills to find a job. Meta-evaluations of JSA programmes in industrialized countries reveal that besides being relatively cheap, they have positive short-term effects with regards to employment outcomes (Kluve 2007). However, during the economic downturn of 2008–09, expanding JSA would require increases in human and financial resources for public employment services, which can be challenging even for OECD countries. Moreover, JSA is likely to be less effective in the short run during periods where labour demand is low, as witnessed during the global financial crisis.

Despite these challenges, many industrialized countries have increased resources for public employment services to facilitate the increased demand for JSA schemes during the economic downturn starting in 2008. For example, Finland has responded by temporarily increasing funding of PES staff and JSA and counselling measures for laid-off workers (OECD 2009a).

Broader than JSA, training measures aim to improve the employability of the unemployed through the enhancement of skills. These programmes typically focus on vocational skills training, taking place either in training institutions or on the job. They are funded either through government revenue, levies, public–private partnerships or official development assistance (in the case of developing countries). These programmes in developing countries are constrained by the lack of resources and appropriate training institutions. For both OECD and developing countries, a major challenge is being able to identify areas for training that will help the unemployed find jobs when the economy picks up again. This involves linking the programme with the current and future skills requirements of employers, which is something that public providers of training courses have not always done correctly or cost-effectively. Indeed, evaluations of training programmes indicate that they work best when conducted on the job and with active employer involvement (Betcherman et al. 2004).

In the context of the crisis of 2007–09, in November 2008 China announced a 4 million yuan (US$586 billion) economic stimulus package for two years, which amounts to 14 per cent of estimated GDP (2008 level). As part of this package, there is an announced nationwide vocational training scheme, which would especially assist laid-off and migrant workers, with a view to easing the pressures on the Chinese job market (Lee 2009).

Related to training measures, work experience and apprenticeship programmes usually target young people who lack skills and experience. Generally, work experience programmes are shorter-term in nature, while apprenticeships offer longer formalized training linked to a particular employer. A challenge for these measures is the poor lock-in effect: after completing a work experience or apprenticeship programme, workers are not retained by the firm. In developing countries, an additional challenge is to improve the effectiveness of apprenticeship schemes in the informal economy, particularly in terms of quality of training.

In addition to these interventions, one common form of support to the unemployed/underemployed, particularly in developing countries, is entrepreneurship incentives, which usually consist of training, credit or a combination of both. Entrepreneurship training focuses on developing skills in business planning, marketing, and product development, often coupled with mentoring. Entrepreneurship credit schemes, usually micro-credit, seek to overcome the barriers faced by the unemployed in accessing funds from a formal lending institution, which are especially severe because these individuals lack credit history and collateral. A major constraint is that these schemes can only assist a small proportion of the unemployed since not all individuals are suited to becoming entrepreneurs (although it can be argued that entrepreneurship skills can be beneficial for a broader range of roles).

Providing income support

Within the labour market package, passive LMPs, particularly unemployment benefit schemes (contributory and non-contributory), aim to maintain income levels after the loss of a job, providing insurance to maintain consumption levels and to keep individuals and their families out of poverty. The flipside of these interventions is the much-discussed disincentive effects of high unemployment benefits, which may discourage workers from taking job offers. Classical theory suggests that 'generous' income support discourages the unemployed from seeking work (by increasing their reservation wage) and reduces the 'fear' of unemployment, hence increasing the upward pressure on wages from employees (via trade unions, for example). Empirical evidence on OECD countries does suggest that high and long-term unemployment benefits may generate long-term unemployment and potentially affect unemployment rates, although this has been disputed by more recent work (Boeri et al. 2008). It is important to stress that the disincentive effects of unemployment benefit schemes are less of a concern during a crisis, because they are not the driver of rising and persistent levels of unemployment.

A collapse in aggregate demand results in job losses and reductions in working hours and wages, which in turn leads to lower demand as there are falls in incomes and hence consumption. In such situations, unemployment benefits act as automatic stabilizers because the overall coverage of assistance to the unemployed increases by design during a recession as more jobless submit claims for benefits, without any specific government intervention.[15] However, during the global financial crisis, large numbers of laid-off workers have been ineligible for unemployment benefits. In response to this aspect, many governments have made changes to unemployment benefit schemes, including extending the coverage and increasing the generosity of payments. For example, some countries have extended unemployment benefits to those who have not previously been eligible (by, for example, reducing the minimum number of months needed to be eligible). Others – for example, Brazil and the Republic of Korea – have extended the duration of unemployment benefits.

In OECD countries, job losers who are not eligible for unemployment benefits are often able to access social assistance and housing support payments. For example, in the United States, federal funding has been provided for social assistance payments to the unemployed who have exhausted their unemployment benefits. The Government of Japan is offering a subsidy to employers to continue providing housing to dismissed workers so they do not become homeless (OECD 2009a).

The main challenge to expanding coverage and increasing unemployment benefits is the cost implication for governments, although these measures are mostly meant to be temporary. Most developing countries do not have unemployment benefit schemes due to their cost, and capacity and institutional requirements such as a functioning public employment service. In Africa, only Algeria, Egypt, Mauritius, South Africa and Tunisia provide any form of unemployment insurance programme (SSA/ISSA 2009). Viet Nam is the only low-income country to establish an unemployment insurance scheme, which commenced in January 2009, although Vietnamese employees can only benefit from this scheme from the beginning of 2010 (Pham 2009). In other countries, new social security systems can only be envisaged over a longer-term horizon, which limits the applicability of this policy option as an immediate response to the crisis in developing economies. Nonetheless, it remains an important goal as a means to protect the welfare of the poor (Townsend 2009). Since most of the poor in developing countries are beyond the reach of formal income protection schemes, countries in Latin America such as Brazil support those in poverty through targeted cash transfers (usually conditional on the participation of children in schools or health-related requirements).[16]

Targeting vulnerable groups

Given the unequal impact of the crisis on the population highlighted in chapter 5, governments have recognized the need to target certain groups such as youth in their labour market response. Indeed, during the global downturn of 2008–09, youth have suffered more in the labour market as reflected by larger increases in unemployment rates than witnessed for the prime-age population. This has been driven by their higher likelihood of being laid off and lack of work experience and job search skills. Young people with low levels of education have been particularly at risk. With many adults seeking employment, young people across the world are facing stiff competition for the few jobs available in the labour market.

A majority of OECD countries have indeed targeted labour market measures at young people to mitigate the impact of the 2008–09 economic downturn (OECD 2009a). This is essential to ensure that youth will not become long-term unemployed, which would reduce their future career and earnings potential, and increase their level of social exclusion. The challenge for policymakers is to implement policies that will effectively assist young people threatened by layoffs, those who have already lost their jobs in such sectors as construction and manufacturing, and new entrants to the labour market.

In addition to the situation in OECD countries, many developing nations already have national youth and gender employment policies and programmes, which are vehicles for implementing policies mentioned above and are listed in Table A8.2. For example, if a government has identified that young men and women are most severely impacted by the crisis, it could respond by expanding the national youth employment programme's training or entrepreneurship support schemes. Alternatively, if a country recognizes that those in a particular region are being hit the hardest, it could implement a public works programme that would hire residents in that region who have lost jobs or are underemployed.

Migrants, whether legal or illegal, are particularly vulnerable during crises because they are typically not provided with the same level of employment protection as native workers and hence are the first to lose their jobs during an economic downturn. Some countries have reacted to the crisis by reducing migrant intake in order to reduce pressures on the labour market. In this regard, (temporary) migrant workers in countries such as Japan and Spain have received incentives to return to their home countries (OECD 2009b). Similarly, to reduce the pressures on the labour market, Australia has decreased its intake of skilled migrants by 18,500 places, representing 14 per cent of the total intake.[17]

The main objective of targeted programmes is to reach those most in need. In any scheme, however, there is the potential to exclude needy beneficiaries and include some who are not in need as a result of imperfect information about their situation. Since administrators cannot accurately determine the eligibility of all beneficiaries, they design schemes that eliminate the risk of including a non-eligible individual or household in the scheme. This is in itself a challenge in developed countries. As indicated above, evaluations of programmes targeting youth in OECD countries reveal that they are less likely to have positive effects on beneficiaries than non-targeted programmes (Betcherman et al. 2004; Card et al. 2009; Kluve 2007). Nonetheless, as argued by Bell and Blanchflower (2009), it is still appropriate for countries like the United Kingdom to undertake a 'temporary, limited and targeted'[18] expansion of active labour market policies addressing the employment challenges of youth, but this in turn requires the piloting of interventions and proper evaluation to identify what programmes work.

The role of social dialogue in promoting effective labour market responses

Constructive and effective social dialogue is an instrumental part of the process of achieving a negotiated outcome between governments, employers and workers on economic and social policy issues (see chapter 9). In the midst of a crisis, social dialogue is crucial to negotiating outcomes that protect the interests of both employers and workers. This involves governments identifying ways of helping firms to adjust to the rapid economic contraction, which entails providing financial support to employers to avoid mass layoffs. For example, as indicated already, the use of subsidized work-sharing schemes in a number of countries, most notably Germany, has avoided layoffs as a result of the global recession and the subsequent increases in unemployment. This outcome involved social dialogue and the financial involvement of the government to subsidize the reduction in income accompanied by a lower number of work hours.

As analysed in chapter 9, however, the involvement of social partners in the design and implementation of national responses to the global financial crisis has generally been limited, especially in the earlier stages of the downturn. Evidence cited in this chapter shows that many governments have been reluctant to undertake nationwide debates on the crisis, and mostly did not involve social partners from the onset to help shape the formulation of the crisis policy response. Notable exceptions were Belgium, Ireland and Spain, which already had tripartite systems in place that then focused on the crisis as part of their institutionalized negotiations. As already stressed above, this highlights the importance of having existing institutions in place in order to effectively respond to an economic crisis.

The position taken by social partners in response to the crisis has also varied depending upon the level of negotiation (Rychly 2009). The focus of negotiations at the enterprise level has been on wage and benefit moderation or freezes along with layoffs, voluntary retirements and other measures. As highlighted earlier in this chapter, in general most employers are reluctant to cut nominal wages, and evidence cited in Rychly (2009) suggests that this remains the case in the downturn of 2008–09. In fact, with falling prices, real wages in many countries have increased since the start of the crisis in 2007. However, firms in badly affected sectors such as the airline, automobile and mining industries have had to resort to more drastic measures to reduce costs. For example, the Toyota Motor Corporation (United Kingdom) reached an agreement with employee representatives to cut base pay and production at its British plants by 10 per cent for a period of one year starting on 1 April 2009, which would nonetheless avoid the layoffs that have been unavoidable for most car manufacturers.[19]

What has been working during the Great Recession of 2008–09?

Since most crisis-related ALMPs are still in progress, it is too early to present findings from evaluations of these programmes. Nonetheless, it is possible to gain an insight into their scope and potential effectiveness by analysing any available information on ALMPs during the crisis of 2008–09 in terms of number of beneficiaries.

In addition to the implications of previous studies on the effectiveness of ALMPs, it is also possible to gain an insight into the coverage of crisis-related programmes using information provided by governments (particularly the public employment services). As illustrated by the examples in Table 8.1, this information indicates that in high-income countries, work-sharing schemes have been utilized for a large number of workers as a response to the crisis. Even if it is too early to 'evaluate' these schemes, it is likely that these measures have helped to prevent further increases in unemployment. Moreover, while these measures work over the short term, they have to be phased out at one point because resources and job reallocation have to take place and because these measures are costly. Generally, these measures should be temporary and well targeted. In some middle-income countries, public works programmes are supporting incomes among a large number of poor households during the downturn.

One key aspect of the role of ALMPs in times of crisis is the enhancement of individual transitions in the labour market. These policies help to keep individuals in touch with the labour market, making sure that they are ready (through training and retraining) when the economy is in better shape. ALMPs are, therefore, crucial tools in the battle to prevent long-term unemployment and avoid discouragement.

Concluding remarks

Since most countries have exited recession and slowly entered a phase of economic recovery, attention has shifted to concerns about exit strategies and the increasing urgency of tackling the crisis-induced fiscal deficit and government debt. At the same time, a premature withdrawal of monetary and fiscal stimulus could endanger the recovery and have further negative implications for the labour market and may even compromise long-term economic gains. As stressed in chapter 2, a jobs-led recovery has not yet materialized (as of the first quarter of 2010). The challenge is hence to ensure that the recovery is accompanied by

Table 8.1 Coverage of selected ALMPs during the crisis: selected examples from G20 countries

Country	Nature of ALMP	No. of beneficiaries
Work-sharing		
France	Activité/Chômage partiel	183,000 workers (June 2009)
Germany	Kurzarbeit	1.43 million workers (June 2009)
Italy	Cassa Integrazione Guadagni (CIG)	716.8 million hours compensated in Jan–Oct 2009
Netherlands	Deeltijd WW	36,000 workers (third quarter 2009)
Japan	Employment Adjustment Subsidy Programme	Over 2.5 million workers (September 2009)
Republic of Korea	Job sharing measure	1,999 enterprises (in firms with more than 100 employees) have utilized this scheme
Wage subsidies		
Argentina	Productive Recovery Program (REPRO)	By September 2009 coverage had extended to 2,317 enterprises and 123,444 workers
Training		
Indonesia	Vocational Training Centres (BLK)	50,000 jobseekers received training
Republic of Korea	Youth internship programme	90,000 interns employed at administrative agencies, public institutions and SMEs
Russia	Vocational training	107,000 workers threatened with lay-off
Public works programmes		
India	National Rural Employment Guarantee Scheme	1.77 million person days generated in 2009/10 financial year (five months)
Spain	State Fund for Local Investment	400,000 jobs created
South Africa	Expanded Public Works Programme	568,224 beneficiaries (2008/09)
Entrepreneurship incentives		
Russian Federation	Support to business start-ups	55,300 persons

Source: Compiled from national sources accessed via websites. Details available from authors on request.

a growth in employment. In addition, ALMPs should continue to play a complementary role in responding to the crisis, so concerted efforts are required to prevent long-term unemployment and to help individuals remain attached to the labour force and find a job.

More specifically, governments should consider the following key priorities during the recovery phase:

- Continue to keep workers in jobs through ALMPs such as work-sharing schemes (depending upon the pace of economic recovery);
- Utilize job/wage subsidies along with tax credits to encourage employers to start taking on new staff. To minimize deadweight costs, these measures should target individuals who are vulnerable to becoming long-term unemployed or losing attachment to the labour force, such as youth and the low-skilled; and
- Strengthen re-employment policies, i.e. job search assistance, training and related measures, that improve the employability of the unemployed. This will reduce the risk of long-term unemployment and discouragement, avoid workers' skills becoming obsolete, and smooth any structural changes in the labour market.

Since financial budget constraints will become increasingly binding, governments should reallocate resources to ensure that labour market policies move in line with developments in the overall economy and the labour market.

Over the longer term, governments should aim to develop a comprehensive and integrated policy and institutional framework that will enable them to respond better to future crises. This involves the development of ALMPs as a counter-cyclical measure. In addition, more efforts need to be made to monitor and evaluate the impact of specific policies to ensure that interventions are effective. It is also necessary to identify potential linkages between different labour market institutions, such as articulating ALMPs properly with unemployment benefit schemes, in line with activation principles in a context of weak labour demand (keeping in mind the role of unemployment benefits as an automatic stabilizer).

Despite their association with OECD countries, ALMPs are also relevant for low- and middle-income countries, but will be different in nature and scope to those utilized in the OECD. Such ALMPs as public works programmes (including guarantee schemes) are important tools for these countries. With the support of the ILO and social partners, these policies will also contribute to efforts to meet larger development goals, including achieving the MDGs.

Finally, mechanisms should be developed to facilitate constructive dialogue between the social partners, the governments, employers and workers, in order to formulate more effective labour market policies during a crisis and to promote a jobs-led recovery.

Notes

1. See G20 Leaders' Final Communiqué, 'The Global Plan for Recovery and Reform', April 2009, available at http://www.g20.org/Documents/final-communique.pdf.
2. See, for example, the case of the East Asian Crisis in Fallon and Lucas (2002).
3. See, for example, Auer et al. (2008), Kluve (2007) and Bell and Blanchflower (2009).
4. See Betcherman et al. (2004), Card et al. (2009), Kluve (2007) and Lechner and Wunsch (2009) for further discussion on these issues.
5. Some have argued that ALMPs could be used as an 'automatic stabilizer' in the economy as passive measures do (Quiggin 2001): spending on active labour market programmes, for example, provides income replacement (wages paid) and generates a consumption-smoothing effect.
6. See Council of the European Union (2009), ECLAC (2009), ILO (2009a, 2009b), Kannan (2009b), Lee (2009), OECD (2009a), and Titiheruw et al. (2009). The information was current as of October 2009.
7. This holds for cases that have applied in 2009. From January 2010, the maximum duration was set at 18 months.
8. See Budget Speech from 22 May 2009, www.gov.mu/portal/goc/mof/files/budspeech09.pdf.
9. Rs 300 million = US$9,255,831 at the exchange rate on 23 June 2009.
10. See http://www.aph.gov.au/budget/2009-10/content/ministerial_statements/deewr/html/ms_deewr-03.htm.
11. See www.epwp.gov.za/index.asp?c=Home.
12. See http://nrega.nic.in/ and Sjoblom and Farrington (2008).
13. The NREG scheme was extended in 2008 to cover 615 districts (previously 330) and provide work for 32 million people (cost of US$4 billion in the 2008–09 budget). There is also a plan to extend this scheme to urban areas; at least one-third of the beneficiaries shall be women (they made half of the beneficiaries in 2008) (ILO 2009a).
14. See the Korea Development Bank, http://www.kdb.co.kr/weblogic/Board?BID=25&NID=35932&ACTION=VIEW.
15. In contrast, most ALMPs have to be increased through actions of policymakers, except for such countries as Denmark and Switzerland where funding for such policies rises automatically with the unemployment rate (OECD 2009a).
16. The Brazilian Minister of Social Development and Fight Against Hunger, Patrus Ananias, announced during his presentation of the programme at the

ILO's Governing Body meeting in March 2009 that the Bolsa Familia scheme will be expanded, www.ilo.org/global/about_the_ILO/Media_and_public_information/Feature_stories/lang—en/WCMS_103947/index.htm. Paraguay also plans to expand its conditional cash transfer programme to benefit 120,000 extremely poor families (ECLAC 2009).

17. See http://www.theaustralian.news.com.au/story/0,25197,25191631-601,00.html.
18. By 'limited', the authors mean that there can only be a modest increase in ALMPs, drawing on pilot studies conducted at the regional level (p. 61).
19. See http://news.bbc.co.uk/2/hi/business/7936397.stm.

Appendix

Table A8.1 Advantages and disadvantages of policy tools/changes to mitigate the impact of economic crisis on the labour market

Policy tool	Advantage	Disadvantage	Financing source	Institutional requirements	Potential challenges for developing countries
Maintaining labour demand – Keeping people in jobs					
Subsidized reduction in working hours (work sharing)	Allows employers to reduce hours worked to avoid layoffs; Helps retain skilled workers; Reduces labour costs for the employers; Enhances job security for workers; Protects incomes of workers; Promotes skills development of workers (if combined with training); No direct financial cost for employer	Requires financial support from government; Imposes administrative costs and changes to company's management practices; Income replacement may not be perfect leading to loss of earnings for workers	Government revenue through unemployment insurance schemes, unemployment funds, or subsidies paid directly to the employers	Social dialogue; legislation	Costly for developing countries
Non-subsidized reduction in working hours	Allows employers to reduce hours worked to avoid layoffs; Helps retain skilled workers; Reduces labour costs for the employers; Enhances job security for workers; Promotes skills development of workers (if combined with training); No direct financial cost for employer	Involves income reduction for employees; Imposes administrative costs and changes to company's management practices	If income is strongly reduced through cut in working hours employees might depend on a social security net and cause thereby further costs		Wages in developing countries are often too low to cut (the lower labour costs would also have a negligible effect for employers); Tool is only relevant for the formal economy, which is usually very small in such countries

(continued)

Table A8.1 Continued

Policy tool	Advantage	Disadvantage	Financing source	Institutional requirements	Potential challenges for developing countries
On-the-job training	Workers remain employed and retain/improve their human capital, which will contribute to improved productivity and growth in the future	Costly; Training is only a temporary measure and does not reduce labour costs for employers; New skills can be of limited use when there are few job vacancies	Government revenue, enterprises, levies	Training institutions (or within-firm training capacity)	There is a low level of training capacity in some developing countries (training institutions and in firms)
Maintaining labour demand – Creating jobs					
Wage subsidies and cuts to employer social contributions (a policy that will not only help to create new jobs but also to maintain existing ones)	Reduces labour costs of existing and new workers, while workers receive the same wage	Costly and difficult to phase out; Can entail deadweight losses in terms of supporting worker who would have otherwise been hired/kept in the job in the absence of subsidies; Such policies can also encourage employers to replace non-subsidized workers with subsidized ones (substitution effect); Maybe ineffective during a crisis when aggregate demand has collapsed; Cuts in social contributions have long-term cost implications for social security funds	Government revenue	Legislation regulating subsidies	The high cost and problems with leakage of resources are major barriers for many developing countries; This tool is only relevant for the formal economy, which is usually very small in such countries

programmes (and cash-for-work, food-for-work and other conditional cash transfer schemes)	particularly in rural areas, and has other longer-term benefits such as the building of infrastructure	in creating long-term jobs; Difficult to phase out; Proven to be not so effective in developed countries	revenue, official development assistance (ODA)		developing countries to mixed success, which is due to poor design and implementation of programmes
Improving the match between labour demand and supply by making the unemployed more employable					
Job search assistance (JSA)	Improves the job search abilities of unemployed at a relatively low cost	Ineffective in times of low labour demand; Can entail deadweight costs because beneficiaries who find work through JSA are often more qualified and perhaps could have found jobs in the absence of assistance	Government revenue	Public employment service or private labour exchanges/ employment agencies	Many developing countries do not have an effective public employment agency or private brokerage services, or lack skilled staff in these organizations
Work experience and apprenticeship programmes	Helps vulnerable persons, particularly youth, build experience and skills	Poor work conditions, including low wages; Lock-in effect is often low	Government revenue, enterprises, ODA	Existing programmes	Programmes in developing countries are often underfunded, and thus, could be difficult to expand. A major challenge for these countries is improving the effectiveness of apprenticeship schemes in the informal economy. In these schemes, the quality of training can be low.
Training programmes	Builds the skills of those out of employment to increase their chances of finding a job	Costly and training is often not linked to the demands of employers (skills mismatch)	Government revenue, ODA, enterprises, levies, public-private partnerships	Training institutions	There is a lack of effective training institutions in developing countries

(continued)

Table A8.1 Continued

Policy tool	Advantage	Disadvantage	Financing source	Institutional requirements	Potential challenges for developing countries
Entrepreneurship incentives (training and microcredit) (a policy not only used to improve employability but also to create SMEs)	Provides capital and skills training to potential entrepreneurs	Costly and not always effective because training does not focus on the correct skills and because the financing is too restrictive; Poorest/women and other vulnerable groups are unable to access programmes; Many recipients do not succeed over the long-term	Government revenue, ODA, private sources including levies, public-private partnerships	Training and microcredit institutions, entrepreneur associations	Existing programmes in developing countries are only available for a small proportion of the population and are not always effective
Providing income support					
Extending unemployment benefits in terms of duration and coverage	Maintains income, assists with consumption smoothing and prevents households falling into poverty	High direct and administrative costs; Potential disincentive effects (if done without activation)	Government revenue	Existing unemployment benefits scheme and administrative structure, including public employment service	Most developing countries do not have a unemployment benefits system; Costly to establish and requires certain administrative structures that are absent in these countries
Expanding other social protection schemes (social assistance)	Maintains income, assists with consumption and prevents households falling into poverty	High direct and administrative costs; Potential disincentive effects (if done without activation)	Government revenue	Existing social protection scheme and administrative structure	Most developing countries do not have a universal social protection system; Costly to establish

Table A8.2 Responding to the crisis through labour market policies: examples from different regions

Policy (changes to policies and new initiatives)	High-income countries	Middle-income countries	Low-income countries
Subsidized and unsubsidized reduction in working hours	Austria, Belgium, Canada, Czech Republic, Cyprus, Denmark, Finland, France, Germany, Hungary, Ireland, Italy, Japan, Luxembourg, Netherlands, Portugal, Republic of Korea, Slovakia[2], Slovenia, Spain, Sweden, Switzerland, United Kingdom, United States	Argentina, Chile, Costa Rica[3], Dominican Republic, Mexico, Poland, Romania, Russian Federation, Serbia, Turkey, Uruguay	
Job/wage subsidies and cuts to employer social contributions (for new or existing workers)	Australia, Belgium, Canada, Czech Republic[2], Finland, France, Germany, Greece, Hungary, Italy, Japan, New Zealand, Portugal, Republic of Korea, Slovakia, Spain, Sweden, United Kingdom, United States	Argentina, Chile, Malaysia[6], Mexico, Poland, Turkey	
Public works programmes including employment guarantee schemes	Hungary, Iceland, Ireland, Japan, Republic of Korea	Chile, India, Indonesia, Malaysia, Mexico, Pakistan, Paraguay, Peru, Philippines, Saint Lucia, Serbia, South Africa, Turkey, Ukraine	Bangladesh
Job search assistance and improved capacity of public employment services	Australia, Austria, Belgium, Canada, Denmark, Finland, France, Germany, Greece, Hungary, Ireland, Italy, Japan, Netherlands, Norway, Republic of Korea, Spain, Sweden, Switzerland, United Kingdom, United States	Argentina, Chile, China, Dominican Republic, Malaysia[6], Mexico, Pakistan, Philippines, Peru, Poland, Romania, Russian Federation, Serbia, Ukraine	Cambodia
Training (including on-the-job training), Work experience and apprenticeship programmes	Australia, Austria, Bahrain, Belgium, Canada[4], Denmark, Estonia, Finland, France, Germany, Greece, Hungary, Ireland, Italy, Japan, Korea, Netherlands, New Zealand, Norway, Portugal, Saudi Arabia, Slovakia[5], Spain, Sweden, Switzerland, United Kingdom, United States	Argentina, Chile, China, Colombia, Costa Rica, Dominican Republic, Egypt, Indonesia, Jordan, Latvia, Malaysia[6], Mauritius, Mexico, Morocco, Nicaragua, Pakistan, Peru, Philippines, Poland, Romania, Russian Federation, Serbia, Thailand, Turkey, Uruguay	Bangladesh, Cambodia, Kenya, Viet Nam

(*continued*)

Table A8.2 Continued

Policy (changes to policies and new initiatives)	**High-income countries**	**Middle-income countries**	**Low-income countries**
Entrepreneurship incentives	Finland, France, Germany, Hungary, Ireland, Italy, Japan, Korea, Portugal, Slovakia, Spain, United Kingdom, United States	Argentina, China, Chile, Colombia, Costa Rica, India, Indonesia, Latvia, Malaysia[6], Mauritius, Mexico, Pakistan, Peru, Philippines, Poland, Romania, Serbia, Turkey, Uruguay	Cambodia, Kenya, Nepal, Tanzania, Viet Nam
Change to unemployment benefits schemes	Australia, Belgium, Canada, Czech Republic, Finland, France[7], Greece, Ireland, Italy, Japan, Korea, Latvia, Norway, New Zealand, Portugal, Sweden, United States	Argentina, Brazil, Chile[8], China, Jordan, Mexico, Romania, Russian Federation, Ukraine, Uruguay	Viet Nam[9]

Sources: Council of the European Union (2009), ECLAC (2009), ILO (2009a, 2009b), Kannan (2009b), Lee (2009), OECD (2009a), and Titiheruw et al. (2009).

Notes: These examples are drawn from various studies on regional responses to the crisis, which may exclude some country responses that have not been addressed in these references. The categories of countries are based on the World Bank classification using gross national income (GNI), see http://go.worldbank.org/K2CKM78CC0.

1 – In these countries, workers are temporarily unemployed, while their employment contract remains binding.

2 – Planned or considering implementation; see (OECD 2009a).

3 – This is only a draft law (ECLAC 2009).

4 – These programmes are not directly linked to an employer (occupational training) (OECD 2009a).

5 – This refers to training for entrepreneurs (OECD 2009a).

6 – Announced by Deputy Prime Minister of Malaysia on March 10, 2009, www.pmo.gov.my/?menu=speech&page=1677&news_id=5&speech_cat=11. Employers are eligible for increased tax deductions when they hire individuals who were retrenched after July 1 2008.

7 – Proposed extension.

8 – Planned enlargement

9 – Due to the crisis, the Government of Viet Nam has agreed to postpone the scheme. As a result, employees will only be able to access unemployment benefits from the beginning of 2010 at the earliest (Pham 2009).

9

Coping with Crises: Easing the Burden of Macroeconomic and Structural Adjustments through Social Dialogue

L. Rychly

Introduction

During the postwar period, in all regions of the world there were numerous critical developments which affected industrial relations, or in which industrial relations played an important role in the recovery effort.[1] This was the case in Europe and in Japan, where industrial relations were an integral part of postwar reconstruction. It contributed to overcoming the consequences of the major recession of the 1970s and 1980s in industrialized countries and also – to some extent – those of the Asian financial crisis in 1997–98. The acceptance of freedom of association, the practice of collective bargaining and, above all, the development of national tripartite consultations, helped to ease the severe economic difficulties related to the transition from central planning to a market economy in Central and Eastern Europe, preventing major social conflicts.

In this broader context, the objectives of this chapter are: first, to discuss the lessons that can be learned in the sphere of industrial relations from past crises in different parts of the world; secondly, to highlight some recent industrial relations developments at the national, sectoral and enterprise levels since the beginning of the global financial crisis in the middle of 2007; and, thirdly, to suggest some preliminary policy options.

Social dialogue during the global financial crisis

Acceleration of national-level social dialogue

A recent ILO survey, which mapped the industrial relations aspects of the global financial crisis of 2007–09, shows that social partners' involvement in the design and implementation of national measures as a response to the crisis has been rather limited during the first stage (summer and autumn 2008).[2] Many governments apparently hesitated to launch nationwide debates as they feared further erosion of confidence in the national financial systems. In some cases, there were hopes that the crisis would remain limited to some sectors or regions or just to highly industrialized countries which were fully involved in the globalized economy. In others, admitting the impact of the crisis and launching public discussions was postponed for political reasons, linked to electoral cycles in some cases or to the general lack of transparency in governance.

It can be stated that in most countries, with notable exceptions,[3] the government's very first reaction was not to involve the social partners in crisis management. However, this picture changed considerably when the crisis deepened. The need to gain support for these policies and to share responsibilities became a very strong motivation resulting, in many instances, in a more positive attitude towards social dialogue. It is evident that since December 2008 and even more since January 2009, crisis-related measures have been increasingly on the agenda of tripartite or bipartite negotiations/consultations. This tendency continued in 2009, considerably improving the originally dim picture.

The form and content of various types of crisis-related social dialogue are reflected in Table 9.1.[4]

As highlighted by the results presented in Table 9.1, it comes as no surprise that those countries with the most developed and institutionalized industrialized systems reacted quickly and proactively, with governments turning to their social partners at the very earliest stages of the crisis. In countries such as Belgium, Ireland and the Netherlands, the first critical developments were simply taken on board in ongoing regular consultations or negotiations. In Ireland, the changing economic conditions were reflected in the "transitional agreement" negotiated and signed within the framework of the joint medium-term programme, Towards 2016. This agreement established rather moderate wage growth, and covered issues such as the employment rights of temporary workers (who were the first victims of the crisis), voluntary arbitration on change at the enterprise level, as well as the government's commitment to modernizing public services.

In the Netherlands, as in Ireland, the last rounds of annual consultations between the government and the social partners on social and economic plans for the coming years took into account the potential economic downturn. Both social partners agreed on the need

Table 9.1 Form and main focus of crisis-related social dialogue at the national level

Country	Tr/Bi	Exp	Agr	Train	Secu	Empl	Tax	LA	Wage	E/W
Albania	x			x	x		x			x
Angola	x							x		
Armenia	x	x	x	x	x	x			x	x
Australia				x		x			x	x
Barbados	x	x				x				
Belgium	x		x		x				x	x
Bosnia and Herzegovina	x		x	x	x	x		x		
Brazil						x			x	x
Bulgaria	x			x	x	x			x	x
Chile			x	x	x	x				
China	x	x		x	x	x		x	x	
Colombia	x									
Croatia	x							x	x	x
Cyprus	x	x		x	x	x				
Czech Rep.	x	x		x	x	x				x
Ecuador	x									
Estonia				x		x	x			x
Finland					x	x			x	x
France	x			x	x	x	x	x	x	x
Germany		x			x	x	x		x	x
Guatemala	x									
Hungary	x				x	x				x
India	x				x	x			x	
Indonesia	x					x	x		x	x
Ireland	x		x	x	x	x	x	x	x	
Japan			x	x	x	x		x	x	x
Kazakhstan	x	x		x	x	x		x	x	x
Korea, Rep. of	x	x	x	x	x	x	x	x	x	
Lithuania							x	x	x	x
Luxembourg	x			x					x	x
Namibia	x					x				
Netherlands	x	x		x	x	x	x	x	x	
Norway				x			x	x		x
Pakistan	x					x			x	
Peru	x					x			x	x
Philippines	x					x		x	x	
Poland	x				x	x			x	x
Romania	x			x	x	x	x	x	x	x
Russian Federation	x	x			x	x				x
Singapore	x		x	x		x			x	
Slovakia	x	x				x	x			x
Slovenia	x			x	x	x			x	
South Africa	x	x	x	x	x	x				

(continued)

Table 9.1 Continued

Country	Tr/Bi	Exp	Agr	Train	Secu	Empl	Tax	LA	Wage	E/W
Spain			x	x	x	x		x	x	x
Sudan		x								
Tajikistan	x		x		x	x			x	
United Kingdom	x	x		x	x	x	x			x
Uruguay	x								x	
United States				x	x	x		x		x
Viet Nam	x	x			x	x			x	
Zimbabwe	x	x								

Notes: Trip/Bi – crisis-related issues discussed in standing or newly created tripartite or bipartite bodies or regular conferences
Exp – crisis-related issues discussed in specific expert bodies dealing with the crisis
Agr – tripartite agreements or similar joint documents reached
Train – training measures
Secu – social security/protection measures
Empl – employment-related measures
Tax – tax-related measures
LA – specific measures related to labour administration
Wage – wage-related measures
E/W – specific initiatives taken by social partners

to maintain purchasing power and asked the government to postpone the planned VAT increase – aside from a series of other measures to cope with the rapidly deteriorating situation. The Dutch government reacted quickly to the crisis by creating Mobility Centres to assist workers in their search for jobs and, as requested by social partners, introduced the a new work-sharing scheme enabling companies to apply for part-time unemployment benefits for some of their employees to neutralize the acute drop in demand and to avoid unnecessary dismissals.

Spain was one of the first countries in which the social partners began to discuss anti-crisis measures. This occurred as early as the summer 2008 in response to the imminent crisis in the Spanish construction sector, exacerbated by external factors related to the tightening of credit conditions. The tripartite Declaration of Principles for the Promotion of the Economy, Employment, Competitiveness and Social Progress of 29 July 2008 suggested a broad range of measures targeting increased liquidity of companies, financing protected housing construction and reforming the vocational training system. This agreement also showed the limits of the compromise and highlighted the major cause of disagreements in many further negotiations throughout the world: employers were calling for greater flexibility and less costly dismissal provisions – proposals vehemently rejected by both union confederations, the CC.OO and the UGT.

In many countries, however, it took much more time for social dialogue to become part of the solution. As stated by one national union leader:

> First we were told that the crisis would pass round our country. Then we were told that consequences would not be hard because we are well protected. Then they admitted that the crisis might take some time and that the worst period will be the first half of 2009. Now, we are being told that the crisis will take two, three or four years... We have to be prepared for everything.

This is not the exception; the crisis took many governments by surprise and their reaction lagged behind people's expectations. Employers and workers facing the first effects of the crisis asked the governments to take urgent measures,[5] or they themselves elaborated suggestions in areas such as tax policy, job security, wages, social protection, training, and so on. In other cases, employers and workers at the national level or in the worst-hit sectors such as finance, construction and the automobile industry presented joint requests to their governments.[6]

Naturally, while employers' and workers' strategies coincided on many macroeconomic measures, in most cases they disagreed about two important points: whether (or how far) wage moderation should be applied, and whether the employment relationship should be more protected or more flexible at times of crisis. Even in the two 'success stories' mentioned earlier (Ireland and Spain), social dialogue later faced serious difficulties during the stage of negotiating the sharing of crisis-induced costs.[7] In Ireland, employers withdrew from the earlier mentioned 'transitional agreement' in December 2009, thus paving the way for a period of company-level bargaining agreements after nearly 25 years of centralized national-level bargaining, arguing that the agreement became 'wholly unsuited to economic circumstances'. At the same time, the government announced that talks with the public sector trade unions over austerity measures had collapsed. For some observers, this meant the 'end of 'social partnership'',[8] one of the elements of Irish prosperity since the 1980s.

In most cases, crisis-related social dialogue was not limited to one communication channel. According to the dynamics of developments, informal and formal meetings alternated and complemented one another. However, regular tripartite and bipartite institutions proved to be very helpful in providing a reliable framework; among the countries observed by the ILO survey, the vast majority used existing tripartite or bipartite bodies to address the crisis. Unsurprisingly, tripartite institutions with a negotiating mandate[9] and composed of members of cabinet and high-level representatives of social partners proved to be much more efficient in this emergency situation than large advisory or consultative councils with cumbersome structures, complicated procedures and limited (mainly advisory) mandates. Many countries[10] decided to entrust the crisis issues to specific bodies, some of them newly created, with the specific task of elaborating anti-crisis action plans or suggesting measures to help governments in making decisions. The motivation for such a step was not only to involve large groups of people in decision-making and benefit from their specific knowledge or experience, but also to enhance the feasibility of suggested measures, making them separate from day-to-day political conflicts. However, the composition of these special anti-crisis teams has been sometimes random, sometimes politically motivated, and in some cases without the participation of organized employers and workers. The status of these bodies also varies greatly, from expert teams composed of academics, government officials of various ranks, managers and bankers to high-level organs created by the highest authorities of the country. Obviously, in the last case, there is the risk that these bodies might overshadow the regular representative institutions already charged with clear and incontestable political mandates.

In the overwhelming majority of cases, consultations and negotiations on crisis-related measures were based on policy documents prepared under the responsibility of governments, most often in the form of policy packages. Almost all the countries surveyed included in these packages – apart from macroeconomic measures – many provisions with a bearing on national labour policies as reviewed in chapter 8. Practically all of them contained provisions dealing with employment, the unanimous opinion being that the key measure is to keep people employed. This is also why specific emergency support was provided to industries directly or indirectly employing large numbers of workers, especially in the automobile and construction sectors which are particularly suffering from the credit crunch and low demand. Some employment measures looked farther into the future and were intended to improve the employability of workers or promote promising new sectors, e.g. in the area of so-called 'green jobs'.

In most cases, social dialogue also dealt with social protection measures, either focused on concrete groups of workers or companies (and provided ad hoc),[11] or with measures to change existing legislation, for example, the laws dealing with unemployment insurance[12] or protection of workers' claims in the event of employers' insolvency. However, in the field of labour legislation there are disagreements between employers and workers, especially in relation to the issue of regulation of dismissal, or where the proposed changes have an impact on the stability of employment or on working hours. Wage policy is another area of frequent and intense national-level dialogue, especially between the social partners themselves. Governments rarely called for a general wage freeze,[13] but calls for moderation and for respect of companies' capability to pay[14] have not been uncommon. In some cases, the crisis was an opportunity to discuss and to adapt the minimum wage.[15] While minimum wage adjustment might be more difficult in times of crisis, contrary to what happened in previous downturns, a large number of countries raised their real minimum wage or are considering improving their minimum wage-fixing systems.[16] In some countries, the crisis revived discussions on the introduction of the national statutory minimum wage,[17] even if the positions of social partners still differ.

Most of the measures contained in the 'packages' are to be implemented through individual laws and by-laws. In some countries, the adoption of a more comprehensive anti-crisis law or laws has also been considered in order to simplify and accelerate legislative procedures. As the crisis developed at the end of the budgetary year, many governments included anti-crisis policies in their budget proposals for 2009; in many cases, these revised state budgets, reflecting spending on new anti-crisis measures and programmes, were also submitted to the social partners for information or consultation.[18] In most cases, these budgetary proposals, seeking cuts in public spending, were subjected to harsh criticism, especially from unions. In many European countries, consultation on the national budget is the usual practice and a regular component of tripartism, not specifically related to the crisis.

In some cases, anti-crisis measures were embodied in tripartite or bipartite documents. Most of them (pacts, agreements, declarations, joint guidelines, opinions and so on) are not enforceable by law but have an undeniable political significance. Not only do they contain concrete recommendations for governments and social partners, but they also send important political messages in sensitive areas such as wages and redundancies, sometimes containing guidelines for socially responsible restructuring.[19] Some of them have strong ethical messages concerning mutual trust and solidarity, the protection of vulnerable sectors, or socially responsible management. Commenting on a recently signed tripartite agreement in Japan, Prime Minister Taro Aso described it as 'a message to the people'.

The crisis of 2007–09 undeniably has a strong moral element. It is widely acknowledged that it is not simply an ordinary cyclical recession caused by the inherent laws of markets; rather, is is seen as strongly related to bad management, a lack of regulation, insufficient supervision, greed, or even straightforwardly criminal behaviour. As expressed in the words of the Secretary-General of the ITUC, there is a 'strong feeling of injustice and anger'.[20] In this sense, this crisis is not just a cyclical economic phenomenon with social consequences, but also a political event.[21] Thus, the solutions are seen to lie not only in traditional macroeconomic fiscal and monetary measures or in active or passive employment policies, but also in the increased responsibility of political leaders and the managers of enterprises, in enhanced transparency and in a system of responsible governance. Many politicians, realising these moral aspects, appealed for the voluntary adoption of policies, such as limiting or avoiding redundancies, restraining from excessive wage requirements, limiting industrial actions or respecting workers' rights and civil freedoms.[22]

The crisis might also have long-term impacts on wage systems, at both the national and company levels, especially in connection with the effort to reduce risk-taking short-term incentives, but only the future will show whether the crisis-related developments will reverse the tendency towards variable pay schemes, especially in the banking sector, described in several recent but pre-crisis studies.[23] As we learn from past crises, economic downturn always represents a challenge for income policies and governments tend to intervene in national-level bargaining, which is a strong impetus for the centralization of wage bargaining. However, if national wage bargaining fails, as it has in the case of Ireland, enterprise-level bargaining can gain some ground.

Limited number of comprehensive tripartite agreements

Only in a limited number of cases did social dialogue on anti-crisis measures result in the adoption of specific, fully-fledged tripartite or bipartite documents,[24] legally binding only in very rare cases[25] but always politically important. In this context, three recent examples of national-level tripartite agreements should be highlighted because of their particular comprehensiveness.

In **South Africa**, as a joint effort of the Presidency and the national tripartite committee (NEDLAC), the government and the social partners agreed on the 'Framework for South Africa's response to the international economic crisis', built on the following principles: (1) the protection of the most vulnerable groups of workers; (2) the growth of the economy to increase employment and guarantee the quality of jobs; (3) high levels of investment in infrastructure; and (4) timely, targeted, tailored and reviewed interventions. Retaining and increasing employment are the core objectives of the agreement. It is estimated that through the expanded public works programme, more than two million full-time jobs for the poor and the unemployed will be created by 2014. In spite of current fiscal pressures caused by lower than expected revenues, the government will maintain social transfers and other key social expenditures.

While the South African agreement focuses on government measures, the 'Agreement by labor, management, civic groups and the government to overcome the economic crisis' reached in the Republic of Korea, contains targeted objectives that are to be achieved through industrial relations, in particular through enterprise-level bargaining. With the objective of sharing the burden between labour and management, 'labour will freeze, return or reduce wages depending upon the business conditions of their companies, while business will refrain from dismissing workers for managerial reasons so as to maintain existing levels of employment'. Labour will also 'refrain from strikes during the economic crisis, will not demand unreasonable participation in managerial matters, while business will try to create trust between labour and management through transparent and ethical management and faithful labour–management consultation'. Similar to the South African agreement, the social safety net would be expanded to protect vulnerable groups and to remove blind spots not covered by social insurance (including protection of temporary workers and the self-employed), and the government will promote employment – for example in the areas of health, social welfare, education, culture, the environment and community development – and will try to make these jobs sustainable. In order to 'spread concession bargaining at the enterprise level, workers' and employers' organizations will provide guidance about job-sharing and job-retaining measures' to their members, and the government will set up and operate a Crisis Support Team. A joint body supported by the Prime Minister's Office will monitor the implementation of the agreement. However, the impact of this agreement might be limited by the fact that one of the national trade union federations did not participate in the negotiation process.

In **Japan**, the tripartite agreement signed on 23 March 2009 assigned specific roles to the government and to the social partners in four areas: maintenance of employment by promoting the Japanese model of work sharing (including reduced working time), expansion and strengthening of the social safety net, support for participants of vocational training programmes and employment creation, with a special focus on growing sectors such as medical services, care work, the environment, agriculture and forestry.

The crucial role of public policies supporting crisis-related social dialogue

As discussed in Rychly (2009), crises usually enhance the state's interest in industrial relations, which are seen either as a problem or as part of the solution. In the latter case, appropriate public policies can make a substantial contribution to the efficiency of social dialogue at various levels. The current crisis has led many governments to intensify their appeals to social partners to negotiate or participate in joint consultations; such appeals are a common practice in northern Europe or in France, but the crisis has led to a more proactive approach towards social dialogue and collective bargaining even in countries with less dialogue-oriented administrations, not only in Europe but also in Asia and Latin America.

Beyond this general political support, social dialogue can benefit from more concrete promotional actions. Above all, governments should promote – by legislation, provision of funds and by providing technical support – social innovation. For example, when negotiating redundancies or, better yet, alternatives to them, the financial involvement of the state is the major factor for success. Following the German example of *Kurzarbeit* (which many times in the past helped to find at least temporary solutions to enterprises' difficulties with fluctuations in demand), several governments decided, in line with the requests of their social partners, to improve the situation of workers who were obliged to accept shorter working hours and to compensate them from unemployment schemes or from other public budgets.[26] This measure has a direct bearing on collective bargaining, as management and unions can offer employees much better pay conditions which make the deal with unions much more plausible. For example, the German state provides compensation for income losses in proportion to the regular working hours in cases of considerable reductions in working time for economic reasons or in relation to structural changes within the company.[27]

In France, the state finances payment for lost working hours. The system was significantly improved following the recent agreement between national employers' and workers' federations. In Belgium, the National Labour Office compensates temporary economic unemployment up to 75 per cent of the maximum wage.[28] In the Netherlands, an amendment to the Unemployment Act extended the protection against partial unemployment (originally applicable only in situations of 'force majeure') to the crisis situation facing the country in 2009. In Sweden, where temporary layoffs are normally prohibited, the central social partners in the manufacturing industry signed an agreement allowing shorter working hours. According to this agreement, employees can be temporarily laid off while keeping their jobs and receiving at least 80 per cent of their normal salary, in proportion to the time actually worked. This agreement, however, has caused disagreements among trade unions.

It is evident that a more rapid response to the crisis was possible in those countries where the legal basis for partial unemployment compensation already existed, where the collective bargaining system was sufficiently sophisticated to include flexible working time arrangements, and where collective bargaining coverage extends to the majority of workers. Recent developments thus seem to confirm the hypothesis that 'bargaining coordination facilitates faster and more flexible responses to shocks'.[29]

As mentioned earlier, many national consultations and enterprise-level agreements deal with the issue of the employability of workers.[30] Once again, this is an area where governments can contribute greatly to the deal between the two sides of industry by providing direct financial contributions or tax incentives to employers and/or workers.[31] These deals can also be supported through the adoption of appropriate legislation, easing the interruption of careers by extending social and pension insurance for workers on training schemes,[32] by including training (accredited by relevant authorities) in the public works programme, and so on. For example, Italy established a Fund for Employment and Training financed from the Employment Fund, and the Fund for Underdeveloped Areas (*Fondo per le Aree Sottosviluppate*).[33] In France, the state will contribute 1.5 billion euros to the *Fonds d'investissement social (FISO)*, destined to support retraining during the crisis period.[34] At the tripartite employment summit on 12 January 2009, the UK government announced the introduction of 'employers' Golden Hellos', incentives of up to £2,500 paid to employers to recruit and train unemployed people. In Romania, the government decided to co-fund 50 per cent of the costs of vocational training provided to unemployed people and employees.[35] The Government of China announced that the vocational training programmes will expand to bring the total number of skilled workers to 110 million nationwide according to the plan for reducing unemployment in 2009–10.[36] Actually, using the period of low demand for the upskilling of workers and thus increasing their chances in the labour market has been one of the most frequently used anti-crisis measures, discussed between social partners themselves and with the state. The loss of skills from downsizing has been identified as one of the biggest threats posed by the crisis in many countries such as Germany, South Africa and the United Kingdom.

No doubt the management of the crisis and its impact will require extraordinary efforts from public authorities in general and from labour administrations in particular. In many countries the social partners count the improvement of labour administration services as one of their objectives. Public employment services, labour inspectorates and vocational training institutions are particularly active during this period, as rapidly rising unemployment creates new challenges for active employment policies in terms of massive restructuring and redundancies affecting specific industries, regions and categories of workers such as agency workers, fixed-term employees, migrants and young workers. Unsurprisingly, the need for the more efficient and innovative functioning of job centres has been part of the consultations. In many countries national authorities have already taken various measures to strengthen national employment services, for example by increasing the number of staff members to reduce unemployment insurance processing time and to improve counselling services,[37] by assisting with the repatriation of returning overseas workers,[38] or by restructuring the system for better efficiency.[39]

In order to help unemployed people back into employment as soon as possible in the Netherlands, in December 2008 the Dutch labour ministry decided to establish 30 mobility centres, promoting cooperation between companies, trade unions and job-finding organizations.[40] The UK government introduced a government-funded scheme that offers individual job seekers one-to-one support and training tailored to their needs (Jobcentre Plus).[41]

Similarly, labour inspection is facing crisis-related challenges, particularly in the employment field as regards control procedures for termination of employment for economic reasons or addressing unregistered or illegal work, often connected with the return of migrant workers.[42] Some countries are therefore strengthening their inspection services to prevent social dumping.[43] In Ireland, the new National Employment Rights Authority (NERA) created in 2008 focuses on wage arrears.[44] In those countries where labour inspection is involved in industrial relations, for example, Spain, inspectors are increasingly involved as mediators in collective bargaining and industrial conflicts. However, the crisis may also reinforce the tendencies already existing in some countries to restrict the number of inspection visits, under the pretext that they create an additional burden for the enterprises. In the long run, the major crisis-related risk for labour administration is linked to major budget cuts that can be expected following the huge investments involved in stimulus packages. The squeeze on public expenditure may result in cuts in the number of labour administration staff, in a higher turnover caused by employment insecurity and low salaries, and thus in a worsening of the quality of services on offer.

Mixed picture of enterprise-level collective bargaining

Most sectors and enterprises where collective bargaining is practised are still covered by collective agreements that were negotiated before the summer of 2008. Despite an increasing number of more comprehensive analytical studies suggesting widespread wage moderation, the aggregated impact of bargaining in the new circumstances on wages and other working conditions will not be fully known until later into 2010.

However, developments reported from all regions, and especially from the most affected sectors (finance, automobile, construction, steel, transport, tourism, mining, retailing, textile and garment, temporary work agencies, export-oriented manufacturing, services), show that *job security, linked to income security, is becoming the crucial issue on the bargaining agenda* in many enterprises.

Collective bargaining in many important enterprises in all regions and in the public sector deals with the urgent need to cut costs, including wage costs. The measures suggested by management, and in many cases bargained with unions, include:

- Freezing or reducing of wages, including the postponement or elimination of bonuses and, in some cases, the reduction of executive pay; Changes in company wage structures.
- Shorter or more flexible working hours, paid or unpaid leave, sabbaticals and other career breaks, working hours accounts, limiting or cancelling overtime or elimination of overtime bonuses, or even shorter breaks for workers.
- Redundancies – forced or voluntary.
- Voluntary retirement.
- Reduction of contributions to health and pensions schemes.
- Elimination of job banks.
- Compensation via shares.
- Provision of training.

- Possibility of rehiring.
- Job security for a certain period.
- Social peace as a condition for government loans.

Wage moderation or even wage freezes or wage cuts are required in many enterprises. However, especially at higher negotiation levels, both partners often agree that purchasing power must be maintained in order to boost demand;[45] there are reports about recent sectoral wage agreements that envisage wage increases despite the crisis.[46] Nevertheless, in many cases there is pressure to renegotiate pre-crisis wage agreements, 'taking into account new circumstances'. In some agreements, social partners introduced clauses that enable the renegotiation of agreements in case of changed economic conditions. In some cases, 'voluntary' wage concession by unions are reported to have saved companies from the threat of bankruptcy, or facilitated the securing of new investment.

The trend towards wage moderation as part of concession bargaining seems to be confirmed by the initial surveys from different regions. The 2009 survey on the prospects of industrial relations elaborated for the Korean Ministry of Labour and the Korea Labour Institute[47] shows that both employers and workers share quite pessimistic expectations, especially in terms of employment insecurity because of the economic recession. A majority of respondents (70 per cent of employers, 60 per cent of workers) responded that it would be desirable to freeze or cut the wage level for 2009. Both parties agreed that labour and management should focus on employment security, refrain from wage increases and find solutions using reduction in working time, unpaid rotational leave with job training, cut in nominal wages and regulated layoffs.

A survey by Towers Perrin shows that 82 per cent of respondents revised their remuneration policies and took cost-saving measures, including the revision of wage levels (21 per cent), the freezing of wages (18 per cent) or the reduction of wages for newly hired workers (4 per cent). Wage increases, initially fixed at 3 per cent on average, were reduced by 0.5 per cent. However, the attitudes vary from extreme rigour to simple prudence, depending on the industry and enterprise involved. According to the same study, enterprises facing the crisis try to maintain internal cohesion and solidarity by granting the same wage increases to all categories of workers.

The problems faced by small and medium-sized companies seem to be similar, if not worse. According to a survey conducted on 475 SMEs undertaken for the Irish Small Firms Association (SFA), 30 per cent of companies have been forced to make redundancies while 28 per cent expect to do so during the next quarter; in addition, 63 per cent of companies have stopped recruiting. To face economic difficulties and avoid layoffs, nearly 70 per cent of small firms expect to introduce a pay freeze in the next three months, while 23 per cent will cut wages.[48]

The forecast for the trend in wages for 2010 does not predict any substantial improvement. In the public sector, austerity measures are supposed to have serious effects on both salaries and on employment prospects and not only in countries which were particularly hit by recession – such as the Baltic states, Greece, Hungary, Ireland and Spain.[49] In the private sector, there is a large gap between employers' and workers' expectations for the next collective bargaining rounds, even in countries with traditionally well-established bargaining practices, such as Denmark, Netherlands or Sweden. At the same time, the differentiation between companies, industries and professions, already apparent from the previous year, seems to be confirmed and even made deeper, as some enterprises are already preparing for recovery and are therefore focusing on retaining or engaging core workers: staff cuts and wage reductions seem thus to be selective,[50] more often affecting low-skilled and low-paid workers and thus contributing to greater wage inequality.

The fact that many companies are facing or planning restructuring seems to be confirmed, for example, by the survey organized among Belgian companies by the human resource consultancy SD Worx.[51] According to this survey, half of the companies expected to undertake restructuring in 2009; smaller companies, however, seemed to be less concerned by restructuring processes. These restructuring processes include mergers, closures or internal company changes which may or may not involve staff cuts. As indicated by the Belgian authorities, the number of bankruptcies during the first three months of 2009 increased by nearly 20 per cent compared to the same period in 2008.

In spite of major economic difficulties, many employers prefer temporary work stoppages, obligatory leave, the cancellation of overtime, drastic shortening of working hours and other forms of interruption of production to immediate layoffs, a point also stressed in chapter 8.[52] Many of them experienced important workforce shortages just before the crisis started and had to invest in employee training, accommodation or transportation; they therefore prefer to keep their employees in case the demand grows again soon.[53] Avoiding layoffs actually might save costs in the long run, as productivity tends to be higher under the work-sharing programmes than it is after layoffs and 'when the company decides to ramp up production again and does not have to hire and train new employees...'[54] However, as discussed earlier, the success of partial unemployment is linked to the capacity of the state to assist companies and workers through the use of passive and active employment policies. Since the crisis started, several governments decided to strengthen the security component of the *flexicurity* approach; for example, the Spanish government is considering temporarily extending the payment of unemployment benefits from two to three years.[55] In Japan, financial aid to jobless workers is part of the rescue package. In the United Kingdom, the government announced a £500 million scheme to help people who have been out of work for more than six months. In the Bahamas, a new unemployment insurance scheme was introduced.

For the time being, it is difficult to predict the consequences of the crisis on national collective bargaining systems. Cases of the further decentralization of collective bargaining systems as a consequence of crisis-related pressures on flexibility exist,[56] but they are probably not representative. On the contrary, in some cases of higher-level bargaining, critical developments have unblocked the bargaining process and facilitated an agreement between the two sides of industry. It is not unlikely that the crisis might bring some tendency to improve the coordination of collective bargaining to avoid unnecessary industrial conflicts, to reduce transaction costs and to avoid wage undercutting, as was the case in the past.[57]

The necessity to coordinate labour conditions in multinational companies will certainly lead to further efforts to extend collective bargaining beyond the boundaries of national states; these developments might be supported by regional groupings, as is already the case in the European Union.

Trends in trade union membership will be a crucial factor in the further development of collective bargaining. The effects of the crisis of 2007–09 on unionization rates are, however, difficult to forecast. On one hand, there are clear signs from many parts of the world that the generalized feeling of insecurity and the need for solidarity can lead to higher levels of union affiliation and participation in union activities,[58] similar to events during the Asian financial crisis; for example, in the United States the unionization rate increased in 2006–07.[59] There are reports about workers joining unions in companies menaced by restructuring in various European countries. Interestingly enough, the role of unions during the crisis has been recently highlighted by many politicians and other authorities, including US President Barack Obama[60] and Pope Benedict XVI.[61] If handled correctly, the global financial crisis may therefore be an opportunity for unions to enhance their authority and prestige and bring in new members. On the other hand, however, unemployment, bankruptcies, mergers or structural changes are reported to have a negative effect on union density.[62]

The crisis (especially its budgetary consequences) will certainly affect employment conditions and industrial relations in the public services. Public sector workers could face freezes or even wage cuts[63] for the next few years,[64] as their pay is often linked to the price index, stagnating or even falling in case of deflation predicted for years to come. Moreover, huge stimulus packages will have a negative impact on public finances with budget deficits spiralling out of control, and with public sector pay accounting for a large proportion of public spending. Recently, there have been several industrial conflicts concerning wages and restructuring, some of them aggravated by the challenges of liberalization and privatization prospects. As in the past, the consequences will be particularly important in countries where public servants are not protected by proper collective bargaining rights. However, in those countries where public servants are better protected than private sector workers, solidarity between these two groups of employees might be severely challenged.[65]

Concluding remarks

General considerations

Current and past experience shows that the economic crisis has numerous effects on the content and form of industrial relations as well as on the behaviour of its actors and of the state.

These effects can be rather paradoxical. On one hand, economic constraints, especially if the result is downsizing, increase tensions between the two sides of industry. They also have an impact on the balance of power, as job insecurity reduces the chances of industrial action. Structural changes may also affect the capacity of employers' and workers' organizations to represent their constituents in affected sectors. On the other hand, economic hardship helps to bridge the interests of employers and workers, as their short-term interests – which are usually contradictory – are overshadowed by shared long-term concerns about the survival of companies or whole industries. As seen in many studies, strike activities generally vary according to the business cycle.[66] It seems that the propensity to strike is related to the divergence of expectations between employers and unions, which reaches a maximum in the boom of the cycle.[67] Another reason for lower strike activity during the crisis seems to be the fact that, in a recession, the reduced expectations of workers facilitates internal consensus within their unions, and the fear of job insecurity leads unions to seek a more consensual relationship with both management and the government.

Collective bargaining during the recession – so-called 'concession bargaining' – can therefore lead to compromises, trade-offs and win–win agreements that would be difficult to imagine in the period of economic stability and growth. It should be noted, however, that this type of bargaining, obviously used more frequently during the crisis period, exists occasionally regardless of the general economic situation. As observed in several research studies,[68] it can hardly be considered a long-term strategy; rather, it creates a new, temporary, more consensual, less adversarial system of industrial relations, weakening the struggle for power which is an inherent characteristic of labour–management relations. However, the evidence shows that collective bargaining is 'responding pragmatically to the conditions of the economic environment, and that when the economy regains its health, collective bargaining will return to its former aggressive and adversarial self'.[69] This does not preclude pragmatic and more or less durable adaptations of whole industrial relations systems, as witnessed, for example, in Sweden in the 1970s–90s (see Rychly 2009).

Also at the national level, serious economic difficulties and other exceptional situations may require solutions reaching beyond the partial interests of employers and workers, and sometimes even across the political spectrum – solutions in favour of the public interest. The feasibility of reforms – especially pro-growth and anti-inflationary fiscal and monetary measures, measures aimed at achieving reductions in public expenditure, the reform of social protection or of labour market policies, privatization or the adoption of investment incentives – may be facilitated by improved communication between the state and the social partners. Moreover, some economic objectives, typically those related to income policies combating inflation and increasing competitiveness, can be implemented successfully only with the cooperation – or at the very least the acquiescence – of employers and workers. Not surprisingly, in the critical periods, *the state tends to intervene in various ways in industrial relations*, which in extreme cases may raise questions concerning the compatibility of such actions with international standards or national laws concerning the freedom of association and the right to bargain collectively.

There is nevertheless a huge difference between the logic of collective bargaining between management and labour, and the logic of a national-level tripartite social dialogue. While collective bargaining is based on differences of interests and the struggle for power between the two sides of industry, with cooperation often limited to crisis periods, at the national level the state, as guardian of the public interest, should have a permanent interest in cooperating with representatives of employers and workers, representing the two major societal groups involved in the production of national wealth. Social dialogue should be the part of governance of any sensible government. But this wisdom is not always applied and, as noted by Wilke and Tarantelli many years ago, 'usually, in a recession, politicians in order to allay restive unions and to reduce losses in mass support, accept bargains which may be symbolic *prima facie* but which imply obligations in the future. Extending, e.g. tripartite arrangements to ever more issue areas including legislation, is intangible at the moment but will have its tangible effects over time.'[70]

It can be argued therefore that *industrial relations at the enterprise and national levels is not merely a passive object* of developments related to the crisis; quite the contrary: *it can be a useful policy tool* which can help mitigate social hardship and facilitate recovery measures, and most of all help rebuild confidence which is the crucial condition for returning to normal economic conditions.

Lessons from the past and the global financial crisis of 2007–09

From the past, we can learn that economic crises have seriously shaken or even temporarily disrupted industrial relations in many parts of the world, including the most advanced countries with the oldest traditions of social dialogue. However, in countries with well-established labour institutions, social dialogue has, sooner or later, managed to adapt to new circumstances, and played a significant role in renewing economic stability and growth. This is also the case in countries transitioning from the planned to the market economy, where social partners' organizations were established on a sound, democratic basis and where governments showed the political will to involve them in the design and implementation of economic and social reforms. In some countries with non-existent or fragile social dialogue traditions, past crises served as catalysts to the creation or strengthening of social dialogue institutions; however, these achievements in some countries did not sustain the return to normal economic conditions. In certain countries, the crisis increased the authority of trade unions and the interest of workers in their functioning. National economic emergencies in most countries generally increase the interest of governments in industrial relations and their involvement in procedural and substantial rules governing relations between employers and workers and employment conditions.

From the global financial crisis of 2007–09, we learn that the social partners' involvement in the design and implementation of national measures in response to the crisis has been rather limited, at least in the early stages (2008). Nevertheless, there are clear signs that crisis-related measures were increasingly on the agenda of national tripartite bodies or ad hoc meetings organized with the participation of social partners over 2009. In many countries, national employers' and workers' organizations criticized the government for inadequate and slow reaction; sometimes they joined together in voicing this criticism.

At the enterprise level, sacrificing pay and benefits to save jobs seems to be a widespread response by trade unions and workers to the deteriorating economic climate. This tendency towards 'concession bargaining' seems to be confirmed by several more comprehensive recent studies.[71] At the national level, however, positions on income policies are divided; while some governments insist on wage moderation, others prioritize maintaining purchasing power and demand.

The global financial crisis underscores the importance of the regular employment relationship with regards to workers' protection in times of crisis, as atypical and other temporary workers are often the first victims of downsizing. Workers whose employment was arranged through illegal job brokers are a particularly vulnerable group. The impact is heavier on outsourced workers in small and medium-sized companies.

The uncertainty about the prospects for future employment is one of the key features of industrial relations during the crisis period, as concession bargaining can only be successful as a transitory strategy. If concession does not prevent redundancies in the long run, this strategy is in danger of weakening the unions that took the risk and recommended it to their members. This crisis was not sparked by low wages and therefore concession bargaining, while beneficial in a concrete company, should not be transformed into a general wage freeze policy.

Policy options

In dealing with the current global financial and economic crisis, governments and the social partners should give priority to negotiated solutions. Social dialogue and collective bargaining have a particular significance at this time and must be promoted as tools not only for handling the social consequences of the crisis but also for addressing – through improved governance – its causes and re-establishing economic growth and stability. Where negotiations are not practicable, other forms of social dialogue should apply, such as consultations or the simple exchange of information or developments of various forms of industrial democracy within enterprises, for example through works councils.

At the national level, the existing institutional framework, as well as newly established consultative bodies, should be used to identify appropriate national policies and their implementation. Where these bodies do not exist, ad hoc high-level meetings should be held to exchange information and consult or negotiate policy measures. Representative organizations of employers and workers should be consulted on legislative and other anti-crisis measures concerning their interests. Where specific anti-crisis expert bodies have been created, they should not replace functioning tripartite or bipartite organs.

It is crucial to build and maintain mutual trust between the state and the social partners and among the social partners themselves, to prevent social unrest, avoid damaging industrial actions and maintain social cohesion. Democratic policymaking and transparency of governance have a particular importance in these circumstances. Measures should be taken to guarantee impartial and efficient judicial, as well as extra-judicial proceedings, to deal with individual and collective disputes, especially in connection with layoffs and wage arrears.

The 'exit' phase of the crisis, addressing the issue of public finances, might represent a particular challenge for national industrial relations systems; every effort should be made to prevent disruption of social dialogue mechanisms that proved to be successful in the past.

Labour administrations systems should be reinforced to ensure the implementation of measures to combat the crisis and its social consequences and to provide services to employers and workers; public employment offices and labour inspection bodies should be strengthened.

At the enterprise level, the exchange of information, consultations and collective bargaining are essential to avoid or mitigate the negative consequences of crisis-related developments. The state and higher bodies of employers' and workers' organizations should assist enterprises in finding solutions and alternatives to cutting jobs and in providing necessary support to workers losing employment and income.

Notes

1. This chapter is based on Rychly (2009), which also provides more details on past experiences.

2. The survey was based mainly on information from ILO field offices, the media and websites of governments, employers' and workers' organizations, as well as websites of national consultative bodies.
3. For example, Belgium, Ireland or Spain.
4. The purpose of this table is to provide a general picture of crisis-related social dialogue, its forms and content. Taking into account the very high dynamics of developments, it cannot provide precise and up-to-date information on individual countries; its value is mainly in illustrating prevailing forms used to deal with the current crisis as well as the main focus of social dialogue in its various forms (information exchange, consultations, negotiations). In some countries, more detailed information on the content of social dialogue within national tripartite bodies was not available at the time of drafting of this chapter.
5. For example, in Barbados, Brazil, Estonia, Romania, the Russian Federation and many other countries.
6. For example, the joint declaration of employers and workers of the automotive industry in the Czech Republic, 2008.
7. http://www.eurofound.europa.eu/eiro/2009/02/articles/es0902029i.htm, http://www.eurofound.europa.eu/eiro/2009/01/articles/ie0901039i.htm, http://www.eurofound.europa.eu/eiro/2010/01/articles/ie1001029i.htm
8. http:// www.eurofound.Europa.ez/eiro/2009/12/articles/ie091201i.htm.
9. For example, in Belgium, the Czech Republic, Hungary, Ireland, the Netherlands, Singapore and Slovenia.
10. For example, Armenia, Barbados, China, the Czech Republic, Kyrgyzstan, Republic of Korea, Russian Federation, Slovakia, South Africa, Sudan, Uruguay and Viet Nam.
11. For example, providing exceptional subsidies to redundant workers, e.g. glass factory workers in the Czech Republic.
12. For example, in the Bahamas, an unemployment insurance scheme was introduced; in Romania, the unemployment benefit period was extended by three months. Spain and even the United States recently expanded unemployment benefits. For example, in Illinois benefits were extended to 59 weeks from 26 as apart of the stimulus measures.
13. For example, in Croatia or Romania.
14. For example, in Australia, Republic of Korea and Singapore.
15. For example, the Philippines, Portugal and Slovakia. In Estonia, the current economic downturn has led to the postponement of the national minimum wage agreement as employers emphasized that the difficult economic situation makes further increases in the minimum wage problematic.
16. Update of the first Global Wage Report, ILO, GB.306/ESP/2.
17. Wage formation in the EU, Eiro, http://www.eurofound.europa.eu/eiro/studies/tn0808019s/tn0808019s_1.htm
18. For example, in Angola, Bulgaria, the Czech Republic, Ireland, Latvia and Romania.
19. For example, China and Singapore.
20. Ryder (2009).
21. However, the 'moral' connotation is not a specific feature of this particular crisis. Already during the Great Depression moral aspects were raised, for example by the Czech industrialist Tomáš Bat'a in 1932: 'Moral poverty

is the main cause of this crisis .... Many people in our country think that economic downturn can be solved by money. I am horrified by the consequences of such an error.... Confidence can be restored only by improved morals and by personal example.'

22. For example, the Australian Prime Minister declared: 'In these times, employers must do their utmost to protect their workers from dismissal, knowing that these workers will serve them well when times turn good again ... Workers, too, must restrain any wage claims.' See www.workplace-express.com.au
23. See http://www.eurofound.europa.eu/eiro/studies/tn0803019s/index.htm
24. For example, Japan, Republic of Korea and South Africa.
25. For example, regular inter-professional agreements in Belgium.
26. For example, Bulgaria, the Czech Republic, Hungary, France, Netherlands, Norway, Poland, Slovenia.
27. Glassner and Galgoczi (2009).
28. Attempts were also made to introduce temporary employment for white-collar workers, but the negotiations between the social partners were not successful.
29. Aidt and Tzannatos (2002).
30. For example, in Albania, Bosnia and Herzogovina, Bulgaria, China, Cyprus, the Czech Republic, Estonia, France, Ireland, Italy, Kazakhstan, the Netherlands, Singapore, South Africa, Spain and the United Kingdom.
31. For example, in Romania the state co-funds 50 per cent of training costs.
32. Bulgaria.
33. www.eurofound.europa.eu/eiro/2008/12/articles/it081209i.htm.
34. *Le Monde*, 10 April 2009.
35. www.eurofound.europa.eu./eiro/2009/02/articles/ro0902039i.htm.
36. *Asia Pulse*, 13 April 2009.
37. For example, 1,400 additional staff members are being hired in Spain, 320 in Norway.
38. For example, in the Philippines.
39. France merged employment services and unemployment insurance systems.
40. www.eurofound.europa.eu.eiro/2009/01/articles/nl090149i.htm.
41. www.eurofound.europa.eu/eiro/2008/12/articles/uk0812039i.htm.
42. Migrant workers seem to be one of the victims of the crisis in both developed and developing countries. Unemployment or cutting the quotas for foreign workers might have significant impact on sending countries; based on Human Rights Watch data, some 3.5 million Uzbeks are working abroad, 80 per cent of them in the Russian Federation. In the Czech Republic, foreign workers from Mongolia, Ukraine and Viet Nam, many of them agency workers, lost their jobs right at the beginning of the crisis. The government offered (mainly in the automotive and construction sectors) free return tickets and a bonus of 500 euros to those who would return to their home country. Japan introduced an emergency scheme, offering \$3,000 towards airfare, plus \$2,000 for each dependent, addressing mainly blue-collar Latin American guest workers. See www.nytimes.com/2009/04/23/business/global/23immigrant.html.
43. For example, Norway.
44. http://www.eurofound.europa.eu/eiro/2009/02/articles/ie0902029i.htm.
45. For example, employers and unions in the metalworking industry in Austria.

46. For example, in the metalworking industry in Bulgaria and in Germany, or in German railways. See http://www.eurofound.europa.eu/eiro/2008/12/articles/de0812049i.htm http://www.eurofound.europa.eu/eiro/2009/01/articles/bg0901059i.htm http://www.eurofound.europa.eu/eiro/2009/02/articles/de0902039i.htm.
47. The survey was executed by the Matrix Corporation among 500 employers and 500 employees of companies with over 100 workers.
48. See www.irishtimes.co/nespaper/breaking/2009/0310/breaking20_pf.html.
49. For example, the Czech government decided to cancel some 14,000 unfilled jobs, which also means cutting wages, as the ministries continued to receive funds allocated from the state budget for these positions which were usually used for increasing wages in the civil service.
50. Mercer's 2009/2010 US compensation Planning Update.
51. See http://www.eurofound.europa.eu/eiro/2009/02/articles/be0902069i.htm.
52. In support, the ILO is updating its 'Guide to worker displacement: Some tools for reducing the impact on workers, communities and enterprises' by G.B. Hansen, published in 2002.
53. This is what happened in Germany and in some Central European countries after the introduction by the German government of a subsidy for disposing of old vehicles. This measure quickly enabled a return to normal working time in Skoda (Czech Republic) and in Dacia (Romania).
54. F. Reid, Director of the Centre for Industrial Relations and Human Resources, University of Toronto. See www. googgle.com/hostednews/canadainapress/article/AleqM5.
55. http://global factiva.com/aa/default.aspx?pp=Print&hc=Publication.
56. For example, the case of German chip-maker Infineon, which decided not to follow the provisions of a higher-level collective agreement.
57. The Great Depression of the 1930s had led some governments to generalize the system of extension of industry-level collective agreements.
58. See, for example, 'Capitalism's crisis gives the labour movement a chance to revive and reinvent itself' in www.economist.com/business.
59. Freeman (2009).
60. Addressing the executive board of the AFL-CIO in March 2009, he declared: 'We need to level the playing field for workers and the unions that represent their interests... I want you to know that you will always have a seat at the table.'
61. 'The great challenge and the great opportunity posed by today's worrisome economic crisis is to find a new synthesis between the common good and the market, between capital and labour... and in this regard, union organizations can make a significant contribution', the Pope told directors of the Confederation of Italian Labour Unions on 31 January, 2009. See www.catholicleader.com.au/index.php?id=4722.
62. For example, according to estimates of the Estonian Trade Union Confederation (EAKL), the rapidly increasing unemployment rate and large collective redundancies in sectors where trade union membership is traditionally higher are causing a decline in trade union membership. Thus, trade union membership, which is already as low as 7.6 per cent of employees, is expected to decrease even further.
    See www.eurofound.europa.eu/eiro/2009/02/articles/ee0902059i.htm.

63. For example, in Estonia (see http://www.eurofound.europa.eu/eiro/2009/02/articles/ee0902049i.htm) or in Ireland (see http://www.eurofound.europa.eu/eiro/2009/01/articles/ie0901039i.htm). In Slovenia, an austerity pay deal was signed in February 2009 in order to reduce the growth in wages in the public sector envisaged for 2009. See also 'A common economic crisis but contradictory responses: The European experience 2008–2009', by R. Kyloh and C. Saget (ILO).
64. For example, Greece is considering a wage freeze of public servants' pay and one-off tax on high salaries; similar measures are envisaged e.g. in Ireland, Lithuania and the United Kingdom.
65. 'It is unacceptable that the public sector should not share this pain. There is already an apartheid between the public and private sectors on pensions. We cannot have apartheid on pay, too.' D. Frost, Director-General of the British Chamber of Commerce.
66. For example, as noted by Wilke and Tarantelli (1981) with relation to the experts' meeting on the impact of the labour market crisis on the conduct of industrial relations: 'A notable feature of our preparatory conversation in 1978 was the general astonishment about the obvious lack of disruptive action of organized labour in response to the most severe labour market crisis in the post-war period. The apparent inability of governments to stabilize their shaky economies and of private enterprise to secure the jobs of millions of people failed to provoke violent attacks from organized labour on the established prerogatives of economic and political decision making.'
67. Idem.
68. For example, Cullen (1987).
69. Derber (1983).
70. Wilke and Tarantelli (1981).
71. Industrial Relations Developments in Europe 2009, see http://eurofound.europa.eu/eiro/studies/tn1004019s/index.htm.

10
The Way Forward

I. Islam and S. Verick

This volume has navigated a wide and diverse terrain. Hence, it would be useful at this juncture to offer a summary of the key findings. This will set the appropriate context to reflect on the likely evolution of a post-crisis future and why one ought to move away from a 'business as usual' mindset.

Summary of key findings

The findings presented in the chapters provide important insights into the crisis in terms of its causes and consequences, how governments have responded to the downturn, prospects for recovery and policy options for a post-crisis world. In summary, the key conclusions are as follows.

- There were different interpretations of the pre-crisis period, delineated by an optimistic view of the global economy (the 'Great Moderation', the 'platinum' age) and a more pessimistic analysis drawing from the situation in developing countries (the 'Lost Decades', the 'crisis-before-the-crisis').
- In any case, the overwhelming (mis-)perception in the boom period (2002–07) was of continuing low levels of risk and volatility, which was a major factor behind the crisis. Despite a long, rich history of calamitous financial and economic episodes in both advanced and developing economies, the crisis that began in the middle of 2007 came as unexpected. A number of commentators did underscore the warning signs that were evident before the onset of the disintegration of the sub-prime housing market, but the prevailing sentiment was one of optimism. However, the crisis quickly revealed that the

global economy was far less robust or stable in 2007 as believed by many academics, investors and policymakers.

- The crisis resulted in the most severe recession the world has seen since the Second World War. Some countries have been affected dramatically, suffering from depression-like contractions of more than 10 per cent in 2009 (Lithuania, Latvia, Armenia, Estonia, Ukraine and Botswana). For this reason, the epithet, the 'Great Recession' seems a fitting description.
- As a consequence of the recession, millions have lost jobs, leading to rising unemployment, discouragement, rising informality and working poverty. The hardest-hit have been mostly young people, men, temporary workers, and unskilled and migrant workers, which is mostly explained by the sectoral composition of the recession.
- At the same time, a range of countries have emerged relatively unscathed, particularly the large developing Asian countries (China and India). Even some countries that have experienced a large economic contraction have avoided a major deterioration of the labour market.
- Developing countries in general have experienced a deceleration of growth rather than an outright recession, but even this has adverse implications for the progress in poverty reduction. The evidence suggests that some transmission channels (such as trade flows) have been more important than others (such as remittances) in causing growth decelerations. The evidence also shows that certain features, such as holding an adequate amount of international reserves and a large domestic economy, can partly explain why some developing countries have been more resilient than others during the Great Recession of 2008–09.
- A key theme of this volume is the diversity of the crisis with respect to the large variation in its impact on the economy and the consequences for the labour market. This diversity can be explained by: (1) differences in initial conditions such as the stage of the business cycle, the presence of a housing bubble, the strength of the labour market, and the degree of fiscal space; and (2) the response of policymakers in terms of macroeconomic stimulus and labour market policies. The aggressive stance taken by most governments of advanced economies and some developing ones has helped avoid a deeper recession. An important lesson is therefore that countries cannot remain passive in the presence of such crises, though this in turn depends on their political resolve and their technical and financial capacity to intervene.

- The long-standing issue of lack of policy and fiscal space in the case of developing countries has attained prominence in the wake of the Great Recession. Surveys show that more than 70 per cent of developing countries are fiscally constrained and cannot engage in adequate counter-cyclical policies to offset the deleterious consequences of external shocks. Enhancing fiscal and policy space will require a combination of national initiatives and international cooperation.
- In terms of labour market impact, there is a distinction between developing and OECD economies. In the former, labour market adjustments have entailed changes in unemployment rates as well as real wages – which is at par with the evidence from previous crises. In the OECD, data availability enables the identification of the labour market consequences by educational attainment, contract status, migration status, age and gender. This has been a recession for the poor and less educated, for migrants, for young men and those with precarious employment status.
- Whether employment will recover quickly in the recovery phase depends significantly upon whether the job losses are cyclical or structural in nature. Past experience shows that when recessions coincide with structural shifts on the economy, the lag between labour market recovery and resumption in GDP growth can be quite long.
- During the crisis, a number of countries have successfully staved off a surge in unemployment through the utilization of labour market policies, particularly work-sharing schemes, which kept workers threatened by layoff in their jobs. A range of middle-income (and some low-income) countries have implemented different labour market policies to help with the adjustment process.
- The social partners' involvement in the design and implementation of national measures in response to the crisis has been rather limited, at least in the early stages (2008). Nevertheless, there are clear signs that crisis-related measures were increasingly on the agenda of national tripartite bodies or ad hoc meetings organized with the participation of social partners over 2009. Social dialogue has played an important role in the development of appropriate policies in response to the crisis. Indeed, countries that have relied on dialogue between social partners as part of their response to the downturn have been able to more rapidly formulate effective policy packages.
- As the global economy entered the recovery phase late in 2009, the question for policymakers turned quickly to competing priorities of maintaining the stimulus and starting to tackle the mountain of debt

incurred as a consequence of interventions since 2007. At the time of writing, two main risks remain: the premature withdrawal of the stimulus resulting in a further economic slump (even a 'double-dip' recession); and the threat of a 'jobless' recovery, which is likely unless policies remain in place to encourage hiring and investment. The path to recovery will be protracted and uncertain, and, ultimately, will hinge on whether China (and to some extent, India) can continue to drive global growth.

- The Great Recession has also engendered a much-needed debate on core issues of macroeconomic management. The ascendency of macroeconomic conservatism entailing a preoccupation with inflation targeting and fiscal consolidation might now give way to a policy framework that can accommodate a renewed commitment to full employment.

These key findings serve as a prelude to the case for moving away from crisis-management mode to a long-term strategic approach in order to shape the post-crisis era. This is the focus of the rest of the chapter.

Delineating a post-crisis future: from short-term management to a long-term, strategic approach

In the quest to secure sustainable growth, policymakers in various parts of the world face two challenges. First, they need to move away from a short-term crisis management mode to a long-term, strategic approach. Second, they need to temper the intellectual influence of a particular paradigm that has dominated the global policy agenda for at least two decades. This pre-crisis paradigm, characterized by such epithets as 'the Washington Consensus', 'market fundamentalism' and the 'neoliberal globalization model', allowed a particular formulation of economic policy to dominate global policy discourse.[1]

Both these challenges are intertwined. If one believes in the pre-crisis paradigm, then short-term management is a rational strategy, as one can go back to a 'business-as-usual' mindset once the crisis is over and thus disengage from the need to reflect on, and enunciate, alternative pathways to a post-crisis future. Hence, those who urge an 'exit strategy' from the current attempts to counter the effects of the global recession of 2008–09 are, in essence, the 'true believers' in the *status quo ante*.[2] To them, the globally coordinated attempts at expansionary macroeconomic policies must now be unwound. Otherwise, they will lead to high inflation and unsustainable debt burdens. Indeed, according to this narrative, governments across the world have to spend time repairing the fiscal distress caused by the crisis.[3]

There are, of course, voices counselling caution against the supporters of the *status quo ante*. The United Nations, in its latest report on the global economy, has warned of the grave consequences of a premature exit strategy. Simulations undertaken by the United Nations Global Policy Model suggest that an early withdrawal could cause the world economy to experience a double-dip recession.[4] There is also a popular aspiration, as reflected in statements by political leaders across the world, that 'more of the same' is no longer an appealing and even a credible option.[5] At the same time, as will be argued later, it is possible to detect a convergence of views among key multilateral agencies on a post-crisis policy agenda.

Elements of a post-crisis policy paradigm: towards a new consensus

What is the way forward? It is possible to identify a convergence of views among a number of multilateral agencies on what a post-crisis policy paradigm would look like. Some of them pre-date the crisis; others have emerged in the wake of the crisis. A range of prominent economists have called for a new paradigm, including Krugman (2009a) and Sachs (2009). Even the IMF has begun to 'rethink' its position on both macroeconomic policy and capital controls (Blanchard et al. 2010; Ostry et al. 2010). Though these commentators are rightly questioning the assumptions underlying policymaking that dominated the landscape prior to the crisis, they are mostly silent on the most important dimension in terms of household welfare: employment. In this respect, to date there has been little discussion (outside the domain of the ILO) on how to restore full employment as an explicit goal of government policies, and how to promote growth in household incomes that would be far more sustainable than the debt-fuelled experience witnessed during the boom years of 2002–07.

Elements of alternative pathways to a post-crisis future, which puts employment back in the centre of the policy agenda, can be found in the ILO's and the Global Jobs Pact, which was endorsed by the International Labour Conference in June 2009.[6] The Decent Work Agenda adopts a holistic approach to the world of work. It emphasizes sustainable and productive employment creation, social protection, rights and standards at work and social dialogue. The Global Jobs Pact is 'based on the decent work agenda' and embodies 'an integrated portfolio of tried and tested policies ... that can be tailored to national and local situations' to attenuate the impact of the 2008–09 global recession on national economies and to craft a pathway to sustainable and equitable growth.[7] Leaders of the G20 agree. In their collective statement issued at the Pittsburgh Summit (24–25 September 2009), they noted: 'We ... welcome the recently adopted ILO Resolution on Recovering from the Crisis: A Global Jobs Pact, and we commit our nations to adopt key elements of this general framework...'.[8] The ILO (2010: 5) justifiably notes that 'the Global Jobs Pact has gained worldwide support at global, regional and national levels'.

Other organizations, such as the World Bank's MILES approach, share significant similarities with the ILO approach.[9] The notion of 'fair globalization' that represented the topic of a 2004 global report done under the auspices of the ILO is now echoed by the World Bank in the form of 'responsible globalization'.[10] The ADB has advanced its agenda of 'rebalancing growth' in the context of the export-oriented economies of East Asia. In addition, the goals and targets for policymaking and monitoring that follow from the ILO's Decent Work Agenda and the Global Jobs Pact share similarities with the OECD's approach to analyzing labour market trends and proposing policy recommendations as reflected by its annual *Employment Outlook* and other publications.

A post-crisis policy paradigm drawing on the above ideas should have the following components:

- Goals and targets that focus on the need for a renewed commitment to full employment.
- A broad-based portfolio of 'tried and tested' policies that covers both macroeconomic and microeconomic components.
- Mechanisms for consultations with social partners on policy design and delivery.
- Monitoring and evaluation entailing a transparent, accountable and rigorous validation process that relies on systematic use of evidence to verify and/or modify existing policies and programmes.
- A periodic 'stress test' (say, every three to five years) to assess evidence of vulnerability to external shocks and global economic downturns (for example, asset price bubbles, excessive reliance on particular sectors) and to ascertain how quickly and effectively policy responses can be crafted to such high-impact, low frequency events.
- A new era of international and regional cooperation that complements national initiatives.

These components add up to an evidence-based approach to policymaking. The primary strength of this approach is that it guards against myopic policy responses driven by populist pressures and ideological proclivities.

Renewed commitment to full employment

There should be fundamental reorientation of macroeconomic policy goals. They need to be anchored in MDG1 (target 1b), which calls for 'full and productive employment and decent work for all'. This goal should be pursued while maintaining macroeconomic stability. This reorientation offers a much-needed corrective to a narrow focus on nominal targets and aligns the macroeconomic policy framework with the global development agenda. There is a diverse range of 'decent work' indicators that can be used to monitor the attainment of MDG1b beyond quantitative expansions in employment and should be part of the labour market information system in all countries.[11]

Monetary and financial policies to support employment creation

Until the outbreak of the global financial crisis in 2007, the monetary authorities of many developing countries were pursuing a policy of inflation targeting. The aim was to attain low, single-digit inflation (usually less than 5 per cent), even though the empirical evidence was not robust enough to support the diligent practice of inflation targeting.[12] The aim of monetary policy should now be to support the attainment of MDG1b while maintaining a moderate (but not necessarily low single-digit) and stable rate of inflation. In advanced economies, the challenge for central banks and financial authorities is not only to focus on price stability in a narrow sense but to also consider the role of monetary and financial policies in tackling asset price bubbles.

Current proposals for fixing the financial system should take account of the need to provide access to finance to SMEs. This view can be endorsed by findings from business environment surveys (covering 10,000 firms in 80 countries) that consistently show lack of bank finance as one of the most important constraints on the growth of SMEs.[13]

Fiscal policy and public investment to support employment creation

The lack of public investment in infrastructure can act as a binding constraint on growth. How to facilitate such public investment in a fiscally sustainable fashion is thus a major policy challenge that transcends the imperatives of the global recession of 2008–09. The ILO's well-established Employment Intensive Investment Programme (EIIP) has also demonstrated under a variety of developing country circumstances how public investment can be used in infrastructure as a significant source of employment creation, including the creation of 'green jobs'.[14] In light of the deficiencies that have stemmed from the practice of focusing on short-run fiscal targets in the past, a long-term agenda that uses public investment in infrastructure as a major tool of fiscal policy can potentially pay rich dividends.

Capital account and exchange rate management to support employment creation

The discussion in this volume made it amply clear that capital mobility can constrain policy options for middle-income developing countries with access to global capital markets. Moreover, capital controls can be effective in staving off the effects of global financial instability. Active capital account management, therefore, should be seen as an important way to enhance the capacity of policymakers to pursue discretionary monetary, fiscal and exchange rate policy without having to worry about the destabilizing influence of short-term capital flows. It is necessary to maintain a competitive and stable real exchange rate – a goal that becomes rather difficult to attain in the presence of a high degree of capital mobility. There is a well-established empirical literature that substantiates this view.[15] In particular, one should draw attention to the prescriptions of UNCTAD (2010), which argue the case for a 'constant real exchange rate rule' (CRER). This will entail an arrangement whereby nominal exchange rates strictly follow inflation differentials among countries. The authors argue that this will: (1) curb excessive currency speculation; (2) prevent unsustainable current account deficits and currency crises; (3) avoid unsustainable debt; (4) avoid the imposition of pro-cyclical conditions by creditors; and (5) reduce the need to hold excessive international reserves.

Protecting workers and vulnerable groups

The focus on time-bound and targeted social safety nets needs to be transcended by an emphasis on the need to provide economic security for all citizens, regardless of where they work and live and also of the state of the business cycle. The aim is to have a holistic approach to social protection that uses complementary instruments to cater to the particular needs of different groups in the formal economy, the informal economy and rural areas. ILO and other studies show that incentive-compatible unemployment compensation programs for formal sector workers are technically feasible and fiscally affordable (financed through 1 to 2 per cent of payroll taxes) even for developing economies.[16]

There is now a menu of 'best practice' social safety nets that have been used in countries ranging from South Asia to Latin America, entailing such instruments as conditional cash transfers, microfinance and rural employment guarantee schemes to cater to workers outside the formal economy.[17] A basic social security package for all is also technically feasible and fiscally affordable for developing economies and requires investment of around 4 per cent of GDP in many cases.[18] Furthermore, greater efforts at domestic resource mobilization, in conjunction with transitional assistance from the donor community, can make such a basic social security package an attainable goal for all developing countries. Once a social security protection system is in place, it is much easier to pursue enterprise-level flexibility and to cope with global economic downturns.

Complementary labour market policies

The crisis has also revealed that governments can keep workers in jobs through such schemes as work-sharing policies. For this reason, a comprehensive social protection system needs to be complemented by various labour market policies that focus on a broad range of interventions including job/wage subsidies, public works programmes, entrepreneurship incentives, training programmes and employment services for displaced workers and the underemployed. An analysis based on 345 studies of well-designed training programmes in more than 90 countries show that they can have a significant impact on the livelihoods of displaced workers.[19] Over the longer term, governments should aim to develop a comprehensive and integrated policy and institutional framework that will enable them to better respond to future crises through labour market interventions. This involves the development of labour market policies as a counter-cyclical measure. In addition, more efforts need to be made to monitor and evaluate the impact of specific policies to ensure that interventions are effective.

Sharing the pain and shaping the future through social dialogue

As argued above, many, if not millions of workers across the world have to cope with downward adjustments to wages and working conditions as firms struggle to save jobs and maintain operations in the wake of a fall in demand. This so-called 'concession bargaining' at the enterprise level cannot really act as a substitute for tripartite dialogue at the national level. Some governments, notably those in Belgium, the Netherlands, Republic of Korea and South Africa, have enacted national plans to respond to the crisis by engaging in social dialogue with both employers and workers. One hopes that other governments will adapt this practice more extensively to their particular circumstances.

Monitoring and evaluation: the role of 'stress tests'

The monitoring and evaluation framework appears at times to rely too much on statistical exercises using cross-country data to validate competing hypotheses on labour market performance and too little on 'field experiments' to ascertain the effectiveness of policies and programmes.[20] Hence, policy and programme evaluations based on country-specific field experiments to supplement the currently dominant cross-country methodology are highly desirable.

There is one important innovation that could be considered by policymakers. The monitoring and evaluation framework should include periodic 'stress tests' (say, every three to five years) to identify emerging vulnerabilities and to assess whether policy responses to external shocks and global economic downturns can occur quickly and effectively.[21]

One prerequisite for developing and maintaining a robust monitoring and evaluation system is to have access to timely and reliable data. It is therefore disappointing to note that only 20 developing countries have semi-annual labour force surveys (and only one in Africa), while only 17 developing countries have up-to-date unemployment data and no poverty data for 2008 and 2009.[22] Unless steps are taken to address this acute paucity of data, the notion of a monitoring and evaluation system will remain merely an aspiration.

International and regional cooperation to complement national initiatives for sustainable recovery

No post-crisis policy agenda is complete without some comprehension of how the international community will embrace globalization after the Great Recession of 2008–09. This will entail a new era of international and regional cooperation to complement national efforts to secure sustainable recovery.

Towards 'fair globalization' in the post-crisis era

The dominant policy paradigm in the pre-crisis period – much of it associated with the Bretton Woods institutions – reflected the tendency to regard globalization as an end in itself rather than a means to an end. There is a case for moving away from a 'cheerleader's' version of global economic integration and reflecting on how one could attain a 'fair globalization' that will create equitable opportunities for all nations to meet their developmental aspirations. An agenda of 'fair globalization' includes, but is not limited to, the following elements: (a) the need for greater policy autonomy in the case of developing countries; (b) a development-friendly multilateral framework to short-term capital flows, FDI and cross-border movement of people; (c) upholding international labour standards; (d) the need for global macroeconomic coordination to sustain full employment; (e) a 'social floor' for the global community through the implementation of minimum social protection for all in all nations; (f) mobilizing additional resources for development assistance; (g) avoiding protectionism; and (h) making institutions of global governance more democratic, accountable and transparent.[23]

Enhancing the developmental role of the state in the developing world

There is a widely shared view that many developing countries lack the necessary fiscal and policy space to cope effectively with global economic volatility.[24] Such volatility in turn can impair long-term development potential. In addition, the dominance of conservative economic ideology over the last 30 years that extolled the virtues of private sector-driven development strategies led to the neglect of the developmental role of the state in the developing world. Such benign neglect needs to be reversed so that the important role that activist trade and industry policies can play in building internationally competitive manufacturing capabilities can no longer be discounted as a return to old-fashioned and counter-productive *dirigiste* regimes.[25] There needs to be a renewed commitment to assist developing countries to fortify their capacity to cope with global economic volatility. This might well require access to quick-disbursing, low-conditionality external financing facilities located at both the regional and global levels. Such facilities can reinforce the 'self-insurance' initiatives (such as accumulation of foreign reserves, setting aside fiscal resources in a stabilisation fund) that several developing and emerging economies have successfully undertaken to cope with global economic volatility.

Avoiding protectionism

One promising development in the wake of the global recession of 2008–09 is that, by and large, the systemically important nations have not responded with onerous protectionist measures. As the review of trade and investment measures prepared for the September 2009 G20 Leaders Summit by the OECD, UNCTAD and WTO shows, there is 'no indication of a descent into high-intensity protectionism as a reaction to the crisis'.[26] Certainly, there has been some slippage in trade policy, with some G20 members raising tariffs and non-tariff barriers to protect domestic production in steel and motor vehicles. At the same time, some G20 countries have taken measures that discriminate against foreign-controlled companies and/or inhibit outward investment flows. The authors of the review warn that G20 member countries could cede ground to protectionist pressures as … unemployment continues to rise'. These developments 'could aggravate the contraction of world trade and investment and undermine confidence in … sustained recovery of global economic activity'.[27]

Taming global financial markets

By now it is widely accepted that cross-border financial flows have been destabilizing and prone to crisis, and have largely bypassed low-income and capital-scarce economies. This means that developing countries should not be coerced into capital account liberalization. The process should be gradual, with appropriate sequencing. These ideas are no longer regarded as heretical in the wake of the crisis of 2008–09. The challenge is to muster the collective political will to reform the international financial architecture so that cross-border financial flows can indeed be tamed and tempered and act as a handmaiden of the real economy. If the necessary collective action can be undertaken, this will fortify the capacity of developing countries to engage in prudent capital account management.

A development-friendly multilateral framework for FDI

When analysing the costs and benefits of private capital flows, there is a tendency in global policy discourse to make a distinction between short-term capital flows and FDI. The former is seen as a hindrance to development while the latter is seen as enabling development. Hence, developing countries are often urged to improve the investment climate to attract FDI. However, independent studies have shown that FDI flows can be quite volatile, posing significant challenges for maintaining policy autonomy.[28] Hence, there is little to be gained in supporting any multilateral framework that places an onus on developing countries to engage in 'incentive competition' through fiscal and other incentives to woo FDI. Developing countries should be encouraged to apply a 'national benefits test' to the pursuit of policies that seek to attract FDI.

A development-friendly multilateral framework for regulating the cross-border movement of people

The 'cheerleaders' of globalization often pay insufficient attention to the benefits of global labour mobility and focus instead on trade and capital flows. Collective action is necessary to build a multilateral framework that provides uniform and transparent rules for the cross-border movement of people. The aim is to balance the interests of both migrants themselves and of countries of origin and destination. Independent scholarly work has corroborated the view that a well-managed process of global labour mobility can engender benefits to the international community that are many times more than, say, the gains that accrue from enhanced foreign aid to developing countries.[29] Such observations have also gained renewed currency in the wake of the global economic crisis of 2008–09. Many developing countries rely heavily on the 'export' of labour services and the revenue stream generated through remittances. The available data show that remittances have been adversely affected in some developing countries, although by no means as badly as trade and private capital flows (Majid 2009). What is of greater concern is the risk that labour market distress and limited employment opportunities in the wake of the global recession in labour-importing countries might induce a xenophobic backlash against migrant workers. At the same time, labour-exporting developing countries might struggle to productively resettle return migrants. Hence, the need for fair rules to deal with international migration is certainly an important element of fair globalization.

Upholding international labour standards

There is always the risk that, when policymakers are in a crisis-management mode, they can, by default, allow the erosion of working conditions and the suppression of the democratic aspirations of workers. Influential voices are calling for a renewed commitment to labour market flexibility as a long-run strategy for dealing with the global jobs crisis.[30] The rationale is that labour market regulations act as a binding constraint on growth and employment creation. Such voices should not be heeded. The uncritical embrace of labour market flexibility should be replaced by an agenda that seeks to uphold international labour standards and empower labour market institutions. This position can be substantiated by several state-of-the-art studies that question the notion that labour market regulations represent a binding constraint on growth and employment creation.[31] Indeed, one of the key lessons from the global financial crisis of 2007–09 is that institutions such as employment protection and unions have played an important role in smoothing the adjustment process. Hence, a sustainable, post-crisis policy paradigm needs to make a renewed commitment to upholding international labour standards.

Global macroeconomic coordination

In the wake of the global recession of 2008–09, there was widespread agreement among professional economists and political leaders that the systemically important countries should coordinate their macroeconomic policy responses to cope with the decline in aggregate demand. This spirit of international cooperation was, by and large, maintained. The challenge lies ahead. There is much more hesitation to mount a second round of stimulus packages to sustain global demand. Some countries might move towards a premature 'exit strategy' on the ground that the global recession has ended. The concern is that a technical recovery in terms of positive GDP growth might turn out to be of little solace to the unemployed and new jobseekers as they are likely to face relatively poor labour market prospects. This is where a renewed commitment to full employment as a global goal needs to be a central part of the post-crisis agenda.

Towards a minimum 'social protection floor' for the global economy

The notion of a 'global social protection floor' has gained renewed momentum in the wake of the Great Recession of 2008–09. It was endorsed by the United Nations system in April 2009.[32] It is not just a case of strengthening social protection systems in developing countries. Even in the industrialized nations that represent the home of the modern welfare state, decades of benign neglect and fiscal conservatism have led to erosion in the quality of social protection coverage. Admittedly, many G20 countries have sought to patch up their social protection system in the wake of the crisis. It is now necessary to move beyond expedient improvisations and 'band-aid' solutions to embrace the idea of a 'global social protection floor' as a worthy goal for all nations.

The need for additional resources for development assistance

The widely proclaimed target of ODA being at least equal to 0.7 per cent of the GDP of donor nations has yet to be fulfilled. Although there is no evidence yet that ODA flows will decline appreciably in the wake of the crisis of 2008–09, it is equally clear that ODA volatility has undermined the ability of developing countries to tap into a predictable source of external finance, especially during times of economic upheaval. There is a case for tapping into new sources of development assistance. This message is fully consistent with the view that a renewed interest in international financial transactions tax as a new source of raising revenue for funding global public goods is an auspicious development.

The reform of global governance

All relevant international organizations should be well resourced, transparent and accountable. This will entail increasing resources in real terms for the United Nations system, increasing democratic oversight of its roles and responsibilities and increasing voice and representation of developing countries in the Bretton Woods institutions and other global institutions, and also providing a forum for other non-state actors, most notably civil society associations that seek to represent the poor.

The agenda of 'fair globalization' resonates with the mood and spirit of the post-crisis era. For example, the World Bank, through its office of the President, has called for the embracing of 'responsible globalization'. It does not explicitly acknowledge the intellectual antecedents of this notion, but both the spirit and substance are in line with the ethos of 'fair globalization' advocated by the ILO. Robert Zoellick, the President of the Bank, argues the need for 'balanced global growth and financial stability… global efforts to counter climate change, and advance opportunity for the poorest' (2009a). Zoellick recognizes that the 'voting shares' of the international institutions '… should reflect the weights and new responsibilities of emerging powers, while assuring a voice for the poor'. The international institutions in the post-crisis era need 'the transparency and agility to work within networks of private business, foundations, and civil societies as well as with one another'. Zoellick makes the important point that, while the 'G20 should become the premier forum for international cooperation', it cannot afford to ignore the voices of the vast majority of countries that are outside the G20. This will entail the latter acting as a 'Steering Group across a network of countries and international institutions'.

Dealing with global imbalances by rebalancing the export-oriented growth model

Among multilateral agencies, the Asian Development Bank (ADB) has become a robust proponent of the notion that a critical post-crisis challenge is to deal with global imbalances – that is, the juxtaposition of the policy tensions created by surplus and deficit countries.[33] Paradoxically, low- and middle-income economies, such as the export powerhouses in East Asia, have become net exporters of capital to rich nations, such as the United States. This unsustainable position emerged primarily after the 1997 Asian financial crisis, as countries built up foreign exchange reserves as self-insurance against economic volatility.

One way of rectifying global imbalances is to revisit the export-oriented growth model that has served East Asia so well and that is so often regarded by other developing economies as a model worthy of emulation. What needs to be recognized, as is pointed out by the ADB, is that '[a]chieving rapid growth by producing ever-larger quantities of an ever-increasing range of manufactured goods is feasible so long as there are markets that can absorb these goods'. Unfortunately, 'the global financial crisis rudely shatters the delusion that there are no limits to external demand and hence to export-led growth'.[34] What needs to be done is to 'rebalance' the export-driven growth model so that there is a greater reliance on domestic and regional markets. This does not mean a return to old-fashioned *dirigiste* policies. It means rectifying the incentive structure that offers excessive rewards to the tradables sector at the expense of the non-tradables sector and the G3 export markets at the expense of regional markets. It also means boosting social protection systems that will reduce the need for the middle classes of China and other countries of developing Asia to forsake consumption for the sake of engaging in precautionary saving. Finally, it means a new era of international cooperation that will reduce the incentives for self-insurance at the national level that lies at the root of building up excessive foreign exchange reserves.

'Rebalancing' the export-oriented growth model needs to start at the national level. It is necessary for policymakers to have the political will to 'wind down the incentive schemes for export promotion that often includes tax breaks, preferential lending, and other explicit and implicit subsidies to exporters'.[35] Beyond that, a determined effort will have to be made in new investments in infrastructure, education, health care, the social protection system and in protecting the environment. These investments will boost domestic living standards and reduce the incentives to engage in precautionary savings at the expense of consumption.

The effectiveness of national initiatives for 'rebalancing' the export-oriented growth model also depends crucially on regional and international cooperation. The establishment of a 'modality of institutions for mutual assistance and policy coordination at the regional level' has been on the agenda of 'ASEAN + 3' since the 1997 Asian financial crisis, although not much has been achieved because of the 'failure of the PRC and Japan to provide leadership for regional cooperation'.[36] Hence, there needs to be a renewed commitment to regional policy coordination. In its absence or ineffective presence, individual countries might hesitate to adopt corrective action to its incentive structure to reduce the bias against the non-traded sector or to use expansionary policies to boost domestic demand because of the concern that other countries might not follow suit.

The contentious issue of the excessive accumulation of foreign exchange reserves by the exporting nations of East Asia is unlikely to be resolved at the national level unless there is reform of the global financial architecture and, more generally, the reform of global economic governance. As the ADB observes:[37]

> Many commentators in developing Asia feel that IMF did a poor job of handling the Asian crisis of 1997–98. Right or wrong, this view has eroded confidence in the institution throughout the region. This, in

> turn, may have encouraged regional countries to... build up a large war chest of foreign exchange reserves that would protect them from another devastating crisis in the future. Measures to restore the region's confidence in IMF, such as governance changes that would give the region a voice proportionate to its role in the world economy, would weaken the incentives for precautionary reserve build-up and thus contribute to global rebalancing.

In sum, the issues that emanate from the ADB-led discussion on the role that policymakers can play in contributing to the attenuation of global imbalances reaffirm the policy agenda for the post-crisis era advanced in this chapter. In essence, one needs to pay a lot more attention to the welfare of domestic constituencies by investing in infrastructure, health, education and social protection and by seeking to reform global governance. These are also key elements in the agenda of 'fair globalization'.

A word of caution. In propagating the thesis of rebalancing the export-oriented growth model of East Asia, it is necessary to avoid an overly hasty approach – such as an abrupt appreciation of the real exchange rate.[38] Rebalancing inevitably takes time as it entails delicate policy decisions with respect to the reallocation of resources between traded and non-traded sectors. Building up the social protection system also takes time. Hence, forcing the pace of change could impose large adjustment costs – an important point that has been made at an earlier juncture.

Concluding remarks

This concluding chapter has highlighted the need to move from a crisis-management mode to a long-term strategic approach in order to shape the post-crisis era. The case for upholding the *status quo ante* is rather weak. The dominant policy paradigm of the last three decades that upheld the ethos of macroeconomic conservatism and extolled the virtues of private sector-driven growth in a context of deep global economic integration failed to spot the storm that was brewing during the so-called global 'platinum age' of the first decade of the twenty-first century. A post-crisis policy agenda needs to focus on a renewed commitment to full employment. This will entail, at the national level, the adoption of a menu of policies that cut across both macro- and microeconomic dimensions. Monetary, financial, fiscal policies and capital account management need to support sustainable employment creation, including the creation of 'green jobs'. There has to be a greater commitment to investments in social protection, the upholding of core labour standards in times of crisis and a more inclusive approach to policymaking through social dialogue. Greater preparedness for economic volatility is warranted. To this end, policymakers across different parts of the world can consider the notion of implementing periodic 'stress tests' to assess the vulnerability and degree of preparedness of national economies to future crises. This will require complementary efforts by national governments to enhance the timely availability of good-quality data.

These national initiatives have to be complemented by efforts to enact a new era of international and regional cooperation. This will mean: (a) the need for greater policy autonomy in the case of developing countries; (b) fair and transparent rules to regulate the cross-border movement of people and flows of foreign capital; (c) upholding international labour standards; (d) reducing unfair barriers to trade in goods and services that affect developing countries; (e) the need for global macroeconomic coordination to sustain full employment; (f) a 'socio-economic floor' for the global community through the implementation of minimum social protection for all national citizens; (g) regulating short-term capital flows by reforming the global financial architecture; (h) mobilizing additional resources for development assistance; and (i) making institutions of global governance more democratic, accountable and transparent.

These elements form an agenda of 'fair globalization' – an agenda that resonates with the mood and spirit of the post-crisis era. Other multilateral agencies, such as the World Bank through its notion of 'responsible notion' and the ADB through its advocacy of 'rebalancing' the export-oriented growth model in order to rectify global imbalances, are also producing the intellectual momentum for a new consensus on an appropriate policy paradigm for dealing with the employment and labour market challenges that have emanated in the wake of the Great Recession of 2008–09. The findings in the various chapters of the book fully endorse the emerging policy paradigm.

Notes

1. The pre-crisis development paradigm is associated with the Bretton Woods institutions, but its core ideas were spawned by intellectuals in the developed world.
2. The term 'exit strategy' has to be used with care as those who believe in the need for a new policy paradigm also use it to define their position. The particular manner in which the term is used pertains to the way conservative thinkers use them.

3. An influential US conservative think-tank, the Heritage Foundation, argues that fiscal stimulus packages are ineffective and lead to unsustainable debt burden. See Foster (2009).
4. UN (2010) WESP 2010, Geneva and New York, Executive Summary.
5. As Martin Wolf puts it, 'The world economy cannot go back to where it was before the crisis, because that was demonstrably unsustainable'. See M. Wolf (2009) 'Why the green shoots of recovery could yet wither', *Financial Times*, 22 April.
6. ILO (2009f) *Recovering from the crisis: A Global Jobs Pact*, Geneva: ILO.
7. Ibid., page iv.
8. Leaders' Statement: The Pittsburgh Summit, 24–25 September 2009.
9. See Holzmann (2006) on the World Bank's MILES approach to development policy. The key point is that labour market and social policies should be seen as part of a holistic development framework. Hence, the MILES approach (the epithet stands for 'macro', 'investment climate', 'labour', 'and education' and 'social safety nets'). The philosophical premise is similar to the ILO's Decent Work Agenda that was unveiled in 1999.
10. See the World Commission report on fair globalization. See Zoellick (2009a,b) on 'responsible globalization'.
11. Although the MDGs are specifically meant to apply to low- and middle-income economies, the statement on full employment is applicable to both rich and poor countries.
12. See, for example, Epstein (2009). IMF research even suggests higher threshold levels of inflation, above which inflation significantly reduces growth (11–12 per cent for developing countries), than what has been prescribed through official country advice (Khan and Senhadji 2001).
13. de Ferranti and Ody (2007).
14. ILO (2004c).
15. See, for example, Rodrik and Subramanian (2009).
16. Lee (1998), Vroman (1999) and Vroman and Brustentev (2005).
17. See Ravallion (2008). See also Lustig (2000) who notes that the well-known Mexican *Progresa* conditional cash transfer scheme costs about 0.2 per cent of GDP and two million households are beneficiaries. The *Trajabar* programme in Argentina reaches 350,000 persons and costs a 0.25 per cent of GDP. The Brazilian Bolsa programme costs about 0.4 per cent of GDP and covered 11.1 million families in 2006 (ILO 2009a). In Indonesia, the social safety net operations during the height of the 1997 financial crisis cost about 2 per cent of the central government's budget and played an effective role in crisis impact mitigation. (Dhanani and Islam 2002).
18. ILO (2009c). A simulation exercise for Nepal, for example, shows that nearly 100 per cent of the basic social security package can be financed from domestic resources, provided the Nepalese government can partly reallocate social expenditure, increase the goods and services tax rate marginally, improve income tax collection and introduce modest health insurance contributions.
19. See World Bank (2009b).
20. Duflo (2005).
21. This point is emphasized by Cavallo and Izquierdo (2009: chapter 1). They call it the need to engage in 'fire drills'.

22. Department of Statistics, ILO, Geneva.
23. See pp. xii–xiv of the World Commission's report on 'fair globalization' (2004). The ILO's Global Jobs Pact calls for international cooperation in the following areas: (1) 'building a stronger, more globally consistent, supervisory and regulatory framework for the financial sector'... (2) promoting efficient and well-regulated trade and markets that benefit all and avoiding protectionism by countries... (7) encourage the international community, including international financial institutions, to make available resources for countercyclical action in countries facing fiscal and policy constraints... (8) keep commitments to increased aid to prevent a serious setback to the Millennium Development Goals... (9) urge the international community to provide development assistance, including budgetary support, to build up a basic social protection floor on a national basis'. See ILO (2009f), pp. 9–11.
24. See, for example, *The Global Monitoring Report 2009*.
25. See, for example, UNCTAD (2010).
26. OECD-UNCTAD-WTO (2009) *Report on* G20 *Trade and Investment Measures*, 14 September, Paris and Geneva, pp. 5–6.
27. OECD-UNCTAD-WTO (2009).
28. Mold (2008).
29. Pritchett (2004).
30. *The Economist* (2009) 'The Jobs Crisis', 12 March.
31. Howell et al. (2007), Freeman (2007), Berg and Kucera (2008), Ghose et al. (2008), Lee and Eyraud (2008).
32. See UN (2009b). 'The United Nations Social Protection Floor Initiative – Delivering Joint Support to National Efforts', New York.
33. Of course, the ADB is not the only agency that argues the case for 'rebalancing'. The United Nations system as a whole has advocated this proposal. See UNCTAD (2010).
34. ADB (2009: 63). Asian Development Outlook, Part 2, Rebalancing Asia's Growth, p. 63.
35. Park (2009) 'The Global Economic Crisis and Rebalancing Growth in East Asia', ADB Institute, Research Policy Brief No. 31, p. 5.
36. Park (2009: 9).
37. ADB (2009: 67).
38. Rodrik (2009). makes the point that the Chinese currency is currently undervalued by 25 per cent. If, in seeking to a make a contribution to the rectification of global imbalances, the Chinese authorities allow the currency to appreciate rapidly, GDP growth will decline by an estimated 2.2 percentage points per annum. This could well threaten political and social stability in China whose authoritarian political regime relies heavily on rapid growth to sustain its legitimacy.

Bibliography

Aaronson, D., S. Brave and S. Schechter (2009) 'How Does Labor Adjustment in This Recession Compare with the Past?', *Chicago Fed Letter*, June, no. 263.

Abela, M. and G. Ducanes (2009) 'The Effect of the Global Economic Crisis on Asian Migrant Workers' and Governments' Responses', Technical Note (Bangkok: ILO).

Acharya, V.V. and M. Richardson (2009) 'Causes of the Financial Crisis', *Critical Review*, vol. 21, no. 2–3, pp. 195–210.

ActionAid (2009) 'A Stimulus Package for Developing Countries', ActionAid factsheet. Available at http://www.actionaid.org/assets/pdf/ActionAid%20Stimulus%20Factsheet.pdf.

Adams, R.H. and J. Page (2005) 'Do International Migration and Remittances Reduce Poverty in Developing Countries?', *World Development*, vol. 33, no. 10, pp. 1645–69.

Aeppel, T. and J. Lahart (2009) 'Lean Factories Find It Hard to Cut Jobs Even in a Slump', *Wall Street Journal*, 9 March, p. A1.

Aidt, T. and Z. Tzannatos (2002) *Unions and Collective Bargaining* (Washington, DC: World Bank).

Aizenman, J. (2009) *On the Paradox of Prudential Regulations in the Globalized Economy. International Reserves and the Crisis: a Reassessment*, NBER Working Paper, no. 14779 (Cambridge, MA: National Bureau for Economic Research). Also published on the website of the University of California.

Akerlof, G.A. and R.J. Shiller (2009) *Animal Spirits: How Human Psychology Drives the Economy, and Why It Matters for Global Capitalism* (Princeton, NJ: Princeton University Press).

Akyuz, Y. (2007) *Global Rules and Markets: Constraints Over Policy Autonomy in Developing Countries* (Penang: Third World Network).

Angeriz, A. and P. Arestis (2008) 'Assessing Inflation Targeting Through Intervention Analysis', *Oxford Economic Papers*, vol. 60, no. 2, pp. 293–317.

Ariyoshi, A.K. et al. (2000) *Country Experiences with the Use and Liberalization of Capital Controls*, IMF Occasional Paper, no. 190 (Washington, DC: IMF).

Asian Development Bank (ADB) (2009) *Asian Development Outlook 2009, Part II, Rebalancing Asia's Growth* (Mandaluyong City: Asian Development Bank).

Astley, M., J. Giese, M. Hume and C. Kubelec (2009) 'Global Imbalances and the Financial Crisis', *Bank of England Quarterly Bulletin*, 2009Q3.

Auer, P. (ed.) (2001) *Changing Labour Markets in Europe* (Geneva: ILO).

Auer, P., U. Efendioglu and J. Leschke (2008) *Active Labour Market Policies around the World: Coping with the Consequences of Globalization* (Geneva: ILO).

Baily, M.N., R.E. Litan and M.S. Johnson (2008) *The Origins of the Financial Crisis*, Initiative on Business and Public Policy at Brookings, Fixing Financial Series, Paper 3, November (Washington, DC, Brookings Institution).

Baker, D. and K. Walentin (2009) 'Money for Nothing: The Increasing Cost of Foreign Exchange Holdings for Developing Countries', November (Washington, DC: Center for Economic and Policy Research).

Baker, G. (2007) 'Welcome to the Great Moderation', *The Times*, 19 January.

Banuri, T.J. (1990) *Economic Liberalization: No Panacea* (Oxford: Clarendon Press).

Barrel, R., D. Holland and D.W. te Velde (2009) 'A Fiscal Stimulus to Address the Effects of the Global Financial Crisis on Sub-Saharan Africa', 25 March (London: Overseas Development Institute and National Institute of Economic and Social Research).

Barro, R.J. and J. Lee (2000) *International Data on Educational Attainment: Updates and Implications*, CID Working Paper, no. 42, April (Cambridge, MA: Centre for International Development).

Bazza, S. and M. Clemens (2009) *Blunt Instruments: On Establishing the Causes of Growth*, CGD Working Paper, no. 171 (Washington, DC: Center for Global Development).

Bean, C. (2009) 'The Great Moderation, the Great Panic and the Great Contraction', Schumpeter Lecture, Annual Congress of the European Economic Association, Barcelona, 25 August.

Bell, D.N.F. and D.G. Blanchflower (2009) *What Should Be Done About Rising Unemployment in the UK?*, IZA Discussion Paper, no. 4040 (Bonn: IZA).

Berg, J. and D. Kucera (eds) (2008) *In Defence of Labour Market Institutions* (Geneva: ILO and Basingstoke: Palgrave Macmillan).

Bergsten, F. (2009) 'Needed: A Global Response to the Global Economic and Financial Crisis'. Presentation before Subcommittee on Terrorism, Non-proliferation and Trade Committee on Foreign Affairs, US House of Representatives.

Bernanke, B.S. (2004) 'Remarks by Governor Ben S. Bernanke: the Great Moderation'. Speech made at the meetings of the Eastern Economic Association, Washington, DC, 20 February.

Besley, T. (2005) 'Introduction', in T. Besley and R. Zagha (eds), *Development Challenges in the 1990s* (New York: World Bank and Oxford University Press).

Betcherman, G. and R. Islam (2001) *East Asian Labor Markets and the Economic Crisis: Impacts Responses & Lessons* (Washington, DC: World Bank and Geneva: ILO).

Betcherman, G., K. Olivas and A. Dar (2004) *Impact of Active Labor Market Programs: New Evidence from Evaluations with Particular Attention to Developing and Transition Countries*, World Bank Social Protection Discussion Paper No. 0402 (Washington, DC: World Bank).

Bewley, T.F. (1999) *Why Wages Don't Fall During a Recession* (Cambridge, MA: Harvard University Press).

Bezemer, D. (2009a) '"No One Saw This Coming": Understanding Financial Crisis Through Accounting Models', Groningen University, 16 June.

Bezemer, D. (2009b) 'Why Some Economists Could See the Crisis Coming', *Financial Times*, 7 September.

Bhaduri, A. (2005) *Macroeconomic Policies for Higher Employment in the Era of Globalization*, Employment Strategy Papers, 2005/11 (Geneva: ILO).

Birdsall, N. (2009) 'How to Unlock the USD 1 Trillion That the Developing Countries Desperately Need to Cope with the Crisis', CGD Notes, February (Washington, DC: Center for Global Development).

Blanchard, O. (2009) Emerging Market Countries and the Crisis – Synchronization and Heterogeneity. IMF Presentation. Available at http://210.193.37.130/pmas/Olivier-J-Blanchard.pdf.

Blanchard, O., G. Dell'Ariccia and P. Mauro (2010) *Rethinking Macroeconomic Policy*, IMF Staff Position Note, February (Washington, DC: IMF).

Blanchard, O. and J. Simon (2001) 'The Long and Large Decline in US Output Volatility', *Brookings Papers on Economic Activity*, vol. 1, pp. 135–64.

Boeri, T., B. Helppie and M. Macis (2008) *Labour Regulations in Developing Countries: A Review of the Evidence and Directions for Future Research*, World Bank Social Protection Discussion Paper, no. 0833 (Washington, DC: World Bank).

Bredenkamp, H. and S. Schadler (eds) (1999) *Economic Adjustment and Reforms in Low-income Countries* (Washington, DC: IMF).

Brown, G. (2002) 'The Conditions for High and Stable Growth and Employment', *The Economic Journal*, vol. 111, pp. 30–44.

Brunnermeier, M.K., A. Crockett, C.A. Goodhart, A. Persaud and H.S. Shin (2008) 'The Fundamental Principles of Financial Regulation', Preliminary Conference Draft, January (Geneva: International Centre for Monetary and Banking Studies).

Bruno, M. (1995) 'Development Issues in a Changing World: New Lessons, Old Debates, Open Questions'. Proceedings of the World Bank Annual Conference on Development Economics 1994 (Washington, DC: World Bank).

Bruton, H.J. (1997) *On the Search for Well-being* (Ann Arbor, MI: University of Michigan Press).

Bulir, A. and A.J. Hamann (2007) *Volatility of Development Aid: An Update*, IMF Staff Papers, no. 4, pp. 727–39.

Bundesagentur für Arbeit (2009) *Monats bericht: Der Arbeits- und Ausbildungsmarkt in Deutschland, July 2009*. Available at http://www.pub.arbeitsagentur.de/hst/services/statistik/000000/html/start/monat/aktuell.pdf.

Bureau of Labor Statistics (BLS) (2009) 'The Employment Situation: August 2009'. Available at http://www.bls.gov/news.release/empsit.nr0.htm.

Card, D., J. Kluve and A. Weber (2009) *Active Labour Market Policy Evaluations: a Meta-analysis*, IZA Discussion Paper, no. 4002 (Bonn: IZA).

Cavallo, E. and A. Izquierdo (eds) (2009) *Dealing with an International Credit Crunch: Policy Responses to Sudden Stops in Latin America* (Washington, DC: Inter-American Development Bank).

Cazes, S., S. Verick and C. Heuer (2009) *Labour Market Policies in Times of Crisis*, Employment Working Paper, no. 35 (Geneva: ILO).

Cecchetti, S.G., M.S. Mohanty and F. Zampolli (2010) 'The Future of Public Debt: Prospects and Implications'. Conference paper presented at the Reserve Bank of India's International Research Conference 'Challenges to Central Banking in the Context of the Financial Crisis', Mumbai, India, 12–13 February.

Central Bureau for Statistics (CBS) (2009) 'More Non-western Immigrants Unemployed Due to Recession', Web Magazine, 17 November. Available at http://www.cbs.nl/en-GB/menu/themas/arbeid-sociale-zekerheid/publicaties/artikelen/archief/2009/2009-2965-wm.htm.

Central Bureau of Statistics of Indonesia (BPS Statistik) website: http://www.bps.go.id.

Chandrasekhar, C.P. and J. Ghosh (2008) 'Employment and the Pattern of Growth', in R. Kapila and U. Kapila (eds), *Economic Developments in India* (Delhi: Academic Foundation).

Chen, S. and M. Ravallion (2009) 'The Impact of the Global Financial Crisis on the World's Poorest', VoxEU, 30 April 2009. Available at http://www.voxeu.org/index.php?q=node/3520.

Clift, J. (2009) 'Questioning a Chastened Priesthood', *Finance and Development*, vol. 46, no. 3, pp. 4–7.

Corden, M. (2009) 'Why the World Needs Fiscal Stimulus', 17 December, University of Melbourne. Available at http://www.eastasiaforum.org/2009/12/17/why-the-world-needs-fiscal-stimulus/.

Cotis, J.P. (2007) 'Overview', *OECD Economic Outlook*, May (Paris: OECD).

Council of the European Union (CEU) (2009) 'Addendum 2 to the Note: Employment Committee's Contribution to the Informal Employment Summit – Analysis Carried Out by the EMCO on Short-time Working Arrangements', 10015/1/09, REV 1, ADD 2.

Cullen, D.E. (1987) 'Recent Trends in Collective Bargaining in the United States', *International Labour Review*, vol. 24, no. 3, pp. 299–322.

Culpeper, R. and N. Kappagoda (2007) 'Domestic Resource Mobilization, Fiscal Space, and the Millennium Development Goals: Implications for Debt Sustainability', 27 March (Toronto: North–South Institute).

Daily Star (Bangladesh) (2009) 'Over 550,000 Chinese laid off by credit crisis', 21 January.

Davis, S.J. and J. Haltiwanger (1999) 'Gross Job Flows', in O. Ashenfelter and D. Card (eds), *Handbook of Labour Economics* (Amsterdam: North-Holland), pp. 2711–97.

de Ferranti, D. and A.J. Ody (2007) 'Beyond Microfinance: Getting Capital to Small and Medium Enterprises to Fuel Faster Development', The Brookings Institution, March, Policy Brief, no. 159 (Washington, DC: Brookings Institution).

de Mello Jr., L.R. (1997) 'Foreign Direct Investment in Developing Countries and Growth: A Selective Survey', *Journal of Development Studies*, vol. 34, pp. 1–34.

de Mello Jr., L.R. (1999) 'Foreign Direct Investment-led Growth: Evidence from Time Series and Panel Data', *Oxford Economic Papers*, vol. 51, pp. 133–51.

Derber, M. (1983) 'Are We in a New Stage?' Proceedings of the 35th Annual Meeting of the IRRA (Geneva: IRRA).

Dervis, K. and N. Birdsall (2006) *A Stability and Social Investment Facility for High Debt Countries*, CGD Working Paper, no. 77 (Washington, DC: Center for Global Development).

Deutsche Bank (2008) 'World Outlook', 5 December (Frankfurt: Deutsche Bank Securities Inc).

Dhanani, S. (2000) *Indonesia: Strategy for Manufacturing Competitiveness* (Jakarta: UNIOD).

Dhanani, S. and I. Islam (2002) 'Poverty, Vulnerability and Social Protection in a Period of Crisis: The Case of Indonesia', *World Development*, vol. 30, no. 7, pp. 1211–31.

Dhanani, S., I. Islam and A. Chowdhury (2009) *The Indonesian Labour Market: Changes and Challenges* (London and New York: Routledge).

Djaja, K. (2009) *Impact of the Global Financial and Economic Crisis on Indonesia: A Rapid Assessment* (Bangkok and Geneva: ILO Regional Office for Asia and the Pacific, ILO Policy Integration and Statistics Department).

Dollar, D. and A. Kraay (2002) 'Growth Is Good for the Poor', *Journal of Economic Growth*, vol. 7, no. 3, pp. 195–225.

Duflo, E. (2005) 'Field Experiments in Development Economics', BREAD Policy Brief, No. 012, December.

Easterly, W. (2001) *The Lost Decades: Developing Countries Stagnation in Spite of Policy Reforms 1980–1998* (Washington, DC: World Bank).
Economic Intelligence Unit (2009a) *Country Report: Indonesia*, May. Available at http://www.eiu.com/report_dl.asp?issue_id=1774523362&mode=pdf.
Economic Intelligence Unit (2009b) *Country Report: Argentina*, May. Available at http://www.eiu.com/report_dl.asp?issue_id=674489652&mode=pdf.
Economic Intelligence Unit (2009c) *World Data online*. Available at http://www.eiu.com/site_info.asp?info_name=ps_WorldData&entry1=psNav.
Edwards, S. (1997) *The Mexican Peso Crisis? How Much Did We Know? When Did We Know It?*, NBER Working Paper No. 6334 (Cambridge, MA: NBER).
Edwards, S. (2004) 'Financial Openness, Sudden Stops, and Current-account Reversals', *American Economic Review*, vol. 94, no. 2, pp. 59–64.
Eichengreen, B. and K. O'Rourke (2009) 'A Tale of Two Depressions', VoxEU, 1 September. Available at www.voxeu.org.
Elmendorf, D.W. (2007) 'Was the Fed Too Easy for Too Long?' Unpublished paper, The Brookings Institution. Available at http://www.brookings.edu/~/media/Files/rc/opinions/2007/11_fed_elmendorf/11_fed_elmendorf.pdf.
Epstein, G. (2003) *Alternatives to Inflation Targeting Monetary Policy for Stable and Egalitarian Growth*, PERI Working Paper, no. 62 (Political Economy Research Institute, University of Massachusetts-Amherst).
Epstein, G. (2009) *Rethinking Monetary and Financial Policy: Practical Suggestions for Monitoring Financial Stability while Generating Employment and Poverty Reduction*, Employment Working Paper, no. 37 (Geneva: ILO).
European Commission (2009) *Employment in Europe 2009* (Brussels: Directorate-General for Employment, Social Affairs and Equal Opportunities, European Commission).
Fallon, P.R. and R.E.B. Lucas (2002) 'The Impact of Financial Crises on Labor Markets, Household Incomes, and Poverty: A Review of Evidence', *The World Bank Research Observer*, vol. 17, no. 1, pp. 21–45.
Fields, G.S. (1994) *Changing Labor Market Conditions and Economic Development in Hong Kong, the Republic of Korea, Singapore, and Taiwan, China* (Washington, DC: The International Bank for Reconstruction and Development/World Bank).
Fischer, S. (1993) 'The Role of Macroeconomic Factors in Growth', *Journal of Monetary Economics*, vol. 32, no. 3, pp. 485–512.
Foreign Policy (2009) 'The Worst is Yet to Come', January 2009.
Forslund, A. and A.B. Krueger (2008) *Did Active Labour Market Policies Help Sweden Rebound from the Depression of the Early 1990s?*, CEPS Working Paper No. 158 (Princeton, NJ: Center for Economic Policy Studies).
Foster, J.D. (2009) *Keynesian Fiscal Stimulus Policies Stimulate Debt – Not the Economy*, The Heritage Foundation Backgrounder, no. 2302. Available at http://www.heritage.org/research/reports/2009/07/keynesian-fiscal-stimulus-policies-stimulate-debt-not-the-economy.
Fosu, A. and W. Naudé (2009) *The Global Economic Crisis*, Discussion Paper No. 2009/03 (Helsinki: UNU-WIDER).
Fox, J. (2009) *The Myth of the Rational Market: a History of Risk, Reward and Delusion on Wall Street* (New York: HarperBusiness).
Freeman, R. (2009) 'Labor Regulations, Unions and Social Protection in Developing Countries: Market Distortions or Efficient Institutions?', in Rodrik,

D. and M. Rosenzweig (eds), *Handbook of Development Economics*, vol. 5, chapter 70, pp. 4657–4702 (Amsterdam: Elsevier).

Galbraith, J.K. (2009) 'Who Are These Economists, Anyway?', *The NEA Higher Education Journal*, Fall, pp. 85–97.

Garnaut, R. (with D.L. Smith) (2009) *The Great Crash of 2008* (Clayton, VIC: Melbourne University Press).

Garnaut, R. and Y. Huang (2007) 'Mature Chinese Growth Leads the Global Platinum Age', in R. Garnaut and L. Song (eds), *China: Linking Markets for Growth* (Canberra: The Australian National University E-Press).

Ghose, A.K. (2000) *Trade Liberalization and Manufacturing Employment*, Employment Paper, 2000/3 (Geneva: ILO).

Ghose, A.K. (2003) *Jobs and Incomes in a Globalizing World* (Geneva: ILO).

Ghose, A.K. (2004) *Capital Inflows and Investment in Developing Countries*, Employment Strategy Paper, 2004/11 (Geneva: ILO).

Ghose, A.K., N. Majid and C. Ernst (2008) *The Global Employment Challenge* (Geneva: ILO).

Glassner, V. and B. Galgoczi (2009) *Plant-level Responses to the Economic Crisis in Europe* (Brussels: ETUI).

Gonzales-Rozada, M. and A. Menendez (2002) *Why Has Poverty and Income Inequality Increased So Much? Argentina 1991–2002* (Princeton, NJ: Princeton University Press).

Government of India, Ministry of Labour and Employment (2009) *Report on Effect of Economic Slowdown on Employment in India (October–December 2008)* (Chandigarh: Government of India).

Green, D., R. King and M. Miller-Dawkins (2010) 'The Global Economic Crisis and Developing Countries: Impact and Response', Working Draft for Consultation, January, Oxfam Research Report.

Griffin, K. (2001) 'Macroeconomic Reform and Employment: An Investment-led Strategy of Structural Adjustment in Sub-Saharan Africa', in McKinley (ed.) (2001).

Groningen database. Available at www.ggdc.net.

Groshen, E.L. and S. Potter (2003) 'Has Structural Change Contributed to a Jobless Recovery?', *Current Issues in Economics and Finance*, vol. 9, no. 8, pp. 1–7.

Gupta, S and S. Tareq (2008) 'Mobilizing Revenue', *Finance and Development*, vol. 45, no. 3, pp. 44–7.

Hailu, D. (2009a) *The Rich Expand, the Poor Contract: The Paradox of Macroeconomic Policy in Ethiopia*, International Policy Centre for Inclusive Growth (Brasilia: UNDP).

Hailu, D. (2009b) 'Is the Washington Consensus Dead?', International Policy Centre for Inclusive Growth (Brasilia: UNDP).

Hailu, D. (2009c) 'The Indonesian Response to the Financial and Economic Crisis: Is the Developmental State Back?', IPC One Pager, no. 86. (Brasilia: International Policy Centre for Inclusive Growth).

Hall, R.E. (2007) 'How Much Do We Understand About the Modern Recession?', *Brookings Papers on Economic Activity*, vol. 38, no. 2007-2, pp. 13–30.

Hansen, G.B. (2002) *Guide to Worker Displacement: Some Tools for Reducing the Impact on Workers, Communities and Enterprise* (Geneva: ILO).

Hanson, G.H. and R. Robertson (2008) *China and the Manufacturing Exports of Other Developing Countries*, NBER Working Paper, no. 14497 (Cambridge, MA: NBER).

Haugh, D., P. Ollivaud and D. Turner (2009) *The Macroeconomic Consequences of Banking Crises in OECD Countries*, OECD Economics Department Working Paper, no. 683 (Paris: OECD).

Heller, P. (2006) 'The Prospects of Creating "Fiscal Space" for the Health Sector', *Health Policy and Planning*, vol. 21, no. 2, pp. 75–9.

Heriawan, R. and W. Imawan (2008) 'Provision of Macro and Micro Data for Anti-poverty Program in Indonesia: Challenges and Responses'. Presented in the Seminar on Measuring Critical Social Issues: Experiences and Challenges, New York, 22 February.

Holzmann, R. (2006) 'More and Better Jobs: A Multi-sector Strategy'. Paper presented at the Preparatory Meeting on the Theme of the 2006 High-Level Segment of ECOSOC, New York, 4–5 April.

Honkapohja, S. and E. Koskela (1999) 'The Economic Crisis of the 1990s in Finland', *Economic Policy*, vol. 14, no. 29, pp. 399–436.

Hooper, P. and T. Sløk (2009) 'Quantifying the Impact of Fiscal Stimulus Packages', *Global Economic Perspectives* 8 April (Frankfurt: Deutsche Bank Securities, Inc.).

Howell, D.R., D. Baker, A. Glyn and J. Schmitt (2007) 'Are Protective Labor Market Institutions at the Root of Unemployment? A Critical Review of the Evidence', *Capitalism and Society*, vol. 2, no. 1, pp. 1–71.

International Bank for Reconstruction and Development (IBRD) (2009) *Commodities at the Crossroads – Key Findings from Global Economic Prospects 2009* (Washington, DC: World Bank).

International Institute for Labour Studies (IILS) (2008) *World of Work Report 2008* (Geneva: IILS).

International Institute for Labour Studies (IILS) (2009) *The Financial and Economic Crisis: A Decent Work Response* (Geneva: IILS).

International Labour Office (ILO) (1997) *World Employment Report 1996/97* (Geneva: ILO).

International Labour Office (ILO) (1999) *Indonesia: Strategies for Employment-Led Recovery and Reconstruction*. Report of the Employment Strategy Mission, 26 April–7 May 1999, Indonesia.

International Labour Office (ILO) (2002a) *Employment Policies for Poverty Reduction during Indonesia's Economic Recovery* (Jakarta and Geneva: ILO).

International Labour Office (ILO) (2002b) *Labour Market Policies and Poverty Reduction Strategies in Recovery from the Asian Crisis*. Report of the ILO-Japan-Government of Indonesia, Tripartite Sub-Regional Seminar, Jakarta, Indonesia, 29 April–1 May (Bangkok: ILO).

International Labour Office (ILO) (2004a) *A Fair Globalization – Creating Opportunities for All*. Report of the World Commission on the Social Dimension of Globalization (Geneva: ILO).

International Labour Office (ILO) (2004b) *Economic Security for a Better World*, Socio-Economic Security Programme (Geneva: ILO).

International Labour Office (ILO) (2004c) *Reducing the Decent Work Deficit in the Infrastructure and Construction Sectors: The Experience and Proposals of ILO's Employment-Intensive Investment Programme* (Geneva: ILO).

International Labour Office (ILO) (2006) *Global Employment Trends for Youth* (Geneva: ILO).
International Labour Office (ILO) (2008a) *Key Indicators of the Labour Market (KILM)*, 5th edition (Geneva: ILO).
International Labour Office (ILO) (2008b) *Global Wage Report – 2008/9: Minimum Wages and Collective Bargaining. Towards Policy Coherence* (Geneva: ILO).
International Labour Office (ILO) (2008c) *Eighth European Regional Meeting Report, 2008*, vol. I, part 2 (Geneva: ILO).
International Labour Office (ILO) (2009a) *Protecting People, Promoting Jobs: a Survey of Country Employment and Social Protection Policy Responses to the Global Economic Crisis*, An ILO report to the G20 Leaders' Summit, Pittsburgh, 24–5 September (Geneva: ILO).
International Labour Office (ILO) (2009b) *The Fallout in Asia: Assessing Labour Market Impacts and National Policy Responses to the Global Financial Crisis*, Background document prepared for meeting on 'Responding to the Economic Crisis – Coherent Policies for Growth, Employment and Decent Work in Asia and Pacific', Manila, 18–20 February.
International Labour Office (ILO) (2009c) *Global Employment Trends – Update, May 2009* (Geneva: ILO).
International Labour Office (ILO) (2009d) 'Is Recovery in Sight? Has the World Economy Turned the Corner?' Report presented at the Committee of the Whole on Crisis Responses, International Labour Conference, 98th Session, Geneva, June.
International Labour Office (ILO) (2009e) *Social Security for All*, Social Security Policy Briefings, Paper 7 (Geneva: ILO).
International Labour Office (ILO) (2009f) *Recovering from the Crisis: a Global Jobs Pact* (Geneva: ILO).
International Labour Office (ILO) (2010) *Global Employment Trends, January 2010* (Geneva: ILO).
International Herald Tribune (2008) 'China Vows to Focus on Jobs as Unemployment Rises', 20 October.
International Herald Tribune (2009) '20 Million Migrant Workers in China Can't Find Jobs', 2 February.
International Monetary Fund (IMF) (2008) *World Economic Outlook Database, October 2008* (Washington, DC: IMF).
International Monetary Fund (IMF) (2009a) *World Economic Outlook Database*, April 2009 (Washington, DC: IMF).
International Monetary Fund (IMF) (2009b) 'Crisis Deals Sharp Blow to Asian Growth'. Accessed at http://www.imf.org/external/pubs/ft/survey/so/2009/car050509a.htm.
International Monetary Fund (IMF) (2009c) *The Implications of the Global Financial Crisis for Low-income Countries* (Washington, DC: IMF).
International Monetary Fund (IMF) (2009d) *World Economic Outlook: Crisis and Recovery* (Washington, DC: IMF).
International Monetary Fund (IMF) (2009e) 'Initial Lessons of the Crisis'. Paper produced by the Strategy, Policy and Review Department, 6 February.
International Monetary Fund (IMF) (2009f) 'Review of Recent Crisis Programs'. Paper produced by the Strategy, Policy and Review Department, 14 September (Washington, DC: IMF).

International Monetary Fund (IMF) (2009g) 'The Size of the Fiscal Expansions: An Analysis of the Largest Countries', February (Washington, DC: IMF).

International Monetary Fund (IMF) (2009h) 'Global Economic Policies and Prospects'. Paper prepared for the Group of Twenty, Meeting of the Ministers and Central Bank Governors, London, 13–14 March.

International Monetary Fund (IMF) (2009i) 'From Recession to Recovery: How Soon and How Strong?' Chapter 3 in IMF (2009) *World Economic Outlook (WEO) Crisis and Recovery*, April (Washington, DC: IMF).

International Monetary Fund (IMF) (2010) *World Economic Outlook Update*, 26 January (Washington, DC: IMF).

International Monetary Fund (IMF) and World Bank (2009) *Global Monitoring Report (2009): A Development Emergency* (Washington, DC: IMF and World Bank).

Islam, I. (2002) 'Poverty, Employment and Wages: An Indonesian Perspective', in ILO (2002a).

Islam, I. (2003) *Avoiding the Stabilization Trap: Towards a Macroeconomic Policy Framework for Growth, Employment and Poverty Reduction*, Employment Paper, 2003/53 (Geneva: ILO).

Islam, I. (2005) 'Circumventing Macroeconomic Conservatism: A Policy Framework for Growth, Employment and Poverty Reduction', *International Labour Review*, vol. 144, no. 1, pp. 55–84.

Islam, I. (2009) *Creating Policy Space for Developing Economies to Cope with the Global Economic Crisis: A Proposed Framework*', Employment Policy Department (Geneva: ILO).

Islam, I. and A. Chowdhury (2000) *The Political Economy of East Asia: Post-Crisis Debates* (Oxford and Melbourne: Oxford University Press).

Islam, I. and A. Chowdhury (2009a) 'The Global Economic Crisis: How to Enhance Fiscal and Policy Space in Developing Countries', VoxEU, 11 May. Accessed at http://www.voxeu.org/index.php?q=node/3555.

Islam, I. and A. Chowdhury (2009b) 'The G20 Declaration at the London Summit: A Global "New Deal"?', VoxEU, 20 April. Accessed at http://www.voxeu.org/index.php?q=node/3473.

Islam, I. and A. Chowdhury (2009c) *Growth, Employment and Poverty Reduction: The Case Study of Indonesia* (Geneva: ILO).

Islam, R. (2003a) *Labour Market Policies, Economic Growth and Poverty Reduction: Lessons and Non-lessons from the Comparative Experience of East, South-East and South Asia*, Issues in Employment and Poverty Discussion Paper, no. 8, Recovery and Reconstruction Department (Geneva: ILO).

Islam, R. (2003b) 'Revisiting the East Asian Model of Economic Growth and Poverty Reduction: A Labour Market Perspective'. Paper presented at the 'Economics for the future' conference, Cambridge, 17–19 September.

Islam, R. (ed.) (2006) *Fighting Poverty: The Development–Employment Link* (London: Lynne Rienner).

Islam, R., G. Bhattacharya, S. Dhanani, M. Iacono, F. Mehran, S. Mukhopadhyay and P. Thuy (2001) 'The Economic Crisis: Labour Market Challenges and Policies in Indonesia', in Betcherman and Islam (2001).

Islam, R. and G. Buckley (2009) 'Rising Food Prices and their Implications for Employment, Decent Work and Poverty Reduction', mimeo, February (Geneva: ILO).

Jha, V. (2009) *The Effects of Fiscal Stimulus Packages on Employment*, Employment Working Paper, no. 34 (Geneva: ILO).
Jitsuchon, S. and A. Siamwalla (2009) *Economic Shocks and Vulnerable Thailand: A Case Study of Rising Food and Fuel Prices* (Bangkok: Thailand Development Research Institute).
Kalter, E., S. Phillips, M. Espinoza-Vega, R. Luzio, M. Villafuerte and M. Singh (2004) *Chile: Institutions and Policies Underpinning Stability and Growth*, Occasional paper, no. 231 (Washington, DC: IMF).
Kang, S.-H., J. Keum, D.-H. Kim and D. Shin (2001) 'Korea: Labor Market Outcomes and Policy Responses after the Crisis', in Betcherman and Islam (2001).
Kannan, K.P. (2009a) *Social Dimensions of the Impact of Global Economic Crisis on India: A First Assessment* (New Delhi: ILO Subregional Office for South Asia).
Kannan, K.P. (2009b) *National Policy Responses to the Financial and Economic Crisis: The Case of India* (Bangkok: ILO Regional Office for Asia and the Pacific).
Kanyenze, G., G.C.Z. Mhone and T. Sparreboom (2000) *Strategies to Combat Youth Unemployment and Marginalization in Anglophone Africa*, ILO/SAMAT Discussion Paper, no. 14 (Harare, Zimbabwe: ILO).
Khan, A.R. (1994) 'Stabilization, Structural Adjustment and the Labour Market: Issues and Evidence from Asia', in R. Islam (ed.), *Social Dimensions of Economic Reforms in Asia* (New Delhi: ILO).
Khan, A.R. (2006) 'Integrating Employment Growth into the PRSP Process: An Analysis of Issues and a Suggested Methodology', mimeo, March 2006 (Geneva: ILO).
Khan, A.R. and M. Muqtada (eds) (1997) *Employment Expansion and Macroeconomic Stability Under Increasing Globalization* (London: Macmillan and New York: St Martin's Press).
Khan, M.S. and A.S. Senhadji (2001) *Threshold Effects in the Relationship Between Inflation and Growth*, IMF Staff Papers, vol. 48, no. 1, pp. 1–21 (Washington, DC: IMF).
Kharas, H. (2008) *Measuring the Cost of Aid Volatility*, Wolfensohn Center for Development Working Paper, no. 3 (Washington, DC: Brookings Institution).
Khatiwada, S. (2009) *Stimulus Packages to Counter Global Economic Crisis: a Review*, IILS Discussion Paper, no. DP/196/2009 (Geneva: IILS).
Kluve, J. (2007) 'The Effectiveness of European ALMPs', in J. Kluve et al. (eds), *Active Labour Market Policies in Europe: Performance and Perspectives* (Berlin and Heidelberg: Springer), pp. 153–203.
Krueger, A.O. (1992) 'Policy Lessons from Development Experience since the Second World War'. Paper presented at the first ADB Conference on Development Economics, Manila.
Krueger, A.O. (2009) 'Development Prospects in Light of the Global Financial Crisis'. Presentation for the ABCDE Conference, Seoul, 23 June.
Krugman, P. (1998) 'What Happened to Asia', mimeo. Accessed at http: //web.mit.edu/krugman/www/DISINTER.html.
Krugman, P. (2009a) 'How Did Economists Get It So Wrong?', *New York Times*, 6 September.
Krugman, P. (2009b) *The Return of Depression Economics and the Crisis of 2008* (New York: W.W. Norton and Company).
Laeven, L. and F. Valencia (2008) *Systemic Banking Crises: A New Database*, IMF Working Paper No. 224 (Washington, DC: IMF).

Lechner, M. and C. Wunsch (2009) 'Are Training Programs More Effective When Unemployment is High?', *Journal of Labor Economics*, vol. 27, no. 4, pp. 653–92.
Lee, C.H. (2009) *National Policy Responses to the Financial and Economic Crisis: The Case of China* (Bangkok: ILO Regional Office for Asia and the Pacific).
Lee, E. (1998) *The Asian Financial Crisis: the Challenge for Social Policy* (Geneva: ILO).
Lee, S. and F. Eyraud (2008) *Globalization, Flexibilization and Working Conditions in Asia and the Pacific* (Geneva: ILO and Oxford: Chandos).
Lensink, R. and O. Morrissey (2006) 'Foreign Direct Investment: Flows, Volatility, and the Impact on Growth', *Review of International Economics*, vol. 14, no. 3, pp. 478–93.
Lewis, W.A. (1954) 'Economic Development with Unlimited Supplies of Labour', *Manchester School of Economic and Social Studies*, vol. 22, no. 2, pp. 139–91.
Lin, J.Y. (2008) 'The Impact of the Financial Crisis on Developing Economies'. Paper presented at Korea Development Institute, 31 October.
Lovén, K. (2009) 'Agreement on Temporary Layoffs Reached in Manufacturing', Eiroline. Available at http://www.eurofound.europa.eu/eiro/2009/03/articles/se0903019i.htm.
Lustig, N. (2000) 'Crises and the Poor: Socially Responsible Macroeconomics', *Economica*, vol. 1, no. 1, pp. 1–30.
Majid, N. (2001) 'The Working Poor in Developing Countries', *International Labour Review*, vol. 140, no. 3, pp. 271–91.
Majid, N. (2008) *The Employment Effects of North–South Trade and Technological Change*, Employment Working Paper, no. 22 (Geneva: ILO).
Majid, N. (2009) *The Global Recession and Developing Countries*, Employment Working Paper, no. 40 (Geneva: ILO).
Majid, N. (2010) 'Poverty, Inequality and Growth: a New Reading of Evidence', mimeo (Geneva: ILO).
Manning, C. (2000) 'Labour Market Adjustment to Indonesia's Economic Crisis: Context, Trends and Implications', *Bulletin of Indonesian Economic Studies*, vol. 36, no. 1, pp. 105–36.
Martin, J. (2000) 'What Works Among Labour Market Policies: Evidence from OECD Countries' Experience', *OECD Economic Studies*, vol. 1, no. 30, pp. 79–113. Available at http://www.oecd.org/dataoecd/31/35/2732343.pdf.
Massa, I. and D.W. te Velde (2008) 'The Global Financial Crisis: Will Successful African Countries be Affected?', ODI Background Note, 8 December (London: Overseas Development Institute).
McKenzie, D.J. (2004) 'Aggregate Shocks and Urban Labor Market Responses: Evidence from Argentina's Financial Crisis', *Economic Development and Cultural Change*, vol. 52, no. 4, pp. 719–58.
McKinley, T. (2001) (ed.) *Macroeconomic Policy, Growth and Poverty Reduction* (Basingstoke: Palgrave).
Messenger, J. (2009) *Work Sharing: A Strategy to Preserve Jobs During the Global Jobs Crisis*, ILO TRAVAIL Policy Brief, no. 1, June (Geneva: ILO).
Meyn, M. and J. Kennan (2009) *The Implications of the Global Financial Crisis for Developing Countries' Export Volumes and Values*, ODI Working Paper, no. 305 (London: ODI).
Milanovic, B. (2009) *Global Inequality Recalculated: The Effect of New 2005 PPP Estimates on Global Inequality*, MPRA Paper, no. 16538 (Munich: University Library of Munich).

Mold, A. (2008) 'The Fallout from the Financial Crisis: Implications for FDI to Developing Countries', *Policy Insights,* no. 86, December (Paris: OECD Development Centre).

Mundell, R. (1968) *International Economics* (New York: Macmillan).

Muqtada, M. (2003) *Macroeconomic Stability, Growth and Employment, Issues and Considerations Beyond the Washington Consensus*, Employment Paper 2003/48 (Geneva: ILO).

Muqtada, M. (2009) 'Rethinking Macroeconomic Policies for Stability, Growth and Employment', in L. Banerjee, A. Dasgupta and R. Islam (eds), *Development, Equity and Poverty: Essays in Honour of Azizur Rahman Khan* (New Delhi: Macmillan Publishers India Ltd).

Nakaso, H. (2001) *The Financial Crisis in Japan During the 1990s: How the Bank of Japan Responded and Lessons Learnt.* Bank of International Settlements (BIS) Papers, no. 6 (Basel: BIS).

Ndikumana, L. and S. Verick (2008) 'The Linkage Between FDI and Domestic Investment: Unravelling the Developmental Impact of Foreign Investment in Sub-Saharan Africa', *Development Policy Review*, vol. 26, no. 6, pp. 713–26.

New York Times (2009) 'The Economic Summit', 2 April.

Obstfeld, M. and K. Rogoff (2009) 'Global Imbalances and the Financial Crisis: Products of Common Causes'. Paper prepared for the Federal Reserve Bank of San Francisco Asia Economic Policy Conference, Santa Barbara, CA, 18–20 October.

Ocampo, J.A. (2002) 'Rethinking the Development Agenda', *Cambridge Journal of Economics*, vol. 26, no. 3, pp. 393–407.

Okun, A.M. (1962) *Potential GNP: Its Measurement and Significance*, Proceedings of the Business and Economics Section (Washington, DC: American Statistical Association), pp. 98–104.

Organisation for Economic Co-operation and Development (OECD) (2007) 'Editorial: The Globalisation Paradox', *OECD Employment Outlook* (Paris: OECD).

Organisation for Economic Co-operation and Development (OECD) (2008) *OECD Employment Outlook 2008* (Paris: OECD).

Organisation for Economic Co-operation and Development (OECD) (2009a) *OECD Employment Outlook 2009* (Paris: OECD).

Organisation for Economic Co-operation and Development (OECD) (2009b) *International Migration Outlook 2009: SOPEMI 2009. Special Issue: Managing Labour Migration beyond the Crisis* (Paris: OECD).

Organisation for Economic Co-operation and Development (OECD) (2009c) *Economic Outlook, Interim Report*, March (Paris: OECD), chapter 3.

Organisation of Economic Co-operation and Development (OECD), United Nations Conference on Trade and Development (UNCTAD) and World Trade Organization (WTO) (2009) *Report on G20 Trade and Investment Measures*, 14 September (Paris and Geneva).

Orphanides, A. (2007) 'Taylor Rules', Finance and Economics Discussion Series, No. 2007-18 (Washington, DC: US Federal Reserve Board).

Ostry, J.D., A.R. Ghosh, K. Habermeier, M. Chamon, M.S. Qureshi and D.B.S. Reinhardt (2010) *Capital Inflows: The Role of Controls*, IMF Staff Position Note, 19 February, SPN/10/04.

Overseas Development Institute (ODI) (2007) *Policy Space: Are WTO Rules Preventing Development?*, ODI Briefing Paper, no. 14, January (London: ODI).

Overseas Development Institute (ODI) (2009) *Fiscal Space for Strengthened Social Protection: West and Central Africa*, February (London: ODI).

Özatay, F. and G. Sak (2002) 'The 2000–2001 Financial Crisis in Turkey'. Unpublished paper.

Park, Y.C. (2009) *The Global Economic Crisis and Rebalancing Growth in East Asia*, ADB Institute, Research Policy Brief, no. 31 (Tokyo: ADBI). Available at http://www.adbi.org/files/2009.12.15.rpb31.global.economic.crisis.east.asia.pdf.

Pham, N.Q. (2009) *Impact of the Global Financial and Economic Crisis on Viet Nam: a Rapid Assessment* (Geneva: ILO Regional Office for Asia and Pacific, Bangkok, and Policy Integration and Statistics Department).

Pilling, D. (2009) 'Export Policy Goes Beyond its Sell-by Date', *Financial Times*, 27 May.

Pollin, R. (2009) 'Tools for a New Economy: Proposals for a Financial Regulatory System', *Boston Review*, January/February.

Pomerleano, M. (2009) 'The IMF's Global Fumble – As the IMF Tries to Please Everyone, it Serves No One', VoxEU, 26 March. Accessed at voxeu.org.

Portes, R. (2009) 'Global Imbalances and the Crisis'. Presentation for the Conference 'Financial Crisis and Its Impact on Developing Countries' Growth Strategies and Prospects', 20–1 April, Cambridge, MA (organized by the Commission on Growth and Development). http://www.growthcommission.org/index.php?option=com_content&task=view&id=108&Itemid=201.

Posner, R.A. (2009) *A Failure of Capitalism: The Crisis of '08 and the Descent into Depression* (Cambridge, MA: Harvard University Press).

Prasad, E. and I. Sorkin (2009) 'Assessing the G-20 Stimulus Plan: A Deeper Look', March (Washington, DC: Brookings Institution).

Pritchett, L. (2004) *Let Their People Come: Breaking the Gridlock on Global Labour Mobility* (Washington, DC: Center for Global Development).

Quiggin, J. (2001) 'Active Labour Market Policy and Macroeconomic Stabilisation', *The Drawing Board – An Australian Review of Public Affairs*, vol. 2, no. 2, pp. 51–66.

Rahman, M., K.G. Moazzem and S.S. Hossain (2009) *Impact of the Global Economic Crisis on the Employment and Labour Market of Bangladesh: A Rapid Assessment* (Dhaka: Center for Policy Dialogue and Geneva: ILO).

Rampell, C. (2009) 'Great Recession: A Brief Etymology', *New York Times*, 11 March.

Ratha, D., S. Mohapatra and A. Silwal (2009) 'Outlook for Remittance Flows 2009–2011: Remittances Expected to Fall by 7–10 Per Cent in 2009', *Migration and Development Brief*, no. 10 (Washington, DC: World Bank).

Ravallion, M. (2008) 'Bailing out the World's Poorest', mimeo (Washington, DC: World Bank).

Razin, A. and E. Sadka (2007) *Direct Investment: Analysis of Aggregate Flows* (Princeton, NJ: Princeton University Press).

Reinhart, C.M. and K.S. Rogoff (2008a) *Banking Crises: An Equal Opportunity Menace*, NBER Working Paper, no. 14587 (Cambridge, MA: NBER).

Reinhart, C.M. and K.S. Rogoff (2008b) 'Is the 2007 US Sub-prime Financial Crisis so Different? An International Comparison', *American Economic Review*, vol. 98, no. 2, pp. 339–44.

Reinhart, C.M. and K.S. Rogoff (2009a) *The Aftermath of Financial Crises*, NBER Working Paper, no. 14656 (Cambridge, MA: NBER).

Reinhart, C.M. and K.S. Rogoff (2009b) *This Time is Different: Eight Centuries of Financial Folly* (Princeton, NJ and Oxford: Princeton University Press).

Riskin, C. (2010) 'Inequality and Economic Crisis in China', in L. Banerjee, A. Dasgupta and R. Islam (eds), *Development, Equity and Poverty: Essays in Honour of Azizur Rahman Khan* (Delhi: Macmillan India).

Rodrik, D. (2009) 'Making Room for China in the World Economy', Harvard Kennedy School. Paper prepared for the American Economic Association (AEA) session on 'Growth in a Partially De-Globalized World'.

Rodrik, D. and A. Subramanian (2009) *Why Did Financial Globalization Disappoint?*, IMF Staff Papers, vol. 56, pp. 112–38.

Romer, C. (2009) 'From Recession to Recovery: The Economic Crisis, the Policy Response, and the Challenges We Face Going Forward'. Testimony before the Joint Economic Committee, 22 October.

Roubini, N. and B. Setser (2004) 'The US as a Net Debtor: The Sustainability of the US External Imbalance', mimeo, New York University.

Roy, R., A. Heuty and L. Letouze (2006) 'Fiscal Space for Public Investment: Towards a Human Development Objective'. UNDP paper presented at the G-24 Technical Meeting, Singapore, 13–14 September.

Rychly, L. (2009) *Social Dialogue in Times of Crisis: Finding Better Solutions*, ILO Industrial and Employment Relations Department Working Paper, no. 1 (Geneva: ILO).

Ryder, G. (2009) Speech delivered at the HL Crisis Meeting, Geneva, ILO, 23 March.

Sachs, J. (2009) 'Rethinking Macroeconomics', *Capitalism and Society*, vol. 4, no. 3, article 3.

Sakong, I. (G20 Summit coordinating committee) (2009) 'The Global Financial Crisis: Causes and Policy Responses'. Speech given at the G20 Summit in Seoul, 22 June.

Schnabel, G. (2002) *Output Trends and Okun's Law*, BIS Working Paper, no. 111 (Basel: Bank for International Settlements).

Sheng, A. (2009) 'From Asian to Global Financial Crisis', Third K.B. Lall Memorial Lecture, Indian Council for Research on International Economic Relations, New Delhi, 7 February.

Sjoblom, D. and J. Farrington (2008) 'The Indian National Rural Employment Guarantee Act: Will it Reduce Poverty and Boost the Economy?', *ODI Project Briefing*, No. 7, January.

Spilimbergo, A., S. Symansky and M. Schindler (2009) *Fiscal Multipliers*, IMF Staff Position Note, 20 May (Washington, DC: IMF).

Stevens, G. (2008) 'Interesting Times', Address made at the Australian Business Economists Annual Dinner, Sydney, 9 December.

Stiglitz, J.E. (1998) 'More Instruments and Broader Goals: Moving Towards the Post-Washington Consensus', WIDER Annual Lecture (Helsinki: WIDER).

Stiglitz, J.E. (2004) 'Capital Market Liberalisation, Globalisation and the IMF', *Oxford Review of Economic Policy*, vol. 20, no. 1, pp. 57–71.

Stiglitz, J.E. (2009a) 'Testimony Before the Congressional Oversight Panel – Regulatory Reform Hearing', 14 January.

Stiglitz, J.E. (2009b) 'The Global Crisis, Social Protection and Jobs', *International Labour Review*, vol. 148, nos 1–2 (Geneva: ILO).

Stiglitz, J.E. (2009c) 'The Anatomy of a Murder: Who Killed America's Economy?', *Critical Review*, vol. 21, nos 2–3, pp. 329–39.

Stiglitz, J.E. (2010) *Freefall: America, Free Markets, and the Sinking of the World Economy* (New York: W.W. Norton and Company).

Sum, A. and I. Khatiwada (2010) 'Labour Underutilization Problems of US Workers Across Household Income Groups at the End of the Great Recession: A Truly Great Depression among the Nation's Low Income Workers Amidst Full Employment among the Most Affluent'. Paper prepared for the C.S. Mott Foundation, February.

Taylor, J.B. (2009) 'Economic Policy and the Financial Crisis: an Empirical Analysis of What Went Wrong', *Critical Review*, vol. 21, nos 2–3, pp. 341–64.

Taylor, L. (1988) *Varieties of Stabilization Experiences: Towards Sensible Macroeconomics in the Third World* (Oxford: Clarendon Press).

te Velde, D.W. (2008) 'The Global Financial Crisis and Developing Countries: Which Countries are at Risk and What Can be Done?', October (London: ODI).

te Velde, D.W. et al. (2009) *The Global Financial Crisis and Developing Countries: Synthesis of the Findings of 10 Country Case Studies*. Working Paper, no. 306 (London: ODI).

The Economist (2009a) 'China's Economy: a Great Migration into the Unknown', 31 January–6 February.

The Economist (2009b) 'The Jobs Crisis', 12 March.

The Economist (2009c) 'The IMF: Battling Stigma', 26 March.

Tinbergen, J. (1952) *On the Theory of Economic Policy* (Amsterdam: North-Holland).

Titiheruw, I.S., H. Soesastro and R. Atje (2009) *Indonesia*, Paper 6, ODI Global Financial Crisis Discussion Series (London: ODI).

Tobin, J. (1996) *Full Employment and Growth: Further Keynesian Essays on Policy* (Cheltenham and London: Edward Elgar).

Tong, H. and S.-J. Wei (2009) *The Composition Matters: Capital Inflows and Liquidity Crunch during a Global Economic Crisis*. NBER Working Paper, no. 15207 (Cambridge, MA: NBER). Available at www.nber.org/papers/w15207.pdf.

Torm, N. (2003) *The Nexus of Economic Growth, Employment and Poverty during Economic Transition: An Analysis of Armenia, Kazakhstan, Kyrgyzstan, Moldova, Tajikistan and Uzbekistan*, Issues in Employment and Poverty Discussion Paper, no. 13, Recovery and Reconstruction Department (Geneva: ILO).

Townsend, P. (2009) *Building Decent Societies: Rethinking the Role of Social Security in Development* (Geneva: ILO).

United Nations (UN) (2001) *Social Dimensions of Macroeconomic Policy*, report of the Executive Committee of the Economic and Social Affairs (New York: United Nations).

United Nations (UN) (2003) *World Youth Report 2003: The Global Situation of Young People* (New York: United Nations).

United Nations (UN) (2009a) *Report of the Commission of Experts of the President of the United Nations General Assembly on Reforms of the International Monetary and Financial System*. Accessed at http://www.un.org/ga/econcrisissummit/docs.shtml.

United Nations (UN) (2009b) *The UN Social Protection Floor Initiative – Delivering Joint Support to National Efforts* (New York: United Nations).

United Nations (UN) (2010) *World Economic Situation and Prospects 2010 (WESP 2010)* (New York: United Nations).

United Nations Conference on Trade and Development (UNCTAD) (2005) *Handbook of Statistics* (Geneva: UNCTAD).

United Nations Conference on Trade and Development (UNCTAD) (2007a) *Asian Foreign Direct Investment in Africa: Towards a New Era of Cooperation among Developing Countries*, UNCTAD Current Studies on FDI and Development No. 3 (Geneva: UNCTAD).

United Nations Conference on Trade and Development (UNCTAD) (2007b) *Economic Development in Africa: Reclaiming Policy Space – Domestic Resource Mobilization and Development States* (Geneva: UNCTAD).

United Nations Conference on Trade and Development (UNCTAD) (2008) *Handbook of Statistics* (Geneva: UNCTAD).

United Nations Conference on Trade and Development (UNCTAD) (2009a) *The Least Developed Countries Report 2009: State and Development Governance* (Geneva: UNCTAD).

United Nations Conference on Trade and Development (UNCTAD) (2009b) *Trade and Development Report, 2009* (Geneva: UNCTAD).

United Nations Conference on Trade and Development (UNCTAD) (2010) *Global Monetary Chaos: Systemic Failures Need Bold Multilateral Responses*, UNCTAD Policy Briefs, No. 12, March (Geneva: UNCTAD).

United Nations Economic Commission for Africa (ECA) (2009) 'The Global Financial Crisis: Impact, Responses and Way Forward'. Background document for the 'Meeting of the Committee of Experts of the 2nd Joint Annual Meetings of the AU Conference of Ministers of Economy and Finance and ECA Conference of Ministers of Finance, Planning and Economic Development' held in Cairo, Egypt, 2–5 June, E/ECA/COE/28/6.

United Nations Economic Commission for Latin America and the Caribbean (ECLAC) (2009) *The Reactions of the Governments of the Americas to the International Crisis: an Overview of Policy Measures up to 31 March 2009* (Santiago, Chile: ECLAC).

United States Social Security Administration (SSA) and International Social Security Association (ISSA) (2009) *Social Security Programs Throughout the World: Africa 2009* (Washington, DC: SSA).

Verick, S. (2009) *Who is Hit Hardest During a Financial Crisis? The Vulnerability of Young Men and Women to Unemployment in an Economic Downturn*, IZA Discussion Paper, no. 4359 (Bonn: IZA).

Verick, S. (2010) *Unravelling the Impact of the Global Financial Crisis on the South African Labour Market*, Employment Working Paper, no. 48 (Geneva: ILO).

Vroman, W. (1999) *Unemployment and Unemployment Insurance in Three Groups of Countries*, Social Protection Discussion Paper, no. 1911, May, Social Protection Unit, Human Development Network (Washington, DC: World Bank).

Vroman, W. and V. Brusentev (2005) *Unemployment Compensation Throughout the World: A Comparative Analysis* (Kalamazoo, MI: W.E. Upjohn Institute for Employment Research).

Weichselbaumer, D. and R. Winter-Ebmer (2005) 'A Meta-Analysis on the International Gender Wage Gap', *Journal of Economic Surveys*, vol. 19, no. 3, pp. 479–511.

Weisbrot, M. (2009) 'G-20 Should Think Twice About Increasing IMF Funding Without Reforms', *The Guardian*, 25 March.

Weisbrot, M., R. Ray, J. Johnston, J.A. Cordero and J.A. Montecino. (2009) *IMF-Supported Macroeconomic Policies and the World Recession: A Look at Forty-One Borrowing Countries*, October (Washington, DC: Center For Economic and Policy Research).

Wickramasekara, P. (2004) *Policy Responses to Skilled Migration: Retention, Return and Circulation* (Geneva: ILO Perspectives on Labour Migration Series).

Wilke, G. and E. Tarantelli (1981) *The Management of Industrial Conflict in the Recession of the 1970s: Britain, Germany and Italy* (Florence: European University Institute).

Williamson, J. (1997) 'The Washington Consensus Revisited', in L. Emmerij (ed.), *Economic and Social Development* (Baltimore, MD: Johns Hopkins University Press).

Woo, W.T. (2008) 'What the US and Asia Should Do: Establish a Global Financial Crisis and Asian Financial Facility', in Brookings Institution (ed.), *The G-20 Financial Summit: Seven Issues at Stake* (Washington, DC: Brookings Institution).

World Bank (2004) *Global Economic Prospects 2004: Realizing the Development Promise of the Doha Agenda* (Washington, DC: World Bank).

World Bank (2005) *Economic Growth in the 1990s: Learning from a Decade of Reform* (Washington, DC: World Bank).

World Bank (2006) *World Development Report 2006: Equity and Development* (Washington, DC: World Bank).

World Bank (2008) 'Labour Market Programs That Make a Difference in a Time of Crisis'. Unpublished paper, Human Development Network and Social Protection, World Bank, Washington, DC.

World Bank (2009a) *Global Economic Prospects 2009: Commodities at the Crossroads* (Washington, DC: World Bank).

World Bank (2009b) 'How Should Labor Market Policy Respond to the Financial Crisis', HD and PREM Labor Market Teams, February. Available at http://siteresources.worldbank.org/INTLM/Resources/Note-LM_Crisis_Response_26April.pdf.

World Bank (2009c) 'The Global Economic Crisis: Assessing Vulnerability with a Poverty Lens', Vulnerable Countries Brief, February, Washington, DC. Available at http://siteresources.worldbank.org/NEWS/Resources/WBGVulnerableCountriesBrief.pdf.

World Bank (2009d) *Global Development Finance 2009: Charting Global Recovery* (Washington, DC: World Bank).

World Bank (2009e) *World Development Indictors 2009* (Washinton, DC: World Bank).

World Bank (2010) *Global Economic Prospects 2010: Crisis, Finance, and Growth* (Washington, DC: World Bank).

World Trade Organization (WTO) (2009) 'World Trade 2008, Prospects for 2009'. Press release, Geneva, 24 March.

Yap, J.T. (2009) *Impact of the Global Financial and Economic Crisis on the Philippines: A Rapid Assessment* (Bangkok and Geneva: ILO Regional Office for Asia and the Pacific and ILO Policy Integration and Statistics Department).

Yelden, E. and H. Ercan (2009) 'Growth, Employment Policies and Economic Linkages: Turkey'. Paper prepared for the ILO–EU joint project on 'Expanding Knowledge Base on Decent Work in Mediterranean Countries', September.

Yun, J.-W. (2009) 'Labor Market Polarization in South Korea: The Role of Policy Failures in Growing Inequality', *Asian Survey*, vol. 49, no. 2, pp. 268–90.

Zhang, Y., N. Thelen and A. Rao (2010) *Social Protection in Fiscal Stimulus Packages: Some Evidence*, UNDP/ODS Working Paper. Available at http://www.undp.org/developmentstudies/docs/socialprotection_fiscalstimulus_march2010.pdf.

Zimmer, R. (2008) 'The Fallout from the Financial Crisis: The End of Public Support for Development?', Policy Insights No. 87, December (Paris: OECD Development Centre).

Zoellick, R.B. (2009a) 'After the Crisis?' Speech given at the Paul H. Nitze School of Advanced International Studies, Johns Hopkins University, 25 September.

Zoellick, R.B. (2009b) 'Time to Herald the Age of Responsibility', Op-ed, *Financial Times*, 25 January.

Index

Bold page numbers indicate tables and figures